BLUE HELMET BUREAUCRATS

This history of colonial legacies in UN peacekeeping operations from 1945 to 1971 reveals how United Nations peacekeeping staff reconfigured the functions of global governance and sites of diplomatic power in the post-war world. Despite peacekeeping operations being criticised for their colonial underpinnings, our understanding of the ways in which colonial actors and ideas influenced peacekeeping practices on the ground has been limited and imprecise. In this multi-archival history, Margot Tudor investigates the UN's formative armed missions and uncovers the officials that orchestrated a reinvention of colonial-era hierarchies for Global South populations on the front lines of post-colonial statehood. She demonstrates how these officials exploited their field-based access to perpetuate racial prejudices, plot political interference, and foster protracted inter-communal divisions in post-colonial conflict contexts. Bringing together histories of humanitarianism, decolonisation, and the Cold War, *Blue Helmet Bureaucrats* sheds new light on the mechanisms through which sovereignty was negotiated and renegotiated after 1945.

MARGOT TUDOR is a postdoctoral research fellow at University of Exeter. She won the BISA Michael Nicolson Thesis Prize in 2021 and her article, 'Gatekeepers to Decolonisation', won the ISA History Section's Merze Tate Award in 2022.

Human Rights in History

Edited by

Stefan-Ludwig Hoffmann, University of California, Berkeley
Samuel Moyn, Yale University, Connecticut

This series showcases new scholarship exploring the backgrounds of human rights today. With an open-ended chronology and international perspective, the series seeks works attentive to the surprises and contingencies in the historical origins and legacies of human rights ideals and interventions. Books in the series will focus not only on the intellectual antecedents and foundations of human rights, but also on the incorporation of the concept by movements, nation-states, international governance, and transnational law.

A full list of titles in the series can be found at:
www.cambridge.org/human-rights-history

BLUE HELMET BUREAUCRATS

United Nations Peacekeeping and the Reinvention of Colonialism, 1945–1971

MARGOT TUDOR
University of Exeter

CAMBRIDGE
UNIVERSITY PRESS

Shaftesbury Road, Cambridge CB2 8EA, United Kingdom

One Liberty Plaza, 20th Floor, New York, NY 10006, USA

477 Williamstown Road, Port Melbourne, VIC 3207, Australia

314–321, 3rd Floor, Plot 3, Splendor Forum, Jasola District Centre, New Delhi – 110025, India

103 Penang Road, #05–06/07, Visioncrest Commercial, Singapore 238467

Cambridge University Press is part of Cambridge University Press & Assessment, a department of the University of Cambridge.

We share the University's mission to contribute to society through the pursuit of education, learning and research at the highest international levels of excellence.

www.cambridge.org
Information on this title: www.cambridge.org/9781009264921

DOI: 10.1017/9781009264952

First published 2023

A catalogue record for this publication is available from the British Library.

Library of Congress Cataloging-in-Publication Data
Names: Tudor, Margot, 1995– author.
Title: Blue helmet bureaucrats : United Nations peacekeeping and the reinvention of colonialism, 1945–1971 / Margot Tudor, University of Exeter.
Description: First Edition. | New York : Cambridge University Press, 2023. | Series: Human rights in history | Includes bibliographical references and index.
Identifiers: LCCN 2022049045 (print) | LCCN 2022049046 (ebook) | ISBN 9781009264921 (Hardback) | ISBN 9781009264938 (Paperback) | ISBN 9781009264952 (epub)
Subjects: LCSH: United Nations–Peacekeeping forces. | Security, International. | Conflict management–International cooperation. | World politics–1945-1955. | World politics–1955–
Classification: LCC JZ6374 .T83 2023 (print) | LCC JZ6374 (ebook) |
DDC 327.1/7–dc23/eng/20230104
LC record available at https://lccn.loc.gov/2022049045
LC ebook record available at https://lccn.loc.gov/2022049046

ISBN 978-1-009-26492-1 Hardback

CONTENTS

FIGURES

ACKNOWLEDGEMENTS

This book is the product of my luck and privilege in meeting a wealth of intellectually generous and profoundly kind people since I began my postgraduate degree in 2017. I started the research for this book as a PhD student at the Humanitarian and Conflict Response Institute (HCRI) at the University of Manchester in September 2017. Materially, I would not have been able to complete my PhD without my studentship from the Economic and Social Research Council (ESRC). I also relied upon bursaries from the Institute of Historical Research, the Global Humanitarianism Research Academy (2018), and the University of Manchester to make my archival research trips possible. I am indebted to the UN Archivists in New York and the UN Library staff for their expertise and speed in aiding my research. Many thanks also go to Jess Farr-Cox for her careful proofreading and thoughtful indexing.

My research grew from model supervision, patience, and constant support from Eleanor Davey, Laure Humbert, Steven Pierce, and Roisin Read. Since the PhD, Laure and Eleanor have kindly guided me through the academic publishing process and given me the confidence to finish this manuscript. I am in awe of them both and endlessly grateful for their friendship. Without Emily Baughan's encouragement, belief, and support (since 2015!), I would not have dived into the history of humanitarianism and pursued a history PhD. I also hugely appreciate Peter Gatrell for advising me during and after my PhD on this project.

Since January 2021, my Postdoctoral Research Fellowship at the University of Exeter has provided me with the financial security to continue to write, revise, and publish this book. Working on the 'Warnings from the Archive: A Century of British Intervention in the Middle East' project with Catriona Pennell and Owen Thomas has been inspiring and shaped this book in many ways. I have also benefited from the friendship of Gemma Clark, Stacey Hynd, and Martin Thomas, as well as many others during my time at Exeter.

Small sections of this book have been published elsewhere in two articles and one book chapter. Receiving reviews and editorial comments on those pieces was critical for the development of my thinking for this book. Thanks go to the editors of the *Journal of Contemporary History* (especially to Giusi Russo for including me in her special section on 'The UN and the Colonial

World') and the *Journal of Global History*, as well as Julius Heise, Maria Ketzmerick, and Jan Lüdert for inviting me to contribute to their edited volume, *The United Nations Trusteeship System: Legacies, Continuities, and Change.*

Throughout the years, I have been lucky to have benefitted from a community of generous academics who have helped me develop my ideas for this book. I am particularly grateful for the detailed advice and support from Meredith Terretta, Bertrand Taithe, and Brian Drohan. I am thankful to Catherine Arthur, Eirik Bjorge, Anna Bocking-Welch, Duncan Bell, Poppy Cullen, Marie-Luce Desgrandschamps, Marianna Dudley, Larissa Fast, Andy Flack, Frank Gerits, Myfanwy James, Swapna Kona Nayudu, Ria Kapoor, Nadia Kornioti, Eva-Maria Muschik, Mark-William Palen, Kseniya Oksamytna, Silke Roth, Eva Schalbroeck, and Rob Skinner, among many others for their kindness and help over the years.

My research was most improved by listening to and learning from my inspiring friends and fellow early career researchers. Joining the union and participating in strikes alongside my colleagues helped me to centre activism and solidarity in my work. I am indebted to my HCRI/Manchester colleagues for sharing their world-class research with me. I am especially lucky to have worked (and laughed) alongside Jenny Chapman, Ben Gittens, Nicola Jones, Kasia Nowak, Margaux Pinaud, Isabelle Schlapfer, Louise Tomkow, Kristina Tschunkert, and Ria Sunga Turner. I was lucky to be a participant in the Global Humanitarianism Research Academy in 2018, organised by Fabian Klose, Johannes Paulmann, and Andrew Thompson, where I met some amazing researchers. Special thanks to Monique Beerli, Jen Carr, Ryan Heyden, Elena Kempf, Emma MacKinnon, Elisabeth Piller, and Jiayi Tao for their friendship. Recent conversations with Alice Chessé and Lou Pingeot have been inspiring and have helped build my confidence as an interdisciplinary researcher. Emma Kluge has been a vital source of support and solidarity in post-doc life. Ceri Fowler will always be my lockdown sister. I am so grateful to academia for introducing me to my close friends, Molly Avery and Matilda Greig: I think the world of you both. Eternal thanks to my wonderful friend Kate Doyle for being there for me since the beginning (Geneva, 2014!).

I am grateful to my parents, Abi and Mark Tudor, for their patience and care during this erratic period of my life. Thank you for never questioning that this was possible. My sister, Emily, has also been a great support. Many thanks also to Jane and Pete Baldwin for their kindness and generosity as I worked on my PhD and this book.

Finally, this book is dedicated to my partner, Owen Baldwin, for grounding me in our life outside work and always bringing me joy.

NOTES ON THE TEXT

Place Names

Many of the places mentioned in this book have been known by different names at different points in time by different individuals and organisations. The United Nations officials used a variety of names to refer to host territories before, during, and after their periods of authority and so relying on the organisation staff's terminologies would not have provided consistency.

As a rule, the names used have been chosen to correspond to how they were most frequently referred to during the mission period. For example, I use the city and regional names 'Leopoldville', 'Elizabethville', 'Jakarta', and 'Hollandia' – unless they have been directly referred to otherwise in the source. These have since been renamed Kinshasa, Lubumbashi, Djakarta, and Jayapura, respectively. Similarly, I use the same rule for country or territorial names – for example, I use 'Rhodesia', 'Burma', 'Ceylon', 'Ruanda-Urundi', 'Republic of Dahomey', and 'Republic of Upper Volta' for the nations that are, at the time of publication, known as Zimbabwe, Myanmar, Sri Lanka, Rwanda and Burundi, Benin, and Burkina Faso, respectively. I use 'Congo' instead of 'the Congo' as the latter term has colonial connotations and is more commonly used to refer to the river. The nation was renamed Zaïre from 1971–1997. The nation has been recognised internationally as the Democratic Republic of Congo since 1997. From 1958 to 1961, Egypt (including Sinai and the Gaza Strip) and Syria formed a political union known as the United Arab Republic (UAR). Syria withdrew from this union in 1961, but Egypt remained known as the UAR until 1971.

With relation to my chapter on West Papua, the choice in terminology is political and in support of Papuan activists seeking independence from Indonesian annexation. West Papua has been given many names in its history: Netherlands New Guinea/Nederlands-Nieuw-Guinea/West New Guinea by the Dutch, West Irian/West Irian Jaya/Irian Jaya Barat/Papua Barat by the Indonesians, and West Irian/West New Guinea by most of the international community, especially UN forums. The UN staff, during the peacekeeping mission, largely referred to the territory as West New Guinea or West Irian. I quote these historical names when necessary but have chosen to use the term

'West Papua' as it was adopted by indigenous independence activists to refer to their territory in 1961.

Translations

All translations are mine unless otherwise indicated, and all errors are my own.

INITIALISMS/ACRONYMS

ANC	Armée Nationale Congolaise
ASEAN	Association of Southeast Asian Nations
CIA	(US) Central Intelligence Agency
ICJ	International Court of Justice
ICRC	International Committee of the Red Cross
MSC	(UN) Military Staff Committee
NATO	North Atlantic Treaty Organization
NGO	non-governmental organisation
ONUC	Opération des Nations Unies au Congo
PRC	People's Republic of China
SBA	Sovereign Base Area
UAR	United Arab Republic
UN/UNO	United Nations
UNAEC	United Nations Atomic Energy Commission
UNC	United Nations Command (in Korea)
UNCCP	UN Conciliation Commission for Palestine
UNEF	United Nations Emergency Force
UNESCO	United Nations Educational, Scientific and Cultural Organization
UNFICYP	United Nations Peacekeeping Force in Cyprus
UNIPOM	United Nations India-Pakistan Observation Mission
UNMOGIP	United Nations Military Observer Group in India and Pakistan
UNOGIL	United Nations Observer Group in Lebanon
UNOKAT	United Nations Operations in Katanga
UNPC	United Nations Palestine Commission
UNRWA	United Nations Relief and Works Agency
UNSCOP	United Nations Special Committee on Palestine
UNSF	United Nations Security Force
UNTEA	United Nations Temporary Executive Authority
UNTSO	United Nations Truce Supervision Organization
WHO	World Health Organization

Introduction

Peacekeepers and Field-Based Global Governance

On a humid July evening in central Cyprus in 1966, peacekeeping officials prepared a private dinner party to celebrate the visit of the special representative to the United Nations (UN) secretary-general to the island. The arrival of Dr Ralph Bunche was an exciting event for the deployed UN peacekeeping troops and the mission's chief of staff, British-national Brigadier Michael Harbottle. After a sweltering day of touring the Old City of Famagusta with Swedish peacekeeping officers and taking meetings with Cypriot political leaders, Bunche and Harbottle returned to the UN mission base, Blue Beret Camp, on the west of the capital city, Nicosia. Once the meal began, Bunche turned to his host and joked, 'You know, Brigadier, if it had not been for your country, I should have been out of a job eighteen years ago!'[1] In his memoirs, Harbottle reflected on this comment and the underlying truth at the centre of the statement. 'A joke maybe', he argued, 'but when one looks at the varied operations and missions that the United Nations have undertaken, and the part that Bunche has taken in them, in so many of the former colonies and mandated territories once administered by the United Kingdom, his words were far from being mere frivolous comment.'[2] As Bunche acknowledged, territorial disputes resulting from decolonisation had afforded the UN with not only an exceptional military and political role for a non-governmental actor, but also a steady supply of work in international peace and security. Bunche, in particular, became integral to the organisation's response to the surge of decolonisation conflicts in the post-war period as one of the key figures in the UN Secretariat inner circle. For UN officials, decolonisation was not just a global political movement; it represented a logistical challenge, a reputational opportunity, and – at its simplest – a stable career.

During the transformative era of decolonisation in the mid-twentieth century, UN peacekeeping staff orchestrated a reinvention of sovereignty and a remaking of colonial-era hierarchies for Global South populations on the front

[1] M. Harbottle, *The Impartial Soldier* (Oxford: Oxford University Press, 1970), p. 48.
[2] Harbottle, *The Impartial Soldier*, p. 48.

lines of post-colonial statehood. Peacekeeping missions perpetuated colonial structures, imaginaries, and staffing into newly independent or politically transitional spaces.[3] Using a humanitarian guise, the organisation set host populations and international community expectations of the rights-based motivations and interests protected by peacekeeping staff. Unelected mid-level UN officials – defined as mission or organisation leadership who were active in the field – employed their direct access to local politicians, populations, and activists to shape governance structures, such as post-colonial territorial borders, that would conform to the organisation's nation-state framework in exchange for technical support and international legitimacy.[4] Mission practices on the ground entrenched a universalist governing ideology of liberal internationalism and paternalism, prioritising regional and international stability over small or marginalised populations' self-determination.

[3] In this book, I chose to use the imperfect terms 'Global North' and 'Global South' as geopolitical categories rather than as fixed geographic territories in order to avoid re-entrenching colonial ideas of dependency, as with terms such as 'developing world' or 'third world'. However, I do agree with Nina Schneider (2017) that simply changing terms whilst producing the same type of intellectual work is insufficient; we must investigate the 'real effects' of these terms and how far they do – or do not – meaningfully denounce injustices and global inequalities. This work does directly challenge geopolitical hierarchies and systems of dependency, but I acknowledge that the language we – as scholars – use in unpicking these processes deserves to be problematised further in order to re-centre subaltern, marginalised, and 'peripheral' voices/knowledge. Although this geopolitical term is more recent in literature, it enables me to address the global hierarchies within international peace and security forums without perpetuating that uneven hierarchy itself. Peacekeepers themselves variously described these nations as 'developing'/'underdeveloped', part of the 'third world', and even 'primitive' during this period, and I have not altered quotes to change these instances. I believe that the use of these terms are themselves vital for understanding the asymmetric power dynamic between peacekeeper and civilian and help to reveal the prejudices held by peacekeepers.

[4] I use the terms 'in the field' and 'on the ground' to refer to the site of humanitarian delivery or military operations as opposed to the organisations' headquarters. This terminology is the norm within the history and practice of humanitarianism, with NGOs establishing roles such as 'Field Director' and scholars such as Emily Baughan (2021) and Eleanor Davey (2015) using these terms in their monographs on INGOs See E. Baughan, *Saving the Children: Humanitarianism, Internationalism, and Empire* (Oakland: University of California Press, 2021); E. Davey, *Idealism beyond Borders: The French Revolutionary Left and the Rise of Humanitarianism, 1954–1988* (Cambridge: Cambridge University Press, 2015). Operations undertaken 'in the field' or 'on the ground' are performed *in context*; using these terms is not an assumption that that context is foreign or local to the worker. These terms instead allow this book and its focus on peacekeeping *practices* to create a distinction between the international staff deployed to the site of conflict (or, in context) versus those situated in the organisation's headquarters (and thus divorced geographically from the conflict), or elsewhere entirely. This distinction is vital in demonstrating the (dis)connections between headquarters staff and field-based staff within the same international organisation, enabling me to tease out the power dynamics and internal hierarchies reinforced by the transnational geographic spread of international workers.

By adopting and reflecting the dominant geopolitical order, UN peacekeeping staff imposed a particular elite, technocratic standard of acceptable statehood and post-colonial political life upon decolonising populations, gatekeeping international representation and protections. Rethinking the mechanisms through which sovereignty was negotiated and renegotiated from the late 1940s onwards allows us to better understand the loci of power that influenced the processes of decolonisation and formation of the post-colonial international order.

Grounded in technocratic exceptionalism and a policy of anticommunism, mid-level peacekeeping personnel took inspiration, often instinctively, from previous imperial administrations or career experiences to establish 'stability' in the host countries and assert paternalistic political authority over the population through peacekeeping mandates. The UN secretary-general recruited these mid-level officials from a variety of past positions – from managing mining corporations to presiding over the General Assembly – but they all became integrated within the UN international civil service and, thus, belonged to the same international epistemic community of liberal internationalists.[5] Through field-based access, peacekeeping staff became knowledge gatekeepers to the global community and held substantial power over how local populations' rights were conceived by international forums, directly impacting on host states' political futures and position within the global geopolitical hierarchy.[6] These field-based peacekeepers were both enabled *and* constrained by issues such as mandate wording, operational logistics, host state obstruction, geopolitical interests, and concerns of organisational reputation. This book tracks the peaks and troughs of these mid-level peacekeepers' power during and across these missions, tracing the UN officials' fluctuating room to manoeuvre *as well as* examining the limitations on their agency during this period of geopolitical rupture. Crucially, it also identifies the hierarchies of rights, race, and political values in anti-colonial thinking during decolonisation, examining how these uneven relations and diplomatic alignments obstructed meaningful anti-colonial solidarity and Afro-Asian bloc unity.

The UN was not just a faceless, bureaucratic international organisation. During decolonisation, UN field-based officials reconfigured the functions of global governance and sites of diplomatic power in the post-war world. Deployed to conflicts across the Global South, peacekeepers helped to reframe

[5] P. M. Haas, 'Introduction: Epistemic Communities and International Policy Coordination', *International Organization*, 46:1 (1992), p. 3.

[6] This power dynamic is similar to that of translators or human rights witnesses. For more on this dynamic, see L. Kunreuther, 'Earwitnesses and Transparent Conduits of Voice: On the Labor of Field Interpreters for UN Missions', *Humanity: An International Journal of Human Rights, Humanitarianism, and Development*, 11:3 (2020), pp. 298–316.

conflict as a stabilising solution to violence – a peaceable solution for the liberal international order – rather than a protracted war. Instead of confirming the belief that post-Cold War peacekeeping missions have strayed from the original, apolitical standards of UN operations,[7] this book examines how Cold War-era peacekeeping missions and staff played an integral role in perpetuating racial hierarchies, international interference, and technocratic supremacy within conflict contexts.

Peacekeepers' armed presence in conflict contexts not only transformed the context and conduct of war. Their mandate also provoked a reimagining of peace and global governance. As Galo Plaza, President of Ecuador (1948–52) and UN official, has argued:

> The presence of armed forces, the presence of foreigners involved in dealing with problems within a country, if it is done by any country is intervention. If it is done by an international organization it is not intervention. It is a new concept of sovereignty that has to be taken into consideration with the existence of the international organizations.[8]

Expanding out of international headquarters to the host state, the UN peacekeeping staff reconfigured expectations of the diplomatic organisation by undertaking decisions from the front line. No longer restricted to the political forums in New York or Geneva, the international peacekeepers embodied a particular authority due to their physical presence on the ground. This devolution of organisational power complicated traditional ideas of the international core/periphery, centring Global South locations and populations in the knowledge production and geopolitical discourses of international peace and security; from the Pacific to the Middle East, South-East Asia, and Africa, peacekeeping officials shaped decolonisation processes on the ground. Their interactions with regional politicians, host communities, and UN headquarters colleagues placed them in a uniquely influential position, empowered as gatekeepers and technocrats within the international peace and security industry. From its origins, the UN leadership characterised the organisation and its employees as humanitarian, impartial, non-aligned, and expert. These apolitical credentials encouraged both Global South *and* colonial actors to appeal for UN-led peacekeeping missions to resolve post-colonial conflicts, rather than seeking the military recourse of a Cold War-aligned neighbouring state or superpower. However, UN international staff – civilian and military – deployed to conflict contexts were not apolitical actors, as advertised by the

[7] C. Stahn and H. Melber (eds.), *Peace Diplomacy, Global Justice and International Agency: Rethinking Human Security and Ethics in the Spirit of Dag Hammarskjöld* (Cambridge: Cambridge University Press, 2014).

[8] 'Transcript: Galo Plaza Interviewed by Diego Cordovez', 28 March 1984, p. 8.

leadership; their previous career experiences and anxiety over threats to the UN manifested in highly partial and ideologically driven practices. Rather than passive intermediaries, mid-level peacekeepers sought to cut through red tape of the UN headquarters in New York and exploit their power to augment the political future of the host territory *and* the post-colonial international order.

By the same token, the communities governed by peacekeeping missions during decolonisation were not simply passive beneficiaries of international aid and security. Local populations were active participants in their political futures, and it was common for groups to directly engage with peacekeepers to communicate ideas, share expertise, and seek greater representation in peace negotiations. Locals were employed by the UN as administrative staff, drivers, translators, or healthcare workers, and many more acted as intermediaries.[9] For those who disagreed with the mission or sought to criticise its practices, community groups and activists used protests, marches, and petitioning campaigns to attract the attention of the media and the international community. Communities experiencing violence, infrastructural instability, and economic distress were vocal and organised in their resistance to war. Although this book focuses on peacekeeping practices, it also reveals the political activity and imagination of 'protected' populations in their efforts to shape missions *and* their own futures.

From the field, mid-level peacekeeping staff set the standards for 'acceptable' or 'credible' nationalist movements and assumed a gatekeeping role. In this book, 'gatekeeping' refers to the processes of inclusion and exclusion in-built in the humanitarian system: for instance, controlling the delivery of aid, data collection and analysis, refugee resettlement, and access to international diplomatic forums. At its simplest, humanitarian gatekeepers decide who eats, who moves, and who speaks. For Étienne Balibar, humanitarian actors become institutional gatekeepers as a result of their intermediary role to police the law during periods of war, revolution, or environmental disaster. Through this protection of the law, humanitarian actors can become political suppressors, governmental spokespersons, and instruments 'in the service of precisely the powers that created the distress'.[10] Thus, rather than supporting 'collective movements of emancipation' which seek to transform 'structures of domination', humanitarian organisations can profit from their role as a global

9 For more research on the dynamic of local workers as humanitarian staff and intermediaries, see M. James, 'Humanitarian Fables: Morals, Meanings and Consequences for Humanitarian Practice', *Third World Quarterly*, 43:2 (2022), pp. 475–493; M. James, '"Who Can Sing the Song of MSF?": The Politics of "Proximity" and Performing Humanitarianism in Eastern DRC', *Journal of Humanitarian Affairs*, 2:2 (2020), pp. 31–29.

10 É. Balibar, *We, the People of Europe?: Reflections on Transnational Citizenship* (Princeton: Princeton University Press, 2004), p. 117.

authority in the 'institutional distribution of survival and death'.[11] For recipients of aid, humanitarians could both *police* borders (conceptual and literal) and *become* the borders themselves.[12] This gatekeeping dynamic between humanitarian and civilian is further amplified in the context of an armed peacekeeping mission whereby UN staff are empowered with governing *and* military authority and infrastructure.

Although many peacekeepers were motivated by what they would describe as 'good intentions' for the affected population and the cessation of violence, their ideas about peace, governance, and self-determination were shaped by decades of colonial knowledge systems and thus promoted paternalistic and racist practices in the field. Priya Satia's extensive work on the relationship between conscience and imperialism has similarly shown how knowledge of the good intentions of liberal interventionists fails to compensate for the exploitation and violence of colonialism. She argues that this humanitarian guise was 'in fact an approach to conquest that pre-emptively insured against ethical doubt'.[13] Indeed, British imperialists' belief in their moral stature further exacerbated their claims of national superiority and therefore rightful role in intervention, suffocating critiques of colonial practices and prejudices. The colonial narrative of the 'civilising mission' justified interventions as 'progressive' enabling colonists to justify their imperial behaviours – and profits – as moral and humanitarian. For them, only through British imperialism and capitalism could Global South societies be 'liberated' into modernity. John Hobson has also highlighted the continuities between the 'good intentions' of nineteenth-century imperialists and present-day liberal interventions.[14] This paternalistic dynamic was mirrored in UN peacekeeping missions as international staff relied upon a humanitarian justification of 'progress' and 'peace' to legitimise officials' gatekeeping, political interference, and racialised decision-making. The logic of peacekeepers' 'good intentions' – underpinned by a patriarchal, racialised, and technocratic sense of superiority – fed into the idea that they were entitled to 'do what needs to be done' and they knew best (or, at least, better than the local population). As Agnieszka Sobocinska has argued in relation to development volunteers, international humanitarian staff helped 'normalize a culture of foreign aid in which good

[11] Balibar, *We, the People of Europe?*

[12] P. Pallister-Wilkins, *Humanitarian Borders: Unequal Mobility and Saving Lives* (London: Verso Books, 2022).

[13] P. Satia, *Time's Monster: History, Conscience and Britain's Empire* (London: Penguin Books, 2022), p. 3.

[14] J. M. Hobson, *The Eurocentric Conception of World Politics: Western International Theory, 1760–2010* (Cambridge: Cambridge University Press, 2012), pp. 114–115.

intentions were considered sufficient to justify Western intervention across vast swathes of the globe'.[15]

The formative peacekeeping missions in this book serve as vital case studies for understanding how particular operations fundamentally and continually remade international cultures of peacekeeping and humanitarianism as well as reworked doctrines of imperial power and sovereignty during the Cold War. The Suez crisis led to the construction of the first armed peacekeeping mission, the United Nations Emergency Force (UNEF), which was established in Egypt in November 1956. Three years into UNEF's operations, the Congo crisis erupted, and the *Opération des Nations Unies au Congo* (ONUC) formally launched in July 1960. The UN secretary-general negotiated the first UN territorial administration, United Nations Temporary Executive Authority (UNTEA), and deployed a peacekeeping mission to West Papua in October 1962. Lastly, just as the ONUC mission was winding down, the UN Security Council authorised the United Nations Force in Cyprus (UNFICYP) on the island of Cyprus in March 1964.

The physical nature of mission deployment empowered mid-level staff, authorising them to take decisions on the ground that would otherwise be outside their purview. Mid-level bureaucrats were faced with different ex-colonial powers – British, Belgian, Dutch – and the intricacies of the political and economics legacies of each colonial administration on the host country's society. Additionally, these territorial disputes erupted at different points in the populations' processes of decolonisation: Egypt had been, nominally, independent from Britain for three decades before the Suez crisis; the Congo crisis developed a fortnight after Congolese Independence Day; West Papua was still colonised by the Dutch when the UNTEA mission arrived; and Cyprus was three years post-independence and precariously 'peaceful' until December 1963. The heterogeneity of the sovereignty disputes faced by UN peacekeeping staff during decolonisation presented a variety of logistical and diplomatic challenges in an increasingly hostile geopolitical environment. As the organisation's global position grew, the oversight of UN missions increased whilst member-states began to question the costs – financial and political – of the peacekeeping project as a whole.

Through an in-depth, comparative consideration of the roles that the original UN peacekeeping missions played during decolonisation, this book follows the evolving agendas and influence of the UN leadership and peacekeeping staff during decolonisation and makes three key arguments. First, the UN leadership used peacekeeping missions deployed to decolonising and post-colonial contexts as a means to protect and restore the reputation of the UN

[15] A. Sobocinska, *Saving the World?: Western Volunteers and the Rise of the Humanitarian-Development Complex* (Cambridge: Cambridge University Press, 2021), p. 4.

and demonstrate its value to the international community. During the Congo mission, the UN staff's political interference in the Congolese constitutional crisis in September 1960 was the first in a series of ONUC crises that ignited international controversy and criticism of the UN leadership's decision-making. Months later, the ONUC mission leadership's reaction to the murder of Congolese Prime Minister Patrice Lumumba and military operations in Katanga further threatened member-states' conceptions of the organisation's ability to manage an armed peacekeeping mission. In the wake of these operations in Congo, the UN leadership perceived the subsequent UNTEA and UNFICYP missions as vital diplomatic and operational opportunities to repair the organisation's standing and encourage member-states to pay their debts to the fiscally stretched UN. In the shadow of ONUC, deploying peacekeepers to the crises in West Papua and Cyprus enmeshed the international bureaucrats in diplomatic discussions about the future of sovereignty in the two disputed territories whilst the UN officials prioritised the repair and rebuilding of the organisation's international value.

This reputational crisis encouraged UN staff to dismiss 'local' elites in the mission's host states and extend control over the public narrative of the conflict. UN bureaucrats collected, transmitted, and omitted information from the field to the international community through their reports to the secretary-general and the Security Council, crafting international understandings of local population to the organisation's advantage. The mid-level UN staff used their bureaucratic mandate and administrative machinery to manage the 'official' narrative of the conflict. Peacekeepers' disengagement from host territories' activists was at odds with the UN leadership's carefully orchestrated identity of the organisation as a bastion of human rights and self-determination.[16] Instead, peacekeeping activities and decision-making, particularly during UNTEA and UNFICYP, were driven by a defensive organisational culture. Throughout this period, peacekeeping practices evolved to prioritise short-term solutions and anti-Soviet strategies, reflecting the trend of using the missions as both reputational repair and a 'quick fix' to prevent any potential Communist acts of aggression.

The second key finding is that peacekeeping missions were, during the height of the Cold War, primary UN instruments for pro-democratic, ideological interference. Moving away from a Cold War historiography traditionally dominated by national, typically Anglo-American, foreign policy,[17] as is particularly evident in scholarship on Western interests and interventions

[16] M. Alleyne, *Global Lies?: Propaganda, the UN and World Order* (New York: Springer, 2003).

[17] Exceptions include O. A. Westad, *The Global Cold War: Third World Interventions and the Making of Our Times* (Cambridge: Cambridge University Press, 2012); C. Dorn and K. Ghodsee, 'The Cold War Politicisation of Literacy: Communism, UNESCO, and the

during the Suez crisis, Congo crisis, and Cyprus crisis, this book reveals the efforts of UN peacekeeping leadership and staff to ensure host territories elected – or were annexed by – a pro-West (or non-aligned) leader. During the early 1950s, the UN weathered a 'McCarthyite' or anticommunist purge of the UN Secretariat, prompted by the investigations and trials led by US Senator Joseph McCarthy and the House Committee on Un-American Activities.[18] To further his political interests within the Secretariat, the UN secretary-general Dag Hammarskjöld cultivated a circle of elite American advisors, including Bunche and Andrew Cordier, to design and implement ways for the organisation to protect 'First World', liberal internationalist interests.[19] Peacekeeping missions offered unique opportunities for ideological interventions under the administrative and technocratic guise of the mission mandate, such as installing pro-West or non-aligned figures in positions of power in newly independent nations. The UN leadership staff justified their determined pursuit of anticommunism and anti-Soviet intrusion as a peace-building tactic rather than a violation of impartiality or an explicitly political act; for them, preventative action would prevent a 'Third World War'. High-level Secretariat staff – in particular, Hammarskjöld, Bunche, and U Thant – were anxious to ensure that the demands of host state politicians and populations would not unbalance their fight against global Communist aggression.

This culture of anticommunism within the UN leadership – in particular, the concept of anticommunism as a strategy for stabilising international peace and security – was inextricably linked with racism. As Richard Seymour argued, anticommunist aims preserved 'a global racial hierarchy in which "Anglo-Saxon" civilisation was seen as the best safeguard of democracy' and liberal peace.[20] This connection between racism and international peace and security is demonstrated in this book's third chapter as it uncovers how UN officials justified their political interference in Congolese infrastructure as necessary for the protection of law and order: a paternalistic choice that they had to make for the stability of the continent. ONUC staff's racialised judgements of Congolese Prime Minister Lumumba's capacity to govern compounded with

World Bank', *Diplomatic History*, 36:2 (2012), pp. 373–398; S. Lorenzini, *Global Development: A Cold War History* (Princeton: Princeton University Press, 2019).

18 M. Cohen, 'The United Nations Secretariat – Some Constitutional and Administrative Developments', *American Journal of International Law*, 49:3 (1955), pp. 295–319.

19 S. Hazzard, *Defeat of an Ideal: A Study of the Self-Destruction of the United Nations* (London: Little, Brown Book, 1973), p. 178; S. R. Weissman, *American Foreign Policy in the Congo, 1960–1964* (Ithaca: Cornell University Press, 1974), p. 60; G. Simons, *The United Nations: A Chronology of Conflict* (New York: Springer, 2016), p. 94.

20 R. Seymour, 'The Cold War, American Anticommunism and the Global "Colour Line"', in A. Anievas (ed.), *Race and Racism in International Relations: Confronting the Global Colour Line* (Abingdon: Routledge, 2014), p. 162.

rumours of his Communist fidelity to create a figure who presented, to them, a significant threat to Congolese stability and, thus, international peace and security. In this way, peacekeeping interventions in host states entrenched the racist assumption that maintaining white supremacy and Western, liberal interests in unstable states was in the greater interests of preserving international peace and security (i.e. anticommunism) *and* part of their mandate to restore law and order. The mid-level peacekeeping officials controlled host states' core structures of governance and intervened in political networks, deviating from and overruling the political demands of the local population, to ensure that the newly independent nation aligned with the organisation's anti-Soviet geopolitical goals.

Thirdly, this book uncovers how mid-level peacekeepers perpetuated colonial structures and took inspiration from imperial administrations. Mid-level UN peacekeepers used the missions to experiment with non-state administration and policing, inspired by imperial laws and executive powers, to establish mission control over host populations. Their reiteration of colonial stereotypes about Global South populations legitimised these unequal dynamics under the guise of peacebuilding and international development. Rooted in the nineteenth-century colonial rhetoric of *mission civilisatrice* and staffed by career diplomats, the peacekeeping bureaucracy on the ground was permeated with a culture of international exceptionalism further exacerbated by a humanitarian power hierarchy of the 'saviour', morally and intellectually positioned above the 'beneficiary' or host population.[21] As will be explored in Chapters 3 and 4, much of the mid-level peacekeepers' feelings of exceptionalism was grounded in a culture of racism and infantilisation of the Congolese and West Papuan populations, thus driving peacekeepers' paternalistic justifications for political interventions in the host countries. Colonial (pre)conceptions and methods of law and order inspired UN stabilising operations and were reinforced by a belief that technocratic judgement over the political direction of the post-colonial nation was superior to the opinions and desires of the local population. This book provides vital insight into how peacekeepers perceived and interacted with local civilians, as well as how peacekeeping practices were shaped by the interveners' perceptions, by illustrating the variety of practical and prejudicial colonial continuities in peacekeeping operations.

[21] P. Brantlinger, *Taming Cannibals: Race and the Victorians* (Ithaca: Cornell University Press, 2011); A. Lester, K. Boehme, and P. Mitchell (eds.), *Ruling the World: Freedom, Civilisation and Liberalism in the Nineteenth-Century British Empire* (Cambridge: Cambridge University Press, 2020); B. Weinstein, 'Developing Inequality', *American Historical Review*, 113:1 (2008), pp. 1–18.

Liberal Internationalism in Practice

The deployment of an armed peacekeeping mission in 1956 following the Suez crisis was the most substantial experiment in liberal internationalism since the drafting of the UN Charter in 1945. Liberal internationalism is defined as a transnational vision that considers 'the state' as the central unit of world politics and justifies interventions in other sovereign states for the propagation of liberal democracy.[22] For Western internationalists, the dominance of liberalism and liberal rules-based norms – such as rule of law, democracy, human rights, and global governance institutions – became an evangelical duty in order to protect international peace and promote global progress. However, as Jeanne Morefield has shown, there is a central paradox in liberal thought: 'liberals have frequently advocated a politics that both proclaims an ideological commitment to human equality and relegates sections of the population to the status of children'.[23] She has argued that liberals have long fancied 'themselves apostles of a radically transformative approach to world politics', whilst also requiring 'little to no change in the global status quo'.[24] This book addresses this paradox and traces the *practical* exercise of liberal internationalism through field-based peacekeeping missions whilst comparing with the rhetoric communicated by the UN headquarters.

Liberal internationalism largely enjoyed a sympathetic academic reading from left-leaning international relations scholars during the twentieth century.[25] Recent efforts to recover liberal internationalism from its crisis in the twenty-first century have inspired right-wing, pro-isolationist critiques that argue liberal internationalism is fundamentally flawed and therefore the entire international project is unworkable.[26] However, although this book critically engages with the liberal internationalist project, it does not seek to undermine *all* internationalisms or achievements of the UN system. Many historians, such as Steven Jensen and Anna Konieczna, have shown how international meetings and organisational forums, like the UN General Assembly and its

[22] D. Bell, *Dreamworlds of Race: Empire and the Utopian Destiny of Anglo-America* (Princeton: Princeton University Press, 2020), pp. 301–344.

[23] J. Morefield, *Covenants without Swords: Idealist Liberalism and the Spirit of Empire* (Princeton: Princeton University Press, 2005), p. 2.

[24] Morefield, *Covenants without Swords*, p. 2.

[25] F. Fukuyama, *The End of History and the Last Man* (New York: Free Press, 1992); G. J. Ikenberry, *A World Safe for Democracy: Liberal Internationalism and the Crises of Global Order* (New Haven: Yale University Press, 2020); T. Smith, *Why Wilson Matters: The Origin of American Liberal Internationalism and Its Crisis Today* (Princeton: Princeton University Press, 2017); G. J. Ikenberry, *Liberal Leviathan: The Origins, Crisis, and Transformation of the American World Order* (Princeton: Princeton University Press, 2012).

[26] P. Cunliffe, *Cosmopolitan Dystopia: International Intervention and the Failure of the West* (Manchester: Manchester University Press, 2020).

subcommittees, catalysed and/or amplified forms of anti-colonial politics, transnational solidarity networks, legal protections, and human rights norms during decolonisation.[27] However, that is not the focus of this book. Instead, it focuses on how liberal internationalist systems – such as peacekeeping – inherited and legitimised colonial structures into the post-colonial international order, thus perpetuating inequalities on the ground and obstructing alternative forms of anti-colonial politics.

Conveying the racialised prejudices at the heart of UN peacekeeping bureaucracies requires a critical approach to the racist underpinnings of international relations.[28] From a theoretical perspective, the tensions between the UN's liberal practices and colonialism are well acknowledged, if not yet historically traced. For instance, Paul Musgrave and Daniel H. Nexon have argued that 'liberal values uphold the inviolability of sovereign politics that are themselves imperial in character … international institutions, often regarded as innately liberal, can themselves act in ways not dissimilar to empires'.[29] Conceptions of racism within international relations has been traditionally limited by the assumption that the 'elite Western subject' was the 'implicit cosmopolitan subject' and central 'agent in the task of global justice',[30] but critical research has begun to examine the racial power dynamics, inequalities, and hierarchies perpetuated through liberal international organisations.[31]

[27] S. L. B. Jensen, *The Making of International Human Rights: The 1960s, Decolonization, and the Reconstruction of Global Values* (Cambridge: Cambridge University Press, 2017); A. Konieczna, '"We the People of the United Nations": The UN and the Global Campaigns Against Apartheid', in A. Konieczna and R. Skinner, *A Global History of Anti-Apartheid: 'Forward to Freedom' in South Africa* (London: Palgrave Macmillan, 2019), pp. 67–103.

[28] For more on the racial underpinnings of the international relations system, specifically the democratic peace theses, see E. A. Henderson, 'Navigating the Muddy Waters of the Mainstream: Tracing the Mystification of Racism in International Relations', in W. C. Rich (ed.), *African American Perspectives on Political Science* (Philadelphia: Temple University Press, 2007).

[29] P. Musgrave and D. H. Nexon, 'States of Empire: Liberal Ordering and Imperial Relations', in T. Dunne and T. Flockhart (eds.), *Liberal World Orders* (Oxford: Oxford University Press/ British Academy, 2013), p. 212.

[30] I. Valdez, 'Association, Reciprocity, and Emancipation: A Transnational Account of the Politics of Global Justice', in D. Bell (ed.), *Empire, Race and Global Justice* (Cambridge: Cambridge University Press, 2019), pp. 121–122.

[31] R. Vitalis, *White World Order, Black Power Politics: The Birth of American International Relations* (Ithaca: Cornell University Press, 2015; B. G. Jones, 'Race in the Ontology of International Order', *Political Studies*, 56:4 (2008), pp. 907–927; W. E. Connolly, 'The Liberal Image of the Nation', in D. Ivison et al. (eds.), *Political Theory and the Rights of Indigenous Peoples* (Cambridge: Cambridge University Press, 2000); L. A. Viola, *The Closure of the International System: How Institutions Create Political Equalities and Hierarchies* (Cambridge: Cambridge University Press, 2020); R. A. Rubinstein, *Peacekeeping under Fire: Culture and Intervention* (Boulder: Paradigm Publishers, 2008).

International organisations, like the UN, behaved as racial structures despite projecting as technocratic, race-neutral bureaucracies.[32] However, it is not the racism of individual international staff that deserves detailed analysis. Instead, we should focus our attention on the organisational mechanisms and interests that supported, benefitted, and disguised the translation of officials' racist beliefs into patterns of inequality within UN systems and agencies, perpetuating violence and discrimination within host populations and normalising racialised 'knowledge' as expert 'facts'.

Through the construction of the UN and the gradual development of peacekeeping, the imposition of liberal ideals through internationalist cooperation and military intervention was transformed from a hypothetical discussion to a practical act. The UN Charter enshrined liberal internationalism as the political norm within the organisation in 1945 as part of the organisation's purpose as an instrument of conflict prevention and democratic hegemony.[33] Globalist thinkers in the 1940s and 1950s traditionally understood post-war liberal internationalism as part of a shift *away* from the nation-state sovereignty framework,[34] the dilution of Westphalian sovereignty facilitating the shift towards the implementation of collective security and a shared global morality.[35] However, liberal peace relied upon the construction of stable democratic units and so the UN's procedures, organs, and functions were dedicated to *protecting* the nation-state paradigm – especially the sovereignty of its permanent member-states (Britain, France, the United States, China, and the Soviet Union).[36] For Thomas Weiss, the era of decolonisation altered the

32 Vitalis, *White World Order, Black Power Politics*; E. A. Henderson, 'Hidden in Plain Sight: Racism in International Relations Theory', *Cambridge Review of International Affairs*, 26:1 (2016), pp. 71–92; Valdez, 'Association, Reciprocity, and Emancipation'; V. Ray, 'A Theory of Racialized Organizations', *American Sociological Review*, 84:1 (2019), pp. 26–53.

33 T. G. Weiss, 'The United Nations: Before, During and After 1945', *International Affairs*, 91:6 (2015), p. 1224.

34 O. Rosenboim, *The Emergence of Globalism: Visions of World Order in Britain and the United States, 1939–1950* (Princeton: Princeton University Press, 2017), p. 177; Q. Slobodian, *Globalists: The End of Empire and the Birth of Neoliberalism* (Cambridge, MA: Harvard University Press, 2018), p. 185.

35 For more on this debate, see S. M. Makinda, 'Sovereignty and International Security: Challenges for the United Nations', *Global Governance*, 2:2 (1996), p. 150; S. M. Makinda, 'The United Nations and State Sovereignty: Mechanism for Managing International Security', *Australian Journal of Political Science*, 33:1 (1998), p. 101; G. J. Ikenberry, 'Liberal Internationalism 3.0: America and the Dilemmas of Liberal World Order', *Perspectives on Politics*, 7:1 (2009), pp. 71–87.

36 E. Muschik, 'Managing the World: The United Nations, Decolonization, and the Strange Triumph of State Sovereignty in the 1950s and 1960s', *Journal of Global History*, 13:1 (2018), pp. 121–144; J. D. Kelly and M. Kaplan, *Represented Communities: Fiji and World Decolonization* (Chicago: University of Chicago Press, 2001), pp. 1–29.

agenda, 'but the UN's basic structure is fundamentally intact, a formidable bastion of state sovereignty'.[37] In the same vein, Amitav Ghosh has described the UN as 'the child of all the world's hierarchies'.[38]

Expanding on the legal and diplomatic powers of the League of Nations and the UN Trusteeship Committee,[39] peacekeeping missions provided liberal internationalists with a legitimate instrument to militarily police the internal affairs of vulnerable states and intervene in territorial disputes without invalidating the sovereign protections of powerful nations. UN staff imposed – or attempted to impose – 'democracy' and other liberal norms onto decolonising and post-colonial territories in order to control their trajectory towards liberal peace, believing that democratic states would be less likely to engage in armed interstate conflict or to align with the Soviet Union.[40] Liberalism's 'capacious' meaning by the mid-twentieth century was the result of its expansion ad absurdum during the Cold War by Western thinkers in opposition to Communist and totalitarian regimes.[41] Indeed, it had become 'the metacategory of Western political discourse'.[42] Liberal internationalist ideals were fundamental to UN Secretariat peacebuilding strategies, but implementation of this ideology had been initially restricted by the organisation's limited functions and military capacity.[43] The UN peacekeeping bureaucrats fostered a specific liberal internationalist imaginary for implementing the stability of post-colonial nations.[44] Thus liberal internationalism – manifested through peacekeeping missions – was a form of colonialism as it justified the international staff's prioritisation of their own anxieties and solutions over the

[37] T. G. Weiss, 'What Happened to the Idea of World Government', *International Studies Quarterly*, 53:2 (2009), p. 255.

[38] A. Ghosh, 'The Global Reservation: Notes toward an Ethnography of International Peacekeeping', *Cultural Anthropology*, 9:3 (1994), p. 413.

[39] C. Storr, *International Status in the Shadow of Empire: Nauru and the Histories of International Law* (Cambridge: Cambridge University Press, 2020).

[40] For more on the democratic peace theory, see D. M. Gibler, *The Territorial Peace: Borders, State Development, and International Conflict* (Cambridge: Cambridge University Press, 2012); Bell, *Dreamworlds of Race*; M. W. Doyle, 'Liberalism and World Politics', *The American Political Science Review*, 80:4 (1986), pp. 1151–1169; A. J. Bellamy and P. Williams (eds.), *Peace Operations and Global Order* (Abingdon: Routledge, 2014).

[41] D. Bell, 'What Is Liberalism?', *Political Theory*, 42:6 (2014), p. 683.

[42] Bell, 'What Is Liberalism?', p. 683.

[43] Although there were many liberal and illiberal international world visions, this book focuses on the hegemonic, mainstream policies of liberal internationalism. For more on the diversity of internationalist visions during the twentieth century, see P. Hetherington and G. Sluga, 'Liberal and Illiberal Internationalisms', *Journal of World History*, 31:1 (2020), pp. 1–9.

[44] R. Wilde, *International Territorial Administration: How Trusteeship and the Civilising Mission Never Went Away* (Oxford: Oxford University Press, 2008), p. 291.

rights, demands, and long-term protection of host populations.[45] Racialised ideas about Global South populations' lack of intelligence and political ignorance combined with international security concerns about the expansion of Soviet power in post-colonial nations to legitimise UN interference as 'for their own good'. This peacekeeping paternalism in the field was thus driven by the moral logic of liberal internationalism; the (liberal) ends justify the (interfering) means. This vision encouraged and entitled mid-level UN staff to use their authority within host states to interfere in the political direction of the territory, perpetuate relationships with ex-colonial powers, and silence activist groups; peacekeeping missions were practical experiments in the Western interests of liberal peace.

There was unequal respect for sovereignty at the heart of the liberal internationalist project and thus peacekeeping practice. This unevenness was driven by the geopolitical position of a state within the international order, differentiating state access to sovereignty and its protections. The UN Secretariat's respect for sovereignty was underpinned by colonial models of 'civilisation' and geopolitical inequality; a state's right to non-intervention was determined by its perceived geopolitical value until it reached a certain racialised 'standard' of liberal politics. As Adom Getachew has argued, 'The protections that guarantees of sovereign equality and nonintervention afforded were unevenly distributed, making new and weak postcolonial states vulnerable to arbitrary interventions and encroachments at the hands of larger, more powerful states as well as private actors.'[46] Member-states' and organisations' compliance with sovereignty was reliant on the perceived geopolitical value of the state in question rather than respect for the principle of sovereignty itself. Therefore, UN peacekeeping practices during decolonisation ensured that liberal internationalism shaped the post-colonial international order; sovereignty became simultaneously inviolable and violable (through multilateral intervention) depending on a state or territory's international value. The UN peacekeepers played an instrumental role in implementing unequal respect for sovereignty within the post-colonial international order as they sought to, counter-intuitively, construct democratic units through political violation and interference. By tracing neglected or obscured sources of power within UN operations, particularly decision-making in the field, this book draws back the curtain on the operations and politics of the opaque organisational bureaucracy. It reveals, at a granular level, how mid-level staff

[45] For more on the individual agency of international interveners versus the homogenous 'international', see J. Wallis, 'It's the Little Things: The Role of International Interveners in the Social (re)Construction of the International Peace Architecture', *Global Society*, 35:4 (2021), pp. 456–478.

[46] A. Getachew, *Worldmaking after Empire: The Rise and Fall of Self-Determination* (Princeton: Princeton University Press, 2019), p. 113.

framed, protected, and expanded the UN's position in the international community whilst protecting liberal standards of 'peace' and 'sovereignty'.

Navigating the Muddy Waters of Decolonisation

It was the specific generation of decolonisation in the mid-twentieth century that catalysed the demand for UN peacekeeping missions as the preferred recourse for protracted territorial and border disputes. As Yoav Di-Capua has identified, 'Whether we examine Latin America, Africa, Asia, or the Middle East, again and again a violent pattern repeated itself, in which a recently decolonized country was bullied into choosing sides and slowly sank into chronic civil war marked by foreign intervention.'[47] Whilst European empires fractured across the Global South in the mid-twentieth century, previously unified colonial dominions splintered into problematic or 'lumpy' territorial units and local activists mobilised to avoid re-colonisation, resist imperial counter-insurgency, and demand liberation.[48] In tandem with this post-colonial mobilisation, many newly independent states sought to assert their nationhood and articulate ideas of citizenship (and distinguish those excluded from its protection), provoking land and border disputes.[49] This is not to say that decolonisation – as a political, cultural, and societal process – began in 1945. Anti-colonial resistance, revolutionary struggle, and Global South nationalism had a long history pre-1945 which

[47] Y. Di-Capua, *No Exit: Arab Existentialism, Jean-Paul Sartre, and Decolonization* (Chicago: University of Chicago Press, 2018), p. 170.

[48] This book builds upon the expanding literature on sovereignty, borders, and the limits of statehood during decolonisation: M. Thomas and G. Curless (eds.), *Decolonisation and Conflict: Colonial Comparisons and Legacies* (London: Bloomsbury, 2017); L. Benton, *A Search for Sovereignty: Law and Geography in European Empires, 1400–1900* (Cambridge: Cambridge University Press, 2010); E. Leake and D. Haines, 'Lines of (In) Convenience: Sovereignty and Border-Making in Postcolonial South Asia, 1947–1965', *The Journal of Asian Studies*, 76:4 (2017), pp. 963–985; N. Wheatley, 'Legal Pluralism as Temporal Pluralism: Historical Rights, Legal Vitalism, and Non-Synchronous Sovereignty', in D. Edelstein et al. (eds.), *Power and Time: Temporalities in Conflict and the Making of History* (Chicago: University of Chicago Press, 2020); C. Lu, 'Decolonizing Borders, Self-Determination, and Global Justice', in Bell (ed.), *Empire, Race and Global Justice*.

[49] Key scholarship on this issue includes F. Cooper, *Citizenship between Empire and Nation: Remaking France and French Africa, 1945–1960* (Princeton: Princeton University Press, 2014); E. Hunter, *Political Thought and the Public Sphere in Tanzania: Freedom, Democracy and Citizenship in the Era of Decolonization* (Cambridge: Cambridge University Press, 2015); J. MacArthur, *Cartography and the Political Imagination: Mapping Community in Colonial Kenya* (Athens: Ohio University Press, 2016); M. Terretta, *Nation of Outlaws, State of Violence: Nationalism, Grassfields Tradition and State Building in Cameroon* (Athens: Ohio University Press, 2014); J. Pearce, *Political Identity and Conflict in Central Angola, 1975–2002* (Cambridge: Cambridge University Press, 2015).

has been addressed in detail by imperial historians such as Michael Goebel, Susan Pedersen, and Kim Wagner.[50] Earlier communal alignments, sovereign imaginaries, and anti-colonial insurgencies formally or informally developed by colonised populations (re)emerged as a consequence of the territorial and geopolitical transformations in the post-Second World War period, galvanised by the newly won independence of others.

However, revolutions and decolonisation did not automatically lead to egalitarian politics in post-colonial settings. Rather than an uncomplicated achievement and victory over imperialism, global decolonisation processes provoked a reframing of international interests and violence in Global South territories as well as opening spaces for new imperialist powers.[51] Some post-colonial nations appointed authoritarian leaders who began to assume their own imperialistic and counter-revolutionary goals, such as annexing neighbouring territories and silencing ethnic minorities, thus mapping difference onto territory.[52] The nature of territorial conquest shifted post-1945 as states focused on seizing smaller areas with reduced risks of defence or international condemnation rather than colonising entire states.[53] As Brad Simpson has argued, 'Many of the countries that deployed self-determination claims with the greatest fervour after 1945, such as India, Indonesia, and Algeria, denied them even more fiercely when made by restive ethnic and regional minorities within their borders.'[54] Anti-colonial authoritarianism had expanded during the Second World War and had achieved further success in the post-war period once decolonisation ascribed territorial power to these new state leaders.[55]

[50] M. Goebel, *Anti-imperial Metropolis: Interwar Paries and the Seeds of Third World Nationalism* (Cambridge: Cambridge University Press, 2015); S. Pedersen, *The Guardians: The League of Nations and the Crisis of Empire* (Oxford: Oxford University Press, 2015); K. Wagner, *Amritsar 1919: An Empire of Fear and the Making of a Massacre* (New Haven: Yale University Press, 2019).

[51] J. Namakkal, *Unsettling Utopia: The Making and Unmaking of French India* (New York: Columbia University Press, 2021).

[52] M. Shahabuddin, *Minorities and the Making of Postcolonial States in International Law* (Cambridge: Cambridge University Press, 2021); K. Senaratne, *Internal Self-Determination in International Law: History, Theory, and Practice* (Cambridge: Cambridge University Press, 2021); M. Fibiger, 'A Diplomatic Counter-revolution: Indonesian Diplomacy and the Invasion of East Timor', *Modern Asian Studies*, 55:2 (2021), pp. 587–628; L. Lopesi, *False Divides* (Wellington: Bridget Williams Books, 2018), p. 14; B. Simpson, 'The United States and the Curious History of Self-Determination', *Diplomatic History*, 36:4 (2012), p. 676; A. Anghie, 'The Evolution of International Law: Colonial and Postcolonial Realities', *Third World Quarterly*, 27:5 (2006), p. 749.

[53] D. Altman, 'The Evolution of Territorial Conquest after 1945 and the Limits of the Territorial Integrity Norm', *International Organization*, 74:3 (2020), pp. 490–522.

[54] Simpson, 'The Curious History of Self-Determination', p. 676.

[55] D. Motadel, 'The Global Authoritarian Moment and the Revolt against Empire', *The American Historical Review*, 124:3 (2019), pp. 843–877.

More than a singular 'moment of possibility', the period of decolonisation broke the world apart, creating an opportunity for a reinvention of sovereignty and a dramatic reimagining of geopolitical hierarchies and power as well as opportunities for liberation and solidarity. Although many national and transnational groups pursued anti-colonial aims as a way of achieving independence or uniting liberationist movements across the Global South during this first phase of decolonisation,[56] many post-colonial nations with their own imperial aspirations also used 'anti-colonial' rhetoric and coalitions to align themselves with other decolonising or newly independent nations.[57] Rather than prompting a common understanding of 'anti-colonialism', this generation of decolonisation saw the emergence of plural 'anti-colonial' movements, with diverse experiences and definitions of colonialism, statehood, self-determination, and territorial sovereignty. Thus, the terms 'anti-colonialism' and 'self-determination' were diversely used and understood by a variety of community, national, and international actors, including European colonial powers.[58]

Whilst seeking imperial expansion across neighbouring territories, many post-colonial nations participated in – and even organised – 'anti-colonial' coalitions, many of which were formalised during the 1955 Bandung Conference, further muddying the politics of the 'anti-colonialist' position within the international community. Post-colonial nations formally organised the Afro-Asian voting bloc in the General Assembly following Bandung and controlled the dominant 'anti-colonial' position in the international community, with some using this alignment to exempt their own expansionist foreign policy from accusations of imperialism.[59] Newly independent states, such as Indonesia and India, argued that any attempts to annex other territories was both distinct from *and* as a result of their experiences of European imperialism; these were regions that had shared pre-colonial histories and they were territories that had been unified under a common colonial ruling power. These post-colonial nations contextualised their expansionist activities as part of a process of restoring the pre-colonial or maintaining colonial borders, thus characterising their imperialism as a natural and righteous part of their

[56] For more on anti-colonial transnational networks and movements during the 1950s and 1960s, see J. Munro, *The Anticolonial Front: The African American Freedom Struggle and Global Decolonisation, 1945–1960* (Cambridge: Cambridge University Press, 2017).

[57] H. Weber and P. Winanti, 'The "Bandung Spirit" and Solidarist Internationalism', *Australian Journal of International Affairs*, 70:4 (2016), p. 403.

[58] V. Kuitenbrouwer, 'Beyond the "Trauma of Decolonisation": Dutch Cultural Diplomacy during the West New Guinea Question', *The Journal of Imperial and Commonwealth History*, 44:2 (2016), p. 309; O. C. Tassinis, '"The Consciousness of a Duty Done"? British Attitudes towards Self-Determination and the Case of the Sudan', *The British Yearbook of International Law* (2019), pp. 1–56.

[59] C. Ewing, 'The Colombo Powers: Crafting Diplomacy in the Third World and Launching Afro-Asia at Bandung', *Cold War History*, 19:1 (2019), pp. 1–19.

post-colonial nationhood under the legal principle of *uti possidetis* (translated 'as you possess').[60] Indeed, many post-colonial states searched through (pre) colonial-era cartography to support their territorial claims and legitimise their annexations.[61] Through this territorial 'scramble' during decolonisation, many middle power nations projected their own, or other Afro-Asian bloc states', imperialist claims as the practical implementation of 'anti-colonial' foreign policy; their expansionism was built on the belief that their shared colonial experience, geographic proximity, or, even, a similar climate qualified them to 'save' territories and populations from European domination through annexation.[62] Thus, these post-colonial states shaped their independent national identity from both their own colonial experiences *and* imperial aspirations.

The increase in decolonising and post-colonial conflicts throughout the 1940s, 1950s, and 1960s presented opportunities for reinventing the functions and mandates of the UN as a political agent in its own right.[63] The UN Secretariat staff assumed a front line role in the construction of the liberal international order as arbiter of international law, collective security, multilateralism, and statehood following the upheaval of the Second World War.[64] Allied foreign policy elites developed the inter-governmental organisation as they reflected on the need for an improved global governance body to police international aggression in response to the impotence of the League of Nations during the 1930s.[65] Many of the League staff and agencies transferred directly into the UN bureaucracy, providing an organisational skeleton and pre-

[60] D. D. Agusman, A. Afriansyah, and I. Fadilah, 'Debunking the Pandora Box of Decolonisation: An Inquiry into Papuan Separatism from the Lens of International Law', in J. Rehman, A. Shahid, and S. Foster (eds.), *The Asian Yearbook of Human Rights and Humanitarian Law: Volume 5* (Leiden: Brill, 2021), pp. 282–308.

[61] P. M. McGarr, 'The Long Shadow of Colonial Cartography: Britain and the Sino-Indian War of 1962', *Journal of Strategic Studies*, 42:5 (2019), p. 631; B. Guyot-Réchard, 'Tangled Lands: Burma and India's Unfinished Separation, 1937–1948', *The Journal of Asian Studies*, 80:2 (2021), pp. 293–315; H. Kumarasingham, *Constitution-Making in Asia: Decolonisation and State-Building in the Aftermath of the British Empire* (Abingdon: Routledge, 2016); K. J. Gardner, *The Frontier Complex: Geopolitics and the Making of the India-China Border, 1846–1962* (Cambridge: Cambridge University Press, 2021); Z. Wang, 'A Troubled Alliance: Sino-British Conflicts over Tibet', *The International History Review*, 44:1 (2022), pp. 1–25.

[62] S. Amrith, *Unruly Waters: How Mountain Rivers and Monsoons Have Shaped South Asia's History* (London: Allen Lane, 2018), p. 157.

[63] Muschik, 'Managing the World', pp. 121–144; O. Turner, '"Finishing the Job": The UN Special Committee on Decolonization and the Politics of Self-Governance', *Third World Quarterly*, 34:7 (2013), pp. 1193–1208.

[64] M. Mazower, *No Enchanted Palace: The End of Empire and the Ideological Origins of the United Nations* (Princeton: Princeton University Press, 2013), p. 195; Kelly and Kaplan, *Represented Communities*, pp. 1–29.

[65] Pedersen, *The Guardians*, p. 396; E. Borgwardt, *A New Deal for the World: America's Vision for Human Rights* (Cambridge, MA: Harvard University Press, 2005); S. Wertheim,

existing international community.[66] The UN provided a post-war locus for national and international decision-making by hosting, deliberating, and implementing new international norms from 24 October 1945.[67] However, inheriting the functions of the League limited the reactivity of the organisation, despite its UN Charter suggesting powers to intervene militarily in sovereign territory in contexts of aggression or breaches of the peace. Whilst the number of UN member-states increased throughout the 1950s, the organisation's utility shifted once more, from a static creation of victors' justice to an important space for Cold War belligerence and colonial oversight.[68] Member-states' anxieties over the unprecedented legal and diplomatic processes of decolonisation, and the lack of international recourse with which to thwart permanent member-states' aggression, emboldened the secretary-general Dag Hammarskjöld to design and deploy the first armed peacekeeping mission in 1956. Through this functional expansion, the field-based UN peacekeeping bureaucracy emerged as not only a reactive military force, but also a successful experiment in liberal internationalism and, as such, a conduit for the perpetuation of colonial structures within decolonising contexts. As peacekeepers experimented with non-state diplomacy in the field and bargained with the warring parties, they reinforced a post-colonial world vision with the UN at the centre of state regulation and the international security paradigm.

The United Nations as a Historical Subject

Diplomatic historians are increasingly reflecting on the pivotal position of international staff and inter-governmental organisations in the construction of the post-colonial world order.[69] This flourishing subfield is a result of what

Tomorrow the World: The Birth of US Global Supremacy (Cambridge, MA: Harvard University Press, 2020).

66 H. A. Ikonomou, K. Gram-Skjoldager, and T. Kahlert (eds.), *Organizing the Twentieth-Century World: International Organizations and the Emergence of International Public Administration, 1920–1960s* (London: Bloomsbury, 2020).

67 P. Gordon Lauren, 'First Principles of Racial Equality: History and the Politics and Diplomacy of Human Rights Provisions in the United Nations Charter', *Human Rights Quarterly*, 5:1 (1983), pp. 1–26; K. W. Stiles, 'The Power of Procedure and the Procedures of the Powerful: Anti-Terror Law in the United Nations', *Journal of Peace Research*, 43:1 (2006), pp. 37–54.

68 J. Pearson, 'Defending Empire at the United Nations: The Politics of International Colonial Oversight in the Era of Decolonisation', *Journal of Imperial and Commonwealth History*, 45:3 (2017), pp. 525–549; A. O'Malley, '"What an Awful Body the UN Have Become!!" Anglo American–UN Relations during the Congo Crisis, February–December 1961', *Journal of Transatlantic Studies*, 14:1 (2016), pp. 26–46.

69 Some recent examples include: J. Martin, *The Meddlers: Sovereignty, Empire, and the Birth of Global Economic Governance* (Cambridge, MA: Harvard University Press, 2022); Ikonomou et al. (eds.), *Organizing the Twentieth-Century World*; E. Roehrlich, *Inspectors*

Erez Manela recently termed the 'turn away from methodological nationalism' in 'new international history'.[70] Methodological nationalism was first identified by Andreas Wimmer and Nina Glick Schiller as 'the assumption that the nation state society is the natural social and political form of the modern world'.[71] A turn away from this lens has fostered more nuanced and expansive understandings of political life beyond national borders. As part of this 'transnational turn', more historians are studying international organisations, such as the UN, for insight into processes of globalisation, cultural circulation, statecraft, and economic development.[72] As Glenda Sluga and Sunil Amrith have asserted, 'the UN and its various international organizations offer a seductive and under-utilized focus for seeking out and resuscitating forms of experience and thinking that transcend the assumption that the political borders of nations determine the nature of experiences.'[73] By expanding beyond the nation-state lens or nationalist discipline, the influence of international organisations is visible not only in transnational diplomatic forums but also in the arenas of domestic politics, law, healthcare, race relations, technical expertise, and human rights. Traditionally, historiographical attention to the UN has largely been limited to examining the key personalities and events involved in the origins of the organisation in the immediate post-war period. However, there has recently been an uptick in scholars, such as Roland Burke and Steven Jensen, who have cast the UN with a principal role in decolonisation's geopolitical, cultural, and conceptual transformations.[74]

There are two main approaches to the history of the UN during decolonisation. The first focuses on the UN's role as a diplomatic forum, a setting for

for Peace: A History of the International Atomic Energy Agency (Baltimore: Johns Hopkins University Press, 2022); L. Humbert, *Reinventing French Aid: The Politics of Humanitarian Relief in French-Occupied Germany, 1945–1952* (Cambridge: Cambridge University Press, 2021).

70 E. Manela, 'International Society as a Historical Subject', *Diplomatic History*, 44:2 (2020), p. 184.

71 A. Wimmer and N. G. Schiller, 'Methodological Nationalism and the Study of Migration', *European Journal of Sociology*, 43:2 (2002), pp. 217–240.

72 S. Kott, 'International Organizations – A Field of Research for Global History', *Zeithistorische Forschungen/Studies in Contemporary History*, 8 (2011), p. 446; C. A. Bayley et al., 'AHR Conversation: On Transnational History', *The American Historical Review*, 111:5 (2006), pp. 1441–1464; A. Iriye, 'The Internationalization of History', *The American Historical Review*, 94:1 (1989), pp. 1–10; J. Reinisch, 'Introduction: Agents of Internationalism', *Contemporary European History*, 25:2 (2016), pp. 195–205.

73 G. Sluga and S. Amrith, 'New Histories of the United Nations', *Journal of World History*, 19:3 (2008), p. 252.

74 N. Eggers, J. L. Pearson, and A. Almada e Santos (eds.), *The United Nations and Decolonization* (Abingdon: Routledge, 2020).

member-state discourse and instrumentalisation.[75] The organisation's public forums provided space for the amplification of 'anti-colonial' voices, such as those of the Afro-Asian bloc, through UN deliberative organs. These diplomatic histories argue the General Assembly, and its supplementary committees such as the Third Committee, were crucial, if ambiguous, incubatory spaces for international human rights, global democracy, and anti-colonial discourses. This book takes a different tack and focuses on the individual decision-making of UN staff, such as international civil servants, in shaping international development discourse and state-building during decolonisation from the field. In line with a second body of work, led by scholars such as Eva-Maria Muschik, Guy Fiti Sinclair, and Meredith Terretta, this book forges a more complicated understanding of the UN and its international staff as historical agents in their own right, investigating how the organisation staff shaped post-colonial nationalism and global governance in often unexpected ways.[76]

It also builds and expands upon the idea of the 'Third United Nations', identified by Thomas Weiss, Tatiana Carayannis, and Richard Jolly.[77] The 'Third United Nations' refers to the 'additional' UN – supplementary to the traditional analysis of a 'first' UN (member-states) and a 'second UN' (UN Secretariat staff). This 'third' network highlights the 'insider-outsider' roles of 'nongovernmental organizations (NGOs), external experts, scholars, consultants, and committed citizens' in supporting the UN's inter-governmental bureaucracy.[78] However, this book demonstrates the fluidity between these

[75] R. Burke, *Decolonization and the Evolution of International Human Rights* (Philadelphia: University of Pennsylvania Press, 2011); Jensen, *The Making of International Human Rights*; Wertheim, *Tomorrow, the World*; G. Garavini, *After Empires: European Integration, Decolonization, and the Challenge from the Global South 1957–1986* (Oxford: Oxford University Press, 2012); M. A. Heiss, *Fulfilling the Sacred Trust: The UN Campaign for International Accountability for Dependent Territories in the Era of Decolonization* (Ithaca: Cornell University Press, 2020).

[76] E. Muschik, 'Special Issue Introduction: Towards a Global History of International Organizations and Decolonization', *Journal of Global History*, 17:2 (2022), pp. 173–190; E. Muschik, *Building States: The United Nations, Development, and Decolonization, 1945–1965* (New York: Columbia University Press, 2022); E. Muschik, '"A Pretty Kettle of Fish": United Nations Assistance in the Mass Dismissal of Labor in the Iranian Oil Industry, 1959–1960', *Labor History*, 60:1 (2019), pp. 8–23; G. F. Sinclair, 'Forging Modern States with Imperfect Tools: United Nations Technical Assistance for Public Administration in Decolonized States', *Humanity*, 11:1 (2020), pp. 54–83; M. Terretta, '"We Had Been Fooled into Thinking that the UN Watches over the Entire World": Human Rights, UN Trust Territories, and Africa's Decolonization', *Human Rights Quarterly*, 34:2 (2012), pp. 329–360.

[77] T. G. Weiss, T. Carayannis, and R. Jolly, 'The "Third" United Nations', *Global Governance*, 15:1 (2009), pp. 123–142.

[78] Weiss et al., 'The "Third" United Nations', p. 123.

supposedly discrete three 'United Nations'. Staff moved between these different networks, with many state representatives serving briefly as UN Secretariat personnel, like UNTEA administrator Djalal Abdoh, or becoming consultants for NGOs, and vice versa. Similarly, it was not uncommon for Secretariat staff to have been previously employed by imperial administrations, especially as positions became scarce during decolonisation. Understanding this fluidity between the different UN networks and 'insider-outsider' positions provides insight into the elite cliques and recruitment cultures within the international organisation; the UN was a bureaucracy constructed from referrals, recommendations, and family connections rather than a meritocracy.

The roles of international staff and agencies in twentieth-century state-building and diplomacy has gained recent historiographical attention, drawing attention to the gatekeeping function of early international organisations.[79] As peace settlements from the conclusion of the First World War constructed different territorial borders, reconfigured administrations sought legitimisation and entry into the 'global community'. Historians of the League of Nations have illustrated the multiple methods that the League used to legitimise the 'statehood' of territories through their membership of the organisation during the interwar period.[80] For instance, as Megan Donaldson has argued, the admission of 'fringe' nations, such as Ethiopia, into the League indicated a tentative shift in international standards of statehood towards governmental stability rather than traditional European standards of 'civility'.[81] However, admission was not in itself an anti-colonial victory. Indeed, Susan Pedersen has demonstrated how the League's eventual acceptance of Iraq's exit from British tutelage and achievement of 'independence' in 1932 marked the beginning of an increase of 'client states' within international society.[82] Thus,

79 For instance, S. Chesterman, *You, the People: The United Nations, Transitional Administration, and State-Building* (Oxford: Oxford University Press, 2005); A. Hurrell, *On Global Order: Power, Values, and the Constitution of International Society* (Oxford: Oxford University Press, 2007).

80 Pedersen, *The Guardians*, p. 50; M. Donaldson, 'The League of Nations, Ethiopia, and the Making of States', *Humanity*, 11:1 (2020), pp. 6–31; S. A. Wempe, 'A League to Preserve Empires: Understanding the Mandates System & Avenues for Future Scholarly Inquiry', *The American Historical Review*, 124:5 (2019), p. 1725; P. Clavin, 'The Austrian Hunger Crisis and the Genesis of International Organization after the First World War', *International Affairs*, 90:2 (2014), pp. 265–278; A. L. Staples, *The Birth of Development: How the World Bank, Food and Agriculture Organization, and World Health Organization Changed the World, 1945–1965* (Ohio: Kent State University Press, 2006).

81 Donaldson, 'The League of Nations, Ethiopia, and the Making of States'.

82 S. Pedersen, 'Getting Out of Iraq – In 1932: The League of Nations and the Road to Normative Statehood', *American Historical Review*, 115:4 (2010), pp. 975–1000.

although the standards of acceptance were shifting, colonial powers remained adept at manipulating international structures for their own interests.[83]

Similarly, marginalised populations' visions of territorial sovereignty became increasingly problematic for the next generation of global leadership during the decades of 1950s and 1960s, especially in cases of border disputes or secession.[84] Religious and ethnic minority populations and indigenous communities used letters, petitions, and the international media to highlight their oppression to the UN leadership and UN public forums, anxious of being 'left behind' in the nation-state system and blocked entry to human rights protections and self-determination during the 1960s.[85] Limited efforts at codifying minority rights within post-colonial constitutions failed to address the international structures that prevented non-state groups from access to the global community and international rights.[86] As Julie MacArthur, George Roberts, Lydia Walker, and Natasha Wheatley have recently shown, territorial disputes over the 'peripheral' – or traditionally marginalised – borders of minority populations highlighted the inadequacies of the nation-state paradigm and the inequalities of sovereign protection during this transformative period.[87] Scholars have also identified the artificiality of nation-state borders, legal protections, notions of 'citizenship', and ethno-political territoriality, especially in (ex-)colonial contexts.[88] Imperial powers drew borders to their

[83] M. Spanu, 'The Hierarchical Society: The Politics of Self-Determination and the Constitution of New States after 1919', *European Journal of International Relations*, 26:2 (2020), pp. 372–396.

[84] J. MacArthur, 'Decolonizing Sovereignty: States of Exception along the Kenya–Somali Frontier', *American Historical Review*, 124:1 (2019); E. Leake, *The Defiant Border: The Afghan-Pakistan Borderlands in the Era of Decolonization, 1936–1965* (Cambridge: Cambridge University Press, 2017); N. Chandhoke, *Contested Secessions: Self-Determination, Democracy, and Kashmir* (Oxford: Oxford University Press, 2011); Gardner, *The Frontier Complex*; S. Gupta, 'Frontiers in Flux: Indo-Tibetan Border: 1946–1948', *India Quarterly*, 77:1 (2021), pp. 42–58; B. D. Hopkins, *Ruling the Savage Periphery: Frontier Governance and the Making of the Modern State* (Cambridge, MA: Harvard University Press, 2020).

[85] L. Walker, 'Decolonization in the 1960s: On Legitimate and Illegitimate Nationalist Claims-Making', *Past & Present*, 242:1 (2019), p. 228.

[86] C. Ewing, 'Codifying Minority Rights', in A. D. Moses, M., Duranti, and R. Burke (eds.), *Decolonization, Self-Determination, and the Rise of Global Human Rights Politics* (Cambridge: Cambridge University Press, 2020), pp. 179–206.

[87] MacArthur, 'Decolonizing Sovereignty'; G. Roberts, 'MOLINACO, the Comorian Diaspora, and Decolonisation in East Africa's Indian Ocean', *Journal of African History*, 62:3 (2021), pp. 411–429; Walker, 'Decolonization in the 1960s'; Wheatley, 'Legal Pluralism as Temporal Pluralism'.

[88] A. Niang, *The Postcolonial African State in Transition: Stateness and Modes of Sovereignty* (Lanham: Rowman & Littlefield International, 2018); P. Saksena, 'Building the Nation: Sovereignty and International Law in the Decolonisation of South Asia', *Journal of the History of International Law*, 23:1 (2020), pp. 52–79; C. Leonardi, 'Patchwork States: The

benefit, for resource extraction or political control, in order to prevent colonised communities from developing solidarity movements against the colonial state; the divide and rule policy relied upon these communities resenting one another rather than the ruling imperial power.

Thus, decolonisation processes reignited sovereign imaginaries over territory and amplified the stakes of inter-communal conflicts, making non-national political communities and ethnic or religious minority groups vulnerable to abuse, neglect, or silencing within the international system. In the same manner as imperial powers, UN peacekeeping governance practices and geographies recoded, legitimised, and perpetuated colonial powers' arbitrary administrative structures, such as artificial territorial borders and forced 'national' unity for disparate communities and permanent minorities. For UN leadership, especially Bunche, the collapse of national unity – however artificial the national borders – was a key threat to international peace and security during decolonisation, offering fertile spaces for instability, war, and Communism.

Moving beyond the Institutional Narrative

Methodologically, this book draws on a wide range of sources from international and state archives. It is built upon analysis of UN public documents (General Assembly and Security Council minutes, emergency meetings, resolutions, letters, reports), internal communications (telegrams, cables, memos, reports, letters, handwritten notes), personal papers (diaries, letters, unofficial photographs, unpublished or drafted memoirs), and published material (information booklets, press releases, press conferences, newspaper articles, obituaries). These files are held by the UN Archives (based in-house in New York and digitised on the UN Archives website) and the International Committee of the Red Cross (ICRC) archives (housed in the Geneva headquarters).[89] The United Nations Oral History Project hosted by Yale provided taped transcripts of interviews with UN bureaucrats during the 1990s, recording their memories and preserving the role of the mid-level international civil servant which is often obscured in the official UN Archives. The Bodleian Library in Oxford maintains the archives of the United Nations Career Records Project which provided access to oral histories, personal papers, and memoirs of British peacekeepers, diplomats, and some of their spouses. For a British imperial perspective, the book draws from British foreign policy reports and communications with

Localization of State Territoriality on the South Sudan–Uganda Border, 1914–2014', *Past & Present*, 248:1 (2020), pp. 209–258; E. Newman and G. Visoka, 'The Geopolitics of State Recognition in a Transitional International Order', *Geopolitics* (2021), pp. 1–29.

89 More information on the history of the UN archives is available in: E. Rothschild, 'The Archives of Universal History', *Journal of World History*, 19:3 (2008), pp. 375–401.

embassies and the UK mission to the UN, held by the British National Archives in Kew. Supplementary sources were provided by the digitised archives of Amnesty International, the World Health Organization (WHO), the United Nations Educational, Scientific and Cultural Organization (UNESCO), and numerous international and national newspapers.

Retrieving local responses or criticism of these missions within organisational or state archives has proved fragmentary and has been obfuscated by an elite or racialised lens. Mission reports and cables provide glimpses into interactions with local populations. However, these expose more about the UN officials' perceptions of the population rather than providing insight into host population's conceptions of the intervention. The silences or gaps in UN reports and private communication speak to the types of voices that were valued – and thus preserved – by the UN bureaucracy. The organisational sources also reproduce colonial discourses and knowledge; they are not 'stories' but 'generative substances with histories … of their own'.[90] By taking a post colonial, critical methodological approach to the archival documents, this book does not attempt to 'speak' for unheard or unpreserved voices. Instead, it situates the UN reports and memos as part of larger patterns of the taxonomy of colonised populations, rather than as products of technocratic 'fact'.[91]

Working 'along the archival grain', with state and non-state official documents, has helped to illuminate UN officials' plans, prejudices, and priorities through their communications within the peacekeeping bureaucracy. The extensive UN administrative files and ICRC archives have provided vital insights into the 'minor' histories of internal debates,[92] private thoughts, secret meetings, scribbled comments in the margin, and discarded drafts otherwise lost in homogenous narratives of missions. These sources have allowed access to the political and organisational anxieties of the UN peacekeeping staff as they were faced with increasingly entrenched political disputes. Seeking clarity or direction from their fellow UN colleagues, these notes speak to the experimental and impulsive nature of decision-making in the field as a peacekeeping bureaucrat. As Ann Stoler has highlighted, 'Against the sober formulaics of officialese, these archives register the febrile movements of persons off balance – of thoughts and feelings in and out of place. In tone and temper they convey the rough interior ridges of governance and disruptions to the deceptive clarity of its mandates.'[93] The UN archival documents in particular speak to the impulses underlying the UN officials' decision-making as they responded to field-based dilemmas; when time was short, resources depleted,

[90] A. L. Stoler, *Along the Archival Grain* (Princeton: Princeton University Press, 2009), p. 1.

[91] For more, see H. Tilley, *Africa as a Living Laboratory: Empire, Development, and the Problem of Scientific Knowledge, 1870–1950* (Chicago: University of Chicago Press, 2011).

[92] Stoler, *Along the Archival Grain*, p. 7.

[93] Stoler, *Along the Archival Grain*, p. 2.

and intelligence unreliable, the UN peacekeepers did what they thought 'needed to be done' with little regard for the long-term consequences or local consultation.

The first half of this book follows the optimistic, aspirational beginnings of the UN peacekeeping project. Chapter 1 outlines how the peacekeeping project became a legitimate function for an international organisation. It examines how the UN Secretariat leadership tentatively experimented with intervening directly in conflict contexts in the post-war period, beginning with statecraft and a non-armed presence in the Israel/Palestine conflict and shifting to the construction of the UN Command in Korea. Chapter 2 offers a new perspective on the evolution of the first armed peacekeeping mission, UNEF, during a period of geopolitical transformation within the UN Security Council and General Assembly. It emphasises the expansion of the Afro-Asian bloc's voting weight and the heightened diplomatic engagement of middle-sized states, such as India and Canada, as involvement in peacekeeping became a source of political power within the international community. Once on the ground, the UNEF mission shifted international perceptions of the organisation from a simply deliberative forum to an active military participant. Reflecting on this shift in the field, mid-level peacekeepers and participating troops began to cultivate a distinctive peacekeeper identity through a mission magazine, underpinned by their Orientalist understandings of their space of deployment and the liberal cosmopolitan ideals of the UN Charter. Chapter 3 turns to the Congo crisis, examining the imperial continuities and neo-colonial character of the infrastructural support provided by the ONUC mission during the first phase of the intervention. This chapter establishes the obstructive and productive influences of the ongoing presence of Belgian capitalists and colonial officials on the UN mission. It also examines how the UN staff used the access of technical assistance projects, such as the radio station and airport, to control the political future of the nation.

The second half of the book follows the long shadow of the Congo mission on UN operations as the UN faced a financial and reputational crisis in 1961 and 1962. Chapter 4 examines how the UN leadership, seeking reputational repair, negotiated a peacekeeping mission to monitor the transfer of West Papua from Dutch administration to Indonesian annexation. Once on the ground, the policies of the UNTEA administration actively delegitimised and dismissed Papuans' political activities as a means of ensuring the success of the mission in the stable transfer of sovereignty from the Dutch to the Indonesians. Rather than passive manipulation by Indonesian or American delegates, the UN peacekeepers were motivated by self-interest and racial prejudice, 'othering' the Papuan population and suffocating Papuan activists' demands for independence. Approaching the mid-1960s, Chapter 5 explores the UN peacekeepers' efforts at maintaining stability and establishing a ceasefire in Cyprus whilst intervening in violent inter-communal hostilities. Despite expanding the functions of the UN mission, the recruitment of a UNFICYP mediator exposed the UN's powerlessness in the face of member-state criticism, igniting internal discussions about the value of UNFICYP's presence and ceasefire strategy. It also demonstrated the incompatibility of functioning as an active military participant on the ground whilst simultaneously leading diplomatic negotiations for the resolution of the conflict. By 1971, the UN leadership and UNFICYP contributing nations began to question the future role of the UN in international conflict response following the organisation's experience in Cyprus.

As relationships of domination and suppression shifted during the Cold War and decolonising period, the UN peacekeeping project won significant diplomatic and political currency for its front line role in a series of geopolitically significant conflicts. This currency empowered field-based UN staff to experiment with innovating global norms, especially as the elasticity of nation-state sovereignty was already being tested by socialist, pan-African, Afro-Asian, Black internationalist, federalist, or separatist thinkers.[94] These plans were not simply utopian dreams. Sovereignty was not monopolised by those in support of the nation-state paradigm; national independence was only one of

[94] For more on alternative – largely federalist – world visions to nationhood, see: Getachew, *Worldmaking after Empire*; Cooper, *Citizenship between Empire and Nation*; L. James, *George Padmore and Decolonization from Below: Pan-Africanism, the Cold War, and the End of Empire* (London: Palgrave Macmillan, 2014); M. Matera, *Black London: The Imperial Metropolis and Decolonization in the Twentieth Century* (Oakland: University of California Press, 2015); M. Fejzula, 'The Cosmopolitan Historiography of Twentieth-Century Federalism', *The Historical Journal*, 64:2 (2021), pp. 477–500; M. Collins, 'Decolonisation and the "Federal Moment"', *Diplomacy & Statecraft*, 24:1(2013), pp. 21–40; I. Milford, 'Federation, Partnership, and the Chronologies of Space in 1950s East and Central Africa', *The Historical Journal*, 63:5 (2020), pp. 1325–1348; S. Pillai, 'Fragmenting the Nation: Divisible Sovereignty and Travancore's Quest for Federal Independence', *Law and History Review*, 34:3 (2016), pp. 743–782; R. Hyam, 'The Geopolitical Origins of the Central African Federation: Britain, Rhodesia and South Africa, 1948–1953', *Historical Journal*, 30 (1987), pp. 145–172; A. Cohen, *The Politics and Economics of Decolonization in Africa: The Failed Experiment of the Central African Federation* (London: Bloomsbury Publishing, 2017); Z. Groves, 'Transnational Networks and Regional Solidarity: The Case of the Central African Federation, 1953–1963', *African Studies*, 72 (2013), pp. 155–175; C. Vaughan, 'The Politics of Regionalism and Federation in East Africa, 1958–1964', *The Historical Journal*, 62 (2019), pp. 519–540; R. Abrahamsen, 'Internationalists, Sovereigntists, Nativists: Contending Visions of World Order in Pan-Africanism', *Review of International Studies*, 46:1 (2020), pp. 56–74; F. Gerits and M. Grilli (eds.), *Visions of African Unity: New Perspectives on the History of Pan-Africanism and African Unification Projects* (London: Palgrave Macmillan, 2020); N. S. Sultan, 'Between the Many and the One: Anticolonial Federalism and Popular Sovereignty', *Political Theory*, 50:2 (2021), pp. 247–274; S. A. Dalberto, 'Hidden Debates over the Status of the Casamance during the Decolonization Process in Senegal: Regionalism, Territorialism, and Federalism at a Crossroads, 1946–62', *Journal of African History*, 61:1 (2020), pp. 67–68; Q. Swan, *Pasifika Black: Oceania, Anti-colonialism, and the African World* (New York: NYU Press, 2022).

the many imagined outcomes of decolonisation. During this period, alternative forms of self-determination and political enfranchisement were debated by activists across the Global South (as well as among radical groups in imperial metropoles), competing for traction whilst battling against the racial and ethnic trappings of nationhood, with many of these thinkers building rights-focused, anti-colonial visions for future generations.[95] However, the same moment of transformation that ignited anti-colonial worldmaking plans also provoked a liberal internationalist push to protect the nation-state paradigm and an anticommunist urgency to suppress the growth of socialism as European empires collapsed. UN peacekeeping missions and practices contributed to the silencing of these alternative plans for worldmaking, imposing inflexible frameworks of liberal internationalism, member-state nationalism, and anticommunism onto decolonising spaces.

Better understanding the roots, politics, and constraints on these international civil servants enables a more comprehensive understanding of how UN peacekeeping missions became the most popular solution for the de-escalation of volatile conflicts in the post-war era. Whilst anxieties about an impending 'Third World War' troubled political elites and communities alike, shared dreams of a liberal global community protected by UN peacekeepers satisfied common calls for greater international recourse and expertise in contexts of escalating conflict. For diplomats, it felt like lessons had been learned about the failures of collective security in the past. UN peacekeeping represented the modern, development-driven approach to future-proof international peace and security. Most crucially for the Second World War victors, the missions shielded the 'Great Power' nations from the impact of post-colonial violence and instability caused by themselves or their imperialist allies.

[95] Getachew, *Worldmaking after Empire*; R. Shilliam, 'What about Marcus Garvey? Race and the Transformation of Sovereignty Debate', *Review of International Studies*, 32:3 (2006), pp. 379–400; Cooper, *Citizenship between Empire and Nation*; G. Wilder, *Freedom Time: Negritude, Decolonization, and the Future of the World* (Durham: Duke University Press, 2015).

1

Testing the Waters, 1945–1955

Introduction: Experiments in an International Military

In the first half of the twentieth century, politicians, diplomats, and international civil servants within collective security and liberal internationalist circles sought to develop new legal norms to experiment in formative versions of peacekeeping. The establishment of an international military force became an increasingly popular prospect in the interwar period as the 'Great Powers' sought to use the League of Nations to stabilise disputed territories in a reconstituted Central Europe.[1] Once the Second World War concluded and burgeoning Cold War tensions increased, the idea of an international military emerged with enthusiasm as a solution to protracted conflicts. Concerned with the need to raise diplomatic favour to implement plans for an international military, many of these early debates centred on the recurring issue of how to reach a Great Power consensus on the design of an international force that could balance the restrictions of global sovereignty norms with the practicalities of confronting violence in the field.[2] This chapter traces these formative debates and draws a thread through the interwar period through to the Korean War, situating later UN peacekeeping missions as part of the longer historical legacies of early twentieth-century statecraft, interventionism, and liberal imperialism.

Beginning with an examination of the formative League of Nations multinational missions in interwar Europe, this chapter tracks the evolution of international plans and experiments in League and UN armament, illustrating parallels with the design and politics of the future armed peacekeeping project. From the multinational troops governed under League auspices in Central Europe to the UN military observers policing the Arab–Israeli War in 1948,

[1] The conclusion of the First World War made Great Britain, France, Italy, Japan, and the United States the 'Great Powers' during the interwar period.

[2] *Revision of the United Nations Charter: Hearings before the United States Senate Committee on Foreign Relations, Subcommittee on Revision of the United Nations Charter, Eighty-First Congress, Second Session, on Feb. 2, 3, 6, 8, 9, 13, 15, 17, 20, 1950* (Washington: US Government Printing Office, 1950), p. 354; G. Murray, 'Interview by James Sutterlin', 10 January 1991, pp. 17–18.

these early experiments in the military sphere helped to – diplomatically and logistically – pave the way for the first armed UN mission in 1956. This chapter concludes with an examination of the deployment of a – limited – multinational military force to Korea in 1950, focusing on how the UN's direct involvement in the field affected the organisation's claims to impartiality in the UN headquarters. Of all these experiments, the war in Korea in particular facilitated the conflation of multilateral military interventions and the pursuit of global peace. However, the victory imperative in conflict contexts increasingly limited the diplomatic agility of the UN, obstructing mediation efforts. As legal commentator Josef Kunz has stressed about the UN's experience in Korea, 'it has shown that an international enforcement action is, for all practical purposes, a war and that the most important thing, as in any war, is to win it'.[3]

But how was it that ideas about arming a humanitarian international organisation evolved into legally and diplomatically acceptable – even popular – proposals for intervention within the post-war international community? The idea of a UN armed force had several different origins. First, it can be situated in the development and institutionalisation of the laws of war. Multilateral deployments, wrapped in UN branding, worked with the logic and permissions of international humanitarian law to reinvent militarism – and military power – as the most effective method of preventing violence, restoring law and order, and preserving world peace. In the late nineteenth century, global militaries were strengthened following the establishment of the ICRC and the development of laws of war which codified the expansion of 'belligerent privileges' and focused on limiting the excesses of war rather than implementing its abolition.[4] This in turn encouraged longer-term or permanent conflicts, stagnating political crises and civilian displacement. For Sam Moyn, these international humanitarian legal 'reformers shifted their attention from opposing the crime of war to opposing war crimes', thus validating 'clean' wars – that is, wars whose conduct complied with international law – as the preferred pacifying tool for modern society.[5] Existing limits on the laws of war were narrowed in the aftermath of the Second World War, entrenching norms like the Genocide Convention in 1948 and Geneva Conventions in 1949, and defining who was – or was not – deemed a legitimate target in conflict. Rather than a mechanism for global pacifism or a tool for liberationist movements, international humanitarian law became a line-drawing exercise that proved inadequate in responding to intra-state conflicts, such as civil wars or colonial (counter)insurgency. Indeed,

[3] J. Kunz, 'Legality of the Security Council Resolutions of June 25 and 27, 1950', *The American Journal of International Law*, 45:1 (1951), p. 137.

[4] P. Kalmanovitz, *The Laws of War in International Thought* (Cambridge: Cambridge University Press, 2017), p. 1.

[5] S. Moyn, *Humane: How the United States Abandoned Peace and Reinvented War* (New York: Farrar, Straus and Giroux, 2021).

'Outlawing illegal conduct in wartime did as much to outline the silhouette of humanized war as to establish the legality of waging war itself.'[6]

Second, peacekeeping drew on ideas about the expansion of the conception of 'collective security' in the aftermath of the First World War within the League of Nations, as Patricia Clavin has articulated in relation to British involvement in the organisation.[7] Similarly, Susan Pedersen's book *The Guardians* highlighted the integral diplomatic and functional roles played by the League in transitioning global society from a world of empires to one of nation-states.[8] During the interwar period, the League's organisational staff and state membership debated many of the same territorial concerns and diplomatic topics that would later trouble the UN in the course of mid-century decolonisation. The League investigated implementing collective security, most promisingly with a (later abandoned) peacekeeping mission to Vilna, a city in Lithuania, in 1920–1921.[9] Vilna had been part of the Russian Empire until it was occupied by the German army during the First World War. Although Lithuanian independence from Russian annexation had been established in 1918, the question of Vilna became a source of conflict between Lithuania and Poland once the Lithuanian government declared Vilna as their nation's capital. While Polish troops occupied the region, the Polish government presented their own claim to Vilna to the League in 1920, hoping that the League Council would affirm the state's authority over the region and end the conflict.[10] The Council planned to construct a Military Commission, with 1,600 troops recruited from nations such as Britain, France, Italy, Japan, and Spain, which would be tasked with policing the provisional border between Poland and Lithuania.[11] However, after what Pierre Bourneuf has described as four months of *tergiversations diplomatiques* (or 'diplomatic dithering'), the League cancelled its plans to send the Commission to the field in preference to the less dangerous option of mediation.[12] Although the Vilna mission was an example of the League's weakness within the nation-state arena

[6] B. van Dijk, *Preparing for War: The Making of the Geneva Conventions* (Oxford: Oxford University Press, 2021). p. 5.

[7] P. Clavin, 'The Ben Pimlott Memorial Lecture 2019: Britain and the Making of Global Order after 1919', *Twentieth Century British History*, 31:3 (2020), pp. 340–359.

[8] S. Pedersen, *The Guardians: The League of Nations and the Crisis of Empire* (Oxford: Oxford University Press, 2015), p. 277.

[9] P. Bourneuf, 'La Société des Nations et la force internationale à Vilna (1920–1921): Un projet précurseur pour le maintien de la paix?' *Relations Internationales*, 166:2 (2016), pp. 87–102.

[10] C. Tessaris, 'Open Diplomacy and Minority Rights: The League of Nations and Lithuania's International Image in the Early 1920s', in L. Clerc et al. (eds.), *Histories of Public Diplomacy and Nation Branding in the Nordic and Baltic Countries* (Leiden: Brill, 2015), pp. 40–41.

[11] A. James, *Peacekeeping in International Politics* (London: Palgrave Macmillan, 1990), pp. 33–34.

[12] Bourneuf, 'La Société des Nations et la force internationale à Vilna (1920–1921)', p. 87.

of international politics, it also revealed the ambition of the organisation's staff to expand the League's functions into collective security. There had been many military alliances made between different countries previously, but this was the first instance of a force constructed from national battalions and united under an international organisation's auspices.

Subsequent efforts by the League to expand into military and political administration were more successful despite their lack of historiographical attention. Pursuant to the provisions of the Versailles Treaty, the League governed the Saar, a coal-rich, disputed region on the border between France and Germany, in the anticipation of a plebiscite, between 1920 and 1935. To reflect this aim, Norrie Macqueen has described this period of League operations as 'plebiscite peacekeeping'.[13] League officials and Western commentators hoped that the vote would 'result in the removal of a danger spot from the political map' and thus demonstrate the value of the League to the international community.[14] In 1934, the League established a multinational military force of 3,300 troops to send to the Saar, 'composed of British, Dutch, Italian, and Swedish contingents', echoing the planned operations for Vilna.[15] This peacekeeping force was established to stabilise the region whilst the League Voting Commission carried out the plebiscite in January 1935 to determine the future sovereignty of the territory. Indeed, the mission was so popular with the local population that, although unification with Germany (and the Nazi Party) achieved 90 per cent of the vote, the option of status quo with the League received almost 9 per cent, beating the 0.4 per cent of voters who chose unification with France.[16]

The plebiscite result was not the impartial victory for democracy and collective security that League officials had promised. Accusations of Nazi coercion and intimidation in the Saar had been widespread since Hitler came to power in 1933.[17] League Plebiscite Commissioners attempted to implement restrictive decrees to limit Nazi spying and influence on the media, but the League struggled to combat the pro-German propaganda campaign. The vote also threatened the security of those who opposed Germany and prompted an exodus of French-supporting refugees into France. Fears of a Nazi takeover in Austria and Switzerland also grew.[18] The French Consulate in Saarbrücken,

[13] N. Macqueen, 'Cold War Peacekeeping versus Humanitarian Intervention: Beyond the Hammarskjöldian Model', in F. Klose (ed.), *The Emergence of Humanitarian Intervention: Ideas and Practice from the Nineteenth Century to the Present* (Cambridge: Cambridge University Press, 2015), pp. 234–235.

[14] H. Callender, 'In the Saar History Writes a Chapter', *The New York Times*, 13 January 1935.

[15] Macqueen, 'Cold War Peacekeeping versus Humanitarian Intervention', p. 235.

[16] Macqueen, 'Cold War Peacekeeping versus Humanitarian Intervention', p. 235.

[17] James, *Peacekeeping in International Politics*, p. 76.

[18] 'Austria Sends Force to Bar Nazi Rioting', *The New York Times*, 12 January 1935.

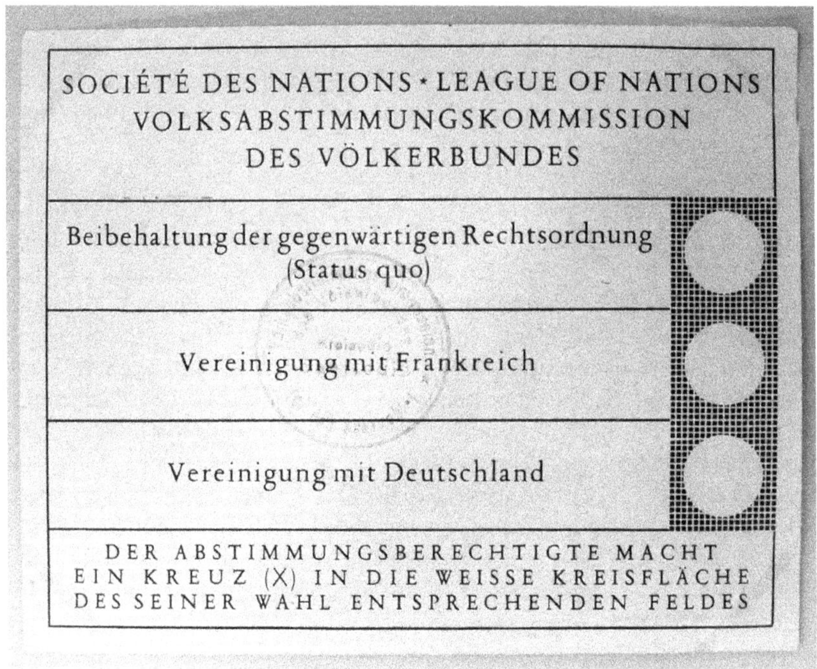
SOCIÉTÉ DES NATIONS • LEAGUE OF NATIONS
VOLKSABSTIMMUNGSKOMMISSION
DES VÖLKERBUNDES

Beibehaltung der gegenwärtigen Rechtsordnung
(Status quo)

Vereinigung mit Frankreich

Vereinigung mit Deutschland

DER ABSTIMMUNGSBERECHTIGTE MACHT
EIN KREUZ (X) IN DIE WEISSE KREISFLÄCHE
DES SEINER WAHL ENTSPRECHENDEN FELDES

Figure 1.1 Ballot card for Saar plebiscite, January 1935.
Credit to Wikimedia.

the regional capital, issued several thousand emergency visas to facilitate the evacuation of the anti-Nazi refugees, and the French Red Cross prepared food aid for those who arrived in the concentration camps on French soil.[19] Within a week, almost 10,000 refugees crossed the border into France from the Saar, and most were resettled in Palestine, France, or Paraguay by the Nansen International Office for Refugees.[20] Although the League administration and multinational force remained in the Saar for the transition period of six weeks, the future security of non-Nazis under the new regime felt uncertain enough to cause the evacuation of tens of thousands of people and provoke fears of Nazi expansion in neighbouring European nations.[21]

These formative peacekeeping proposals and operations provided blueprints for future political, legal, and technical preparations as UN leadership

[19] 'Refugees Shot at from Saar Side', *The New York Times*, 17 January 1935.

[20] V. Caron, *Uneasy Asylum: France and the Jewish Refugee Crisis, 1933–1942* (Palo Alto: Stanford University Press, 1999), pp. 51–56.

[21] C. K. Streit, 'Saar and League Face Tense Period', *The New York Times*, 20 January 1935.

and external international representatives debated the design of a similar force under UN command. The choice to build upon the League Council's ambition and expand into the possibility of military deployment – as outlined in Chapters 6 and 7 of the UN Charter – demonstrated the centrality of reactive collective security in the new organisation's mandate. The failure of the League's policy of appeasement to curb the ethno-nationalist aggression of the Nazi state in the late 1930s provoked calls for an international military or policing force that could improve upon the League's sluggish reaction to interstate aggression. Foundational League experiments in collective security, such as the Vilna mission and the administration of the Saar, thus helped to pave the way for the UN's role in conflict response, inspiring a greater military role for the successor organisation and prompting diplomatic calls for a standby international force.

Building upon the reframing and policing of 'acceptable' interstate war in the 1940s, following the criminalisation and prosecution of Axis personnel for the crime of aggression,[22] Western liberal internationalists conceived of an international military as the most viable, *peaceable* solution for intervening, managing, and resolving conflicts (especially against fascist states). By 1945, the nascent idea of an international peacekeeping force had been circulating for decades in European and North American liberal internationalist networks, especially those aligned with Wilsonian ideals of collective security, and had been further kindled by the successful establishment of the UN on 24 October 1945.[23] This emerging epistemic community in peacekeeping promoted the ideas of a UN-led transnational police, military, or air force, drawing on the foundational cosmopolitan ideals of the organisation.[24] The US State Department believed that these forces would distribute the burden of protecting international security across several contributing nations and would provide a guise of legitimacy to military actions in US interests.[25] During this transformative moment in international politics, the UN's first secretary-general Trygve Lie tangled himself in conversations about the use of force, an issue that had traditionally been the domain of nation-state militaries in quests for territorial, geopolitical, or economic domination. Keen to impress and prove the organisation's value in the shadow of the League, Lie sought to employ the UN's full powers, as mandated in the UN Charter, and embed the

[22] F. Hirsch, *Soviet Judgment at Nuremberg: A New History of the International Military Tribunal after World War II* (Oxford: Oxford University Press, 2020), p. 53.

[23] E. Manela, *The Wilsonian Moment: Self-Determination and the International Origins of Anticolonial Nationalism* (Oxford: Oxford University Press, 2007), p. 35.

[24] The Soviets had insisted on the inclusion of an international air force because of a belief that this would be the 'best guarantee against German revanchism', J. Soffer, 'All for One or All for All: The UN Military Staff Committee and the Contradictions within American Internationalism', *Diplomatic History*, 21:1 (1997), p. 52.

[25] Soffer, 'All for One or All for All', p. 57.

organisation as the primary expert in global issues of international peace and security.

Academics, activist groups, and lawyers also began to discuss the legal, financial, and diplomatic ramifications of a military function within the UN bureaucracy. Many highlighted the benefits of an international force for maintaining world peace in the nuclear age, especially in the volatile context of decolonisation in the post-war period.[26] Increasingly, military measures were conceived as the most practical, humane, and immediate solution to thwart issues which threatened international peace and security. Trust in the UN to perform this central role in global governance led to popular support for a militarised international institution that could execute the functions suggested in the UN Charter and prevent a 'Third World War'. This would push the international order beyond collective security and into a new era of UN-led conflict response. Not simply a multilateral arrangement between allied states, peacekeeping would accelerate the political credentials and position of the UN as a diplomatic *and* military power in its own right whilst also projecting its core identity as a rights-focused international organisation.

International Security Debates in a Nuclear Age

In the early twentieth century, Western internationalists and military figures called for aviation and atomic energy to be centralised under League and – later – UN power to prevent further state aggression.[27] Pleas for disarmament and mobilisation of the international community became particularly common in the aftermath of interstate violence, following the economic and emotional horrors of war.[28] Although the League failed in interwar general disarmament, due to Great Power suppression, the creation of the Disarmament Section established an important precedent for multilateral security that was strengthened in the post-Second World War period.[29] The technological advances of the two world wars had ignited fears across the globe of what future conflicts could look like and prompted questions about what role nuclear weapons would necessarily

[26] H. Kelsen, 'Recent Trends in the Law of the United Nations', *Social Research*, 18:2 (1951), pp. 135–151.

[27] W. H. Zaidi, *Technological Internationalism and World Order: Aviation, Atomic Energy, and the Search for International Peace, 1920–1950* (Cambridge: Cambridge University Press, 2021).

[28] J. Horne, 'Demobilizing the Mind: France and the Legacy of the Great War, 1919–1939', *French History and Civilization*, 2006 Seminar Papers (Published 2009), 2, pp. 1–19, available at https://h-france.net/rude/vol2/horne2/, accessed on 8 August 2021.

[29] H. A. Ikonomou, 'The Administrative Anatomy of Failure: The League of Nations Disarmament Section, 1919–1925', *Contemporary European History*, 30 (2021), pp. 321–334.

play in any potential future aggression.[30] As Europe began to recover from the widescale violence and destruction of the Second World War, politicians, military officials, and activists returned to the topic of an international military as part of discussions on how to practically prevent the advent of another world war. The possibility of nuclear attack eliminated any reasonable provision for incremental or partial military engagement – or, indeed, surrender. These anxieties were gradually compounded by the freezing of diplomatic relations between the United States and the Soviet Union during the late 1940s and an escalation of post-war competition between the two superpowers as the burgeoning Cold War developed.[31] In this shifting geopolitical context, the UN became the preferred institution for those interested in establishing a more robust system of international recourse in the event of future aggression or nuclear warfare. By 1945, the possibility of empowering the international organisation, conceived as a 'world government', with military authority became less of a hypothetical debate and more of a practical discussion of legal permissions, financial resources, and military scope.

The conclusion of the Second World War and the repercussions of the US bombings of Hiroshima and Nagasaki encouraged many to express a shared desire for a UN-led international agency or world government that would manage all nuclear weapons and their potential deployment.[32] The idea that nations should surrender their weapons to the organisation was not unpopular during the immediate post-war years. Indeed, some felt it was an integral aspect of the UN Charter. The World Federation of United Nations Associations met in September 1948 to criticise the lack of 'implementation of Article 54 of the [UN] Charter which provides for the setting up of United Nations armed forces' and recalled the previous year's meeting's efforts to establish a 'system of international inspection and supervision sufficiently comprehensive to make possible the destruction of existing arms or their surrender to an international body'.[33] The US historian James T. Shotwell went as far as to publicly appeal for an international force that should 'control all bombs and possible bombs in the world' to obstruct warring powers and prevent the destruction of the earth.[34] This was also an idea promoted by the Federation of Atomic Scientists, a group of some of the Manhattan Project researchers, resulting in the creation of a popular book and a short documentary

30 M. Krepton, *Winning and Losing the Nuclear Peace: The Rise, Demise, and Revival of Arms Control* (Stanford: Stanford University Press, 2021).

31 Hirsch, *Soviet Judgment at Nuremberg*, p. 14.

32 R. A. Musto, '"Atoms for Police": The United States and the Dream of a Nuclear-Armed United Nations, 1945–1962', NPIHP Working Paper #15, October 2020.

33 UN Archive (UNA, henceforth), S-0472-0098-04-00001, 'World Federation of United Nations Associations (WFUNA) Resolutions on Article 43 of UN Charter (Plenary Assembly held in Rome, 5–10 September)', September 1948, pp. 3–4.

34 J. T. Shotwell, 'Control of Atomic Energy', *Survey Graphic* 34 (October 1945), p. 408.

film, *One World or None* in 1946.[35] For Petra Goedde, the *One World or None* book and documentary drove home the belief that the 'only option available to humanity was to place the atomic bomb under the control of a world government body, preferably the United Nations'.[36]

Although disengaged from the Manhattan Project Albert Einstein held similar beliefs about nuclear pacifism and disarmament. In 1946, he contributed a piece to the 1946 book, asserting his belief in the need for a 'supranational' institution or council that would 'wage peace' and control the world's nuclear weapons.[37] After the nation-state competition of the Second World War and the nationalist ideology that had driven the crimes of the German state, Einstein saw world governance and international cooperation through the UN as fundamental to humanity and justice.[38] Einstein wrote for *The Atlantic* in 1947:

> I believe that the United Nations should have the atomic bomb when it is supplied with its own armed forces and weapons. But it too should have the bomb for the sole purpose of deterring an aggressor or rebellious nations from making an atomic attack. It should not use the atomic bomb on its own initiative any more than the United States or any other power should do so.[39]

As part of his plan, the UN would need to be empowered to control nuclear weapons and take an active role in protecting international peace and security; the organisation would behave with the same political *and* military power as a nation-state. For Einstein and his fellow Manhattan Project scientists who opposed the post-war US nuclear strategy,[40] the UN represented a singular opportunity to prevent global war and to harness nuclear power for its unifying qualities – a humbling realisation of humanity and individual insignificance and supposed power of deterrence rather than in weaponisation of its destructive capacity.[41]

35 D. Masters and K. Way, *One World or None: A Report to the Public on the Full Meaning of the Atomic Bomb* (New York: McGraw-Hill, 1946).

36 P. Goedde, *The Politics of Peace: A Global Cold War History* (Oxford: Oxford University Press, 2019), p. 72.

37 A. Einstein, 'Atomic War or Peace', *The Atlantic*, November 1947.

38 G. Mercer, 'Albert Einstein, Power, the State, and Peace: The Physicist as Philosopher-King in a World State', *International Social Science Review*, 69:3/4 (1994), p. 23.

39 Einstein, 'Atomic War or Peace'.

40 For example, Robert Oppenheimer. However, other Manhattan Project scientists John von Neumann and Edward Teller were famously supportive of US nuclear policy. For more, see S. Carvin and M. J. Williams, *Law, Science, Liberalism and the American Way of Warfare: The Quest for Humanity in Conflict* (Cambridge: Cambridge University Press, 2015), p. 89.

41 The peacemaking attributes of nuclear power and nuclear scientists are further explored in J. D. Hamblin, *The Wretched Atom: America's Global Gamble with Peaceful Nuclear Technology* (Oxford: Oxford University Press, 2021); R. van Munster and C. Sylvest,

Scientists and antinuclear activists were not alone in calling for the UN to take responsibility over the world's nuclear weapons. For Bernard Baruch, US financier and presidential advisor, the establishment of an international police force 'strong enough to halt aggression' would strengthen the UN and safeguard world peace in a nuclear era.[42] Building on the internationalist ideas of the earlier Acheson-Lilienthal Report, Baruch promoted his idea of 'World Peace or World Destruction' – since termed the 'Baruch Plan' – as serving US delegate and temporary chairman to the UN Atomic Energy Commission in June 1946.[43] Although only the United States possessed nuclear weapons, fears of global destruction and the 'black portent of the new atomic age' loomed.[44] For the Truman Administration, the Baruch Plan presented a proposal that could pre-empt war by bolstering international institutions like the UN and codifying cooperation between the permanent member-states. For Baruch,

> The peoples of these democracies gathered here have a particular concern with our answer, for their peoples hate war. They will have a heavy exaction to make of those who fail to provide an escape. They are not afraid of an internationalism that protects; they are unwilling to be fobbed off by mouthings about narrow sovereignty, which is today's phrase for yesterday's isolation.[45]

In developing this internationalist proposal, the Truman Administration demonstrated their recognition that the United States' atomic monopoly would not last and that their 'head start' would not protect their country from aggressors.[46] The British and Canadian governments supported early draft proposals, and the Soviet Union agreed initially with the stipulation that the responsible UN specialised agency (the United Nations Atomic Energy Commission or UNAEC) would be subject to the Security Council veto. Baruch insisted that the authority of the UN and the UNAEC should be

Nuclear Realism: Global Political Thought during the Thermonuclear Revolution (London: Routledge, 2016).

42 'Baruch Urges Curb on Veto Powers in U.N. with World Force to Halt Aggression', *The New York Times*, 15 February 1950.

43 For a more extensive examination of the Baruch Plan, see D. W. Kearn Jr, 'The Baruch Plan and the Quest for Atomic Disarmament', *Diplomacy & Statecraft*, 21:1 (2010), pp. 41–67; L. G. Gerber, 'The Baruch Plan and the Origins of the Cold War', *Diplomatic History*, 6:1 (1982), pp. 69–95; J. I. Lieberman, *The Scorpion and the Tarantula: The Struggle to Control Atomic Weapons, 1945–1949* (Boston: Houghton Mifflin Company, 1970); E. Roehrlich, 'Negotiating Verification: International Diplomacy and the Evolution of Nuclear Safeguards, 1945–1972', *Diplomacy & Statecraft*, 29:1 (2018), pp. 29–50.

44 B. Baruch, 'The Baruch Plan', presented to the United Nations Atomic Energy Commission, 14 June 1946, available at www.atomicarchive.com/resources/documents/deterrence/baruch-plan.html, accessed on 10 May 2021.

45 Baruch, 'The Baruch Plan'.

46 Kearn Jr., 'The Baruch Plan and the Quest for Atomic Disarmament', pp. 43–44.

protected, and that the organisation should be able to sanction violating member-states. However, the power of the Soviets' veto would immediately negate the authority of the organisation to sanction the member-state. This realisation prompted Baruch to call for the suspension – and, even, abolition – of the UN Security Council veto as part of his plan for global nuclear disarmament. For the Soviets, their attention to US 'atomic diplomacy' and preliminary approval of the Baruch Plan was part of a strategy to prevent diplomatic isolation in the post-war period; Stalin had no intention of slowing down his efforts to build an atomic bomb, nor to surrender the weapon to the UN.[47]

However, within the international arena in 1946, Baruch and others' hopes for an international force were obstructed by diplomatic stagnation within the UN. Whilst political figures, such as Baruch, discussed the topic and lobbied the hypothetical of arming the organisation, the practical issue of making the permanent member-states agree on the political and logistical design of a UN military had fallen on the UN's Military Staff Committee representatives. The MSC held its first meeting on the design of a UN military in February 1946. Inspired by the Anglo-American Combined Chiefs of Staff command structure during the Second World War, the British proposed the construction of a UN Military Staff Committee (MSC). Its operations were later codified in Articles 46 and 47 of the UN Charter in 1945.[48] The MSC was conceived as an advisory group staffed by the Chiefs of Staff of the five permanent members of the UN Security Council.[49] It was designed to assist on 'plans for the application of armed force' and was made 'responsible under the Security Council for the strategic direction of any armed forces placed at the disposal of the Security Council'.[50]

Initial MSC proposals considered a UN armed force that would be constructed from permanent member-states' national militaries. However, divergent ideas about how the UN would access the national contingents, the numbers required from each member-state, and concerns about how this would violate national sovereignty led to a stalemate. The US representatives submitted a paper to the MSC in 1946, describing their draft plan for a UN force:

> [E]ach permanent member would maintain special UN units at operational strength and in combat readiness. These forces would remain under national control until the Security Council called them into UN

[47] Kearn Jr., 'The Baruch Plan and the Quest for Atomic Disarmament', p. 59.

[48] Soffer, 'All for One or All for All', p. 52.

[49] H. W. Baldwin, 'Armed Forces for UN Still a Remote Idea', *The New York Times*, 27 October 1946.

[50] UN Doc, UN Charter, 24 October 1945, available at www.un.org/en/sections/uncharter/index.html, accessed on 14 May 2018.

> service. The Security Council would designate an overall commander to act under the strategic direction of the MSC.[51]

In contrast to the future UN peacekeeping project, the permanent members would be the majority – if not, sole – contributing nations included in the international UN force. It also placed the power of choosing a UN force commander with the Security Council rather than, as would be the custom in future missions, the secretary-general. This plan revealed the diplomatic optimism felt by the US government during this period as they sought to build upon the operational strength of the Allies rather than prioritise the obstruction of the Soviet Union's military strength. As Jonathan Soffer has argued, 'That a four-star American general still considered the possibility of joint manoeuvres with the Red Army indicates that as of May 1946 anti-Sovietism had not yet hardened into universal American dogma.'[52]

Whilst MSC deliberations were ongoing in June 1946, Baruch delivered his speech to the international representatives at the UN Atomic Energy Commission. Publicising their position on the UN military, British and French representatives 'violently' opposed Baruch's plan to centre the UN in global denuclearising policy and blocked any further public discussions on the topic. They refused to dilute their sovereign powers or to sacrifice unilateral control of their own military forces, foreshadowing their joint veto during the Suez crisis in 1956.[53] For Britain and France, this erosion of sovereignty would threaten the integrity of their empires and disempower their own nations from military recourse. Their discussions in the MSC focused on how a UN force could enable legitimate interventions in *other* nations, rather than serve as a means to impede their own national foreign policy. This position resulted in the creation of only one agreement during the MSC's years of meaningful operation, 1945–1949: that once the UN force is established – and this was yet to be achieved – it would be 'limited to a police force capable of dealing with conflicts between small and medium nations, but not large enough to stop the aggression by any of the Great Powers. . .'[54] Although this policy would have given the UN more military power than the League, the ultimate failure of MSC negotiations meant that this restriction – one that would have prevented a UN intervention in the Suez crisis – was never tested practically.

Throughout the next two years of negotiations, mistrust solidified between the two superpowers. The Soviets consistently rejected the US representatives' 1946 plan, citing concerns about the potential use of the UN force to intervene

51 Soffer, 'All for One or All for All', p. 58.

52 Soffer, 'All for One or All for All', p. 60.

53 'Baruch Urges Curb on Veto Powers in U.N. with World Force to Halt Aggression', *The New York Times*, 15 February 1950.

54 'U.N. and Its Police Force', *The New York Times*, 21 April 1947.

in socialist regimes or to quash revolutions across the Global South. Soviet representatives also emphasised their issue with the United States seeking to measure contributions by comparable strength rather than units of equal size. This deadlock was not eased by enthusiasm for the international force from Western Europe or China. As Eric Grove has noted, 'Given the difficulties that the French and the Chinese governments were facing internally, it was understandable that both were concerned that they should be allowed to withhold forces in cases of "National Emergency".'[55] By January 1949, the MSC was unable to maintain the attention of the permanent members as alternative regional security arrangements were developed in alignment with new Cold War alliances, such as the North Atlantic Treaty Organization (NATO). Ultimately, for similar 'Realist reasons' to the British and French, the United States and Soviet Union rejected the idea of weakening their sovereignty and legal protections of non-interventionism, anxious that the UN force could become a conduit for one power to militarily overwhelm the other.[56] Thus, in the post-war era, the permanent member-states forged a hierarchical internationalism within the UN, competing against alternative forms of globalism.[57] This enabled them to prioritise the protection of their own sovereignty whilst enjoying the diplomatic privileges of participating in – and, largely, controlling the whims of – the international community.

Unfazed by the position of the permanent members and the effective collapse of the MSC, Baruch rejuvenated his plan for world peace and supported a US Senate resolution that would promote the addition of a 'supplementing' article to the UN Charter in 1950: 'Under the agreement, participating countries would contribute armed forces to an international peace-keeping force which could be ordered into action instantly by the Security Council.'[58] This resolution, termed the 'Thomas-Douglas Resolution' after the two sponsoring Senators,[59] was part of a trend of resolutions during the immediate post-war period that called for the revision of the UN Charter – in particular, the veto powers of the permanent five member-states and the prevention of war.[60] Seeing the UN as an important tool in tackling Soviet aggression, Baruch sought to communicate to fellow

[55] E. Grove, 'UN Armed Forces and the Military Staff Committee: A Look Back', *International Security*, 17:4 (1993), p. 179.

[56] C. Craig, *Glimmer of a New Leviathan: Total War in the Realism of Niebuhr, Morgenthau, and Waltz* (New York: Columbia University Press, 2003), p. 29.

[57] O. Rosenboim, *The Emergence of Globalism: Visions of World Order in Britain and the United States, 1939–1950* (Princeton: Princeton University Press, 2017).

[58] 'Baruch Urges Curb on Veto Powers in U.N. with World Force to Halt Aggression', 15 February 1950.

[59] United States Senate, 'Senate Concurrent Resolution 52'.

[60] United States Senate, Report No. 2501, *Revision of the United Nations Charter* (Washington, Government Printing Office, 1950).

Americans the value of the international organisation for protecting US interests. In North America, Baruch was aligned with a group of liberal American elites in his demands for the construction of a UN military or police force to safeguard international peace and security, with many calling for a simultaneous review of the abusive veto system.[61] They believed that the strengthening of international human rights and collective security institutions – what Elizabeth Borgwardt described as a 'new deal for the world' – would concretise the United States' national interests at the centre of international politics.[62] Stephen Wertheim has similarly identified how many US politicians in the post-war period conceived of the UN as an instrument to give 'the United States the new power to cast its rivals as enemies of the world – against whom all is permitted … American supremacy could not only be obstructive but also destructive, the more so if it paid false homage to international law and order'.[63] With this level of oversight over the organisation, Baruch and many others believed the United States did not need the veto to protect its interests within the UN.

Indeed, for many internationalists, the creation of the veto was in itself a technical mistake and an obstacle to the UN's primary function to safeguard international peace and security. On 17 January 1946, at the first Security Council meeting based in London, one *New York Times* reporter commented on the fifty-one delegates' attitude towards the veto, its role in the international politics of 1946, and its likely impermanence within the UN system:

> They admit that the veto is a political necessity at the moment. They concede that it is better to restrict the veto to five that to give it to everybody, as in the League of Nations, and they agree that the great nations which furnish most of the men and material [sic] to fight the wars should have some special authority in the task of preventing wars. But they can concede all this and still feel that the veto greatly weakens the new organization. At any rate, they say, don't ask us to be enthusiastic about it or believe we have found the ideal formula for keeping the peace.[64]

Across the Atlantic, a group of American politicians were also hoping that the veto would be a short-term diplomatic solution whilst the UN grew from a fledgling institution to a powerful global government. One Senate hearing report submitted that 'It is possible that in the early days of the United

[61] 'Liberals Urge End of the Veto in UN: Party Gives Stand on World Issues and Its U.S. Goals in National Platform', *The New York Times*, 31 October 1949.

[62] E. Borgwardt, *A New Deal for the World: America's Vision for Human Rights* (Cambridge, MA: Harvard University Press, 2005).

[63] S. Wertheim, *Tomorrow the World: The Birth of US Global Supremacy* (Cambridge, MA: Harvard University Press, 2020), p. 172.

[64] J. B. Reston, 'Fifty-One Nations in Search of Unity', *The New York Times*, 27 January 1946.

Nations it was "oversold". The [American] people wanted to believe that the United Nations would be able to back up its decisions by armed force.'[65] Some US politicians, such as Senator Robert Taft, also felt that the veto had meant that 'the United Nations had put the cart before the horse in its approach to the question of maintaining the peace'.[66] Fifty-six Soviet Union vetoes from 1946 to 1954 had triggered disappointment in the UN functions. These concerns prompted the first secretary-general Trygve Lie to write personally to all five permanent-member representatives in December 1949 to call for them to 'broaden progressively their co-operation and to exercise restraint in the use of the veto in order to make the Security Council a more effective instrument for maintaining peace'.[67]

Fearful of Soviet military superiority in Europe and Asia, the choice to put nuclear arms and equivalent weapons into the ownership of the UN became an increasingly mainstream opinion in Anglo-American diplomatic circles during the early Cold War. In 1955, Thomas K. Finletter, former secretary of the air force and US military official, declared his support for total nuclear disarmament enforced 'by a peace-keeping international army' as this would be the 'only way to obtain world peace' in a context where powerful nations were developing their own nuclear weapons.[68] He denounced 'Soviet and Western plans for "unenforceable" disarmament as illusory and critically dangerous for the free nations if put into effect.'[69] He continued that 'Only through it is there any hope that we can come through this hydrogen phase of civilization without destroying our country and most of the rest of the world with us.'[70]

However, schisms within diplomatic, political, and scientific groups prevented meaningful action and the armament of the UN. As Goedde has argued, 'Agreement on the environmental consequences of nuclear testing was much easier to come by than agreement on the nature and efficacy of nuclear deterrence.'[71] Although ultimately unsuccessful, these post-war debates about disarming powerful nations of their nuclear weapons and transferring them into UN ownership help shed light on the evolution of the organisation out of a powerful effort in US politics to establish collective security. These discussions were heavily grounded in new anxieties about nuclear warfare and hopes to

[65] United States Senate, Document No. 87, *Review of the United Nations Charter: A Collection of Documents. Hearing before a Subcommittee of the Committee on Foreign Relations, United States Senate, Eighty-Third Congress, Second Session on Proposals to Amend or Otherwise Modify Existing International Peace and Security Organizations, Including the United Nations* (Washington: Government Printing Office, 1954), p. 825.

[66] 'Ban on the Veto Favored by Taft', *The New York Times*, 16 September 1947.

[67] UNA, S-0472-0103-25-00001, 'Letter from Trygvie Lie, 6 December 1949', pp. 20–24.

[68] 'Finletter Urges Full Disarmament', *The New York Times*, 28 June 1955.

[69] 'Finletter Urges Full Disarmament'.

[70] 'Finletter Urges Full Disarmament'.

[71] Goedde, *The Politics of Peace*, p. 82.

weaponise the UN to limit Soviet military assets. The repeated efforts of a vocal group of US politicians and elite commentators throughout the late 1940s and early 1950s provided a foundation for the UN peacekeeping project at a transformative moment for American international power thus preparing the organisation's expansion into the military sphere.

Observer Origins: Establishing a Presence in the Middle East

Whilst activists and politicians debated the future of nuclear power and its management by an international government, the UN became a key field-based actor in the post-war crisis in Palestine. Initially focused on developing a state-building strategy for Israel, the UN secretary-general, Trygve Lie, shifted from shaping the diplomatic debates around the partition's territorial borders and the resettlement of Jewish refugees on Palestinian land to implementing the deployment of a transnational unit of military observers to Palestine. These activities were closely related, however, as the UN's functional expansion into deploying military observers evolved from Lie's desire to ensure that the formation of the Israeli state – even if not in the design originally approved by Lie – would be a process supported and stabilised by the international organisation.

The United Nations Special Committee on Palestine (UNSCOP) was tasked with developing a territorial solution to the 'Palestine Question' in May 1947. Within UN forums, the question prompted debates on the timeline for the withdrawal of the British Mandate in Palestine and the resettlement of hundreds of thousands of displaced Jewish refugees in the aftermath of the Holocaust and material damage of the Second World War.[72] Arieh Kochavi has shown that the refugee crisis split Anglo-American allies in the post-war period with the British government initially afraid to harm its relations with neighbouring Arab states and Palestinians by accepting European Jews,[73] whilst the US vote on the Palestine Question was dependent on the resettlement of Jews in Palestine.[74] However, Zionist political pressure underpinned by decades of propaganda and galvanised by the tragedy of the Holocaust also

[72] O. Yehudai, *Leaving Zion: Jewish Emigration from Palestine and Israel After World War II* (Cambridge: Cambridge University Press, 2020).

[73] A British plan for partition in Palestine had been considered following the Peel Commission in 1937 but was abandoned later that year and subsequently supplanted by the 1939 White Paper which signalled the British government's intention to 'forego support of a Jewish state and to assert her authority over an undivided Palestine'. A. S. Klieman, 'The Resolution of Conflicts through Territorial Partition: The Palestine Experience', *Comparative Studies in Society and History*, 22:2 (1980), p. 299. For more on British policy on Palestine, see: C. Beckerman, *Unexpected State: British Politics and the Creation of Israel* (Bloomington: Indiana University Press, 2020).

[74] A. J. Kochavi, *Post-Holocaust Politics: Britain, the United States, and Jewish Refugees, 1945–1948* (Chapel Hill: The University of North Carolina Press, 2001).

fundamentally shaped the process of Israeli state formation, complicating the humanitarian resettlement 'narrative' emphasised by representatives of UNSCOP in 1947.[75] Although the Palestine Question began as a resettlement issue for both British and US governments, it was soon sidelined by fierce debates over the splitting up of Palestinian territory and the cartographic logistics of nation-building.[76] Instead of conceiving – and prioritising – the resettlement of Jewish refugees as a political problem requiring attention, both British and US governments restricted the topic to a humanitarian context and focused on improving their own strategic interests in the region.[77]

UNSCOP was a large multilateral committee composed of fifty-five representatives from eleven 'neutral' non-permanent UN member-states: Australia, Canada, Czechoslovakia, Guatemala, India, Iran, Netherlands, Peru, Sweden, Uruguay, and Yugoslavia.[78] The committee visited Palestine and Lebanon in June and July 1947 and flew to Geneva to be given tours of displaced persons camps constructed in American and British occupation zones in Germany and Austria, interviewing Jewish refugees throughout August. Following committee deliberations in late August, the UNSCOP report was published to the General Assembly on 3 September 1947.[79] The committee recommended the end of the British Mandate in Palestine and suggested that Palestine be swiftly partitioned between Israel and Arab Palestinian territories: 'In view of the special circumstances of the Palestine question, however, [the committee] has felt justified in proposing a measure which is designed to ameliorate promptly the condition of the Jewish segments of the displaced persons as a vital prerequisite to the settlement of the difficult conditions in Palestine.'[80] The UNSCOP report also designated the city of Jerusalem as a '*corpus separatum* under a special international regime' to be 'administered by the United Nations' via the Trusteeship Council, dividing the governing territory between Palestinian and Israeli authorities,[81] and operating through Arab and Jewish provisional Councils of Government.[82]

[75] C. Nicault, 'La Shoah et la création de l'État d'Israël : Où en est l'historiographie?', *Les Cahiers de la Shoah*, 2002/1 (no. 6), pp. 161–204.

[76] C. Leuenberger and I. Schnell, *The Politics of Maps: Cartographic Constructions of Israel/ Palestine* (Oxford: Oxford University Press, 2020).

[77] S. Waldman, *Anglo-American Diplomacy and the Palestinian Refugee Problem, 1948–1951* (London: Palgrave Macmillan, 2016), pp. 40–41.

[78] UN Doc, A/RES 106 (S-1), '106 (S-1) Special Committee on Palestine', 15 May 1947.

[79] UN Doc, A/364, 'Official Records of the Second Session of the General Assembly, Supplement No. 11: United Nations Special Committee on Palestine, Report to the General Assembly, Vol. 1', 3 September 1947.

[80] UN Doc, A/364, 'Official Records of the Second Session of the General Assembly, Supplement No. 11: United Nations Special Committee on Palestine, Report to the General Assembly, Vol. 1', 3 September 1947.

[81] UN Doc, A/RES/181 (II), 'Resolution 181 (II). Future Government of Palestine', 29 November 1947.

[82] UN Doc, A/RES 106 (S-1), '106 (S-1) Special Committee on Palestine', 15 May 1947.

Secretary-general Lie supported this partition plan and the UN's role in its implementation, and helped to lobby for its authorisation throughout October and November 1947, building upon his earlier discussions with British representatives in March and April.[83] Ellen Jenny Ravndal's analysis of Lie's personal papers has helped to reveal the special relationship that the secretary-general had to the birth of Israel – and the role that the UN would have as midwife in this process. In his memoirs, Lie entitled the chapter on the Arab–Israeli conflict as 'The First Major Test', referring to the crisis as a 'crucial test … to the wisdom and statesmanship' of the new organisation.[84] Ravndal has argued that 'Lie would later regard the State of Israel "as his child" and he took pride in the part he played in helping to establish the Jewish state. He stated in his memoirs that when the question was first brought to the UN, he did not have much knowledge of the region and its Arab inhabitants, but believed that the Jewish state would be a positive experience.'[85] In his mind, Lie's role as Norwegian foreign minister in exile during the Second World War further predisposed the secretary-general to solving the 'problem of hundreds of thousands of refugees languishing in European camps'.[86] That the partition policy would create another refugee crisis in Palestine did little to shake this foundational belief. Rather than an ardent Zionist, however, Lie was focused on how the 'Palestine Problem' could promote the UN as an expert in other post-colonial, territorial crises. In 1948, the conflict remained relatively disconnected from Cold War politics, suggesting that, in his words, Palestine was a case where the Great Powers 'should still be able to act in unison' and 'do something positive through the United Nations'.[87] His dismissal of the Arab Palestinian population was a by-product of his desire to demonstrate the institution's expertise in state-building and conflict response and his – confessed – ignorance on the politics of the region.

Although most of the Arab Palestinian population and neighbouring Arab nations rejected the UNSCOP plan, the resolution passed in the General Assembly with thirty-three to thirteen votes (and ten abstentions)[88] in favour of partition on 29 November 1947.[89] It was agreed that the British Mandate period would end and that the partition would enable the construction of an Israeli state on Palestinian territory. Several Arab countries formally proposed to request an International Court of Justice (ICJ) advisory comment on the

83 M. J. Haron, 'The British Decision to Give the Palestine Question to the United Nations', *Middle Eastern Studies*, 17:2 (1981), pp. 241–248.

84 E. J. Ravndal, '"The First Major Test": The UN Secretary-General and the Palestine Problem, 1947–9', *The International History Review*, 38:1 (2016), p. 197.

85 Ravndal, '"The First Major Test"', p. 197.

86 Ravndal, '"The First Major Test"', p. 197.

87 Ravndal, '"The First Major Test"', p. 198.

88 At this time, the UN General Assembly was comprised of fifty-six member-states.

89 UN Doc, A/RES/181(II), 'Resolution 181 (II). Future Government of Palestine', 29 November 1947.

legal competency of the General Assembly to partition a state, hoping to challenge the partition plan.[90] Their proposal was narrowly rejected, and the UNSCOP plan was authorised as legal. As Victor Kattan has pointed out, 'Had the Soviet Union or just one of its satellite states voted in favour ... it would have been submitted to the ICJ for an advisory opinion.'[91] In 1948, Pitman B. Potter, an American jurist, argued that it was likely that war would break out in Palestine if the UNSCOP plan was implemented as planned. He stated that 'it would be politically very difficult if not impossible for the United Nations to dictate a solution in Palestine not acceptable to both Arabs and Jews, and practically impossible execute such a program in the absence of United Nations armed forces'.[92] Although many politicians and populations were opposed to the UNSCOP partition plan, such as the British Secretary of State for Foreign Affairs, Ernest Bevin, many commended the UNSCOP committee for developing a solution to a question that had lingered since the Balfour Declaration in 1917.

However, factional violence between Israeli forces and Arab militias escalated in the aftermath of the UNSCOP resolution vote in late November 1947. This conflict is known as the civil war in Mandatory Palestine, or the first phase of the 1947–1948 Palestine war, as Palestinians fought against their displacement. Scholars have maintained that it was only because Britain remained in effective control of Palestine during this period that neighbouring Arab states did not intervene during the winter of 1947.[93] Violence from Arab Palestinians remained largely improvised, limited to sticks and stones, and only escalated into militia-led aggression following the Israeli armed forces' use of firearms. Alan Cunningham, British High Commissioner of Palestine, cabled London in December 1947 to emphasise, 'The initial Arab outbreaks were spontaneous and unorganized and were more demonstrations of displeasure at the UN decision than determined attacks on Jews ... although pleased at the strong response to the strike call [the Arab Higher Committee] were not in favour of serious outbreaks.'[94] The UNSCOP plan and resolution provoked violence between the two groups as it attempted to reframe Palestinian displacement as a 'humanitarian' solution to the Jewish refugee crisis in Europe.

[90] V. Kattan, *From Coexistence to Conquest: International Law and the Origins of the Arab-Israeli Conflict, 1891–1949* (London: Pluto Press, 2009), p. 149.

[91] Kattan, *From Coexistence to Conquest*, p. 151.

[92] P. B. Potter, 'The Palestine Problem before the United Nations', *The American Journal of International Law*, 42:4 (1948), p. 860.

[93] Kattan, *From Coexistence to Conquest*, pp. 177–178.

[94] M. Palumbo, *The Palestinian Catastrophe: The 1948 Expulsion of a People from Their Homeland* (London: Quartet Books, 1987), pp. 35–36.

However, in early 1948, violence between the two communities became more organised and threatened to engulf neighbouring Arab states, prompting US President Harry Truman to reconsider his country's position on the partition plan and suggest the construction of a UN Trusteeship over the entirety of Palestine – not just the city of Jerusalem.[95] Whilst American representatives lobbied for a Trusteeship in New York during March and April, Israeli militant groups Irgun and LEHI (meaning 'fighters for the freedom of Israel') perpetrated a series of massacres in areas assigned to Palestinians by the UNSCOP plan as well as in Jerusalem, most notably the Deir Yassin massacre, attempting to further expel or eradicate Palestinian Arabs from their homes.[96] Inspired by the UNSCOP plan, and undeterred by British Mandate soldiers, armed groups on both sides sought to protect and isolate their communities, implementing a de facto partition that would be mirrored in Cyprus in little more than a decade. One member of the Jewish Agency commented, 'It does not matter what Americans say; the Jews in Palestine have already put a sort of partition into force, and we are maintaining it.'[97] Inspired by the upcoming withdrawal of British troops, from March to May the Jewish leadership mobilised to implement a formal partition and demolition process that would remove any and all traces of Palestinians from designated Jewish areas, regardless of legal rights or cultural heritage.

During this unstable period, the Security Council established a UN Truce Commission, composed of consuls from Belgium, France, and the United States in Jerusalem in response to the United Nations Palestine Commission's (UNPC) inability to operate within the territory.[98] Building upon the consuls existing connections and diplomatic relationships within Jerusalem, it was hoped that the consuls of the Truce Commission would have more success at achieving a ceasefire than the UNPC, whose mandate was explicitly attached to the implementation of the UNSCOP partition plan – to which the Arab states were directly opposed. This tangle of UN commissions and representatives in Palestinian territory was only going to get more complicated once the British Mandate period concluded.

[95] 'United States Proposal for Temporary United Nations Trusteeship for Palestine: Statement by President Truman, March 25, 1948', available at https://unispal.un.org/UNISPAL.NSF/0/C3AFF48D711D26158525715400730A30.

[96] M. Hogan, 'The 1948 Massacre at Deir Yassin Revisited', *The Historian*, 63:2 (2001), pp. 309–333; Kattan, *From Coexistence to Conquest*, p. 168.

[97] 'Plan to Drop Partition of Palestine', *The Times*, 20 March 1948.

[98] The other nation with a consul based in Jerusalem, Syria, 'indicated that his Government [was] not prepared to serve on the Commission'. UN Doc, S/727, 'Establishment of a United Nations Truce Commission for Palestine', 23 April 1948. The UNPC was officially relieved of its duties on 14 May 1948. UN Doc, A/553, 'Further Consideration of the Question of the Future Government of Palestine', 14 May 1948.

The withdrawal of British troops and the expiry of the British Mandate on 14 May 1948 prompted David Ben-Gurion, as leader of the Jewish ruling authorities the World Zionist Organization and the Jewish Agency, to announce Israeli independence in the 'Declaration of the Establishment of the State of Israel'.[99] The 14th May witnessed the violent displacement and expulsion of hundreds of thousands of Palestinian people from their livelihoods and homeland by the Israeli army, termed the 'Nakba(h)' or 'catastrophe'.[100] The next day, a group of Arab states – Jordan, Egypt, Syria, and Lebanon – invaded Palestinian territory in defence of the Arab Palestinian population and in opposition to the creation of a state of Israel on Palestinian land.[101] Benny Morris has described this event as the 'pan-Arab invasion', as neighbouring states reacted to the violent massacres against Arab Palestinians and the arrival of tens of thousands of Jewish refugees.[102] The Egyptian government wrote to the President of the Security Council to declare that this 'pan-Arab invasion' was 'to establish security and order in place of chaos and disorder which prevailed and which rendered the country at the mercy of Zionist terrorist gangs who persisted in attacking the peaceful inhabitants, with arms and equipments [sic] amassed by them for that purpose'.[103]

Although the General Assembly met on 14 May to appoint a UN mediator to resolve the crisis,[104] within two weeks the issue was further escalated to the Security Council, where a ceasefire was declared for a month.[105] The five permanent members met on 20 May to agree on a suitable mediator, unanimously appointing Count Folke Bernadotte as United Nations Mediator on Palestine.[106] Bernadotte, a Swedish diplomat and aristocrat, was the recently appointed President of the Swedish Red Cross. His promotion to this role was in response to recent international praise for his bravery and front line role as a negotiator for the Swedish White Buses mission.[107] The mission – named for the colour of the vehicles with a Red Cross symbol painted on the sides –

[99] 'Declaration of Establishment of State of Israel', 14 May 1948, available at www.mfa.gov.il/mfa/foreignpolicy/peace/guide/pages/declaration%20of%20establishment%20of%20state%20of%20israel.aspx.

[100] Kattan, *From Coexistence to Conquest*, pp. 147, 194–202.

[101] B. Morris, *1948: A History of the First Arab-Israeli War* (London: Yale University Press, 2008), pp. 180–181.

[102] Morris, *1948: A History of the First Arab-Israeli War*, pp. 180–181.

[103] UN Doc, S/743, 'Cablegram addressed to the President of the Security Council dated 15 May from the Minister of Foreign Affairs of Egypt', 15 May 1948.

[104] UN Doc, A/RES/186 (S-2), '186 (S-2) Appointment and Terms of Reference of a United Nations Mediator in Palestine', 14 May 1948.

[105] UN Doc, S/801, '50 (1948) Resolution of 29 May 1948'.

[106] UN Doc, A/RES/186 (S-2), '186 (S-2) Appointment and Terms of Reference of a United Nations Mediator in Palestine', 14 May 1948.

[107] A. Ilan, *Bernadotte in Palestine: A Study in Contemporary Humanitarian Knight-Errantry* (New York: Palgrave Macmillan, 1989), p. 35.

rescued over 17,000 concentration camp prisoners from many camps in German territory towards the end of the Second World War and brought Bernadotte to the attention of the Swedish government.[108] Bernadotte also briefly acted as an intermediary between Heinrich Himmler and the Allies during April 1945, further impressing the international community with his mediatory skills and political objectivity.[109] It was this experience and expertise that Bernadotte was expected to employ in Palestine on behalf of the UN.

The Security Council resolution also decided Bernadotte should be 'provided with a sufficient number of military observers',[110] prompting the construction of what would later be formalised as the United Nations Truce Supervision Organisation (UNTSO).[111] Thus, preliminary steps towards an UN-led peacekeeping mission began with the design and deployment of UNTSO in response to the escalating violence of the Arab–Israeli conflict on 29 May 1948.[112] The military observers were employed to defend the truce or ceasefire on the ground whilst the mediator undertook political negotiations with leaders.[113] Bernadotte was already supported by the consuls from the UN Truce Commission and five officers from his nation, Sweden, to serve as his personal staff. However, once he arrived he required more personnel in Palestine. He requested that the Truce Commission representatives donate additional military observers from their nations to enable his plan for an:

> elaborate control machinery to make sure that no fighting personnel or military material [sic] reaches Palestine or the seven members of the Arab League, and to guarantee that those men of military age who are admitted are not mobilized or trained.[114]

The first fifty military observers who arrived in Palestine in June 1948 were 'experienced international civil servants with a background of service with the United Nations Secretariat at Headquarters', with most having served as security guards in the New York building.[115] Their primary duty was to

108 S. Persson, 'Folke Bernadotte and the White Buses', *The Journal of Holocaust Education*, 9:2 (2000), pp. 237–268.

109 UN Doc, UN Public Information, Press Release PAL/290, 'Count Folke Bernadotte – Activities as Mediator and Biography', 17 September 1948.

110 UN Doc, A/RES/186 (S-2), '186 (S-2) Appointment and Terms of Reference of a United Nations Mediator in Palestine', 14 May 1948.

111 UN Doc, S/801, '50 (1948) Resolution of 29 May 1948'.

112 UN Doc, S/801, '50 (1948) Resolution of 29 May 1948'.

113 T. J. Hamilton, 'Tight Plan Sought: Bernadotte for controls that will make truce in Holy Land work', *The New York Times*, 3 June 1948; M. Brown, 'Jews, Arabs Adopt Jerusalem Truce in Old Walled City', *The New York Times*, 29 April 1948.

114 T. J. Hamilton, 'UN Rejects Move to Send Soviet Observers to Palestine', *The New York Times*, 16 June 1948.

115 UN Doc, UN Public Information, Press Release PAL/189, 'Fifty UN Guards to Go to Palestine', 17 June 1948.

maintain the ceasefire along the supply route from the coastal city of Tel Aviv to Jerusalem, on the eastern side of the territory, which ran along the 'Green Line' between Israeli and Jordanian-Iraqi forces.[116] Under the leadership of Bernadotte, the military observers were to act as his eyes across the region and to investigate any violations of the ceasefire, often putting themselves in dangerous positions on the front line. This unarmed group of military observers and mediatory staff tested the practical implementation and political popularity of a non-governmental international organisation deployed to a conflict context. A UN Press Release also stressed that 'While on duty in Palestine, they were to continue to wear United Nations guard uniforms',[117] beginning the practice of distinguishing UN-employed staff in conflict spaces through the use of the General Assembly-approved light blue uniforms (in the same colour as the UN flag).[118] All observer vehicles were painted white with the large 'UN' initialism covering the roof in black ink, to further differentiate the observers from other parties in the conflict.[119] UNTSO's formative construction was far from an organised peacekeeping mission, as would be developed for UNEF; UNTSO's staffing was informal, fragmentary, and incremental as Bernadotte made an increasing number of requests from Palestine in order to execute his plan for peace.

Just like when recruiting state representatives for UNSCOP, Bernadotte and his UN Truce Commission colleagues chose staff from so-called 'neutral' nations for the UN observer group (soon to be re-constituted into UNTSO).[120] This caused upset from the Soviet Union and Ukraine in the Security Council. The USSR had repeatedly attempted to donate Soviet military observers and had been ignored in debates on Palestine.[121] On 10 June, Andrei Gromyko, USSR permanent representative, insisted on a response from the Security Council following an impassioned speech from his Ukrainian ally, Vasyl Tarasenko:

[116] UN Doc, UN Public Information, Press Release PAL/191, 'United Nations Guards Leave for Cairo', 19 June 1948.

[117] UN Doc, UN Public Information, Press Release PAL/189, 'Fifty UN Guards to Go to Palestine', 17 June 1948.

[118] UN Doc, A/RES/167, 'Resolutions Adopted on the Reports of the Sixth Committee', October 1947.

[119] Although this has led to dangerous instances of copy-cat branding. For instance, in 1992 the Russian army painted its helmets blue in Moldova. The Russian army also painted their vehicles white, 'UN style', during the conflict in Tajikistan in 1993. For more, see I. Hurd, *After Anarchy: Legitimacy and Power in the United Nations Security Council* (Princeton: Princeton University Press, 2008), p. 126.

[120] UN Doc, S/PV.317, '317th Meeting of Security Council. 121. Continuation of the discussion on the Palestine question', 10 June 1948, p. 41.

[121] T. J. Hamilton, 'Russia Insists UN Send Soviet Group to Palestine: US and Canada in Security Unit Oppose Moscow Military Observers', *The New York Times*, 11 June 1948; Hamilton, 'UN Rejects Move to Send Soviet Observers to Palestine', 16 June 1948.

> Why were Belgium, the United States of America and France to be the members of the Truce Commission? Was it because these countries were the most impartial or the most interested, or had some special qualifications which are essential for this particular task? No, it was purely a matter of chance and was due to the fact that these countries had their consuls on the spot.[122]

Tarasenko additionally argued that a continuation of this principle of 'ready, willing, and able' might be an unhelpful way to secure competent or qualified observers. Emboldened from this support, Gromyko added:

> On what grounds can the United States object to the utilization of a small group of Soviet military observers in Palestine? There are no legitimate grounds for this objection. No one in his right mind can understand why United States, French and Belgian military observers should be present in Palestine, while USSR observers may not. Why have the United States, France and Belgium more grounds for sending their observers to Palestine, than the USSR?[123]

In response to this argument, the Canadian permanent representative General Andrew McNaughton argued that it was not in the spirit of the original resolution from April that observers from nations other than the UN Truce Commission would be deployed to Palestine. He insisted that 'the members of the Truce Commission are under an obligation to provide the assistance and the facilities which are needed for this task ... there cannot properly be any question of the right of a country to participate ... the resolutions ... are being properly, correctly and wisely interpreted by our Mediator on the spot.'[124]

On the basis of a lack of Soviet observers in Palestine, the Soviet Union rejected the idea that the 29th May resolution, which had authorised the deployment of military observers to support the operations of Bernadotte, now empowered 'the Mediator to make any such requests or to settle the question of the despatch of military observers'.[125] On 15 June, Gromyko put forward a proposal to vote on sending USSR military observers to Palestine but struggled to gain any support within the Security Council. José Arce, the Argentinian permanent representative, insisted that Bernadotte's decision to not only recruit from solely UN Truce Commission nations but also hire personal staff from his own nation 'which is not a member of the Security

122 UN Doc, S/PV.317, '317th Meeting of Security Council. 121. Continuation of the discussion on the Palestine question', 10 June 1948, p. 43.

123 UN Doc, S/PV.317, '317th Meeting of Security Council. 121. Continuation of the discussion on the Palestine question', 10 June 1948, p. 44.

124 UN Doc, S/PV.317, '317th Meeting of Security Council. 121. Continuation of the discussion on the Palestine question', 10 June 1948, p. 44.

125 UN Doc, S/PV.320, '320th Security Council Meeting. 130. Continuation of the discussion on the Palestine Question', 15 June 1948, p. 6.

Council and has no consul at Jerusalem' must have been 'the course he thought best and we, I deliberately repeat, must respect the wishes of the Mediator and try to interfere as little as possible with the work entrusted to him in Palestine, if we do not wish to put obstacles in his way for one reason or another'.[126] The Soviet resolution failed to pass with only two votes in favour and nine abstentions. This appeared to conclude the issue in the Security Council, frustrating the Soviet Union and their allies. It also demonstrated a significant diplomatic disagreement over *who* should legitimately be deployed under UN auspices and under *what* logic; expertise or neutrality, proximity to conflict or non-permanent member.

Lie sought to enable the construction of the Israeli state through the military observers' assistance, even if its establishment had infringed his preferred UNSCOP partition plan. Instead, he intended to use the UN to bring the permanent members together and to establish the UN deliberative forums as unique spaces for international cooperation across political divisions in the endeavour of global peace. Fearful of the ramifications if the UN was unable to 'solve' the Israel–Palestine crisis, Lie personally visited US and British ambassadors to encourage a united front in support of Bernadotte and the observers, attempting to resolve Anglo-American disagreement on the Palestine 'problem'.[127] During this meeting, he outlined the global and organisational consequences if the conflict was left unresolved:

> If effective action cannot be taken quickly to deal with the situation in the Middle East, the Secretary-General fears (i) a spread of armed intervention in the Middle Eastern area; (ii) possible repercussions in Kashmir, Indonesia and the Balkans following clear proof of the ineffectiveness of the Security Council; (iii) grave reactions on U.K./U.S. relations; (iv) the *beginning of the end of the United Nations.*[128]

By May 1948, Lie recognised that the situation was fraught with complications. He knew that if the UN could not orchestrate a solution in Palestine, it could prove the ineptitude of the institution in conflict response and conclude the young organisation's operations.

Asserting Expertise, Proposing a UN Guard

Although his efforts at uniting diplomats across the Atlantic on the Palestine question had failed, Lie pivoted to use the Arab–Israeli conflict to promote his

[126] UN Doc, S/PV.320, '320th Security Council Meeting. 130. Continuation of the discussion on the Palestine Question', 15 June 1948, p. 10.

[127] Waldman, *Anglo-American Diplomacy and the Palestinian Refugee Problem.*

[128] British National Archives (henceforth, BNA), FO 371/72676, 'Jackson Memo, 21 May 1948' [author's own emphasis].

idea of formally constructing a UN Guard to foster public faith in the organisation. The escalating violence in the region had convinced Lie that UN staff were at risk of attack, and the current security measures were insufficient in providing a professional environment despite the precarious ceasefire in June 1948. On 10 June 1948, in a commencement speech for Harvard University, he first publicly outlined his aspirations for a 'small guard force, as distinct from a striking force'.[129] Those within the inner circle of the UN Secretariat felt that the lack of a UN armed force had 'hampered the work of the Security Council and diminished the prestige of the Organization', especially in protecting international peace and security.[130] In his speech at Harvard, Lie urged the formation of a smaller force 'very soon', pending the 'formation of a larger body as envisaged in the Charter of the United Nations'.[131] Lie proposed a force of '1,000–5,000 men, largely drawn from the smaller member states, to be recruited by the Secretary-General and placed at the disposal of the Security Council, the General Assembly, and the Trusteeship Council'.[132] His desire to draw from smaller member-state nations would be later adopted in UNEF and other future missions as a solution to concerns about Great Power instrumentalisation and interference. Citing Lie's personal memos and papers to fellow UN Secretariat staff, Ravndal has highlighted the driving motivation for Lie in his plans for a UN Guard:

> The proposal also emphasised that 'even more important than the practical usefulness of such a Guard would be the fact that it would symbolize the authority of the United Nations in troubled areas of the world', and could help counteract the growing doubts of the international public regarding the abilities of the UN, as 'the provision of even a very modest Guard force would give people the feeling that the United Nations was being given strength to fulfil its purposes.

In plans to construct an 'international Jerusalem' or an UN Trusteeship administration as part of the partition, Lie and his colleagues in the Secretariat sought to extend the role of the organisation in the protection of the new state through his new UN Guard and thus benefit from the subsequent reputational boon. In a June 1948 memo, UN assistant secretary-general Robert Jackson gushed, 'I do not under-estimate the difficulties of creating this force – but, if you, as Secretary-General, could in fact become the saviour of Jerusalem I believe that the effect on the world as a whole would be electrifying, and the prestige of the United Nations

[129] Ravndal, '"The First Major Test"', p. 205.

[130] Ravndal, '"The First Major Test"', p. 205.

[131] Hamilton, 'Russia Insists UN Send Soviet Group to Palestine', 11 June 1948.

[132] E. J. Ravndal, 'Trygve Lie, 1946–1953', in M. Fröhlich and A. Williams (eds.), *The UN Secretary-General and the Security Council: A Dynamic Relationship* (Oxford: Oxford University Press, 2018), p. 32.

would be vastly increased.'[133] Although Lie had yet to formally present his proposal to the Security Council in June 1948, already Secretariat staff were excited to use the conflict in Palestine to send armed UN guards to Jerusalem. These internal discussions revealed the core motivation behind the Secretariat leadership's inventive approach to the crisis in Palestine: institutional authority.

However, initial plans for the UN Guard shifted as violence on the ground escalated and threatened the security of UN staff, especially the UN mediator Bernadotte and his personal staff. Having accepted the position as UN mediator in Palestine from Lie, Bernadotte had arrived in Rhodes in May 1948 to set up his headquarters on the Greek island.[134] As part of his mediator activities, he travelled to Cairo, Tel Aviv, and other major Arab cities to consult with representatives from both sides and to establish a truce. He also visited Palestinian displacement camps and witnessed the humanitarian crisis.[135] His first progress report, frequently referred to as the Bernadotte plan, was published to the General Assembly on 16 September 1948, condensing his findings from the previous months into fifty-seven pages.[136] It outlined on his plans for a long-term ceasefire or settlement between the two communities, a two-state solution, and the return of displaced Arab Palestinians to their homes. Bernadotte emphasised, 'the right of [Arab Palestinian] refugees to return to their homes at the earliest practical date should be established' and argued that it would be

> 'an offence against the principles of elemental justice if these innocent victims of the conflict were denied the right to return to their homes while Jewish immigrants flow into Palestine, and, indeed, at least offer the threat of permanent replacement of the Arab refugees who have been rooted in the land for centuries'.[137]

Bernadotte's report angered the Israeli government, who became convinced that Bernadotte was an agent of the British, prompting the pro-Israeli LEHI militia to organise the assassination of the UN mediator on 17 September 1948, the day after his progress report was published to the General Assembly.[138] UN observer Colonel Andrew Serot, a French-national, was also

[133] Ravndal, '"The First Major Test"', p. 206.

[134] UN Doc, UN Public Information, Press Release PAL/290, 'Count Folke Bernadotte – Activities as Mediator and Biography', 17 September 1948.

[135] Kattan, *From Coexistence to Conquest*, pp. 218–219.

[136] UN Doc, A/689, General Assembly, 'Progress Report of the United Nations Mediator on Palestine Submitted to the Secretary-General for Transmission to the Members of the United Nations', 16 September 1948.

[137] UN Doc, A/689, General Assembly, 'Progress Report of the United Nations Mediator on Palestine Submitted to the Secretary-General for Transmission to the Members of the United Nations', 16 September 1948.

[138] C. D. Stanger, 'A Haunting Legacy: The Assassination of Count Bernadotte', *Middle East Journal*, 42:2 (1988), pp. 260–272.

murdered during the shooting. In a statement to the Security Council, Bunche revealed that the LEHI group had issued 'general threats against United Nations observers' since the first truce began in June 1948.[139] The subsequent failure of the Israeli police to capture and prosecute the three men involved in the shooting (those arrested were acquitted) led to the UN seeking monetary damages from the Government of Israel via an ICJ case. Having ruled in the UN's favour, the ICJ instructed Israel to remit $54,628.00.[140] In doing so, the Israeli government expressed 'its most sincere regret that this dastardly assassination took place on Israeli territory, and that despite all its efforts the criminals have gone undetected' although it refused to admit responsibility for the mediator's death.[141] Bernadotte's death underlined the risk for UN officials in international conflict zones, further kindling debates about the creation of a UN military but also galvanising a broader discussion about the safety of aid workers and humanitarians in the field.

Taking advantage of Bernadotte's murder, Lie published his UN Guard plan to the member-states, provoking debate within the Security Council and the General Assembly, especially so soon after the disagreement with the Soviets on the nationalities of military observers in Palestine. Just over a week following Bernadotte's assassination, he presented his plans for a UN Guard in a thirteen-page report to the General Assembly titled, 'Demonstrated Need'.[142] He argued that recent crises in Palestine had stressed the UN's functional inability to fully protect its own personnel without an armed force; its diplomatic efforts were disempowered without the protection and, most importantly, defence of a UN military:

> Availability of international protective personnel is a *sine quo non* of a Mission's ability to proceed with the necessary confidence and authority to arrange for the free movement of observers and other mission personnel in troubled areas without the suspicion of partiality which the use of local police or national foreign militia engenders. Absence of an independent international body representative of the authority of the United Nations and capable of offering minimum personal protection to United Nations staff has seriously embarrassed the work of the United Nations

[139] UN Doc, S/1018, 'Cablegram dated 27 September 1948 from Ralph Bunche to the Secretary-General Transmitting Report Regarding the Assassination of the United Nations Mediator', 28 September 1948.

[140] ICJ, 'Reparations for Injuries Suffered in the Service of the United Nations: Advisory Opinion of April 11th, 1949'.

[141] UN Doc, S/1506, 'Letter dated 14 June from the Minister for Foreign Affairs of the Government of Israel to the Secretary-General concerning a claim for damaged [sic] caused to the United Nations by the assassination of Count Folke Bernadotte and a reply thereto from the Secretary-General', 14 June 1950.

[142] UN Doc, A/656, 'United Nations Guard. Report of the Secretary-General. "Demonstrated Need"', 28 September 1948.

> Missions both in the course of hearings and enquiries as well as in the operation of truce arrangements and the rendering of good offices. In Palestine the Mediator emphasized again and again the need to assure to him adequate facilities to enable him to guard mission personnel as well as neutralized buildings and objectives in specified areas. Had even a small security or protective force been available, some injury and loss of life of United Nations personnel might have been avoided, as might also the destruction of vital neutralized objectives, the loss of which could have permanently jeopardized the whole of the Mediator's work.[143]

For Lie and his Secretariat colleagues, the creation of an armed UN Guard would strengthen the organisation and remove any uncertainty that the UN was able to effectively respond to conflict. However, Lie's plans were tentative in comparison with future peacekeeping missions, and he chose to limit the mandate of Guard personnel to safeguarding UN observer staff, equipment, and buildings:

> The Secretary-General clearly recognizes that both on practical as well as on legal grounds such a Guard could not be used for enforcement purposes as envisaged under the Charter, nor for the purpose of maintaining law and order. It is, however, his view that the provision of a Guard such as he proposed would immeasurably strengthen the hands of United Nations missions which are established for the express purpose of assuring pacific settlements without recourse to the use of force and would assist them to expedite peaceful settlements.[144]

Lie had also sketched out some practical details for the UN Guard. The Guard would be a 'normal unit' or department of the UN Secretariat and would be overseen by the secretary-general.[145] It would be emphatically, '*entirely non-military*'.[146] Although hoping that the Guard could increase to 'several thousand' in response to deployment to a conflict, Lie expected approximately 'eight hundred strong' for the core or 'nucleus' Guard staff, 300 for the permanent staff, and 500 in reserve in their respective countries.[147] To limit the costs of the Guard, Lie suggested that the personnel should be recruited from 'physically fit men without dependants, preferably between the ages of twenty-two to thirty

143 UN Doc, A/656, 'United Nations Guard. Report of the Secretary-General. "Demonstrated Need"', 28 September 1948, p. 1.

144 UN Doc, A/656, 'United Nations Guard. Report of the Secretary-General. "Demonstrated Need"', 28 September 1948, p. 2.

145 UN Doc, A/656, 'United Nations Guard. Report of the Secretary-General. "Demonstrated Need"', 28 September 1948, p. 7.

146 UN Doc, A/656, 'United Nations Guard. Report of the Secretary-General. "Demonstrated Need"', 28 September 1948, p. 7. [emphasis in original].

147 UN Doc, A/656, 'United Nations Guard. Report of the Secretary-General. "Demonstrated Need"', 28 September 1948, p. 3; UN Doc, General Assembly, A/AC.24/SR.30, 'Ad Hoc Political Committee, 30th Meeting', 7 April 1949.

years. (This proviso will tend to reduce the burden of expense associated with the maintenance of dependants and will generally be conducive to the ready availability of personnel for movement into the field'.[148] Under Article 100 of the Charter, Guard personnel would promise obedience to the UN alone, in a similar manner to future peacekeeping missions whereby troops were instructed to show deference to the UN Force Commander, rather than their home nation. Lie noted that 'it will not be organizationally of such a size or character as to be susceptible of use as an aggressive force ... No tranks [sic], artillery or major offensive weapons will form part of the regular equipment', although the guard members will be provided with 'personal emergency weapons and emergency technical equipment'.[149] Predicting later political complications and delayed deployments, Lie sought for the UN Guard to 'be so recruited, trained and equipped as to be able to furnish supplementary technical service requirements to a United Nations Mission whenever lack of immediate alternative facilities renders this necessary or desirable'. He believed this would also help strengthen the organisation, preventing the repetition of past disorganised or ill-equipped UN missions – as in Palestine – which had 'not only impaired the efficiency of Missions but the authority of the United Nations [...] lost in dignity thereby'.[150] 'Though small in numbers', Secretariat official and UN legal counsel Abraham Feller noted to the General Assembly, the UN Guard's 'training and devotion to the international ideal would soon make it a potent assistant in the development and strengthening of the United Nations'.[151]

It took almost a year for Lie's UN Guard report to be considered until it was finally debated during the Third Session in the General Assembly in April 1949.[152] However, that year the situation in Palestine had changed. Following Bernadotte's assassination in September 1948, Dr Ralph Bunche became acting UN mediator on Palestine in addition to his existing roles as Head of the UN Trusteeship Division and Chief of the Secretariat. Israeli officials, such as Moshe Sharett Foreign Minister of the Provisional Israeli Government, feared that 'a dead Bernadotte might be more powerful and influential than Bernadotte alive',

[148] UN Doc, A/656, 'United Nations Guard. Report of the Secretary-General. "Demonstrated Need"', 28 September 1948, p. 10.

[149] UN Doc, A/656, 'United Nations Guard. Report of the Secretary-General. "Demonstrated Need"', 28 September 1948, pp. 7–11.

[150] UN Doc, A/656, 'United Nations Guard. Report of the Secretary-General. "Demonstrated Need"', 28 September 1948, p. 3.

[151] UN Doc, General Assembly, A/AC.24/SR.30, 'Ad Hoc Political Committee, 30th Meeting', 7 April 1949, p. 24.

[152] UN Doc, General Assembly, A/AC.24/SR.30, 'Ad Hoc Political Committee, 30th Meeting', 7 April 1949; UN Doc, General Assembly, A/AC.24/SR.31, 'Ad Hoc Political Committee, 31st Meeting', 11 April 1949; UN Doc, General Assembly, A/AC.24/SR.32, 'Ad Hoc Political Committee, 32nd Meeting', 11 April 1949.

thus making the late mediator's plan popular to the other key conflict actors.[153] However, Bernadotte's plan was deemed unfavourable by Israeli *and* Arab nations, as well as the United States and Britain and failed to receive enough support in the General Assembly. And so, Bunche arrived in Palestine to re-start negotiations.

As UN mediator, Bunche worked closely alongside the mediator's Chief of Staff, William E. Riley, a fellow American, to travel around the Middle East and negotiate the Armistice Agreements with the Arab–Israeli belligerent parties throughout 1949.[154] Bunche was an academic, international civil servant, and prominent African American activist and had had a long career in teaching political science in the United States before he participated in the establishment of the UN in 1944.[155] His most enduring legacy – and the reason for his 1950 Nobel Peace Prize – was his mediation of the Middle East conflict for the UN.[156] Bunche's diplomatic negotiations and presence in the Middle East throughout late 1948 and early 1949 helped to recover some of the reputational damage that Lie had weathered in May 1948 following his inability to unite Anglo-American representatives on the 'Palestine Question'. During this year of mediation, Bunche helped to restore international confidence in the organisation as a valuable tool for protecting international peace and security, and, most importantly, inserted the UN as an integral forum *and* agent in the navigation of post-colonial statehood and sovereignty.

Following the adoption of all five Armistice Agreements in July 1949 – representing a set of agreements signed by Israel, Egypt, Lebanon, Jordan, and Syria that established a permanent ceasefire and formal Israeli-Palestinian borders – the functions of the acting UN mediator on Palestine were officially transferred to the UN Conciliation Commission for Palestine (UNCCP). The UNCCP was staffed by three state representatives from France, Turkey, and the United States (elected by the UN permanent member-states) and was located in a demilitarised zone in Jerusalem to enable direct consultation with Israeli and Arab state leadership.[157] These agreements marked the official end of the

153 J. Heller, 'Failure of a Mission: Bernadotte and Palestine, 1948', *Journal of Contemporary History*, 14:3 (1979), p. 525.

154 T. J. Hamilton, 'Riley Carries Plan', *The New York Times*, 2 June 1949.

155 B. Urquhart, 'The Evolution of the Secretary-General', in E. R. May and A. E. Laiou (eds.), *The Dumbarton Oaks Conversations and the United Nations, 1944–1994* (Cambridge, MA: Harvard University Press, 1998), p. 25.

156 E. Ben-Dror, 'Ralph Bunche and the 1949 Armistice Agreements revisited', *Middle Eastern Studies*, 56:2 (2020), pp. 274–289; N. Caplan, 'A Tale of Two Cities: The Rhodes and Lausanne Conferences, 1949', *Journal of Palestinian Studies*, 21:3 (1992), pp. 5–34.

157 UN Doc, A/819, General Assembly, 'United Nations Conciliation Commission for Palestine: First Progress Report', 15 March 1949.

Figure 1.2 Ralph Bunche talking with Ben Gurion, U1102496INP, 12 December 1948.
Reproduced with permission from Bettmann/Getty Images.

conflict for the UN officials, although thousands of Palestinians remained displaced from their homes and disconnected from their livelihoods.

This ongoing context of displacement enabled the UN to retain a presence on the ground to monitor compliance with the agreements' terms and to further encroach itself into field-based governance in the region. Over his last few months as acting mediator, Bunche oversaw the disbanding of the previous military observer system and the transition of international staff into a formal UNTSO structure from 11 August 1949.[158] Riley, previously the UN mediator's Chief of Staff, became UNTSO's Chief of Staff, and the – almost 700 – military observers under the mediator became the permanent staff of UNTSO.[159] The shift to a more permanent force in the wake of the agreements expanded the

[158] UN Doc, S/1376 II, '73 (1949). Resolution of 11 August 1949', 11 August 1949.
[159] T. Lie, 'Statement before the General Assembly', 29 April 1949, cited in A. W. Cordier and W. Foote, *Public Papers of the Secretaries-General of the United Nations. Volume I: Trygve Lie, 1946–1953* (New York: Columbia University Press, 1969), p. 188.

observers' roles and area of operations from their previous duties of monitoring and investigating breaches of the ceasefire along the supply line between Tel Aviv and Jerusalem. Observers would now focus on protecting the terms of the Armistice Agreements in the whole region, policing border skirmishes and smuggling as well as supervising the ceasefire between belligerents. Bunche returned to his role in the Trusteeship Division in New York (having rejected the position of Assistant Secretary of State from President Truman) and later became the first African American to receive the Nobel Peace Prize for his work as acting UN mediator on Palestine in 1950.[160] During his acceptance speech, Bunche noted his UN colleagues and Bernadotte in contributing to the 'return' of the Arabs and Jews to peace: 'I am but one of many cogs in the United Nations, the greatest peace organization ever dedicated to the salvation of mankind's future on earth.'[161] He did not mention any of the Arab or Jewish diplomats who participated in the Armistice Agreements in his speech.

It was the eventual success of Bunche's UN mediation efforts and the Armistice Agreements negotiations that inadvertently foiled Lie's UN Guard plans. Following the publication of Lie's September 1948 'Demonstrated Need' report, diplomatic support for the plan was unstable. The Soviet Union feared that Lie's proposal would breach the UN Charter and circumvent the Security Council – and, therefore, their veto power.[162] As UN officials Andrew Cordier and Wilder Foote commented, 'Quite probably [the USSR's] experience with the military observers sent to Palestine further hardened the Soviet position and fed its suspicions. All the Communist countries were carefully shut out from participating, as they were from UNTSO and similar operations thereafter, with the single exception of the Yugoslav contingent in UNEF.'[163] Support was also lacking from the United States and Western European nations. Although tentatively supportive of Lie's proposal, Western nations were more dedicated to post-war material recovery and rearmament through policies like the Marshall Plan as the answer to Soviet aggression, rather than to the additional financial burden and military risk of a UN Guard.[164]

However, Lie's proposal merited further investigation. The deaths of Thomas C. Watson, a UN Truce Commission member and US-national, and René de

[160] T. J. Hamilton, 'Bunche Ends Task as UN Mediator', *The New York Times*, 28 July 1949.

[161] R. Bunche, 'Acceptance Speech, 10 December 1950', available at www.nobelprize.org/prizes/peace/1950/bunche/acceptance-speech/.

[162] T. J. Hamilton, 'The UN and Trygve Lie', *Foreign Affairs*, 29:1 (1950), p. 75.

[163] Cordier and Foote, *Public Papers of the Secretaries-General of the United Nations. Volume I*, p. 186.

[164] Cordier and Foote, *Public Papers of the Secretaries-General of the United Nations. Volume I*, p. 186.

Labarrière, a military observer and French-national,[165] in addition to the assassination of Bernadotte during the first few months of UNTSO operations prompted international concerns about the security of UN staff in Palestine without an armed UN presence in 1948–1949.[166] There were also ongoing questions about the ability of UN military observers and the mediator to even undertake their role *without* military support from an international force. For instance, in July 1948, the ceasefire had become so fractured that military observers and UN equipment were withdrawn from Palestine to Rhodes with the aid of the US army and navy until the violence was de-escalated.[167] But by April 1949, Bunche's Armistice Agreement negotiations were progressing well and fighting in the region had decreased. On 10 May 1949, Israeli Foreign Minister Moshe Shertok's request for statehood was formally accepted, and Israel became a member-state of the UN General Assembly as a 'peace-loving state' following its third application to the organisation on the condition of its compliance with the Armistice Agreements.[168]

Therefore, by the Third Session meeting on the UN Guard in the General Assembly in April 1949,[169] for many member-states, 'the question of the UN Guard was not as urgent as it had been earlier',[170] prompting Lie to instruct a Special Committee to investigate the possibility of a UN Guard rather than build on the momentum of an emergency.[171] His revised proposal resulted in the construction of the United Nations Field Service in 1949, a technical service of 300 unarmed personnel and the creation of a panel of standby military observers.[172] The failure of Lie's UN Guard to achieve diplomatic popularity in 1948–1949 demonstrated that the concept of an armed UN force would require the international pressure and anxiety of an ongoing crisis in

165 UN Doc, UN Public Information, Press Release PAL/208, 'UN Military Observer in Palestine Fatally Hurt while Investigating Report of Truce Violation; Another Observer Wounded', 6 July 1948.

166 UN Doc, General Assembly, A/AC.24/SR.30, 'Ad Hoc Political Committee, 30th Meeting', 7 April 1949, p. 23.

167 UN Doc, UN Public Information, Press Release PAL/210, 'UN Personnel Withdraws from Palestine', 8 July 1948.

168 UN Doc, A/RES/273 (III), General Assembly, '273 (III). Admission of Israel to Membership in the United Nations', 11 May 1948.

169 UN Doc, General Assembly, A/AC.24/SR.30, 'Ad Hoc Political Committee, 30th Meeting', 7 April 1949; UN Doc, General Assembly, A/AC.24/SR.31, 'Ad Hoc Political Committee, 31st Meeting', 11 April 1949; UN Doc, General Assembly, A/AC.24/SR.32, 'Ad Hoc Political Committee, 32nd Meeting', 11 April 1949.

170 UN Doc, General Assembly, A/AC.24/SR.30, 'Ad Hoc Political Committee, 30th Meeting', 7 April 1949.

171 UN Doc, A/AC.24/45, 'Draft Resolution adopted by the *Ad Hoc* Political Committee at Its 32nd meeting, 11 April 1949'.

172 UN Doc, A/RES/297 (IV), 'United Nations Field Service and United Nations Panel of Field Observers', 22 November 1949.

Figure 1.3 Israeli Foreign Minister Moshe Shertok (centre) and Trygve Lie (right), SAPA980314325180, 29 November 1948.
Reproduced with permission from Gaillourdet/AFP/Getty Images.

addition to a widespread diplomatic lobbying campaign in order to achieve the necessary votes – as would be witnessed during the Suez crisis in 1956.

Although Lie acknowledged in his memoirs that this solution was 'not at all what [he] had originally intended',[173] his UN Guard proposal inspired later calls for a 'stand-by UN Force' from military and diplomatic figures, especially following the spate of individual armed peacekeeping missions emerged in the 1950s and 1960s. US Ambassador to the UN, Adlai Stevenson, insisted that the slow construction of the Cyprus mission in 1964 had 'vividly exposed the frailties of the existing machinery' and called for a standby UN force of national military units to respond immediately to global conflict.[174] He argued, 'In short, when time is of the essence, there is a dangerous vacuum

[173] Ravndal, '"The First Major Test"', p. 206.

[174] R. N. Gardner, 'Needed: A Stand-by UN Force: In Cyprus, the U.N. has been called upon for the fourth time on a large scale to keep peace by military means. Here is the case for institutionalizing that capacity.' *The New York Times*, 26 April 1964.

during the interval while military forces are being assembled on a hit-or-miss basis.' Stevenson pushed beyond Lie's initial Guard plans, however, and called for an UN force entirely divorced from national training or politics: 'we further risk an erosion in the political and moral authority of the UN if troops trained only for national forces are thrust without special training into situations unique to the purpose and methods of the United Nations.'[175]

However, as would be similarly seen in India and Pakistan in 1949, with the establishment of the United Nations Military Observer Group in India and Pakistan (UNMOGIP), military observers along ceasefire lines led to an entrenchment of hostilities between two opposing communities in a post-colonial (or post-mandate) context.[176] The ongoing Palestinian refugee crisis evolved throughout the 1950s, and an additional UN agency (the United Nations Relief and Works Agency, or UNRWA) was founded in December 1949 to respond to the humanitarian emergency that had been left unresolved through the Armistice Agreements and UN mediation.[177] Although considered a diplomatic success for the UN, UNTSO would remain in Palestine indefinitely due to the continual threat of violence and instability along the armistice borders.

During this post-war period, formative UN arrangements – in Israel and Palestine, India and Pakistan – entrenched an organisational preference for partitions as the best form of conflict response. This principle, in combination with long-term ceasefires and truce agreements, served to isolate the warring parties and populations from one another and further delineate their personal lives and political demands. Partition became the favoured solution as it slowed a conflict down for the international community, creating time for diplomats and technocrats to meet and negotiate. But partition also froze crises for the affected populations, preventing displaced communities from returning home, accessing their old place of work, or interacting with people from the other community in a non-militarised context. By separating families and villages along ethno-nationalist lines and policing their segregation through international forces, the UN constrained the freedom of movement to those dressed in blue and perpetuated colonial forms of division and categorisation. Carving out international spaces or 'buffer zones' in contested territories empowered UN personnel, rather than protected the host communities.

175 United States Mission to the United Nations, Press Release No. 4374, 'Dag Hammarskjöld Memorial Lecture by Ambassador Adlai E. Stevenson. "From Containment to Cease-Fire and Peaceful Change', 23 March 1964.

176 For more on UNMOGIP, see C. Shucksmith and N. D. White, 'United Nations Military Observer Group in India and Pakistan (UNMOGIP)', in J. A. Koops, N. MacQueen, T. Tardy, and P. D. Williams (eds.), *The Oxford Handbook of United Nations Peacekeeping Operations* (Oxford: Oxford University Press, 2015), pp. 133–143.

177 For more on UNRWA, see A. E. Irfan, 'Petitioning for Palestine: Refugee Appeals to International Authorities', *Contemporary Levant*, 5:2 (2020), pp. 79–96.

Partitions forced affected groups to build lives in liminal spaces without recourse for complaint or self-determination and 'move on'; for the UN leadership, partition was the solution, not the source of further conflict.

In the case of Israel and Palestine, geopolitical concerns about how the territorial conflict could threaten international peace and security overwhelmed Palestinian and Arab states' efforts to reject territorial partition and displacement. Instead, establishing UNTSO to police the protracted ceasefire and partition provided the international community with the solution to a problem of its own creation. For some commentators, the longevity of UNTSO has been demonstrative of the mission's success in keeping the peace and the UN's ability to separate 'peacekeeping' from 'peacemaking'. For instance, Marrack Goulding has argued that 'a long-standing peacekeeping operation may sometimes be the least bad option available to the international community if renewed war is to be avoided'.[178] But this rationale implicitly approves of protracted or 'frozen' conflicts as a political solution to violence for the international community. Instead, displacement and partition are forms of violence themselves, fostering inter-communal hostility and ever-divergent sovereign imaginaries for the trapped populations. As Aaron Kleiman observed, 'yesterday's partitioned country will become tomorrow's trouble-spot and center of international crisis'.[179]

Imitating Military Responsibility in Korea

In the aftermath of the UN's perceived success in resolving the crisis in Palestine, the organisation had proven itself capable of deploying and managing military staff in conflict settings to the international community. The deployment of UNTSO observers ensured an organisational reaction to threats on the ground, pushing beyond the diplomatic limits of the New York headquarters and establishing value in the field. This value was tested in Korea, as the US government sought to experiment with the functional and political benefits of waging war under a UN flag. Focusing on the innovations and geopolitics of the construction of the UN Command (UNC), this section traces how the UN's involvement in the Korean War cemented the organisation's role in field-based military response during the Cold War.

Not long after Bunche's departure from Palestine, the UN became engulfed in another disputed partition, this time in Korea. Whilst diplomatic battles between the Soviet Union and the United States raged in the UN Security Council and General Assembly during 1950, the Cold War manifested on the ground in North and South Korea, threatening to include the People's

178 M. Goulding, 'The Evolution of United Nations Peacekeeping', *International Affairs*, 69:3 (1993), p. 457.

179 Klieman, 'The Resolution of Conflicts through Territorial Partition', p. 300.

Republic of China (PRC) and expand into a 'Third World War'.[180] Rather than providing military observers and a mediator for this crisis, however, the UN became militarily involved in the Korean War, allying with the US army and providing a command structure for the additional international units in the form of the UNC. The UNC positioned the UN as a belligerent actor within the Korean War, building upon the institutional character practiced during the Arab–Israeli conflict. By restoring stability and maintaining South Korea's sovereignty, the UNC compounded the success of the organisation during UNTSO and demonstrated the military efficacy of an international military under a UN flag. As Jiyul Kim has argued, the Korean War 'established the enduring principle that the UN has a key political and military role in resolving conflicts through peace enforcement and peacekeeping operations'.[181]

The conflict in Korea erupted following years of border disputes between the North and South states, as partisan skirmishes threatened to destabilise the fragile ideological context. Following the conclusion of Second World War and the withdrawal of the Imperial Japanese Army in 1945, Korea was partitioned arbitrarily by the United States and Soviet Union along the 38th parallel in what both sides believed would be a temporary arrangement of five years until a Korean Trusteeship could be established.[182] Anxious about the power vacuum in Korea following the evacuation of Japanese and keen to maintain stability in Asia, the United States sought to learn from the collapse of British and French forms of traditional colonialism in the region and impose their own form of neocolonialism onto post-colonial Korea.[183] US Secretary of State, Dean Rusk recalled the improvised partition in August 1945:

> We finally reached a compromise that would keep at least some US forces on the mainland, a sort of toehold on the Korean peninsula for symbolic purposes ... Working in haste and under great pressure, we had a formidable task: to pick a zone for the American occupation. Neither Tic nor I was a Korea expert, but it seemed to us that Seoul, the capital, should be in the American sector. We also knew that the U.S. Army opposed an extensive area of occupation. Using a National Geographic map, we looked just north of Seoul for a convenient dividing line but could not find a natural geographical line. We saw instead the thirty-

[180] 'Moscow Charges US Plot in Korea: Says Dulles Gave Signal for Hostilities There with View to Launching World War III', *The New York Times*, 2 July 1950.

[181] J. Kim, 'United Nations Command and Korean Augmentation', in D. W. Boose and J. I. Matray (eds.), *The Ashgate Research Companion to the Korean War* (Milton Park: Taylor and Frances, 2016), p. 283.

[182] B. Shin, 'The Decision Process of the Trusteeship in Korea, 1945–1946: Focusing on the Change of U.S. Ideas', *Pacific Focus*, 19:1 (2004), pp. 169–211.

[183] A. R. Millett, *The War for Korea, 1945–1950: A House Is Burning* (Lawrence: University Press of Kansas, 2005), pp. 12–13.

> eighth parallel and decided to recommend that ... [Our commanders] accepted it without too much haggling, and surprisingly, so did the Soviets.[184]

As part of this military compromise, the Cold War powers cut through '75 streams and 12 rivers, intersected many high ridges, crossed 181 small cart roads, 104 country roads...', thus dividing 'a nation which had been united and independent for centuries before Japanese colonisation'.[185]

Despite the partition initially providing a temporary solution to Cold War interests in Asia, this separation led to the election of two independent Korean states – North Korea and South Korea (or the Republic of Korea) – on 15 August 1948.[186] Following these elections, the UN established the United Nations Commission on Korea in 1948,[187] taking over from the activities of a Temporary Commission in Korea,[188] to encourage the 'unification of Korea and the integration of all Korean security forces' and observe the 'actual withdrawal of the occupying forces'.[189] From 1948 to 1950, the majority of Soviet Union and American troops evacuated from Korea, leaving behind advisory groups in command of both Korean militaries. However, three years of partition had cultivated two independent states with ideologically opposed governmental politics, superpower interests, and hardening nationalist imaginaries: both advocated forced reunification and each claimed to be the legitimate Korean government.

As Korean re-unification became a remote prospect with this dual declaration of independence, partisan violence between South Korean Labour (or Communist) Party and groups of conservative and authoritarian Koreans – US supported – erupted across the southern state in 1948 and 1949, threatening to push beyond the 38th parallel and endanger thousands of Koreans in the process.[190] After years of partisan conflict in Republic terri-

[184] D. Rusk cited in J. J. Lee, *The Partition of Korea after World War II: A Global History* (New York: Springer, 2006), pp. 37–38.

[185] C. Forbes, *The Korean War* (Sydney: Macmillan, 2010), pp. 49–50.

[186] L. Gordenker, *The United Nations and the Peaceful Unification of Korea: The Politics of Field Operations, 1947–1950* (New York: Springer, 2012), p. 5.

[187] The United Nations Commission for the Unification and Rehabilitation of Korea (UNCURK) was established to replace the United Nations Commission on Korea on 7 October 1950 in order to establish an independent democratic government for all of Korea: UN Doc, A/RES/376(V), '376 (V). The Problem of the Independence of Korea', 7 October 1950.

[188] UN Doc, A/RES/112(II), '112 (II). The Problem of the Independence of Korea', 14 November 1947.

[189] UN Doc, A/RES/195(III), '195 (III). The Problem of the Independence of Korea', 12 December 1948.

[190] Millett, *The War for Korea, 1945–1950*, p. 2.

tory,[191] the conflict between the two Korean nations erupted in the early hours of 25 June 1950 as the North Korean government saw an opportunity to reunify Korea under their authority.[192] North Korean troops, trained and equipped by the Soviet Union,[193] launched an artillery attack into South Korean territory and an amphibious intervention on the island's eastern coast, surprising the Southern Koreans and the US army.[194] In the PRC, Mao released thousands of Koreans from the People's Liberation Army in order for them to fight with the North Korean People's Army and sent over 300,000 Chinese troops to fight on the 38th parallel, instructing them to remove Chinese Army insignia from their uniforms.[195] This organised act of aggression breached an existing General Assembly resolution that instructed both Korean governments to 'refrain from any acts derogatory to the purposes of' removing 'barriers to economic, social and other friendly intercourse caused by the division of Korea'.[196] The same day, the Security Council voted to call upon UN member-states to 'render every assistance to the United Nations' in the execution of ceasing hostilities in Korea and restoring peace to the region.[197] This condemnation was extended on 27 June as the Security Council voted to recommend that the UN member-states 'furnish' the Republic of Korea with military support against the invasion.[198]

Trygve Lie was personally insulted by the North Korean intervention, conceiving it as a violation of the UN Charter and a direct attack on the UN, as the organisation had overseen the two states' elections in 1948.[199] Over the next fortnight, US representatives met with Lie and his Secretariat officials to develop a plan for the UN to respond militarily to the crisis and to counteract the communist intervention, seeking to expand the existing

191 B. Hwang, 'Revolutionary Armed Struggle and the Origins of the Korean War', *Asian Perspective*, 12:2 (1988), pp. 123–138.

192 'War Is Declared by North Koreans', *The New York Times*, 25 June 1950.

193 M. O'Neill, 'Soviet Involvement in the Korean War: A New View from the Soviet-Era Archives', *OAH Magazine of History*, 14:3 (2000), p. 20.

194 M. E. Henke, *Constructing Allied Cooperation: Diplomacy, Payments and Power in Multilateral Military Coalitions* (Ithaca: Cornell University Press, 2019), p. 66.

195 X. Li, 'China's War for Korea: Geostrategic Decisions, War-Fighting Experience and High-Priced Benefits from Intervention, 1950–1953', in J. Blaxland, M. Kelly, and L. B. Higgins (eds.), *In from the Cold: Reflections on Australia's Korean War* (Canberra: ANU Press, 2020), p. 65.

196 UN Doc, General Assembly, A/RES/293 (IV), 'The Problem of the Independence of Korea', 21 October 1949.

197 UN Doc, S/1501, 'Resolution Concerning the Complaint of Aggression upon the Republic of Korea Adopted at the 473rd Meeting of the Security Council on 25 June 1950'.

198 UN Doc, S/1511, Security Council, '83 (1950). Resolution of 27 June 1950'.

199 E. J. Ravndal, '"A Force for Peace": Expanding the Role of the UN Secretary-General under Trygve Lie, 1946–1953', *Global Governance*, 23:3 (2017), p. 454.

Security Council permissions. Despite the constraints of the UN Charter, the UN could potentially deploy armed forces under Security Council authorisation in reaction to a breach of the peace, as Lie had attempted with his UN Guard proposal. However, for seven months of 1950, the Soviet Union had chosen to boycott the UN Security Council as the UN had accepted a representative of Taiwan to take the PRC's chair.[200] The absence of the Soviets from the Council meant that the five permanent members of the UN were reduced to four; an absence that legally had never been accounted for in the drafting of the UN Charter. This prompted a legal and diplomatic issue: should a resolution be authorised by the Security Council if all permanent members of the Security Council are not present and voting, especially one authorising the deployment of an armed international force to combat a sovereign nation? For legal scholar Josef Kunz, the option of *not* responding to the invasion of South Korea likely presented more of a threat to the organisation than the legal complications of voting without a permanent-member present. He argued that 'to have done nothing in the case of a flagrant armed attack would have meant the end of the United Nations, just as to have done nothing in the case of Japan's invasion of Manchuria in 1931 was the beginning of the end for the League of Nations'.[201] Organisational prestige had motivated the secretary-general's decision-making during the Arab–Israeli conflict, and, in the context of Korea, it combined with anger over the North Korean attack to encourage Lie to plan UN military action with the US government.

Whilst the international community waited for the US and UN representatives to negotiate the design of the UNC and develop a draft resolution for the Security Council, public commentators contributed their own imaginaries of an international military.[202] One example published in *The New York Times* on 7 July 1950 suggested that 'even the smallest of [UN member states] can provide at least a token force, either of regular troops or volunteers, to form a United Nations army which would comprise many nations, races and creeds, and which would contain a substantial contingent of Asiatic troops whose mere presence would refute any charge of "white imperialism"', thus predicting later UN efforts to avoid accusations of colonialism during the peacekeeping mission in Congo.[203]

By July, the legal quandary of the Soviet Union's boycott was disregarded by UN officials and formally recorded as an absence the UN Security Council,

[200] M. Share, 'From Ideological Foe to Uncertain Friend: Soviet Relations with Taiwan, 1943–82', *Cold War History*, 3:2 (2002), pp. 5–6.

[201] Kunz, 'Legality of the Security Council Resolutions', p. 138.

[202] T. J. Hamilton, 'Most UN Delegates Favor Use of Land Force in Korea', *The New York Times*, 1 July 1950.

[203] 'For a UN Army', *The New York Times*, 7 July 1950.

allowing the attending states to authorise the UNC.[204] The UNC resolution approved the force under Chapter 7 of the UN Charter, making it an 'agent' of the Security Council, and authorised it to undertake forceful action for the settlement of the conflict in the name of world peace. The same legal provision would not be undertaken by the UN until the post-Cold War era following the Iraq invasion of Kuwait in 1991.[205] The decision to allow the vote without the Soviet Union representative demonstrated the procedural gatekeeping power held by UN bureaucrats and legal advisors. By choosing to provide a physical and diplomatic forum to host the vote, the UN staff functionally legitimised the process. Numerous legal scholars addressed this issue in 1950–1951, highlighting the troubling context of an international organisation deciding to pursue a vote on international military action *before* independent jurisprudential interrogation of the UN Charter.[206] For the USSR, Poland, and Czechoslovakia, the Security Council votes on the Korean War were illegal and invalid due to the absence of the Soviet representative.[207] They pointed out that Article 28 of the UN Charter states that 'Each member of the Security Council shall for this purpose be represented at all times at the seat of the Organization', with 'for this purpose' meaning the continuous function of the Security Council. In opposition, the United States asserted that the first sentence of Article 28 prohibited intentional absences within the Council. The US State Department released a statement which specified their interpretation of the UN Charter: 'The Security Council shall be so organized as to be able to function continuously ... injunction is defeated if the absence of a representative of a permanent member is construed to have the effect of preventing all substantive action by the Council.'[208]

Once the resolution passed, UNC staffing and strategy was developed and approved by US officials in Washington rather than the UN leadership or a UN commission in New York, despite the name of the force. As this would be the first coordinated military mission under UN auspices, the United States sought to restrict the UN Secretariat's involvement in the recruitment arena, exploiting the organisation's limited experience and military machinery. As Marina Henke has argued,

204 UN Doc, S/1588, '84 (1950). Resolution of 7 July 1950'.

205 D. H. Finnie, *Shifting Lines in the Sand: Kuwait's Elusive Frontier with Iraq* (Cambridge, MA: Harvard University Press, 1992).

206 Kunz, 'Legality of the Security Council Resolutions', pp. 137–142; Y. Liang, 'Abstention and Absence of a Permanent Member in Relation to the Voting Procedure in the Security Council', *The American Journal of International Law*, 44:4 (1950), pp. 694–708; H. Kelsen, *The Law of the United Nations: A Critical Analysis of Its Fundamental Problems* (London: London Institute of World Affairs, 1950).

207 Kunz, 'Legality of the Security Council Resolutions', p. 141.

208 *United States Policy in the Korean Crisis* (US Department of State Pub. 3922, Far Eastern Series 34), pp. 61–63.

> Andrew Cordier, the executive assistant to the UN secretary-general, proposed that a 'Security Council Committee' should be in charge of the process. This committee would meet in private and decide which coalition offers could be accepted. US officials, however, largely disagreed with this idea. They felt that it was 'not practical for the United Nations to get into the actual use and control of [military] assistance ... and it was unthinkable to use the [UN] Military Staff Committee in any way.' Rather, the UN and, in particular, Secretary-General Lie should operate as no more than a 'post office'. They would transmit to the United States information submitted to them by UN member states about their deployment preferences.[209]

Beginning with the recruitment of the Force Commander, the United States sidelined the UN Secretariat officials from the UNC staffing process, preventing the organisation from shaping the character of the force as they would in later missions. On 8 July 1950, US President Truman assigned General Douglas MacArthur as commanding general of the UNC, impressed with MacArthur's success during the Second World War.[210] In contrast to future UN missions, permanent members of the Security Council were encouraged to donate troops to Korea and the United States, Britain, and France all participated militarily. The UN did supply ten destroyers and frigates (types of warships) from its own stores to the UNC, establishing that the organisation had begun to invest in arms for its own participation in conflict by 1950.[211] Ultimately, despite Lie's best efforts to influence the design of the UNC and increase the power of the UN Secretariat in shaping strategy in the field, the US government refused to compromise their authority in commanding the force.[212]

Once on the ground in September 1950, this multilateral force was militarily and strategically led by the pre-existing US personnel on the ground and heavily reliant on US Army logistical support.[213] The ten countries who militarily unified against the 'communist invasion' from the North under the UN flag by the end of 1950 – Britain, the Philippines, Australia, Turkey, Thailand, the Netherlands, France, Greece, Canada, and New Zealand – had been extensively lobbied by the US government to donate troops to the Korean War through the use of 'personal appeals, incentives, and threats'.[214] Instrumentalising existing diplomatic ties and bullying tactics, the United States was able to organise

[209] Henke, *Constructing Allied Cooperation*, p. 70.

[210] T. J. Hamilton, 'Action by Council: American Troops on Their Way to the Front in Korea', *The New York Times*, 8 July 1950.

[211] G. L. Roffman, *Korean War Order of Battle: United States, United Nations, and Communist Ground, Naval, and Air Forces, 1950–1953* (Westport: Greenwood Publishing Group, 2002), p. 118.

[212] Ravndal, '"A Force for Peace"', p. 455.

[213] Kim, 'United Nations Command and Korean Augmentation', p. 289.

[214] Henke, *Constructing Allied Cooperation*, p. 67.

donations from forty-eight (out of a possible fifty-nine) UN member-states, 'including personnel, cash, food, and medicine' as well as support from an additional nine non-member-states that also sent provisions – this number included Japan and West Germany, which were both occupied in 1950.[215]

The Soviet Union broke their boycott of the UN Security Council in August 1950 and vetoed any resolution relating to the support of the UNC, rejecting Lie's as secretary-general in retribution for his involvement in the construction of the force. The USSR representatives used their veto to fire Lie as the end of his first five-year term as secretary-general approached in October.[216] In a humiliating process where Lie struggled to lobby definitive support from any of the permanent members, the vote on the new secretary-general was moved to the General Assembly after the Soviet Union made clear that they would veto any vote supporting Lie in the Security Council.[217] On 2 November, Lie attained the most votes in the second round of elections, and the General Assembly extended his term by three years, although the Soviet Union refused to recognise the election as legal and thus Lie as secretary-general.[218] This, to date, has been the only example of a secretary-general election held by the General Assembly in response to questions on the legality of the vote.[219] Following two years of denunciations from the Soviet Union and PRC, Lie resigned from the office in November 1952. He was replaced by Dag Hammarskjöld the following April. This experience damaged Lie's confidence and, he believed, affected his ability to negotiate an armistice in the Korean War. In his resignation speech, he stated,

> 'The United Nations has thrown back aggression in Korea. There can be an Armistice if the Soviet Union, the Chinese People's Republic and the North Koreans are sincere in their wish to end the fighting. If they are sincere then the new Secretary-General who is the unanimous choice of the five permanent members the Security Council and of the General Assembly, may be more helpful than I can be.'[220]

Following the procedural complications of the secretary-general elections, the United States admitted concerns that the UNC would be eternally held

[215] Kim, 'United Nations Command and Korean Augmentation', p. 285.

[216] T. J. Hamilton, 'UN Council Meets Today on Lie Term: Takes Lead in Proposed 2 or 3 Year Extension but Soviet Stand Is Unknown', *The New York Times*, 9 October 1950; G. Barrett, 'Position of UN Chief Aide Is Thrust into Uncertainty: Council Tells Assembly of Failure to Agree on a Secretary General', *The New York Times*, 13 October 1950.

[217] 'Soviet to Shun Lie If He Stays in Post', *The New York Times*, 31 October 1950.

[218] T. J. Hamilton, 'Lie Term Extended as US Secretary for 3 Years', *The New York Times*, 2 November 1950.

[219] F. T. P. Plimpton, 'Everyone Knows What A Secretary Is, and What a General Is, but: What Is a Secretary General?', *The New York Times*, 27 November 1966.

[220] T. Lie, 'Trygve Lie, Secretary-General of the United Nations, Announces His Resignation', *British Pathe*, Film ID: 2636.23, 10 November 1952, available at www.britishpathe.com/video/trygve-lie-resigns.

hostage by the UN voting system. The multilateral character of the UNC required a functioning voting forum in order to maintain the authorisation of the force in Korea. To remedy this, the United States introduced a transformative legal precedent that would shift the power of permanent members within the UN. The creation of the 'Uniting for Peace' General Assembly resolution in November 1950 permitted other member-states to circumvent a permanent member's right to veto in cases of a breach to the peace and to introduce the resolution to the General Assembly.[221] This innovation would later enable the deployment of UNEF in 1956 despite the veto of two permanent member-states (Britain and France). The combination of the procedural demands of the UNC and the diplomatic hostility of the USSR led to the expansion of General Assembly functions from exclusively deliberative to potentially operational; capable of authorising 'appropriate measures' for the resolution of international peace.

However, although fighting under the UN flag, the UNC was far from an UN-led armed mission.[222] Although transnational in design, the UNC was directed towards the protection and supremacy of pro-US, anticommunist interests in Korea. As Kim has suggested, 'A cynic might say that the UN flag was merely an imprimatur of international cooperation and support that legitimized US policy to contain communism' as the military responsibility of the UN for the force was minimal.[223] The UNC mandate characterised the United States and the Republic of Korea as the parties fighting for international peace and demonised North Korea as communist aggressors, seeking the destabilisation of the region. In the Soviet Union, the government attempted to counteract this narrative and characterise North Korea and its communist allies as those fighting for world peace, pushing back against Western imperialism in Asia and using the Korean War to highlight the military aggression of the United States.[224] Neither superpower acknowledged their own role in the historical foundations of this crisis and their geopolitical interests in perpetuating the war for propaganda. However, the UN auspices of the UNC provided the US army's strategy in Korea with international legitimacy, counteracting Soviet denunciations and casting the force with a moralising guise; the UNC waged war in the name of peace.

221 A. J. Carswell, 'Unblocking the UN Security Council: The Uniting for Peace Resolution', *Journal of Conflict and Security Law*, 18:3 (2013), pp. 453–480.

222 P. Biddiscombe, 'Branding the United Nations: The Adoption of the UN Insignia and Flag, 1941–1950', *The International History Review*, 42:1 (2020), p. 20.

223 D. Kritsiotis, 'The Elusive Peace of Panmunjom', in M. Craven, S. Pahuja, and G. Simpson (eds.), *International Law and the Cold War* (Cambridge: Cambridge University Press, 2019), pp. 65/66.

224 Goedde, *The Politics of Peace*, p. 16.

But the UNC was also a transformative step for an organisation previously limited to mediatory solutions and observer missions, such as UNTSO and UNMOGIP. The military character of the UNC and its construction in the UN headquarters provided legal, diplomatic, and operational precedents for future UN missions, demonstrating the potential value of the organisation as a field-based agent as well as a forum for nation-state debates. It was also a symbolic extension of UN diplomatic activities into a conflict zone, providing inspiration for later missions' efforts to emulate and prioritise symbols of occupation and military authority.[225] The UNC served as a vital platform for the UN to *imitate* military responsibility, drawing the public's attention to UN branding and authorisation whilst the US benefitted from the UN mandate and 'playing the part' of an army fighting for peace. Although the organisation was highly restricted in shaping the conflict on the ground and managing the force independently, the UNC was an important experiment for the UN Secretariat. It provided lessons in staffing multilateral military coalitions and legal precedents for UN forums; these principles would be integral in establishing later UN peacekeeping operations.

Conclusion

Following the creation of the UN, liberal internationalists called for the organisation to test the waters and explore the military potential in-built in the UN Charter, using the Military Staff Committee and the UN's public forums to push the institution further into the military sphere.[226] Powerful member-states began to see that the UN's encroachment into the conflict zones – and more broadly the militarisation of 'international peace' – opened up potential for state collaboration, collusion, and interference on the ground. By tracing the history of peacekeeping through early plans for international military operations, this chapter has shown how the idea of an international reputation was emerging by the mid-1950s and integral the function was to the growing authority of the UN as the leading international organisation in peace and security. As Boutros Boutros-Ghali assessed in his 1992 *Agenda for Peace*, the authority of the UN to deploy military action 'is essential to the credibility of the United Nations as a guarantor of international security'.[227]

[225] The use of the UN flag by the UN Command was authorised under UNSC Resolution 84: UN Doc, S/1588, 'Resolution 84: Complaint of Aggression upon the Republic of Korea', 7 July 1950.

[226] A. Novosseloff, *The UN Military Staff Committee: Recreating a Missing Capacity* (Abingdon: Routledge, 2018).

[227] UN Document (henceforth, UN Doc), A/47/277, 'Agenda for Peace: Preventative Diplomacy, Peacemaking and Peace-Keeping', 17 June 1992, para. 43.

The escalation of experiments in an international military from the formative operations in the Saar in the interwar years to the development of the international armed force under US command in Korea helped pave the way for an UN-led, armed peacekeeping mission in 1956.[228] These tentative steps in a range of different conflict contexts and territorial settings legitimised the international organisation as a leader in conflict response, securing its position within military, diplomatic, humanitarian, and development spheres of influence. The perception of UNC success – for those aligned with the Western member-states – intensified in an international demand for a militarised UN that had been reinvigorated by post-war disarmament debates and reimagined by Trygve Lie's plans for the UN Guard in Palestine. As the new secretary-general, Dag Hammarskjöld, attempted to bury past antagonism between the UN and the Soviet Union, as well as quash developing anti-colonial tensions within the Afro-Asian bloc in the General Assembly, the geopolitical hierarchy of the UN forums faced a dramatic transformation that would have implications for the next twenty years of operations. The decisions and designs from past international military debates and experiments would now be put into practice.

[228] For more specifically on the UN involvement in the Korean crisis, see R. Barnes, 'Chief Administrator or Political "Moderator"? Dumbarton Oaks, the Secretary-General and the Korean War', *Journal of Contemporary History*, 54:2 (2019), pp. 347–367.

2

Reckoning with Suez, 1956–1959

Introduction: The Birth of Peacekeeping in Egypt

On the cool New York evening of 24 October 1956, UN secretary-general Dag Hammarskjöld rehearsed his speech in preparation for the eleventh UN Day celebrations. The UN Public Information Office had organised pamphlets, commemorative stamps, music, and radio presentations to promote and broadcast the festivities to all member-states' populations around the globe.[1] At 8.30 p.m., the New York Philharmonic began its performance on the stage of the General Assembly hall as a preface to Hammarskjöld's celebratory statement.[2] As was customary in UN Day celebrations, the orchestra would also perform the last movement of Beethoven's Ninth Symphony to conclude the event.[3] This year, Hammarskjöld chose to comment directly on the spirit of the piece in his speech. He stated:

> The faith to which Beethoven wished to give expression in his Ninth Symphony ... was the dream of a poet. To translate this dream into action, and thus to give mankind the security it can achieve only through cooperation and the strength it can win only through fusion, is the task of realists.[4]

Hammarskjöld's positive attitude towards the fruits of cooperation was driven by his recent private talks with Britain, France, and Egypt over the nationalisation of the Suez Canal Company.[5] He believed that these meetings had been effective in preventing an escalation in aggression in Egypt and that his involvement had helped shift the parties towards the first step of a two-part

[1] United Nations, *To Live Together in Peace with One Another as Good Neighbors: For United Nations Day, Questions and Answers, 24 October 1956* (New York: United Nations Department of Public Information, 1956).

[2] 'Concert Will Mark United Nations Day', *The New York Times*, 24 October 1956.

[3] 'Concert Will Mark United Nations Day', 24 October 1956.

[4] R. Lipsey, *Hammarskjöld: A Life* (Ann Arbor: University of Michigan Press, 2013), pp. 295–296.

[5] R. Withana, *Power, Politics, Law: International Law and State Behaviour during International Crises* (Leiden: Brill Publishing, 2008), p. 147.

solution.[6] However, whilst he enjoyed the classical music and waited patiently for the second phase of interstate talks to recommence on 29 October, a group of British, French, and Israeli leaders colluded inside a villa in the Parisian suburbs.[7] On UN Day 1956, the three parties secretly signed the Protocol of Sèvres, a document confirming their joint decision to violate the UN Charter and invade the Suez region in east Egypt. In the Charter, under Article 2(4), UN member-states are prohibited from the use of force against one another.[8] Within a week of signing the Protocol, on 29 October, the Israeli army breached the Armistice Lines and Egyptian sovereignty, pushing beyond the borders of the Armistice Agreement (which had been mediated by Ralph Bunche less than a decade earlier). Two days later, on 31 October, Anglo-French forces joined them.[9] As French, British, and Israeli squadrons bombarded Egyptian airfields, the international community demanded that the UN secretary-general respond to the Suez crisis and negotiate a ceasefire to prevent the escalation of violence.[10]

A decade after its creation, the UN found itself at a crossroads in November 1956. With the violence in Egypt, its leadership struggled to respond to this act of aggression by two of its founding members. As discussed in Chapter 1, the UN's reactive capacity was limited to deliberative forums (such as the Security Council and the General Assembly), rhetorical condemnations, and observer missions (as with UNTSO). As territorial and political disputes erupted from decolonising nations in the Global South, these UN responses proved inadequate in resolving complicated sovereignty disputes and violent conflicts. However, recent transformations to the UN General Assembly strengthened the voices of middle power member-states within the UN forums. Between 1955 and 1965 almost fifty former colonial territories joined the General Assembly as member-states, giving them the majority of votes.[11] This expansion in member-states intersected with the complicated global allegiances and politics of the Cold War, as the Afro-Asian bloc and other member-states, such as Yugoslavia, positioned themselves between the two superpowers as the Non-Aligned Movement.[12] 'Anti-colonial'

[6] This 'Six Principle' solution was then accepted by France and Britain in a Security Council resolution on 13th October 1956: UN Doc, S/3671, 'France and United Kingdom of Great Britain and Northern Ireland: Joint Draft Resolution', Security Council, 13 October 1956.

[7] S. Ilan Troen, 'The Protocol of Sèvres: British/French/Israeli Collusion against Egypt, 1956', *Israel Studies*, 1:2 (1996), p. 123.

[8] UN Doc, 'Charter of the United Nations and the Statute of the International Court of Justice', 26 June 1945.

[9] UN Public Information Office, 'Chapter I: Questions Concerning the Middle-East: The Palestine Question December 1955–October 1956', in *Yearbook of the United Nations, 1956* (New York: United Nations Public Information Office, 1956).

[10] UN Doc, General Assembly, A/RES/997 (ES-I), 'Resolution 997, 2 November 1956'.

[11] Y. El-Ayouty, *The United Nations and Decolonization: The Role of Afro-Asia* (New York: Springer, 2012), p. xxiii.

[12] For more on the Non-Aligned Movement, see: J. Dinkel, *The Non-aligned Movement: Genesis, Organization and Politics (1927–1992)* (Leiden: Brill Publishing, 2019); J. M.

nations, led by Indonesia, India, and Ghana, formed the Afro-Asian bloc at the Bandung Conference in 1955 to capitalise on this shift in member-state numbers, concentrating their voting weight in the General Assembly to challenge European imperialism and Western hegemony and to support one another within the international community.[13] This geopolitical transformation within the General Assembly not only shifted the politics of successful Assembly resolutions, it also inspired functional innovations in the toolkit of the international organisation.

With the emergence of post-colonial states radically reshaping the international order, the UN Secretariat leadership questioned what the organisation's role would be and how it could demonstrate value in this increasingly volatile geopolitical context. The conflict in Egypt presented an opportunity for liberal internationalist visionaries to implement an expansion of UN responsibilities from hosting deliberative forums and observing truces to actively designing and deploying an UN-led international military to the front line. These growing responsibilities, as a result, shifted the organisation's leadership towards militarism. As addressed in Chapter 1, the ongoing, shared discourse between Western diplomats and international civil servants since 1945 provided the impetus for the UN Secretariat to construct a military function within the UN's jurisdiction. Such a force would have the authority to enforce liberal norms and political hierarchies as peacebuilding strategies in unstable contexts. Following the invasion of the Suez region in October 1956, these ideas about an UN international force gained popular traction among Afro-Asian delegates, horrified by the tripartite aggression into Egyptian sovereign territory. Recalling the UN's history in the region and its retention of military observers in the Middle East as part of the UNTSO mission, many member-state delegates supported the expansion of the UN into the military sphere to re-establish the violated armistice lines along the Egyptian-Israeli border. The Suez crisis presented the diplomatic impetus that Lie had failed to sustain with his UN Guard plan in 1948.

Schaufelbuehl et al., 'Non-alignment, the Third Force, or Fence-Sitting: Independent Pathways in the Cold War', *The International History Review*, 37:5 (2015), pp. 901–911.

13 A. O'Malley, 'Ghana, India, and the Transnational Dynamics of the Congo Crisis at the United Nations, 1960–1', *The International History Review*, 37:5 (2015), pp. 970–990; G. McCann, 'From Diaspora to Third Worldism and the United Nations: India and the Politics of Decolonizing Africa', *Past & Present*, 218:suppl_8 (2013), pp. 276–277; C. Ewing, 'The Colombo Powers: Crafting Diplomacy in the Third World and Launching Afro-Asia at Bandung', *Cold War History*, 19:1 (2019), pp. 1–19; C. J. Lee, *Making a World after Empire: The Bandung Moment and Its Political Afterlives* (Athens: Ohio Press, 2010); A. Phillips, 'Beyond Bandung: the 1955 Asian-African Conference and Its Legacies for International Order', *Australian Journal of International Affairs*, 70:4 (2016), pp. 329–341.

The invention of an armed peacekeeping mission in response to the Suez conflict transformed the UN into an authority that would empower its staff with responsibility for orchestrating and commanding an armed military force in an active conflict zone. With the deployment of the United Nations Emergency Force (UNEF) to Sinai and the Gaza Strip, the traditional state-actor monopoly on war would be unsettled and the normative imaginaries of warring parties reconstituted. The authorised intergovernmental armed force would intervene directly alongside other military actors as a representative of collective global interests in 'peace'. This intervention would result in a significant diplomatic shift in the international relations of conflict. The beginning of this transformation started with the events in Egypt in 1956.

Overcoming Betrayal, Reconfiguring the UN Charter

The UN peacekeeping mission to the Middle East was a response to a series of violent invasions in the Suez region of Egypt, known collectively as the 'Suez crisis'. Egyptian President Abdel Nasser's decision to nationalise the Suez Canal Company, as part of a broader policy of reclaiming Egyptian sovereignty, threatened British neo-colonial interests and challenged their right to maintain post-colonial authority over the resources of independent Egypt. Decades of nominal independence coupled with international interference had built up widespread Egyptian hostility towards Britain's continued profit from their land and waterways.[14] The canal had been a vital route for colonial transport and extraction since it opened in 1869.[15] Imperial occupation of the area from 1882 onwards was a demonstration of Britain's colonial economic and political power to their electorate and imperial populations.[16] Other powerful nations also sought to regulate the movement and mobility of people, goods, and ideas through the canal, from 'east' to 'west', demonstrating the canal's centrality in the process of globalisation. Britain was one of many states and private companies that struggled for control of the waterway during the increased popularity of the 'global shortcut'.[17] Thus, British occupational power was, in practice, less enforceable than the government encouraged the

[14] J. P. Jankowski, *Nasser's Egypt, Arab Nationalism, and the United Arab Republic* (Boulder: Lynne Rienner, 2002), p. 68.

[15] A. Booth, 'The Economic Development of Southeast Asia: 1870–1985', *Australian Economic History Review*, 31:1 (1991), pp. 20–52; M. E. Fletcher, 'The Suez Canal and World Shipping, 1869–1914', *The Journal of Economic History*, 18:4 (1958), pp. 556–573.

[16] V. Huber, 'Connecting Colonial Seas: The "International Colonisation" of Port Said and the Suez Canal during and after the First World War', *European Review of History*, 19:1 (2012), p. 141.

[17] V. Huber, *Channelling Mobilities: Migration and Globalisation in the Suez Canal Region and Beyond, 1869–1914* (Cambridge: Cambridge University Press, 2013).

home electorate to believe.[18] This historical context of colonial extraction underpinned Nasser's decision to nationalise the Suez Canal Company in 1956: long-existing ideological interests were compounded with more immediate economic constraints imposed by the World Bank.[19] The violent Anglo-French-Israeli response to Nasser's nationalisation policy shocked the international community and the UN General Assembly became a popular forum for nations to voice their outrage or support for the invading forces.

The origin of the idea to construct an UN-led peacekeeping mission to resolve the Suez crisis became a point of contention between Britain and Canada. British Prime Minister Anthony Eden was the first to publicly suggest that a UN international force might be the solution to stabilising the canal region and preventing Egyptian retaliation.[20] However, telegrams between Ottawa and London offices demonstrate that Canadian officials were also making the same suggestions within their Cabinet on the same day. In a telegram from British diplomat G. D. Anderson to Robert Belgrave, Office of the British High Commissioner in Ottawa, the authorship was shared: 'Clearly, therefore, the idea of a UN Force was independently present in both our own and in Canadian minds on 1st November.'[21] As Canadian diplomats sought to establish a new national identity through the humanitarian guise of authorship of peacekeeping, Britain sought to cling to its old national identity of a benevolent interventionist imperial power through connection to the mission's origin story.[22]

The absence of UN officials in the early proposals for an UN peacekeeping force in Suez challenges the dominant narrative presented by the organisation. Hammarskjöld has been typically presented as centrally involved in the nascent phase of UNEF's creation.[23] Indeed, the combined efforts of Hammarskjöld and Canadian diplomat Lester B. Pearson have become

[18] E. A. Haddad, 'Digging to India: Modernity, Imperialism, and the Suez Canal', *Victorian Studies*, 47:3 (2005), p. 363; A. Bulfin, 'The Fiction of Gothic Egypt and British Imperial Paranoia: The Curse of the Suez Canal', *English Literature in Transition, 1880–1920*, 54:4 (2011), p. 438.

[19] W. J. Burns, *Economic Aid and American Policy toward Egypt, 1955–1981* (Albany: SUNY Press, 1985), p. 42.

[20] BNA, FO 371/118885/JE.1074/234, 'Letter from G. D. Anderson to Belgrave', 4 December 1956.

[21] BNA, FO 371/118885/JE.1074/234, 'Letter from G. D. Anderson to Belgrave', 4 December 1956.

[22] I. McKay, *Warrior Nation: Rebranding Canada in an Age of Anxiety* (Between the Lines, 2012); C. McCollough, *Creating Canada's Peacekeeping Past* (Vancouver: University of British Columbia Press, 2016).

[23] K. Kyle, *Suez: Britain's End of Empire in the Middle East* (New York: I.B. Tauris, 2011), p. 850; C. Bildt, 'Dag Hammarskjold and United Nations Peacekeeping', *UN Chronicle*, 2 (2011).

fundamental to historical retellings of the force's design.[24] Pearson had been considered for the job of secretary-general in 1946 (against Lie) and again in 1953 (against Hammarskjöld) and had since been heavily involved in Canadian foreign policy. Despite his failed attempts at becoming secretary-general, his efforts in the mediation process during the Korean War[25] positioned him as a well-respected, trusted diplomat within UN circles as well as domestically as Prime Minister of Canada in 1963–1968.[26] Eventually Pearson won the 1957 Nobel Peace Prize for drafting the UNEF General Assembly resolution, cementing his reputation as one of the forefathers of UN peacekeeping.[27]

Hammarskjöld's contribution and reputation has undergone a significant revision in the last decade. Better understanding his personal and political ideologies has contextualised his recruitment choices and political influence on peacekeeping bureaucracies, thus shaping the staffing and cultures of a mission on the ground. Following his death in 1961, Hammarskjöld's image was sanctified by the UN staff who worked with and succeeded him.[28] However, recent scholarship has treated him as a more controversial figure, particularly his anticommunist politics and his approach to UN conflict resolution.[29] Scholars, such as Edward Johnson, have challenged the institutional view that Hammarskjöld was a martyr for UN principles.[30] Instead, Hammarskjöld sought to '[play] with the ambiguities of the Charter' in order to extend the power of his office and expand the involvement of the organisation in international negotiations and conflict resolution.[31] Stabilisation of post-colonial states or disputing nations through diplomatic or operational means became the institution's policy for preventing escalation into Cold War instrumentalisation and, as he saw it, the beginning of a 'Third World War'.

24 M. Carroll, *Pearson's Peacekeepers: Canada and the United Nations Emergency Force, 1956–67* (Vancouver: University of British Columbia Press, 2009), p. 57.

25 J. Barros, 'Pearson or Lie: The Politics of the Secretary-General's Selection, 1946', *Canadian Journal of Political Science*, 10:1 (1977), pp. 65–92.

26 Murray, 'Interview Transcript', pp. 10–11

27 M. B. Oren, 'Faith and Fair-Mindedness: Lester B. Pearson and the Suez Crisis', *Diplomacy and Statecraft*, 3:1 (1992), pp. 48–73.

28 B. Urquhart, *Hammarskjold* (New York: Knopf, 1972).

29 See P.-M. Durand, 'Leçons congolaises: L'ONUC (1960-1964) ou "la plus grande des operations": Un contre-modèle?', *Relations internationales*, 3:127 (2006), pp. 53–70; J. Troy, 'Dag Hammarskjöld: An International Civil Servant Uniting Mystics and Realistic Diplomatic Engagement', *Diplomacy & Statecraft*, 21:3 (2010), p. 435.

30 E. Johnson, '"The Umpire on Whom the Sun Never Sets": Dag Hammarskjöld's Political Role and the British at Suez', *Diplomacy and Statecraft*, 8:1 (1997), p. 250.

31 Durand, 'Leçons congolaises', p. 56.

The General Assembly voted the Swedish diplomat, 'the darkest of dark horses',[32] into the role in 1953,[33] after Trygve Lie resigned from the role in November 1952 and Lester Pearson was vetoed by the Soviet Union.[34] Hammarskjöld's background in the Swedish aristocracy, economics, and public service led member-state representatives to hope that he would focus on administration rather than political showmanship.[35] Emery Kelén wrote that the new secretary-general had an unthreatening presence, making him attractive to the UN permanent member-states, excluding the PRC, as 'a brilliant economist, an unobtrusive technician, and an aristro-bureaucrat'.[36] Although not a first choice of the Soviets, their UN representative Valerian Zorin was reportedly in a hurry to elect Hammarskjöld.[37] His perceived success as a mediator in 1954 during the Korean War further confirmed to the UN member-states that his 'behind the scenes' approach could be instrumental in resolving future international disputes.[38]

However, Pearson and Hammarskjöld did not construct UNEF in a vacuum. Once the British and Canadians proposed the force, the two men consulted UN civil servants and US officials to ensure that the design of the mission met the requirements of the permanent members. Taking the lead on sketching out the force, Pearson worked in collaboration with US Secretary of State John Dulles to produce the original proposal for a Security Council resolution to vote on the creation of an international force. The first few drafts of Pearson's proposals were rejected by Dulles. Subsequently, Pearson sought to construct 'a halfway house at the crossroads of war', and to expand the UN's functions with, 'an intermediate technique between merely passing resolutions and actually fighting'.[39] Pearson wanted the force to be operational as swiftly as possible and so proposed a 'putting the umbrellas up' force, whereby the invading British and French troops would be used to combat their own

32 P. B. Heller, *The United Nations under Dag Hammarskjold, 1953–1961* (Lanham: Scarecrow Press, 2001), p. 14.

33 'Hammarskjoeld [sic] Elected Successor to Lie as U. N. Secretary General: Swede Gets 57 of 60 Votes and Will Take Oath on Friday', *The New York Times*, 8 April 1953; UN Doc, A/2380, 'Appointment of the Secretary-General to the United Nations', 7 April 1953; UN Doc, A/PV.423, 'Appointment of the Secretary-General to the United Nations', 7 April 1953.

34 T. J. Hamilton, 'Soviet Veto Blocks Pearson UN Boom', *The New York Times*, 14 March 1953.

35 A. M. Rosenthal, 'New UN Secretary Cautious on Issues', *The New York Times*, 10 April 1953.

36 E. Kelén, *Hammarskjöld* (New York: Putnam, 1966), p. 27.

37 US DoS, '315/3-3053. Telegram: The United States Representative at the United Nations (Lodge) to the Department of State', 30 March 1953, *Foreign Relations of the United States, 1952–1954*, Volume III.

38 C. Y. Pak, *Korea and the United Nations* (Leiden: Martinus Nijhoff, 2000), pp. 103–104.

39 UNA, S-0313-0005-06, 'Department of Information Publication: UNEF report', undated.

occupation.[40] Shrewdly, he disguised this use of the deployed resources in the draft as 'forces immediately available' to avoid public criticism.[41] However, Dulles had openly denounced the Anglo-French invasion and recognised that President Eisenhower would be similarly scornful of such a plan to involve the invading forces in the peacekeeping mission.[42] Although leading American officials within the Eisenhower administration had been made aware of the Anglo-French-Israeli plot via National Security Agency (NSA) intelligence before the invasion, US officials chose to deny this and pursue an aggressive policy against the Protocol of Sèvres alliance.[43] In Canadian diplomat Geoffrey Murray's recollection of these meetings with Dulles, he commented, 'The [US] President was not going to rake the Anglo-French chestnuts', indicating that the Suez invasion remained at the forefront of Dulles's decision-making.[44] Pearson revised the draft proposal to ensure the support of the US President ensuring that US interests and critique of the Western European nations remained central in the international UNEF project.

Hammarskjöld's absence from these initial processes is stark, in comparison. Whilst Pearson drafted the Security Council resolution, the Suez crisis upset the secretary-general and his cosmopolitan aspirations for the organisation. In the details of the discussions surrounding the creation of UNEF, Hammarskjöld emerges as personally upset. He publicly questioned the value of the UN if two of its permanent members could so flagrantly violate its Charter and reject his efforts to resolve the situation.[45] Hammarskjöld and his inner circle perceived the use of force in invading Egypt, breaching Article 2(4) of the UN Charter, as not only a personal betrayal, but a betrayal of the UN project. Indeed, Hammarskjöld obliquely offered his resignation to the Security Council on 31 October 1956 in response to the invasion, revealing the level of his frustration.[46] Murray, emphasised the emotional fallout during meetings between the Canadian representatives and the UN Secretariat following the Suez invasion: 'It's not some sort of legalistic approach, it's simply that this was what the organisation was all about, that [Hammarskjöld] didn't see how he could really

40 Murray, 'Interview Transcript', p. 28.

41 Murray, 'Interview Transcript', p. 28.

42 US Department of State (Henceforth, DoS), '455. Memorandum of Discussion at the 302d Meeting of the National Security Council, Washington, November 1, 1956, 9 a.m.', *Foreign Relations of the United States, 1955–1957, Suez Crisis, July 26–December 31 1956*, Volume XVI.

43 Office of Archives and History, National Security Agency/Central Security Service, 'The Suez Crisis: A Brief Comint History (U)', United States Cryptologic History, Special Series, Crisis Collection, Volume 2, 1988, p. 32.

44 Murray, 'Interview Transcript', p. 28.

45 UN Doc, S/PV.751, '751st Plenary Meeting', Security Council, 31 October 1956, pp. 1–2; M. Kidron, 'Interview transcript', *Yale-UN Oral History Project*, 17 April 1991, p. 6.

46 UN Doc, S/PV.751, '751st Plenary Meeting', Security Council, 31 October 1956, pp. 1–2.

make much of this mess . . . he believed so much in the Charter and the sanctity of the Charter commitment.'[47] Hammarskjöld's personal involvement in the crisis, and his belief that his talks with both British and French representatives over the summer of 1956 had been successful in maintaining the peace in Suez, served to paralyse the secretary-general.[48]

Hammarskjöld was not alone in his reaction. The Egyptian UN Representative Mahmoud Fawzi predictably condemned the invasion and highlighted the hypocrisy of the founding members for their acts of aggression:

> Israel has been saying time and again that it owes its existence to the United Nations. France and the United Kingdom are among the authors of the Charter, are constituent Members of the United Nations, and are, moreover permanent members of the Security Council. It was therefore to be assumed and expected that they would show particular respect for this Organisation and particular care for its purposes and ideals. Yet what have they done? . . . Have they shown respect for the Charter of the United Nations, or is the Charter groaning in anguish because of their actions?[49]

His sentiments were shared by many other states in the Afro-Asian bloc, such as Indonesia, who framed it as a betrayal of the UN Charter, the international community, and the vision of cosmopolitanism that was foundational to the organisation's purpose.[50] This revealing, if brief, moment of concern and anxiety for the organisation's future role within the international community has been lost from the UN's official narrative of the 'first peacekeeping mission' in order to reinstate the secretary-general as a diplomatic hero during the Suez crisis. However, this moment represents a significant period of self-reflection within the young organisation. The UN staff's functional and diplomatic reliance on its member-states, particularly the permanent members, was highlighted; if the states did not comply with the UN Charter, what power did the organisation have to call them to account?

The betrayal of Anglo-French governments in Suez encouraged Hammarskjöld to support plans to functionally expand the UN's powers from rhetorical condemnations to military action in defence of the principles of international security outlined in the UN Charter. Hammarskjöld was initially dubious about Pearson and Dulles' peacekeeping proposal.[51] They had designed a UN mission that would facilitate not only a ceasefire between combatants but also the withdrawal of the invading forces. Yet, repeated

[47] Murray, 'Interview Transcript', p. 26.

[48] W. Beeley, 'Interview Transcript', *Yale-UN Oral History Project*, 20 June 1990, p. 7; Murray, 'Interview Transcript', p. 26.

[49] UN Doc, A/PV.600, '600th Plenary Meeting', General Assembly, 28 November 1956, p. 397.

[50] UN Doc, A/PV.600, '600th Plenary Meeting', General Assembly, 28 November 1956, p. 398.

[51] Urquhart, 'Interview Transcript', p. 17.

meetings with the Canadian diplomat, in addition to the confirmation of US support, buoyed the secretary-general. The crisis of confidence within the UN Secretariat in the aftermath of the Anglo-French invasion served to intensify Hammarskjöld's perception of his role as protector of the Charter. Hammarskjöld felt reinvigorated by the expanded mandate in the draft peacekeeping proposal. Arthur Lall, Ambassador for India to the UN, described Hammarskjöld as '[seeming] to feel that he was on a superior plain, that he was appointed by God to resolve this crisis'.[52] However, the authorisation of the force was complicated by the diplomatic and procedural hurdles of the Security Council. The structure of the Council prioritised the protection of permanent members' interests over those of all other member-states through the permanent members' veto.[53] As explained in Chapter 1, the veto was an unpopular aspect of UN politics and had been since the origin of the organisation. Concerns about the future impotence of the Security Council in the context of permanent member abuses had been voiced by representatives at Dumbarton Oaks, who warned that the international community could find itself echoing the powerlessness of the League of Nations in the face of German and Japanese aggression in the 1930s.[54] The obvious bias of the permanent members in these votes also ignited dormant condemnations of the veto from the Afro-Asian bloc. Victor Andrés Belaunde, Peruvian representative to the UN, demanded in the Security Council that the UN complied with its responsibility to collective security and 'peaceful measures', to avoid being paralysed by the veto(s).[55] As predicted, Britain and France were quick to use their veto in all Security Council resolutions calling for their withdrawal from Egyptian territory, preventing the acceptance of any resolutions on the Suez question within the UN's primary forum and obstructing the implementation of a ceasefire in Egypt.

Belaunde was one of many Afro-Asian representatives who supported the use of the 'Uniting for Peace' resolution (377A) in General Assembly in order to resolve the Suez crisis. As addressed in Chapter 1, 'Uniting for Peace' was a procedure put in place on 3 November 1950 by the United States as a means of circumventing Soviet vetoes during the Korean War.[56] The General Assembly was authorised to consider instances of international peace and security – and make recommendations – if unanimity between the permanent members in

[52] A. Lall, 'Interview Transcript', *United Nations Oral History Project*, 27 June 1990, p. 30.

[53] The permanent members of the Security Council were the USA, Britain, France, China (PRC), and the Soviet Union.

[54] R. C. Hilderbrand, *Dumbarton Oaks: The Origins of the United Nations and the Search for Postwar Security* (Chapel Hill: UNC Press Books, 2001), pp. 183–184.

[55] UN Doc, S/PV.749, 'Security Council Official Records: 11th Year: 749th Meeting, 30th October 1956, New York', pp. 19–20.

[56] A. J. Carswell, 'Unblocking the UN Security Council: The Uniting for Peace Resolution', *Journal of Conflict & Security Law*, 18:3 (2013), p. 455.

the Security Council was unachievable.[57] Thus, the processes established during the Korean War served to guide the development of the Suez peacekeeping mission. The 'Uniting the Peace' resolution was used again in 1956 as a result of procedural frustration by member-states.[58] By the 1950s, it was becoming clear that the frameworks for the acceptance of resolutions within the Security Council had been formed without contingency for post-war divisions between the permanent members. It was only through support for the US-led 'Uniting for Peace' resolution in 1956 that the British-French-Israeli invaders were prevented from holding the entire legislative process ransom through the procedural legacies of post-Second World war victory.[59]

Following these discussions, debate on the Suez crisis moved from the Security Council to the General Assembly, shifting the power dynamic between permanent members and non-permanent member-states. In the General Assembly emergency sessions on the Suez crisis in early November 1956 the planned peacekeeping mission was characterised by representatives within the Afro-Asian bloc as a functional requirement to hold permanent members or major powers to account.[60] Internal telegrams within the Foreign Office between the UK Mission to the UN and government offices in London showed that these emergency sessions in the General Assembly were unfriendly environments for British and French representatives. British Foreign Secretary Selwyn Lloyd commiserated with a British diplomat and representative to the UN writing:

> I know that the two Emergency Special Sessions of the General Assembly must have been a more gruelling time than any which the Delegation has had to face, and your task must have been all the more difficult because of the position of isolation and hostility in which we found ourselves.[61]

[57] UN Doc, A/RES/377(V), 'Uniting for Peace', General Assembly 5th Session, 3 November 1950.

[58] Carswell, 'Unblocking the UN Security Council', p. 455.

[59] The procedural circumvention of the Security Council permanent member's veto became an increasing cause of concern for the Soviet Union, the member-state that the Uniting for Peace resolution was initially constructed to restrict. The Soviet Union continued to question the legitimacy of the UNEF due to its authorisation in the General Assembly under the Uniting for Peace resolution and refused to pay for the 'illegally authorised' forces. US DoS, 'The United Nations Financing and Peacekeeping Problems', SC 00680/65A, 23 July 1965.

[60] UN Doc, A/3289, 'First Report of the Secretary-General on the Plan for an Emergency International United Nations Force Requested in the Resolution Adopted by the General Assembly', 4 November 1956.

[61] BNA, FO 371/118884/JE.1074/223, 'Lloyd to Pierson Dixon Internal Telegram', December 1956.

The deployment of the 'Uniting for Peace' resolution against British and French governments demonstrated a growing assertiveness in the Afro-Asian bloc in the General Assembly. The legislation expanded the post-colonial accountability mechanisms available for non-permanent members within UN forums and communicated a rejection of the procedural protections traditionally afforded to permanent members. UNEF's construction was the result of diplomatic shrewdness on the part of the Afro-Asian bloc and the United States to protect the democratic principles underlined within the UN Charter and its values of non-aggression. The criticism of the Security Council veto and use of the 'Uniting for Peace' legislation challenged the foundational power hierarchies within the organisation and shifted power away from a permanent member-state hegemony.

During these debates, Hammarskjöld mediated a ceasefire before the Anglo-French-Israeli invasion completely encompassed the canal region and drafted a mandate for an UN force that would oversee the withdrawal of the invading troops from Egyptian territory. However, by 19 November 1956 invading forces had yet to withdraw despite several international condemnations of the invasion. This inaction prompted complaints from Fawzi on the futility of the UN in dealing with breaches of sovereignty.[62] In a meeting between Nasser, Fawzi, and Hammarskjöld, the secretary-general acknowledged this problem and was concerned that 'These armed forces are [. . .] consolidating their positions in Egyptian territory in complete disregard for Egypt's sovereign rights and in defiance to the United Nations and to the world.'[63] Now that he had the legal authorisation from the 'Uniting for Peace' resolution, Hammarskjöld would have to staff and deploy the mission swiftly if he was to prevent Egypt from breaching the ceasefire and mounting their own defence against the occupiers.

Challenging Hegemony and Designing an 'Acceptable' Force

Acceptance of the 'Uniting for Peace' resolution by the international community restored Hammarskjöld's reputation for most member-states, but the practicality of recruiting national contingents became a delicate point of diplomatic negotiation. For the secretary-general, the price of expanding the functions of the UN was navigating existing diplomatic practices and customary law that restricted the international use of force. Hammarskjöld needed to ensure that the initial donations of troops for the construction of UNEF were sufficient for the foreseeable length of the mission. The force did not require

[62] BNA, FO 371/118874/JE.1074/27, 'Cypher from New York to Foreign Office', 19 November 1956.

[63] BNA, FO 371/118874/JE.1074/27, 'Cypher from New York to Foreign Office', 19 November 1956.

regular three- or six-monthly renewals, unlike future missions, so therefore the burden was on the mission's logistical needs rather than on diplomatic lobbying. Hammarskjöld's senior advisor Brian Urquhart recalled that '[UNEF] had no time limit, and all that had to be done was once a year to report on it to the General Assembly. But it didn't have to be renewed or anything, so the bureaucratic end of it was much easier, too.'[64] The unprecedented nature of the mission allowed Hammarskjöld to experiment and adapt to legal, diplomatic, and operational hurdles. He argued, 'I would rather see [UNEF] as a kind of experimental prototype from which we learn a great deal and which, I hope, will make it easier at a later stage to renew the discussion and reach results concerning a United Nations force as a formal part of our equipment.'[65] Hammarskjöld saw UNEF as a blueprint from which he and his inner circle could formulate all future peacekeeping missions.

However, Hammarskjöld had to act quickly. Rumours began to circulate that Nasser was planning on inviting the Soviets to Egypt if the violence persisted and the UN did not engage militarily.[66] Nasser had allegedly warned Hammarskjöld that he 'had not much confidence in the organisation' but was reluctant to invite the Soviets to defend Egyptian territory as this would likely start 'world war three' and so his options were limited to trusting UNEF.[67] Regardless, the UN leadership remained anxious about the international repercussions in the region if the ceasefire was not installed and patrolled by UN troops by December. The urgency of the conflict on the ground and the Suez Canal's strategic importance for global trade encouraged Hammarskjöld to deploy the mission as soon as possible.

One of Hammarskjöld's first decisions was his choice of UNEF Force Commander: Canadian officer, General 'Tommy' Burns. In early November, Murray witnessed Hammarskjöld's eagerness to confirm his appointment: '[hiring Burns] would show both the British and the French, who, don't forget, were still sailing down the [Mediterranean] toward the Canal zone, that the UN meant business – that they were going to get that force in there as smartly as they could'.[68] Burns had held the position of Chief of Staff for UNTSO for two years when he was recruited by Hammarskjöld as UNEF Commander. Canadian historian Michael Carroll describes Burns's recruitment as 'both appreciated and respected' by local observers in the Middle East due to the general's past

64 Urquhart, 'Interview Transcript', p. 22.

65 UNA, S-0370-0051-05, 'Press Conference with Dag Hammarskjöld, Note 1571 of 4 April 1957, cont.'.

66 BNA, FO 371/118874/JE.1074/29, 'Telegram from New York to Foreign Office', 20 November 1956.

67 BNA, FO 371/118874/JE.1074/29, 'Telegram from New York to Foreign Office', 20 November 1956.

68 Murray, 'Interview Transcript', p. 39.

involvement in local mediation in the region.[69] The secretary-general authorised Burns's appointment overnight following the passing of the General Assembly resolution, demonstrating the immediacy of Hammarskjöld's decision-making.

Burns's past experience in the Canadian military was not without controversy, however, and there were two efforts by superior British and Canadian officers to oust him for his poor leadership during the Second World War.[70] Burns has been described in military histories of the Second World War as having a 'notoriously brusque and anti-social manner with subordinates'.[71] He was relieved of his command after a second complaint in October 1944, reduced in rank to major-general, and relegated to 'unimportant rear area positions'.[72] However, Burns's humiliation in 1944 has been reviewed by Will Lofgren, who has argued that Burns's operational skill on the front line in Italy made him 'one of the most successful Canadian corps commanders in the entire Second World War' and that it was others' affront to his atypical leadership style and interpersonal skills that caused him to be 'pilloried'.[73] Similarly, Douglas Delaney has emphasised Burns's academic brilliance and military skill but acknowledged that Burns's 'uncanny knack for making everyone around him uncomfortable' stunted the General's career.[74] His second life as a UN commander was an opportunity to regain the rank of lieutenant-general and reassert himself in a leadership position unprejudiced by past criticism.

Having recruited a competent – although controversial – military commander, Hammarskjöld moved on to the diplomatically sensitive issues, such as choosing which nations would participate in UNEF's first mission. The construction of the UN force was inherently tied to the nation-state paradigm of the UN organs, agencies, and forums. The force was an alliance of distinct national battalions rather than an international integrated or 'mixed' unit (as had been deployed to Korea) which enabled troops to operate alongside those similarly trained to them – a rupture from the original cosmopolitan design. The choice of national battalions was a decision that Hammarskjöld was keen to protect from political aspersions. Recalling the cosmopolitan vision of the UN founders, UN leadership required UNEF troops to be agile in swapping

[69] Carroll, *Pearson's Peacekeepers*, p. 34.

[70] J. L. Granatstein and P. Suedfeld, 'Tommy Burns as a Military Leader: A Case Study using Integrative Complexity', *Canadian Military History*, 3:2 (1994), p. 64.

[71] C. Jennings, *At War on the Gothic Line: Fighting in Italy 1944–1945* (London: Bloomsbury, 2016), p. 133.

[72] Jennings, *At War on the Gothic Line*, p. 133.

[73] W. Lofgren, '"In Defence of "Tommy" Burns"', *Canadian Military History*, 7:4 (2006), p. 93.

[74] D. E. Delaney, *Corps Commanders: Five British and Canadian General at War, 1939–1945* (Vancouver: UBC Press, 2011), p. 3.

between their national and international allegiances while ensuring that neither became either too dilute or dominant. However, ultimately the UNEF troops were under the authority of Commander Burns despite remaining within their national battalions.

Hammarskjöld also attempted to pre-empt accusations that the mission perpetrated imperial interests in the Suez region or that it was a 'face-saving' exercise by absorbing the existing invading forces on the ground.[75] Hammarskjöld announced that there would be no troops deployed from permanent member-states to UNEF and that the final decision on UNEF contingent recruitment would be by himself and Burns.[76] By late November 1956, Hammarskjöld recognised that amalgamating the invading British and French troops into UNEF would be militarily unviable and politically unpopular. Ralph Bunche recorded Indian representative Arthur Lall arguing at an UN Advisory Committee meeting that it was 'not likely that any Asian forces will participate [in UNEF] if Anglo-French forces are included – they must be treated as untouchables'.[77]

The exclusion of permanent member-states from the mission was a factor in the transition of power away from permanent member hegemony towards the increased diplomatic weight of middle powers.[78] This shift was linked with the UN leadership's assumption that these nations would not complicate the mission with imperial or Cold War politics, as the permanent members had during this period. UNEF presented a unique opportunity to associate their nation with the first UN mission and benefit from that mission's diplomatic and peacebuilding credentials. Middle power nations, such as Canada, India, Ireland, and Indonesia, acknowledged the political influence this would provide for their governments in the context of a rapidly transforming international community. Twenty-one nations offered to donate military contingents to UNEF 'without any prompting', seemingly a pleasant surprise to Ralph Bunche, who commented that it was the 'most popular army ever'.[79]

[75] This accusation has been made by several scholars, including: M. Cohen, 'The Demise of UNEF', *International Journal*, 23:1 (1968), pp. 18–51.

[76] Specifically, the resolution, 'Authorizes the Chief of the Command immediately to recruit, from the observer corps of the United Nations Truce Supervision Organization, a limited number of officers who shall be nationals of countries other than those having permanent membership in the Security Council, and further authorizes him, in consultation with the Secretary-General, to undertake the recruitment directly, from various Member States other than the permanent members of the Security Council, of the additional number of officers needed'; UN Doc, A/RES/1000 (ES – 1), 'Resolution 1000', 5 November 1956.

[77] UNA, S-0370-0028-08, 'Bunche Notes on UNEF Advisory Committee Meeting', undated.

[78] Using a contemporaneous definition from: G. D. Glazebrook, 'The Middle Powers in the United Nations System', *International Organization*, 1:2 (1947), pp. 307–318.

[79] BNA, FO 371/118873/JE.1074/1, 'Report of Talk with Dr Bunche, 14 November 1956'.

Hammarskjöld constructed an international UN Advisory Committee to determine which nationalities should be deployed to the UNEF mission, but the committee itself triggered diplomatic hurdles. It was authorised on 7 November 1956 to:

> undertake the development of those aspects of the planning for the Force and its operation not already dealt with by the General Assembly and which do not fall within the area of the direct responsibility of the Chief of Command [Burns].[80]

The creation of a committee permitted the secretary-general to delegate accountability and responsibility if future operations provoked regional or international criticism. The committee predominantly included Afro-Asian and South American countries: Brazil, Colombia, Ceylon, and Pakistan, as well as Canada and Norway. India was a late addition following criticism of the mission as an imperialistic trick designed to indoctrinate the Afro-Asian nations from Krishna Menon,[81] India's Permanent Representative to the UN.[82] However, deciding that he could police this 'trap' from the inside, Menon accepted a seat on the committee and offered Indian battalions for UNEF.[83] He later became one of the mission's most vocal supporters and argued that UN peacekeeping was a practical furtherance of the Charter's principles: a blossoming of UN functions.[84] In sharp contrast to India's experience with UNEF, middle powers associated with the Warsaw Pact were excluded from the committee, illustrating the Cold War biases present in the UN Secretariat. The UN leadership rejected a Czechoslovakian representative on the committee on the grounds that, 'nobody wanted the east bloc dabbling in all this business'.[85] The committee discussions prepared national representatives for their continued support through the procedural, principled, and practical constraints on the ground. As Hammarskjöld commented in the minutes of one UNEF Committee meeting, 'I trust that you will keep in touch with us and help us, because we certainly want to run this as team-wise [sic] as possible.'[86]

[80] UN Doc, A/RES/1001 (ES-1), 'Resolution 1001', 7 November 1956.
[81] Murray, 'Interview Transcript', p. 47.
[82] For more on India and the UN, see D. Gorman, 'Britain, India, and the United Nations: Colonialism and the Development of International Governance, 1945–1960', *Journal of Global History*, 9:3 (2014), pp. 471–490.
[83] T. Ramakrishna Reddy, *India's Policy in the United Nations* (Madison: Fairleigh Dickinson University Press, 1968), p. 96.
[84] UN Doc, A/PV.703, '703rd Plenary Meeting', General Assembly, 8 November 1957, p. 318, para. 75.
[85] Murray, 'Interview Transcript', p. 49.
[86] BNA, FO 371/125551/JE.1427/104, 'Minutes of UNEF Advisory Committee', 19 January 1957, p. 11.

It was the executive role of the secretary-general to negotiate and vet the suggested contingents and leadership officers once the committee representatives had submitted their opinions. However, Hammarskjöld and Bunche had to ensure that they did not overly dominate the process, nor appear as if they were letting Nasser design UNEF. The force was only permitted in Egyptian territory due to Nasser's consent but the UN leadership had to consider his requests in the context of an international audience.[87] In a meeting with the staff of the UK Mission to the UN and the British Secretary of State, Hammarskjöld affirmed his independence from Nasser: 'The Egyptians still claim the right to refuse individual contingents, but [Hammarskjöld] was quite firm that his is the determining authority, though he can take account of Egyptian views.'[88] Nasser was reported to have asked Hammarskjöld not to accept the contingents offered by Pakistan and Iran, indicating that regional tensions and alliances were reflected in the design of the Force.[89] The leak of Nasser's preferences had diplomatic ramifications for the Egyptian government, and it was quick to deny such reports. The British Embassy in Iran reported that the Egyptian government had argued that 'Iran was such a friendly power that they would prefer to not have an Iranian contingent'.[90] The Egyptian Embassy also rejected press reports that they had a 'ban' on Pakistan troops being included in UNEF, stating that 'Pakistan was not one of the countries suggested by the Secretary General of the United Nations to participate'.[91] Despite Egyptian representatives addressing these reports, Iran and Pakistan did not contribute contingents to the 1956 UNEF mission. This wrangling indicates the level of detail and concern applied to UNEF's construction and the relevance of regional politics to the middle powers' attainment of increased geopolitical power within the UN.

The Egyptian government was also hesitant about Canadian involvement in the Force due to its NATO affiliations with the invading forces.[92] Nasser was keen to ensure that the UNEF troops did not simply 'take over' from the

[87] UNEF only patrolled on the Egyptian side of the demarcation line as it was refused access by the Israeli government despite efforts by Bunche to engage with the Israelis about this issue: 'therefore, the Force is found only on the Egyptian side': UNA, S-0316-0012-06, 'Letter from Bunche to Secretary-General', 6 August 1957.

[88] BNA, FO 371/118874/JE.1074/25, 'Telegram from New York to Foreign Office', 20 November 1956.

[89] BNA, FO 371/118874/JE.1074/38A, 'Cypher from UK High Commissioner in Pakistan to New York', 17 November 1956; BNA, FO 271/118873/JE.1074/6, 'Telegram from Tehran to Foreign Office', 15 November 1956.

[90] BNA, FO 371/118873/JE.1074/6, 'Telegram from Tehran to Foreign Office', 15 November 1956.

[91] BNA, FO 371/118874/JE.1074/38A, 'Cypher from UK High Commissioner in Pakistan to New York', 17 November 1956.

[92] UNA, S-1066-0003-05, 'UNEF and Relations with the Government of Egypt, Memo', 29 October 1962.

Anglo-French invasion and reportedly suggested that the Canadian contribution to the mission begin on restricted terms.[93] However, the concerning dearth of civilian staff submissions required for the management and support of the mission on the ground presented an opening for the Canadian military.[94] As UNEF logistical support was provided by the US and the Canadian army used the same systems, Hammarskjöld and Burns determined that the Canadians would provide military 'housekeeping' for the mission, as well as supplying personnel for the UNEF air force and civilian operations.[95] Participating in UNEF also gave Canada an opportunity to call the permanent members to account for their violation of international law during the Suez crisis. In a press conference, Canadian Prime Minister Louis St. Laurent, commented as follows in an exchange with a reporter:

> ST LAURENT: I have been scandalised more than once by the attitude of the larger powers, the big powers as we call them, who have all too frequently treated the Charter of the United Nations as an instrument with which to regiment smaller nations and as an instrument which did not have to be considered when their own so-called vital interests were at state. I have been told, with respect to the veto, that if the Russians had not insisted upon it the United States and the United Kingdom would have insisted on it, because they could not allow this crowd of smaller nations to deal decisively with questions which concerned their vital interests.
>
> REPORTER: Why should they?
>
> ST LAURENT: Because the members of the smaller nations are human beings just as are their people; because the era when the supermen of Europe could govern the whole world has and is coming pretty close to an end.[96]

The UNEF 'housekeeping' role placed the Canadians at the centre of the mission and empowered the middle power nation to develop its reputation within the international community and build on Pearson's diplomatic prestige.

Within a fortnight of the Suez invasion, mid-November 1956, Bunche announced that UNEF was successfully constructed. It boasted, 'contingents so far accepted [totalling] 4,278. In addition to the Canadians [of 1,200] this is made up as follows: Colombians 550, Indians 800, Swedes 300, Norwegians 200, Danes 350, Finns 250, Yugoslavs 700', with Indonesian and Brazilian

93 BNA, FO 371/118874/JE.1074/25, 'Telegram from New York to Foreign Office', 20 November 1956.

94 Murray, 'Interview Transcript', p. 52.

95 Murray, 'Interview Transcript', p. 52.

96 BNA, FO 371/118880/JE.1074/161 (F), 'Minutes of Canadian Cabinet', 26 November 1956.

contingents also added to the initial deployment over the next fortnight.[97] The inclusion of the Yugoslav contingent did not raise any objections within the UN leadership due to the nation's post-war split from Stalin and founding role in the Non-Aligned Movement under leader Josip Tito.[98] The UN airlifted over 2,000 UNEF troops from Naples into the Suez Canal area on 1 December 1956. Despite the diplomatic hurdles involved in the design of the force, Hammarskjöld deployed the mission in under a month from the adoption of the 'Uniting for Peace' resolution.[99]

'This a Great Test for the UN': Post-invasion Diplomacy and Obfuscation

The successful construction of the mission and its popularity within the General Assembly prompted the British Secretary of State, Selwyn Lloyd, to characterise the British invasion as foundational to UNEF's development. On 14 November, Pierson Dixon, leader of the UK Mission to the UN, defended the British invasion to American UN Ambassador Henry Cabot Lodge Jr. and argued that Britain was acting in self-defence during the invasion of Egyptian territory.[100] Dixon reported his meeting to his colleagues in the Foreign Office:

> [Lodge] spoke of the shock which our action had been and the pain which it had caused him. We had been guilty of aggression and what we had done was indefensible. I said that I did not agree with him at all. We had acted to stop a wider conflagration. We had done so quickly because otherwise Syria and Jordan would have been in the war before we knew where we were. Our intention to protect our national interests in the Canal area was, in my view, legitimate self-defence. . .[101]

Lodge's response indicated that he was not persuaded on this point, and Dixon reported that '[He] really had no answer to that argument'.[102]

Additionally, repeated condemnations by the Afro-Asian bloc nations throughout November led to the adoption of General Assembly resolution which directly called upon the invading forces to withdraw behind the 1949

[97] BNA, FO 371/118876/JE.1074/74 (A), 'Telegram from Foreign Secretary in New York to Foreign Office', 14 November 1956.

[98] R. Neibuhr, 'Nonalignment as Yugoslavia's Answer to Bloc Politics', *Journal of Cold War Studies*, 13:1 (2011), pp. 146–179.

[99] BNA, FO 371/118878/JE.1074/127, 'Proposed Statement to the Press by Secretary-General', 28 November 1956.

[100] BNA, FO 371/118873/JE.1074/1G, 'Telegram from UK Delegation to Foreign Office – Memo of Discussion between Dixon and Lodge', 14 November 1956.

[101] BNA, FO 371/118873/JE.1074/1G, 'Telegram from UK Delegation to Foreign Office – Memo of discussion between Dixon and Lodge', 14 November 1956.

[102] BNA, FO 371/118873/JE.1074/1G, 'Telegram from UK Delegation to Foreign Office – Memo of Discussion between Dixon and Lodge', 14 November 1956.

Armistice Lines.[103] The resolution frustrated the Foreign Office diplomats in London and New York.[104] Lloyd and Dixon felt that the resolution crystalized an unfair characterisation of British operations in Egypt. Foreign Office documents described the Afro-Asian resolution as impractical and a deliberate move by anti-imperialists within the General Assembly.[105] This defensive position was a central strategy of British post-Suez international communications as the popularity of UNEF became an unavoidable geopolitical reality. Lloyd made the same argument in the General Assembly on 23 November 1956. He insisted on the beneficial consequences of the conflict – that is, UNEF and the development of a peacekeeping project – were instigated by the Anglo-French-Israeli forces. He alleged that the invasion was undertaken with a humanitarian impulse to prevent the spread of hostilities following the earlier Israeli operations: that Britain 'wished to put, as rapidly as possible, a protective shield between combatants' through their invasion.[106] Thus, he asserted that any criticism of British actions during the Suez crisis, and 'out of the painful discussions regarding them', were excused and justified by the development of UNEF.[107] Lloyd bestowed the British invasion with the humanitarian and security credentials of a peacekeeping mission by minimising the violence of the occupation, insisting that the ends justified the means. Indeed, he asserted that it would be the British government that would be responsible for the restoration of peace in the Middle East following the Suez crisis if UNEF was successful:

> We believe that we have stopped a small war spreading into a larger war. We believe that we have created the conditions under which a United Nations force is to be introduced into this troubled area to establish and maintain peace. We believe that thereby we have given this Assembly, and the world, another opportunity to settle the problems of the area. We believe that we brought matters to a head, to a crisis, and we have cast down a challenge to world statesmanship of this Assembly to achieve

[103] Reference is to a draft resolution cosponsored by 20 Afro-Asian nations, which was circulated to members of the General Assembly on 22nd November (UN doc A/3385). This draft resolution reiterated previous calls to Great Britain, France, and Israel to comply with UN resolutions requiring withdrawal from occupied territories. This draft resolution was then accepted and published as: UN Doc, A/RES/1120 (XI), 'Resolution 1120', General Assembly, 24 November 1956.

[104] BNA, FO 371/118879/JE.1074/142, 'Secret Memo from Foreign Office to United Kingdom Delegation to the United Nations', 29 November 1956.

[105] BNA, FO 371/118879/JE.1074/142, 'Secret Memo from Foreign Office to United Kingdom Delegation to the United Nations', 29 November 1956.

[106] UN Doc, A/PV.591, '591st Plenary Meeting', General Assembly, Eleventh Session, 23 November 1956, p. 258, para. 87.

[107] UN Doc, A/PV.591, '591st Plenary Meeting', General Assembly, Eleventh Session, 23 November 1956, p. 258, para. 88.

results. We believe that there is in this a great test for the United Nations and on the powers upon whose continued support the United Nations ultimately depends.[108]

Lloyd's position was a blatant attempt to reassert Britain's international reputation as a trustworthy 'great power' with a strategic motivation rooted in political and moral supremacy. This defence – and the state's representatives' expectation that the international audience would accept it – was a legacy of colonial bravado and belief in British righteousness and entitlement in its foreign policy.

In the same speech, Lloyd attempted to assign Britain's invading troops an international policing role. He suggested that as a precaution British troops should remain on the ground until the British government deemed that the UNEF mission staff were 'effective and competent to discharge the tasks' as they did not want UNEF to 'be laughed at'.[109] Lloyd concluded by reminding the UN that the British government was indulging in an 'act of faith' in the mission, the secretary-general, and the organisation as a whole.[110] This was a poorly concealed attempt to pre-emptively shift responsibility for future instability in the Middle East towards the UN leadership rather than the invaders. France did not speak in this session, but the Israeli representative Abba Eban concluded the meeting by reiterating his defence of tripartite aggression in Sinai and the Gaza Strip. He argued that Egypt had endangered Israeli citizens for the past eight years and 'Israel had arisen to defend its life and its future against the perils threatening its existence from every side'.[111] Thus, like the British, Israel had no intention of displaying regret for its invasion of the Suez Canal and its breach of Armistice Lines, as agreed in 1949. Indeed, Israel's compliance with the Armistice Agreements was a condition of their membership of the UN, but they remained a member-state regardless.

Rebuttal of Lloyd's argument dominated the next day in the General Assembly. Countless nations, including Syria,[112] Poland,[113] and Iraq,[114] ridiculed the British explanation that their invading forces should evaluate the competence of the UN mission before withdrawing. Menon challenged Lloyd's

[108] UN Doc, A/PV.591, '591st Plenary Meeting', General Assembly, Eleventh Session, 23 November 1956, p. 259, para. 94.

[109] UN Doc, A/PV.591, '591st Plenary Meeting', General Assembly, Eleventh Session, 23 November 1956, para. 96.

[110] UN Doc, A/PV.591, '591st Plenary Meeting', General Assembly, Eleventh Session, 23 November 1956, para. 95.

[111] UN Doc, A/PV.592, '592nd Plenary Meeting', p. 272, para. 104.

[112] UN Doc, A/PV.591, '591st Plenary Meeting', p. 260, para. 109.

[113] UN Doc, A/PV.592, '592nd Plenary Meeting', General Assembly, Eleventh Session, 23 November 1956, p. 269, paras. 75/76.

[114] UN Doc, A/PV.592, '592nd Plenary Meeting', General Assembly, Eleventh Session, 23 November 1956, p. 271, para. 91.

confidence, rationale, and pseudo-legal justifications for the British invasion: 'I do not see any provision in the Charter indicating that it is given to one nation to use armed might in the defence of any principles. . .'[115] Menon suggested that the history of colonial violence across the Global South had desensitised populations to European violations of sovereignty and that the Suez crisis could not be divorced from these longstanding imperial practices. He stated that 'it has almost become part of the racial memory of men to regard these aggression as though they were less sinful, less criminal, less against the Charter of the United Nations, than any other.'[116] Defending the authority of the UN mission and deriding the arrogance of the British government's attempt to recast their invading forces as de facto peacekeepers, Menon emphasised that 'France and the United Kingdom have no right to tell us: "We will decide, when your forces come in, whether they are big enough and whether they can take over".'[117] However, these rebuttals made little difference to the confidence of the British government in their internal communications and their narrative of the crisis. Lloyd and Dixon's conceptions of Britain's involvement in the 'creation' of the UNEF mission and, more broadly, their humanitarian efforts to have, 'stopped a small war which might quickly have spread into a major war' appeared unshaken.[118] The Security Council veto and availability of military equipment from the past British occupation permitted the Anglo-French-Israeli forces to retain the military upper-hand in the region, despite the transformative shifts within the international community. The timeline of their withdrawal remained their own until the UNEF deployment challenged their presence directly on the ground.

However, once the UNEF troops began arriving on the ground, leadership realised that the force was ill-resourced and poorly prepared to install a ceasefire in the region. Through talks with Ralph Bunche and his UN office, British representatives offered technical and administrative support, particularly for clearing the canal of scuttled vessels during the early months of UNEF's operations, to balance out UNEF's deficit.[119] Although permanent members could not contribute battalions of troops to the mission, Hammarskjöld accepted materiel and administrative support from the British government. For the local population, UNEF perpetuated the presence of the invading

115 UN Doc, A/PV.594, '594th Plenary Meeting', General Assembly, Eleventh Session, 24 November 1956, p. 303.

116 UN Doc, A/PV.594, '594th Plenary Meeting', General Assembly, Eleventh Session, 24 November 1956, p. 303.

117 UN Doc, A/PV.594, '594th Plenary Meeting', General Assembly, Eleventh Session, 24 November 1956, p. 305.

118 BNA, FO 371/118879/JE.1074/142, 'Secret Memo from Foreign Office to United Kingdom Delegation to the United Nations', 29 November 1956, p. 2.

119 BNA, FO 371/118880/JE.1074/163G, 'Suez Canal Clearance: Discussion between Sir P Dixon and Mr Hammarskjöld', December 1956.

personnel in Sinai and Gaza. By borrowing their equipment and seemingly forgiving the invading forces for their violence, the UN leadership angered the civilian population in Sinai and Gaza who supported Egypt. Protests erupted in the Gaza Strip as local people directly challenged the politics and decision-making of UNEF.

Despite these protests, UNEF remained dependant on the logistical and materiel support provided by the British government. Dixon wrote to the Foreign Office in London to discuss their involvement in transferring technical equipment 'such as transport, food stocks and other stores' from their invading position in Port Said to UNEF troops once they arrived.[120] The next week, Bunche delivered a 'shopping list' to Dixon confirming the 'order' of:

> 1) Vehicles for a Norwegian medical company; 2) Vehicles for the Indian infantry battalion. They [Bunche's office] understood that the scale of equipment should be similar to that of a British infantry battalion. 3. POL [petroleum, oils, and lubricants], medical supplies and food.[121]

UNEF's reliance on British technical support and resources legitimised British diplomats' efforts to insert their government in the narrative of UNEF and benefit from the diplomatic credentials of association with the mission, despite their official exclusion from providing a military contingent donation. Hammarskjöld recognised that the UN needed to maintain a civil relationship with the British government, especially while they were still occupying the region. In December 1956, Hammarskjöld covertly requested that the UK Mission the UN influence the Israelis to keep a portion of their invading troops in the Gaza region due to the refugees residing there. A memo from the UK Mission to the Foreign Office reported that:

> Legally, of course, the Israelis were under an Assembly injunction to withdraw completely behind the armistice lines. But Hammarskjöld had privately indicated that the last thing he wanted to see was an early Israel evacuation from Gaza, which would leave all the refugees there with no adequate administration[122]

The UN leadership's use of withdrawing – or supposedly withdrawing – invading troops in the early months of a new mission prioritised organisational concerns above the psychological violence of an occupying force and paved the way for future missions' reliance on ex-colonial powers for technical and administrative support. It also demonstrated that Hammarskjöld would

120 BNA, FO 371/118873/JE.1074/8, 'Telegram from New York to Foreign Office', 11 November 1956.

121 BNA, FO 371/118873/JE.1074/12, 'Telegram from New York to Foreign Office', 19 November 1956.

122 BNA, FO 371/118884/JE.1074/216, 'Memo from United Kingdom Delegation to the UN to Foreign Office', 8 December 1956.

Figure 2.1 Gaza protest, J112923611, 18 March 1957.
Reproduced with permission from Keystone/Hulton Archive/Getty Images.

prioritise the appearance of a swift deployment over the construction of a properly staffed and resourced mission, preferring to substitute with British equipment and Israeli governance.

Crafting a Peacekeeper Identity from Orientalist Imaginaries

Despite these initial obstacles, by December 1956, UNEF installed a sizable military presence along the canal region and the Armistice Demarcation Line(s) and extending across the disputed territories from the Suez Canal region to the Sinai Peninsula and the Gaza Strip. 'Fluttering blue flags, indicating UN control' were 'dotted all along the Line', with troops placing them 'as far as the eye can see', physically marking UNEF's presence on the ground to the local population and remaining occupiers.[123] Once on the ground, the mission staff and troops began to craft, exchange, and project their own conception(s) of UNEF and what it meant to be an international 'peacekeeper', building on the cosmopolitan ideals encouraged by the spirit of the UN Charter. Maintaining a working relationship with the Egyptian government proved difficult for UN staff, who had been instructed by UN leadership to remain suspicious of Egyptian politicians. Bunche wrote to Force Commander Burns in early 1957 to remind him to rely on information solely from other UN agencies rather than Egyptian sources: 'I consider it *inadvisable* [Bunche's emphasis] to approach Gaza Egyptians on questions. Suggest reliance on UNRWA [The United Nations Relief and Works Agency for Palestine Refugees in the Near East] and UNEF sources only.'[124] Through these instructions, the UNEF bureaucracy became culturally insular and disconnected from the Egyptian government in its authority over Sinai and Gaza, influencing the peacekeeping staff's conceptions of the region, the local population, and each other.

The UN leadership emphasised that the UNEF troops were to be held to higher moral and humanitarian standards than their own nations' militaries. The mission leaders expected the troops to represent the ideals of the UN and exposed the peacekeepers to saviour-complex rhetoric from the mission's origin. Once deployed, Hammarskjöld broadcast a message to the new UNEF troops that reflected this shared, moralistic culture:

> You are the frontline of a moral force which extends around the world, and you have behind you the support of millions everywhere. Much will depend upon the example that this force sets. Your success can have profound effect for good, not only in the present emergency, but on future prospects for building a world order of which we may all one day be truly proud.[125]

Similarly, General Burns, asserted:

> We are not a great military force but we are a symbol of a moral force – the force embodied in the Charter of the United Nations, the principles of which we have helped to make effective in this place. Perhaps history will cite our force as the first effective use of the armed forces of many nations to implement the principles of non-aggression which all member nations of the UN are bound to by their adherence to the Charter. If this sort of peace by using armed forces continues, grows and becomes more effective, then the whole human race will have benefited.[126]

[123] British Library (henceforth, BL), U.N.A.466., UN Public Information Office, *Sand Dune: The UNEF Weekly*, ed. 6, 3 April 1957, p. 1.

[124] UNA, S-0316-0009-23, 'Outgoing Code from Bunche to Burns, GA-34', 1 April 1957.

[125] UNA, S-0313-0002-12, 'UN Pamphlet on UNEF', 1 March 1957, p. 17.

[126] BL, U.N.A.466., UN Public Information Office, *Sand Dune: The UNEF Weekly*, ed. 12, 15 May 1957, p. 3.

UN leadership rhetoric entrenched a narrative of the 'chosen' and morally-superior peacekeepers within UNEF and then projected it to the international audience.

The scale of the deployment across such great distances led to the production of a weekly UNEF newsletter, *The Sand Dune*, intended to foster community and provide updates for troops when isolated on their patrols. The UNEF Public Information Office published and distributed the first edition on 26 February 1957 from the UNEF headquarters in Abu Suweir, an airbase to the west of the Suez Canal. The magazine relied heavily on contributions and letters from UNEF troops for content, providing insight into the dynamic relationships between ever-changing troops and national battalions. Jokes littering the pages and stories of masculine camaraderie fostered the collegial tone of the magazine, reflecting its purpose to entertain the thousands of men deployed across the Sinai Peninsula. Regular features included 'UN News', fact sections on the different national battalions deployed, operational updates, letters of thanks from people around the world for their 'preservation of peace',[127] and 'personalities' – a section detailing the previous accomplishments of UNEF leadership figures. This collegial effort was emphasised by the first editor, Major V Longer, an Indian peacekeeper, who stated that the magazine

> recorded the history [of UNEF's deployment] . . . as seen from the inside. It has presented a picture of the various national contingents, of the jobs they are doing on the ADL and of the countries from which they have come. It has become a 'family magazine' and perhaps like the blue berets and helmet liners has contributed something to a sense of unity in the force.[128]

The Sand Dune continually encouraged UNEF troops to engage and send in their opinions so that the publication could adapt to the soldiers' needs and requests, likes, and dislikes. In response, UNEF troops often wrote in to compliment or correct various features, demonstrating its widespread reach and its popularity among the troops. Many used their spare time to write short entertaining pieces about their patrols, other UN troops, or their past military experiences in their home country. One of the Yugoslav troops sent a note to the Editor commenting that the language barrier of *The Sand Dune* (which was published in English) was no longer an issue for his battalion's enjoyment and education:

> The paper 'Sand Dune' is read very much by all the members of our battalion and they like it. We have taken all necessary measures that this

[127] BL, U.N.A.466., UN Public Information Office, *Sand Dune: The UNEF Weekly*, ed. 6, 3 April 1957, p. 4.

[128] BL, U.N.A.466., UN Public Information Office, *Sand Dune: The UNEF Weekly*, ed. 14, 29 May 1957, p. 4.

Figure 2.2 The Suez Crisis 1956: UN Troops in the Sinai Desert, K016700-A4, 9 January 1956.
Reproduced with permission from Keystone-France/Gamma-Keystone/Getty Images.

> our common paper is accessible to all our soldiers. The paper is therefore being translated into our language, and this enables each member of our battalion to become familiar with the efforts and life of their friends from other contingents and at the same time they learn much about the countries which have sent their contingents to take part in UNEF.[129]

The magazine became an accessible and tailored space for the mission troops to promote and reinforce the image of the peacekeeping mission as a successful, humanitarian, and cosmopolitan operation. By 28 March 1957, the UN headquarters in New York increased their order of editions from six to eight copies, with the extra magazines 'being distributed (1) to the library and (2) to the Secretariat News'.[130] The troops' curated reports of their experiences had a transnational reach from the field, shaping international imaginaries of the mission and the conflict.

[129] BL, U.N.A.466., UN Public Information Office, *Sand Dune: The UNEF Weekly*, ed. 5, 27 March 1957, p. 4.

[130] UNA, S-0530-0016-0008, 'Administrative Report No. 55. 8, To Gaza, 28 March 1957'.

The unsophisticated nature of the magazine revealed the political and ideological prejudices of the troops through their portrayal of and engagement with the host population and territory. For instance, stereotypical and colonial beliefs about the region were dominant in the magazine's descriptions of UNEF troops' operations. Edward Said's work on European 'invention' of the Orient has unpacked the variety of practical and rhetorical tools utilised by Western actors in their descriptions of colonised populations, specifically in the Middle East.[131] Said argued that an Orientalist perspective encourages Western visitors to exaggerate the differences between their home country and the Arab-Asiatic region, distorting and homogenising their conceptions of the local population to assume 'the Orient's difference with its weakness'.[132] *The Sand Dune*'s narrative of the troops' experiences in the Middle East replicated the century-old colonial European imagination. The region was seemingly 'timeless', simultaneously 'exotic', but also 'primitive': its 'untouched' nature supposedly providing evidence for both its underdevelopment *and* its unique beauty. Although the troops were constructed from a range of middle power nations, many in the Global South, the very act of intervention – and the moralising power dynamic imposed by the UN leadership of the peacekeepers as 'saviours' – authorised an 'othering' of the host population. The troops reproduced 'the Orient' as they attempted to communicate their intervention in the territory through the magazine by 'making statements about it, authorising views of it, describing it, but teaching it, settling it, ruling over it…'[133] Thus, the symbolism and language used by the troops within *The Sand Dune* as they patrolled the region, reproduced *and* legitimised colonial imaginaries of the post-colonial Middle East within the mission despite the vast geographic spread of the different UN national contingents.

The publication encouraged the UNEF soldiers to conceive of the peacekeeping context through an Orientalist lens of Egyptian culture which had been long popularised through colonial ethnographic publications,[134] archaeological excavations,[135] and tourist literature of the region.[136] The magazine legitimised Orientalist fantasies of Ancient Egypt and 'exoticised' the troops' shared peacekeeping experience. For example, a Norwegian doctor Major Muri was interviewed in *The Sand Dune* and described how he volunteered

[131] E. Said, *Orientalism* (New York: Random House, 1979), p. 1.

[132] Said, *Orientalism*, p. 204.

[133] Said, *Orientalism*, p. 3.

[134] O. El Shakry, *The Great Social Laboratory: Subjects of Knowledge in Colonial and Postcolonial Egypt* (Palo Alto: University of Stanford Press, 2007). W. Carruthers, *Flooded Pasts: UNESCO, Nubia, and the Recolonization of Archaeology* (Ithaca: Cornell University Press, 2022).

[135] D. M. Reid, *Whose Pharaohs?: Archaeology, Museums, and Egyptian National Identity from Napoleon to World War I* (Oakland: University of California Press, 2002).

[136] F. R. Hunter, 'Tourism and Empire: The Thomas Cook & Son Enterprise on the Nile, 1868–1914', *Middle Eastern Studies*, 40:5 (2004), pp. 28–54.

'to come to Egypt for the love of seeing the Nile, the Pyramids, the [Sphinx] and the ancient mysteries of Luxor. To him it was an exciting experience. . .'[137] Similarly, other sections in the magazine frequently referred to their sightings of ancient historical monuments and experiences whilst patrolling 'exotic' landscapes, seemingly trying to connect the region's past with their present operations. As Ali Behdad has argued, the Orientalist's melancholic 'desire' for a past paradise is challenged by 'the emptiness of the signifieds in the subject's encounter with the real ... The subject's desire of the Orient begins to take shape in the gap between the "reality" of the Orient emerging before him from dust and dream and the phantasm of the Orient conveyed to him through the symbolic field of the orientalist intertext'.[138] Behdad articulates the paradoxical challenge for the Orientalist when put in contact with the object of 'desire or fantasy'. For the UNEF troops, they remedied this paradox by exaggerating their pre-conflict fantasies of the region through sharing and reading letters and articles published in *The Sand Dune*. Seeing that other troops conceived of the landscape and people similarly helped to flesh out their Orientalist fantasies and fill the perceived gaps of the 'real' Egypt.

Improvements to communications technology allowed troops to report home their experiences on the frontline and, thus, encouraged the troops to view their environment through a tourist framework as they sought to best translate their foreign surroundings to their friends and family. This tourist framework involved positioning themselves as external to the environment. Debbie Lisle has conceived of this dynamic as a 'tourist lens' and has examined its effect on troops deployed to conflict contexts in foreign spaces. She has argued that the institutionalisation of recreation and relaxation on the frontline, established during the First World War, entrenched 'tourist sensibilities' in the trenches as the troops had longer periods to 'relax'.[139] Lisle has posited that pre-conflict 'dispositions of leisure and travel periodically reorient fighting forces toward foreign battlefields and enemy territory', which serve to '[frame] their off-duty experiences through a familiar prewar tourist gaze'.[140] The troops held a liminal mindset as they were simultaneously part of *and* separate from the field; their pre-conflict or pre-war expectations and fantasies of the region clashing with the realities of deployment to a conflict zone or battlefield. Orientalist fantasies required the production of encounters and interactions in order for an 'authentic' experience of Egyptian culture for UNEF troops. United in their Orientalist expectations for the mission, the

[137] BL, U.N.A.466., UN Public Information Office, *Sand Dune: The UNEF Weekly*, ed. 6, 3 April 1957, p. 2.

[138] A. Behdad, *Belated Travelers: Orientalism in in the Age of Colonial Dissolution* (Durham: Duke University Press, 1994), p. 29.

[139] D. Lisle, *Holidays in the Danger Zone: Entanglements of War and Tourism* (Minneapolis: University of Minnesota Press, 2016), p. 73.

[140] Lisle, *Holidays in the Danger Zone*, p. 71.

troops reconstructed aspects of their fantasies of the region for one another through writings in *The Sand Dune* and organising recreational activities, such as belly-dancing, in order to fulfil their – and their families' – imaginaries of the region and population.

The troops' descriptions of the landscape published in *The Sand Dune* were central to troops' descriptions of patrols, invoking 'othering' comparisons to their homelands. Paradoxically, Sinai was described as both a barren desert *and* an 'exotic' Arab fantasy depending on whether the magazine was intending on projecting UNEF troops as bravely weathering a harsh landscape,[141] or happily enjoying the opportunity to travel to such a new environment.[142] The title of the magazine, for example, encouraged an exoticisation of the landscape and revealed the troops' intimacy with sand and local animals, in particular camels, which were both sources of excitement and frustration.

In their submissions to the magazine, the UN troops reflected on the 'primitive' host country:

> Looking at the rolling downs, the fertile emerald fields and undulating countryside – now polluted with mines and the ravages of war – nothing much seems to have changed from the days of the Bible. The Shepherds and the sheep still emphasise the idyllic, pastoral peace; the donkey is still a convenient mode of conveyance; and Bedouins travel miles and miles of sandy tracks either on foot or on Camel back.[143]

In another instance in this edition, the author combined ancient myths with descriptions of the landscape as if they were real events, imbuing the environment with a greater sense of Orientalist fantasy:

> Heavy vehicles, jeeps, cars and nail-studded boots of UNEF soldiers roll and tread on streets and sands through mud villages and cities replete with Biblical history. Little does one realise that he may be on the very spot where Samson lost his strength. . .[144]

These 'exotic' conceptions of the landscape led to reports of troops mailing grains of sand from Sinai as souvenirs to their families at home, indicating the

[141] A particularly poetic instance of this martyring projection: 'There is a feel about the desert which only those who trod the soft sands know. The Sun beats pitilessly, sand particles sparkle in the light, the sand laden wind cuts into your flesh like sharp needle points. There is an eternal silence and loneliness accentuated by howling winds and endless contours of sand': BL, U.N.A.466., UN Public Information Office, *Sand Dune: The UNEF Weekly*, ed. 11, 8 May 1957, p. 1.

[142] BL, U.N.A.466., UN Public Information Office, *Sand Dune: The UNEF Weekly*, ed. 6, 3 April 1957, p. 2.

[143] BL, U.N.A.466., UN Public Information Office, *Sand Dune: The UNEF Weekly*, ed. 4 (Special Gaza Edition), 20 March 1957, p. 1.

[144] BL, U.N.A.466., UN Public Information Office, *Sand Dune: The UNEF Weekly*, ed. 4 (Special Gaza Edition), 20 March 1957, p. 1.

Figure 2.3 *Sand Dunes*, an early edition of *The Sand Dune* header with camel and sunset cartoon, UNA, S-1724-0000-0007.
Reproduced with permission from the UN Archives.

physical importance of the landscape to the troops' Orientalist fantasies of the region and their experience of peacekeeping.[145]

The magazine's descriptions of Sinai as a 'timeless' desert revealed troops judgements on the 'backwardness' of rural Egypt, placing the peacekeepers in – what they perceived – as a superior 'civilised' position. For the Scandinavian battalions in particular, the novelty of the hot landscape was greater than the troops whose home nations had similar climates or conditions, such as those from the Indian and Columbian battalions. This diversity in national experiences led to a piece in *The Sand Dune* which emphasised the challenge of the desert for the Scandinavian troops, highlighting the transnational range of personnel in UNEF and its cosmopolitanism. The piece compared the climate between their Scandinavian home region and Sinai, evolving into poetic analysis of the host country landscape's inhabitability and undesirability:

> There is no snow; no icey [sic] sheeted lakes; no forests of spruce and pine; no woods and jungles; no midnight sun. And that is what the Finns are used to. Sheram El Sheikh has bare rocks and sands on which the Sun beats pitilessly. There are big, bleak boulders without any vegetation except a few hardy, gnarled, pigmy shrubs. Lots of rats, many more flies, black and brown scorpions and plenty of sharks in the Gulf of Aqaba which touches the shores of Sheram el Sheikh. It's hot, very hot for the tall, fair, light-haired, blue-eyed Finnish soldiers.[146]

As part of an effort to exaggerate the sacrifice of the peacekeepers, lyrical descriptions of the environment reinforced negative political imaginaries of

[145] BL, U.N.A.466., UN Public Information Office, *Sand Dune: The UNEF Weekly*, ed. 2, 5 March 1957, p. 4.

[146] BL, U.N.A.466., UN Public Information Office, *Sand Dune: The UNEF Weekly*, ed. 8, 17 April 1957, p. 3.

the Arab world as paradoxically inferior to the troops' host countries despite their appreciation of its ancient heritage.

This 'othering' process encouraged troops to externalise themselves from the region and reinforce UNEF as temporary in their minds; they were only short-term visitors to the region and their commitment was thus limited. International relations scholars, such as Cynthia Enloe, have drawn attention to the consumptive and objectifying lens of international and national troops in foreign conflict spaces and targeted, in particular, towards local women.[147] During UNEF, troops visited Leave Centres in Cairo and Beirut and organised mission trips to belly-dancing performances and bars. These activities were included in UNEF's budget as Burns considered these recreations as 'necessary for the maintenance of morale and continued efficient operation of the Force'.[148] In one instance, a belly-dancer was employed for the farewell celebrations for the Norwegian battalion transfer at the UNEF headquarters in Abu Suweir:

> All Norwegian boys whistled, smiled and clapped. With the jiggling of breasts, the supple movements of the belly, the provocative hip flights, the sensual thrusts of arms and legs, appreciative roars [rose] the tent roofs. Only the Norwegian doctors were not happy. Their suspicion [sic] minds were not satisfied. Their intimate knowledge of feminine anatomy was jarred. But what suspicions when there is belly dancing ... The belly dancer was an Arab dressed as a woman...[149]

Local men and women became entangled in the heterosexual, hyper-masculine cultural activities and were 'consumed' as part of the mission's 'welfare' activities. This particular instance reveals the emasculation of Arab men and the eroticisation of the UNEF space. The troops' gender and participating in UNEF fed into perceptions of superiority and control within the peacekeeping troops. As Enloe writes about such heterosexual activities in conflict zones, 'Though he may think of himself as simply bolstering his own manly credentials, his attempts to compensate for his insecure, masculine identity help shape power relations between his country's military and the society it is supposed to be protecting.'[150] The peacekeeper identity in UNEF was informed and structured by Orientalist perceptions of the location, landscape, and population. UNEF's peacekeeping identity was thus *both* top-down and bottom-up in its development, reconstituted from transnational imaginaries and colonial-era cultural concepts whilst also developed from gendered experiences between the troops on the frontline.

[147] C. Enloe, *Bananas, Beaches and Bases: Making Feminist Sense of International Politics*, Second Edition (Oakland: University of California Press, 2014).

[148] UNA, S-0530-0011-0011, 'Letter from Burns to Malik, Minister for Lebanese Foreign Affairs', 20 April 1957.

[149] BL, U.N.A.466., UN Public Information Office, *Sand Dune: The UNEF Weekly*, ed. 8, 17 April 1957, p. 4.

[150] Enloe, *Bananas, Beaches and Bases*, p. 7.

Figure 2.4 First Israeli occupation of Gaza 1956–1957, 52983588HO039_gaza, 7 March 1957.
Reproduced with permission from GPO/Hulton Archive/Getty Images/Handout.

The Sand Dune was also an important vehicle for advancing the UN's liberal internationalist project. The publication framed the mission as an experiment in cosmopolitan operational collaboration. Bunche wrote in a draft booklet about UNEF that, despite 'differences in language, training methods, these men of UNEF joined together with great efficiency and carried out the task entrusted to them in a spirit that is truly that of the United Nations'.[151] The magazine provided a forum for troops to write in and verify the success of the UN project in practice by crafting an image of peacekeeping missions as a cosmopolitan utopia. It contained weekly updates on operational movements and efforts by all the battalions so troops could stay informed whilst deployed in a different region. UNEF hospitals became transnational spaces, and doctors regularly proudly commented on the international character of their wards on the ground.[152] The creation of international friendships became a popular feature of *The Sand Dune*. The results of football matches and chess games were included. The editors even

[151] UNA, S-0313-0002-12, 'Draft Introduction to Booklet on UNEF by Ralph J. Bunche', 24 May 1957.

[152] BL, U.N.A.466., UN Public Information Office, *Sand Dune: The UNEF Weekly*, ed. 3, 14 March 1957, p. 3.

created blank space on the back page for readers to record the score of their favourite teams from wherever they were stationed.[153] They also encouraged more battalions to create football teams, and, as language barriers remained a problem for many of the troops, sport soon provided a means for different nationalities to build relationships during their deployment.[154] Language problems were also overcome during the UNEF socials through the distribution of alcohol: 'All kinds of drinks were offered and some good speeches were made in all the languages. In spite of the different languages everybody understood each other, even before the drinks!'[155] Transnational gatherings helped to cement perceptions within UNEF that the mission was an 'authentic' force, gelling and performing like a traditional national army.

Troops shared the same base camps and patrolled alongside one another leading to cross-cultural interactions and relationships developing although the battalions remained in their national companies. For example, one Canadian soldier reportedly asked to remain in a position as he had built a friendship with some Indonesian troops at the same post. *The Sand Dune* reported that 'Canadian soldiers living in three desolate outposts in the Sinai with cheery Indonesian soldiers – despite language difficulties – have become good palls [sic]. One Canadian soldier requested that he be left at the outpost because, he said, he was learning Indonesian.'[156] Battalions were also mobilised due to these relationships as they travelled significant distances across demilitarised areas to compete in football matches against teams they had yet to meet naturally as neighbours on the Armistice Lines.[157] As the troops completed their operations, patrolled the borders, and played football, they exchanged imaginaries of the mission and the UN, developing their 'peacekeeper' identity through communication and comradeship with other national battalions. However, these battalions were subject to regular changes as troops were swapped back and forward from their home country. This created an odd form of permanence for some of the mission staff as relationships and understandings were forged, navigated, and broken on six-month cycles whilst the perpetuity of the mission remained a constant. Copies of *The Sand Dune* were retained to provide newer troops with information and entertainment

[153] BL, U.N.A.466., UN Public Information Office, *Sand Dune: The UNEF Weekly*, ed. 7, 10 April 1957, p. 1.

[154] BL, U.N.A.466., UN Public Information Office, *Sand Dune: The UNEF Weekly*, ed. 2, 5 March 1957, p. 4.

[155] BL, U.N.A.466., UN Public Information Office, *Sand Dune: The UNEF Weekly*, ed. 15, 7 June 1957, p. 4.

[156] BL, U.N.A.466., UN Public Information Office, *Sand Dune: The UNEF Weekly*, ed. 2, 5 March 1957, p. 4.

[157] BL, U.N.A.466., UN Public Information Office, *Sand Dune: The UNEF Weekly*, ed. 2, 5 March 1957, p. 3.

about their new deployment, educating them about the mission and shaping their understanding of being a UN peacekeeper.

The magazine also emphasised the efficacy of having different national troops under one international Force Commander. Towards the end of 1957, ceremonies to grant awards to Force Commander General Burns became a popular demonstration of the battalion's respect for the UN mission and its leadership. His first national award was from Sweden and Burns was reported as 'the first non-Swedish officer for many centuries to receive a sword from the Swedish army. . .'[158] Bunche complimented Burns on the receipt of the sword as a personal aside on a draft progress report, stating, 'The presentation to you of the Swedish sword was a fine and well-merited tribute'.[159] The Swedish sword symbolically verified the success of the UN authority over a diverse mission of national battalions and was swiftly followed by another 'sword of honour' from the Brazilian Minister of War.[160] During this ceremony, other UNEF Commanders and civilian officials were also presented with 'miniatures of the sword' whilst 'Lady Guests of the UNEF staff were presented with silver trays'.[161] *The Sand Dune*'s promotion of these diplomatic displays between national leaders and mission commanders suggested that the cosmopolitan vision between troops on the ground could also be translated to world politics and society.

The magazine's weekly editions characterised UNEF as critical to safeguarding world peace beyond their patrolling role in Egypt. Functionally, it maintained the ceasefire along the DL. But critically, it brought troops of different nations together and forged transnational connections between individuals. Troops regularly reported instances of cross-cultural relationships and field-based activities across national lines in *The Sand Dune*. Publishing small stories of friendships between battalions of different nations were entertaining for the reader, but also fulfilled a secondary function of exemplifying – and making real – an idealised portrayal of global diplomatic peace between all nations. The canal region itself had long held connotations of modernity in the eyes of Western observers who saw the innovation as a demonstration of globalisation and the economic future of imperial Europe.[162] The cosmopolitan collaboration within the international force echoed these globalised imaginaries as the transnational battalions worked together to ensure the

[158] BL, U.N.A.466., UN Public Information Office, *Sand Dune: The UNEF Weekly*, ed. 27, 30 August 1957, p. 4.

[159] UNA, S-0313-0001-01, 'Letter from Bunche to General Burns', 26 August 1957.

[160] BL, U.N.A.466., UN Public Information Office, *Sand Dune: The UNEF Weekly*, ed. 29, 13 September 1957, p. 5

[161] BL, U.N.A.466., UN Public Information Office, *Sand Dune: The UNEF Weekly*, ed. 29, 13 September 1957, p. 5.

[162] Haddad, 'Digging to India', pp. 363–396.

operationality of the canal. Through UNEF, the internationalist project was not only a positive step towards world peace, but it was also practically feasible whilst remaining within the nation-state paradigm.

By the spring of 1958, the UNEF mission was securely installed across the disputed borders. There was a permanency to the UNEF's presence by this point in the mission with some nations bringing in their third contingents for a six-month tour of duty.[163] Hammarskjöld reported the successful implementation of the ceasefire along the Armistice Lines to the General Assembly. Britain seconded the secretary-general during the plenary debate, commenting that 'there has been a notable and encouraging absence of incidents [where the United Nations Emergency Force has been in operation]'.[164] Bunche visited the UNEF troops in the Gaza Strip in mid-1959 and commented on his pride in the mission in a press release, further projecting an image of the UN as a confident, reactive, and expert authority in conflict response and resolution. He stated that, 'The United Nations Emergency Force, now in its third year in the Sinai Peninsula and the Gaza Strip, is probably the most extraordinary operation ever undertaken by the United Nations, and is certainly among the most successful...'[165] By 1959, the growing positive international perception of these early successes validated the 1956 'Uniting for Peace' resolution to expand the functions of the UN beyond those outlined in the UN Charter.

Conclusion

As the first armed peacekeeping mission, UNEF demonstrated that the nature of peacekeeping identity would be both 'top-down' and 'bottom-up', informed by both the messaging from its diplomatic headquarters *and* through the orientalist perceptions of the troops themselves. The geopolitical context drove Hammarskjöld to emphasise the 'moral' character of the force and the peacekeepers worked hard to build a cosmopolitan camaraderie on the ground. These dynamics fostered an inwards-facing mission and an 'othering' relationship with the local population that would be replicated in subsequent missions. Whilst UNEF demonstrated the UN's adaptation to new cosmopolitan imaginaries of transnational cooperation and cross-cultural exchange, the force also replicated Orientalist thinking and justified the continued presence of hegemonic states, such as Britain, and new imperialist powers, like Israel, in ex-colonial territories.

163 BNA, FO 371/134302/VR.1082/6, 'Telegram between Canadian Ambassador in Cairo and Secretary of State in Ottawa', 2 April 1958.

164 BNA, FO 371/129792/UN.1117/108, 'Telegram from New York to Foreign Office: Text of Minister of State for Foreign Affairs' Speech in Today's Plenary Debate', 22 November 1957.

165 UNA, S-0316-0010-01, 'UN Press Release: Dr Bunche Leaves Gaza for Jerusalem, EMF/289', 29 April 1959.

Ultimately, UNEF reflected the shifting place of the UN in the post-war world, as European empires fractured and collapsed in the wake of the new international order. The geopolitical and organisational stakes of the Suez crisis were potentially explosive in November 1956. Hammarskjöld was deeply upset and on the verge of resignation, the US government was insecure about the future of its diplomatic relationship with Britain, and the Afro-Asian bloc nations were questioning the very value of the institution itself. However, UNEF provided a confident beginning in, what would become, a series of post-colonial territorial conflicts inviting a 'stabilising' intervention from an armed UN peacekeeping force. Post-Suez, there was a significant uptake in nations achieving independence from European colonial powers, such as Ghana in 1957 and Guinea in 1958. Nationalist movements and geopolitical transformations within the Global South ignited Cold War anxieties for Western diplomats, especially those in Washington, who worried that these newly independent nations could be vulnerable to communism.[166] However, peacekeeping now offered an alternative to conflict resolution that could pursue anticommunist aims with a peacebuilding guise.

Within diplomatic circles, UNEF had proved its sceptics wrong. Its deployment in Sinai and Gaza demonstrated the value of an international, multilateral peacekeeping function for the de-escalation and resolution of a territorial crisis. The mission leadership reframed UNEF's continued presence on the ground as a demonstration of the value of the UN peacekeeping project, rather than as evidence of the unfinished conflict between Israel and Egypt and the ongoing violence of international interference in the region. The priority, for international observers, was that UNEF had reduced violence in a conflict that could have witnessed a Soviet invasion. UNEF had earned the UN Secretariat immense reputational credit and galvanised public support for UN peacekeeping. Hammarskjöld would soon test that trust on a much larger mission.

[166] J. Kent, 'The United States and the Decolonization of Black Africa, 1945–1963', in D. Ryan and V. Pungong (eds.), *The United States and Decolonization: Power and Freedom* (Abingdon: Springer, 2000), p. 169.

3

Imperial Aspirations, 1960–1961

Introduction: Paternalism and Violence in Congo

The UN Security Council authorised the *Opération des Nations Unies au Congo* (ONUC) a fortnight after thirteen million Congolese achieved independence from Belgium on 30 June 1960.[1] Within days of Independence Day celebrations, the Congolese Prime Minister Patrice Lumumba and President Joseph Kasavubu called upon the UN secretary-general to militarily intervene following the escalation of tensions and violence across the country. This instability was the result of a rebellion of sections of the Congolese Army against their white Belgian officers and the subsequent illegal intervention of Belgian troops in Congolese sovereignty. Belgium's military intervention further antagonised the citizens of the recently independent state, prompting an exodus of Belgian settlers from the country.[2] The evacuation created a personnel vacuum as Belgian colonial administrators had been running most governmental and infrastructural departments during the transition period, threatening core facilities such as food distribution, radio stations, power stations, water and sanitation services, and air traffic control.[3] A fortnight following independence, there was no stable handover to Congolese control but an immediate loss of skilled personnel and institutional memory, prompting a crisis in governance. The conflict expanded to global proportions as imperial economic interests in the mining regions combined with Cold War geopolitical rivalries and undermined Congo's existence as a unified nation.

This violent instability and administrative collapse became popularly known as the 'Congo crisis' in the media and UN debates as the international community called for a UN-led intervention.[4] As the secretary-general

[1] UN Doc, S/4387, 'United Nations Security Council Resolution 143', 14 July 1960.

[2] H. Gilroy, 'Belgium Ignores Congo on Troops', *The New York Times*, 14 July 1960.

[3] UN Doc, S/4389, 'First Report by the Secretary-General on the Implementation of Security Council Resolution S/4387 of 14 July 1960', p. 10; UN Doc, S/4531, 'First Progress Report to the Secretary General, from His Special Representative in the Congo, Ambassador Rajeshwar Dayal', p. 16.

[4] H. Gilroy, 'The Congo Crisis as the Belgians See I', *The New York Times*, 17 July 1960.

hurriedly negotiated the national contingents for the Congo mission, Secretariat leadership also innovated peacekeeping practices by assembling a large-scale civilian presence to manage Congolese governance and infrastructure in the aftermath of the post-independence handover crisis. Ralph Bunche articulated this dual mandate of military and civilian administration to the deployed ONUC staff in July 1960: 'You are here to pacify and then to administer the Congo'.[5] UN Security Council debates on the Congo crisis and the subsequent construction of the ONUC mandate intersected with the economic and diplomatic interests of multiple nations, including the Cold War superpowers, Britain, and the Afro-Asian bloc. The ONUC mission also served the organisational aims of the UN Secretariat staff by providing an opportunity for the UN to demonstrate its value in establishing and maintaining military *and* civilian order during a rapidly escalating conflict.[6] The ONUC mission benefited from the reputation of the UNEF mission which was perceived to have successfully de-escalated the violence in Suez and re-stabilised the Sinai and Gaza regions.[7] However, the UNEF mission was dwarfed by the operations mandated for the ONUC mission, and the Congo crisis presented an administrative and military challenge that would test the operational and diplomatic dexterity of UN peacekeeping personnel.

Focusing on UN imaginaries of the mission, this chapter investigates the state-building aspirations of the ONUC mission staff during the first phase of the Congo mission, tracing the UN operations from its confident beginnings in July 1960 to its humbled second phase in September 1961. ONUC was the largest UN peacekeeping mission during the Cold War period with at its height over twenty thousand UN-employed staff on the ground; a transnational mix of troops, military officers, civilian personnel, politicians, and technicians.[8] As Winifred Tickner, wife of UN representative Fred Tickner, wrote in her diary, 'At United Nations HQ in New York, a breeze of expectancy swept through the Secretariat Building', indicating the prevailing feelings of member-state delegates and UN staff at the prospect of launching another armed peacekeeping mission.[9] However, the deployment of ONUC also came with significant reputational risk. The mission staff were severely disorganised

[5] H. Tanner, 'U.N. IN CONGO: Some Resentment Found among Congolese at World Agency's Large Role', *The New York Times*, 31 July 1960.

[6] A. O'Malley, *The Diplomacy of Decolonisation: America, Britain and the United Nations during the Congo Crisis 1960–1964* (Manchester: Manchester University Press, 2018).

[7] BNA, FO 371/134302/VR.1082/6, 'Telegram between Canadian Ambassador in Cairo and Secretary of State in Ottawa', 2 April 1958.

[8] UN, 'Republic of the Congo – ONUC: Background', available at: www.un.org/Depts/DPKO/Missions/onucB.htm#Establishment.

[9] BL, MS. Eng. c. 4704, Special Collections United Nations Career Records Project, Winifred Tickner, fol 132, *A Spectator in the Congo. Memories from the Diary of an Onlooker at the Violent Birth of the Democratic Republic of the Congo*, p. 7.

during ONUC's early months, as *The New York Times* reported 'the civilian staff . . . mushroomed so fast that nobody either inside or outside the organisation is able to tell exactly how many there are, who is here and what he is doing'.[10] Knowledge of this incompetence could threaten to undermine the reputational credit that the organisation had won during the first years of UNEF. In December 1960, James Pitman MP stated in the House of Commons that:

> In this Congo case, however, there is a new situation which we seem to fail to realise is a usurpation by the United Nations of the authority of the local national government. This is a tremendous danger because this new development could involve the very survival of the United Nations.[11]

The international interests in the crisis heightened expectations of the UN mission; all eyes were on Leopoldville, the capital of Congo, in July 1960.

Post-colonial State Formation and Belgian Interference

In the months before the conflict erupted, European anxieties surrounded Congolese politicians' plans for decolonisation as they feared the potential destabilisation of central Africa if a power vacuum was exposed in June 1960. Following failed Belgian-controlled elections and a series of riots in November 1959,[12] a Congolese alliance of political groups and tribal representatives, including Kasavubu and Lumumba, arrived in Brussels for the Belgo-Congolese Round Table Conferences in January 1960 to negotiate Congolese self-governance. Within five days of the conference beginning, the representatives had agreed a date for Congolese independence: 30 June 1960.[13] The speed of Belgo-Congolese negotiations for Congolese independence left little time for meaningful preparations to ensure a smooth post-colonial transition to Congolese autonomy and administration, neglecting to fully acknowledge the pervasive roots of settler colonialism in the country and the implications this would have for the Congolese infrastructure and population post-independence. The Belgian government used the talks to shore up their economic interests in the territory with an intention (although little idea of

[10] Tanner, 'U.N. IN CONGO'.

[11] UNA, S-0845-0001-02-00001, I. J. Pitman, 'House of Commons Speech: United Nations, the Congo and a World Security Authority', Wednesday, 21 December 1960, p. 7.

[12] '24 KILLED IN RIOT IN BELGIAN CONGO: Troops Sent to Stanleyville to Quell Outbreak Laid to African Nationalists', *The New York Times*, 1 November 1959.

[13] P. Lumumba, 'Statement at the Closing Session of the Belgo-Congolese Round Table Conference', 20 February 1960, available at: www.marxists.org/subject/africa/lumumba/1960/02/statement.html.

how) to extend de facto rule over the nation post-independence.[14] As Crawford Young has argued, the political future of the nation, 'surged . . . on a tide over which neither the coloniser nor the colonised had much control'.[15]

Whilst Belgians in Congo were anxious to maintain legal and political authority over the Congolese natural resources, the Belgian representatives in Brussels were privately confident that independence would be in name only; the act of supporting Congolese nationalism would be a gamble or *le pari congolais* (the Congolese bet).[16] David Gibbs has shown that the Belgian government had strong economic and military incentives to retain its influence over the country post-independence.[17] Indeed, the Belgian government continued to renovate its military bases in May 1960 and dedicate funds to improving these facilities despite the agreed date for Congolese independence.[18] The efforts of the Belgian government to performatively support independence reassured the new Congolese leaders and encouraged them to permit Belgian social, financial, and military 'assistance and cooperation', as outlined in the Treaty of Friendship between Belgium and the Congo.[19] The diplomatic understanding between the parties and the terms of the Treaty allayed Congolese suspicions and bolstered Belgian neoimperial hopes for continued resource extraction and military occupation post-independence.

In the months following the Round Table agreement, Ralph Bunche visited Belgium as the first stop on his longer journey to Congo, where he would attend Independence Day celebrations and provide consultation on post-colonial administrative organisation. Since Bunche's appointment to head of the UN Trusteeship Division in 1946, he had pursued a policy of tutelage towards colonised populations, believing that – although the colonial state was an exploitative and extractive system – imperialist governments could be transformed into instruments for the 'modernisation' and 'advancement' of colonised African populations that were deemed as not yet ready for self-governance or independence.[20] His elite perspective on colonisation and self-determination for Africans was developed further during his role as the architect UN trusteeships and informed his approach to peacekeeping and post-colonial territorial disputes; for Bunche, (ex)imperial administrations in

[14] D. Gibbs, *The Political Economy of Third World Intervention: Mines, Money, and U.S. Policy in the Congo Crisis* (Chicago: University of Chicago Press, 1991), p. 78.

[15] C. Young, *Politics in Congo: Decolonization and Independence* (Princeton: Princeton University Press, 2015), p. 4.

[16] Young, *Politics in Congo*, p. 4.

[17] Gibbs, *The Political Economy of Third World Intervention*, p. 78.

[18] Gibbs, *The Political Economy of Third World Intervention*, p. 78.

[19] *United Nations Peacekeeping in the Congo: 1960–1964: Appendices* (Washington: Brookings Institution, 1966), Appendix C.

[20] C. P. Henry, *Ralph Bunche: Model Negro or American Other?* (New York: NYU Press, 1999), p. 247.

Africa could, and indeed should, be used in the tutelage of (post)colonial populations in their process of 'becoming' a 'civilised' nation.[21] His later appointment as under-secretary-general for special political affairs in 1957 gave him lead responsibility for UN peacekeeping missions and international security, directing the organisation on issues of decolonisation and human rights from the New York UN headquarters. As part of this new role, he would regularly visit the field to inspect peacekeeping operations and discuss the political context with the mid-level UN staff on the ground, providing advice on mediation and conflict resolution based on his experiences of the Arab–Israeli conflict and UNEF. This intermediary position between the UN Secretariat and the operational level in the field cultivated an internal organisational hierarchy that encouraged a filtering of field-based knowledge; this devolved dynamic evolved out of the headquarters staff's confidence in the expertise of those deployed under a UN flag.

Once he had arrived in Brussels, Bunche immediately witnessed the Belgian politicians behaving contemptuously towards visiting Congolese politicians and community leaders. Although the Round Table talks had been 'peaceful and friendly', as Lumumba noted in his official speech, in informal settings the mask slipped and revealed the racist attitudes of those who had just helped to facilitate the nation's independence.[22] Bunche attended meetings in Brussels on 25 June before flying to Leopoldville for the independence celebrations, meeting with several Congolese and Belgian representatives during his trip. Bunche's visit was intended to build upon the relationships developed during Hammarskjöld's earlier trip to Congo in January 1960 and to further embed UN officials in the process of shaping a 'modern', independent Congo.[23] In Leopoldville, Bunche wrote an informal, tipsy letter to Hammarskjöld to complain about 'the banter back and forth across the table between the Belgian officials in the presence of several Congolese, in the most outmoded paternalistic and condescending tone', stating that it 'was downright embarrassing', although he does not mention correcting or chastising any of the officials, publicly or privately.[24] These glimpses of Belgian politicians' behaviour towards Congolese politicians, witnessed by a UN representative, confirmed the ongoing racist attitudes of the Belgians despite the ostensible

[21] Bunche quote cited in W. Ofuatey-Kodjoe, 'Ralph Bunche: An African Perspective', in B. Rivlin (ed.), *Ralph Bunche: The Man and His Times* (New York: Holmes & Meier, 1990), pp. 98–102.

[22] Lumumba, 'Statement at the Closing Session of the Belgo-Congolese Round Table Conference'.

[23] E. Muschik, *Building States: The United Nations, Development, and Decolonization, 1945–1965* (New York: Columbia University Press, 2022), p. 224.

[24] UNA, S-1069-0012-11, 'Letter from Ralph Bunche to Dag Hammarskjöld from Leopoldville', Monday, 27 June 1960.

equality of the political representatives. The withdrawing power seemed convinced of its ability to covertly retain its influence despite the loss of its official authority marked for 30 June 1960.

Bunche was also made aware of a 'seriously threatening situation' in Katanga during his pre-Independence Day visit.[25] Disagreements between the Belgian diplomats in Brussels and mining businessmen based in Katanga, the mineral-rich southern province, over Congolese governance sparked hostility. Katanga-based Belgians were concerned over the speed of independence, and these fears were compounded further by the realisation that there was no established plan for the future of the mining company *Union Minière du Haut Katanga* (or, *Union Minière*) post-independence. Belgians working for Union Minière took umbrage with their exclusion from the Round Table conferences, highlighting how the Belgian representatives in attendance were solely government ministers and advisors who had spent little, if any, time in Congo and were, therefore, perceived as detached from the reality on the ground. Katanga-based Belgians mockingly described the Brussels politicians as 'Dry-season pilgrims'.[26] Endeavouring to protect the company's interests and profits, the funds that Union Minière had marked for tax were instead transferred to Katangan leader Moise Tshombe in the hopes of stoking a secession movement following independence.[27] As Wolf Radmann has uncovered in his research on Union Minière, 'the new, independent Congo would become automatically the most important single shareholder of [Union Minière] without any decree of nationalisation and without paying any indemnity'.[28] In the eyes of those running Union Minière, this would be an unjust economic benefit for the new Congolese government. During these pre-independence months, Union Minière's leaders financially supported and prepared the nascent Katangan secessionist movement to maintain their resource extraction and profit in Central Africa regardless of the decolonisation of the central Congolese government. Bunche's awareness of Belgium's complex involvement in Katanga and the plans to secede from post-independence Congo in June 1960 was limited but extant.[29] Hammarskjöld's future decision to define the Katangan crisis as an internal political issue, and thus

[25] UNA, S-1069-0012-11, 'Letter from Ralph Bunche to Dag Hammarskjöld from Leopoldville', Monday, 27 June 1960.

[26] D. van Reybrouck, *Congo: The Epic History of a People* (London: Harper Collins, 2015), p. 256.

[27] G. Vanthemsche, *Belgium and the Congo, 1885–1980* (Cambridge: Cambridge University Press, 2012), p. 210.

[28] W. Radmann, 'The Nationalization of Zaire's Copper: From Union Minière to Gecamines', *Africa Today*, 25:4 (1978), p. 29.

[29] Awareness was also building within the international media; see H. Gilroy, 'The Congo: Problems of Independence: Struggle for Control of Belgian Colony grows amid Regional and Tribal Controversy', *The New York Times*, 19 June 1960.

outside the mission's mandate, omitted Bunche's discoveries from his June visit in order to defend ONUC's lack of engagement with Belgium's participation in – and financing of – the Katangan secessionist movement.[30]

Businessmen within Union Minière and a number of evacuating colonial administrators united in the goal of disturbing the process of independence directly from within Congo.[31] Many remaining Belgian colonists sought to destabilise the impending independence process by intervening in Congolese attempts to prepare for the transition to independence. For instance, colonist Belgians 'out of spite' destroyed all technical blueprints and instruction manuals for many of the government buildings and facilities in Leopoldville in the weeks before independence.[32] ONUC Chief of Civilian Operations Šture Linnér argued this scorched earth policy was 'crucial' to the subsequent collapse of law and order following independence as the country was left without documentation of its own equipment or employees.[33] Obstruction by Belgians based in Congo aimed to encourage instability and thus substantiate racist Western predictions of Africans' inability to self-govern, intensifying the administrative chaos.[34]

The political volatility in Congo grew as Independence Day approached, and Lumumba and Kasavubu's alliance became tenuous. The two men worked in coalition for the independence of the nation and the establishment of *loi fondamentale*, the draft constitution, during the negotiations with the Belgian government. Alongside fellow Congolese politicians, including future Katangan secessionist leader Tshombe, Kasavubu, and Lumumba attended the Belgo-Congolese Round Table Conferences as leaders of their respective parties, *Alliance des Bakongo* (ABAKO) and *Mouvement National Congolais-Lumumba* (MNC-L). However, the partnership between the two appeared to weaken to those around them as their political visions for post-colonial Congo diverged. Unfortunately, as Redie Bereketeab has highlighted, 'The first feature of the Congo crisis was the failure of the [*loi fondamentale*] to define adequately the division of powers within the executive branch', meaning that 'both the president and the prime minister could dismiss one another with a majority vote in the parliament'.[35] This oversight would soon undermine

[30] T. F. Brady, 'Lumumba Angered by Use of Whites as Katanga Force: Assails Hammarskjöld Stand that U.N. Will Not Help to Subdue Secessionists', *The New York Times*, 14 August 1960.

[31] J. Kent, 'The Neo-colonialism of Decolonisation: Katangan Secession and the Bringing of the Cold War to the Congo', *The Journal of Imperial and Commonwealth History*, 45:1 (2017), p. 96.

[32] Š. Linnér, 'Interview Transcript', *Yale-UN Oral History Project*, 8 November 1990, p. 9.

[33] Linnér, 'Interview Transcript', p. 9.

[34] Linnér, 'Interview Transcript', p. 8.

[35] R. Bereketeab, *Self-Determination and Secession in Africa: The Post-Colonial State* (Abingdon: Taylor and Francis, 2014), p. 171.

their alliance and provoke a power struggle for the position of Congolese Head of State. In his hastily scribbled letter to Hammarskjöld, Bunche emphasised his concern about the 'temporary relief' of the coalition between the incoming President and Prime Minister.[36] He perceived their relations as 'strained, even hostile…', noting that they 'studiously ignore each other, exchange no words beyond those absolutely necessary and, through their cohorts, at times openly squabble about protocol precedence. The compromise that makes a government here possible is almost certainly a temporary one'.[37] The biggest point of division appeared to be 'Lumumba's desire to change the Constitution so as to assume full power [over the Congolese parliament] and Kasavubu's resistance to this', which Bunche believed would provoke a 'showdown'.[38] It appeared that the united front presented by the two men during the Round Table conferences had dissolved in the face of the practicalities and external pressures of post-colonial governance.

Bunche's opinions would, following the deployment of the mission, become integral to the construction of the future ONUC mandate and bureaucracy. Bunche noted that Kasavubu 'is friendly and by reputation a man of integrity…' although 'not an impressive personality'.[39] Bunche was also pleased to hear the incoming President give a 'strong endorsement of the UN' at his oath ceremony in the joint session of Congolese parliament on 27 June and suggested that Kasavubu's intention for Congo to seek membership of the UN indicated that 'Kasa-Vubu [sic] has matured into true nationalist thinking'.[40] Bunche was present to advise the new government, but he was also in the country to see that the future Congo would be led by a politician who would neatly fit into the UN's nation-state paradigm. Bunche's conceptions of the incoming Prime Minister Lumumba were largely determined by the rumours and impressions of those around him, such as Belgian ministers Ganshof van der Meersch and August Edmond de Schryver. He spent significantly less time in the company of Lumumba during his first weeks in Congo in June than he did with Kasavubu and his allies. Bunche reported to Hammarskjöld that 'Everyone agrees that Lumumba is quick and politically agile, but he is obviously young and untried and many consider him lacking in integrity, this being based mainly on his conviction for embezzlement when he

36 UNA, S-1069-0012-11, 'Letter from Ralph Bunche to Dag Hammarskjöld from Leopoldville', Monday, 27 June 1960.

37 UNA, S-1069-0012-11, 'Letter-Report from Dr. Ralph Bunche to Dag Hammarskjöld from Leopoldville', 4 July 1960.

38 UNA, S-1069-0012-11, 'Letter from Bunche to Hammarskjöld', 27 June 1960.

39 UNA, S-1069-0012-11, 'Letter-Report from Bunche to Hammarskjöld', 4 July 1960.

40 UNA, S-1069-0012-11, 'Letter from Bunche to Hammarskjöld', 27 June 1960.

was in the post office'.[41] Although he heard from van der Meersch that Lumumba had 'met his first test' of a 'seriously threatening situation in Katanga' over the past weekend 'with strength, wisdom and decisiveness',[42] Bunche remained suspicious of Lumumba's capabilities and trustworthiness in office.[43] Lumumba appeared to him as a 'man of plural faces', 'the most recent version of God's angry young man', and was already indicating concerns about the 'suspect sources' of Lumumba's campaign funds and rumours of connection to Moscow.[44] Although he had no proof for these accusations, these internal communications between Bunche and Hammarskjöld, pre-ONUC, reveal the ease with which Bunche accepted and escalated negative rumours about the democratically elected Prime Minister.

Lumumba's Independence Day speech at celebrations in late June further intensified Bunche's concerns about the Prime Minister. During the celebrations at the *Palais de la Nation* in Leopoldville, the Belgian King Baudouin III opened the independence ceremony with a boastful speech chronicling the 'genius' of the Belgian colonial system. *The Guardian* reported that the speech 'contained no apologies for the colonial system, but was instead intended as a vindication of it'.[45] In a letter to Hammarskjöld, Bunche reported it as 'maladroit and ill-advised to say the least'.[46] Of Lumumba, special assistant to Bunche, F. T. Liu recalled how, in response to Baudouin:

> Lumumba rose and he made a hard speech, fierce. He started with the history of the Congo; he recalled the very cruel way Leopold II [. . .] had treated the Congolese. They were cutting their arms sometimes when they didn't pay the tax, and so on. A very harsh speech.[47]

Lumumba's speech was particularly ill-received by Bunche, who described it as an 'acid, hard-hitting anti-colonial speech' and wrote that '[Lumumba] overdid it, especially with regard to his emphasis on the great struggle waged by the Congolese for their independence. To the contrary, of course, it [independence] came to them easily and swiftly on the wings of Belgian panic. . .'[48] Bunche felt that the Congolese population had achieved independence

41 UNA, S-1069-0012-11, 'Letter from Bunche to Hammarskjöld', 27 June 1960.

42 This 'serious incident' was a result of the Katangan leader Tshombe's, reaction to the composition of the central government in the week before independence. For more details, see R. Lamarchand, 'The Limits of Self-Determination: The Case of the Katangan Secession', *The American Political Science Review*, 56:2 (1962), p. 414.

43 UNA, S-1069-0012-11, 'Letter from Bunche to Hammarskjöld', 27 June 1960.

44 UNA, S-1069-0012-11, 'Letter-Report from Bunche to Hammarskjöld', 4 July 1960.

45 'Marred: M. Lumumba's offensive speech in King's presence', *The Guardian*, 1 June 1960.

46 UNA, S-1069-0012-11, 'Letter-Report from Bunche to Hammarskjöld', 4 July 1960.

47 'The Congo Crisis / F.T. Liu; Interviewer, Sutterlin', *Yale-UN Oral History Project*, 23 March 1990, p. 9.

48 UNA, S-1069-0012-11, 'Letter-Report from Bunche to Hammarskjöld', 4 July 1960.

relatively easily and that it was 'ungracious' of the Prime Minister to 'make big political capital by lambasting the departing masters'.[49] Similarly, a number of leading Western newspapers, shocked by Lumumba's 'ungrateful' tone, led with the 'pugnacious' speech in their reporting.[50] Indeed, the economic impact of Lumumba's speech was visible through a decline in Union Minère's share prices.[51] Bunche sent these impressions to the Secretariat in New York. His early senses of the Prime Minister further prejudiced the UN leadership against Lumumba and reinforced racist conceptions of the African nationalist as an 'angry young man' rather than a credible, elected political leader who was entirely justified in his criticism of Belgian colonists' violent rule over Congo..

Four days after the independence ceremony, twenty-five thousand Congolese soldiers mutinied from the Congolese army (previously known as the *Force Publique* and recently renamed *Armée Nationale Congolaise* or ANC). The mutiny erupted in Thysville (a western region of Congo) in response to Belgian officers' insistence that independence would not affect the ANC and that there would be no 'africanisation' process for the officer cadres. To emphasise this, ANC Commander General Janssens wrote on a blackboard in a meeting with ANC personnel: 'before independence = after independence'.[52] Putting the *le pari congolais* in practice, the Belgian leadership in the ANC attempted to ignore the independence process and continue running the military as a colonial system. As Kevin Spooner has argued, 'Janssens was typical of many Belgians who fully expected that nothing, if anything, would be changed by independence'.[53] Reports of violence and attacks on Belgian settlers rapidly spread and prompted the panicked flight of thousands of Belgian doctors, technicians, scientists, missionaries, and teachers, or 'isolated whites', from the 'feverish' violence throughout July.[54] *The New York Times* reported on Belgian 'refugees' being 'liberated' from 'Africans' the Ruanda-Urundi border.[55] This exodus created a professional vacuum and infrastructural chaos in the Congolese civil service and technical services. However, much of the purported violence against Europeans (or

49 UNA, S-1069-0012-11, 'Letter-Report from Bunche to Hammarskjöld', 4 July 1960.

50 For example H. Gilroy, 'Lumumba Assails Colonialism as Congo Is Freed', *The New York Times*, 1 July 1960; 'Marred: M. Lumumba's Offensive Speech in King's Presence'.

51 'Dispute over Lumumba's Insult to Belgium Shakes Congo Cabinet', *The Washington Post*, 2 July 1960.

52 K. Spooner, *Canada, the Congo Crisis, and UN Peacekeeping, 1960–64* (Vancouver: UBC Press, 2010), p. 27.

53 Spooner, *Canada, the Congo Crisis, and UN Peacekeeping, 1960–64*, p. 27.

54 S. Cloete and T. Spencer, 'White Men Flee in Terror from Chaos of the Congo: Fear, Sorrow and Farewells and End of Era with Threat of the Jungle Taking Over, but from U.N. Resolute Step', *LIFE Magazine*, 1 August 1960, vol 49, no 5, pp. 10–17.

55 'Belgium's Forces Fight Congolese to Quell Risings', *The New York Times*, 11 July 1960.

'whites') was widely considered to have been exaggerated and a product of racism, as UN official Brian Urquhart has himself admitted.[56] Looting was widespread in some Congolese cities, and there were instances where European settlers were held hostage, but the reality on the ground was far from the frenzied reports of extreme violence and murder.

Indeed, the violence rapidly escalated following the Belgian government's intervention to quash the rioting and 'anarchy' of the mutiny. The Belgian government deployed eight hundred paratroopers and commandos across Congo on 10 July.[57] As the ANC soldiers fought against the invading Belgian forces, the numbers of deaths grew – especially for Congolese soldiers.[58] Lumumba and Kasavubu flew to different regions of Congo to attempt to pacify the mutiny and call for peace, but the Belgian intervention reinvigorated fears of re-colonisation, provoking greater violence and the breakdown of law and order. On 14 July in the Security Council, the Belgian representative resisted accusations of violating Article 2(4) of the UN Charter (prohibiting the use of force against another state) and justified his government's military invasion as a 'humanitarian' intervention, 'with the sole purpose of ensuring the safety of European and other members of the population and of protecting human lives in general'.[59] In the same week, Moise Tshombe attempted to take advantage of the preoccupied Congolese government and declared the Katangan region was seceding, declaring his support for the Belgian's intervention.[60] The military invasion, Katangan secession, and rhetoric of a humanitarian intervention all illustrated the Belgian government's intention of maintaining economic interests and military control on the ground in Congo in violation of the Treaty of Friendship.[61]

Using a crude version of the 'unwilling or unable' international law doctrine,[62] the Belgian government argued that its 'humanitarian' intervention

[56] B. Urquhart, *Hammarskjold* (New York: Knopf, 1972), pp. 402–403.

[57] 'Belgium's Forces Fight Congolese to Quell Risings'.

[58] 'Belgium's Forces Fight Congolese to Quell Risings'.

[59] UN Doc, S/PV.873, 'United Nations Security Council Official Records, 13/14 July 1960', p. 34.

[60] For more on the Katanga secession, see R. M. Irwin, 'Sovereignty in the Congo Crisis', in L. James and E. Leake (eds.), *Decolonization and the Cold War: Negotiating Independence* (London: Bloomsbury, 2015), pp. 203–218; R. Declercq, '"From Cape to Katanga": South African Expansionism, White Settlers and the Congo (1910–1963)', *South African Historical Journal*, 72:4 (2020), pp. 604–626.

[61] M. Tudor, '"The Re-establishment of Satisfactory Conditions in the Congo": Examining the UN's Response to the Belgian Military Intervention in July 1960', *The King's Student Law Review and Strife Journal*, Issue I (2018), pp. 1–13.

[62] This refers to the self-defence doctrine in international law (referring to Article 51 of the UN Charter) whereby a state is permitted to intervene in the territory of another sovereign state that is 'unwilling or unable' to police non-state actor violence or aggression that is based within its borders.

was necessary because they had deemed the Congolese government 'unable' to control the violence of the ANC against European settlers. If accepted by the international community, this would recast the Belgian intervention as self-defence rather than an explicit breach of Congolese sovereignty. European colonial powers with vested interests in Congolese mining companies dominated the debate and shifted the narrative from a breach of sovereignty to the incompetence of an independent African government, deemed unable to stabilise their nation. Stuart Cloete, a reporter for Life *Magazine*, reinforced this racist argument, writing:

> The Congo was a black giant whose bones, sinews and nerves were white. Now, unsupported by the bone, the nerves destroyed, the sinews cut, the giant has collapsed and lies writhing in the jungle from which he had almost risen. The effort was too much for him.[63]

This narrative burdened the Congolese government with the responsibility of satisfying the Belgian government (and their allies within the international community and media) with the safety of the territory *before* Brussels would agree to withdraw its invading troops. Echoing the manipulative techniques of the British government during the Suez crisis, Belgium used its occupying presence on the ground as a position of authority. The Belgians were free to move the goalposts in terms of defining 'security' in Congo as they wished.

The Cold War context intensified Belgium's interests in retaining control over natural resources in central and southern Africa, building upon its prior efforts to thwart Hitler's acquisition of Congolese uranium ore.[64] With rumours circulating about Lumumba's links to the Soviet government, many Western nations were economically and ideologically invested in 'protecting' Congolese natural resources from Communists.[65] Bunche repeatedly complained in his personal reports to Hammarskjöld that Congolese actors, especially Tshombe, did not recognise the international implications of this conflict, including the potential regional destabilisation.[66] The Congo revolution had inspired leftist activists across the globe, catalysing existing movements and forging new international connections between students and political groups.[67] European colonial governments, particularly the British

[63] Cloete and Spencer, 'White Men Flee in Terror from Chaos of the Congo', p. 14.

[64] S. Williams, *Spies in the Congo: The Race for the Ore that Built the Atomic Bomb* (London: Hurst, 2016).

[65] UN Doc, S/4557, 'Second Progress Report to the Secretary-General', p. 50.

[66] UNA, S-0845-0001-03-00001, Cable from Ralph Bunche to Dag Hammarskjöld, 'Report from Elizabethville, Katanga, 4 August, 1960', p. 14.

[67] P. Monaville, 'Making a "Second Vietnam": The Congolese Revolution and Its Global Connections in the 1960s', in C. Jian et al. (eds.), *The Routledge Handbook of the Global Sixties: Between Protest and Nation-Building* (London: Routledge, 2018); L. Passemiers, *Decolonisation and Regional Geopolitics: South Africa and the 'Congo Crisis', 1960–1965*

government, feared the 'domino effect' of decolonisation as a threat both to international security and political stability across the continent and beyond.[68] Robert Vitalis has revealed fears of a 'race war' during this period within elite Western circles, unearthing concerns that aid or military support to decolonising states could support Black aggression against whites. He has argued that these race fears combined with anxieties of Soviet expansion, stating that 'Issues of *Foreign Affairs* in the 1950s and 1960s include matter-of-fact descriptions of the hatred for whites that drives decolonization and the psychological impairments that communists so masterfully exploit.'[69] These racist anxieties underpinned the Belgian intervention in June and continued to shape international reporting on the crisis throughout its duration.

Congo's decolonisation also presented an opportunity for superpower interference violence in the nation's neighbours.[70] For instance, Alan James's work on the British government's reaction to the Congo crisis has argued that British foreign policy decisions were driven by fears of how Congolese independence would bolster anti-colonial activism within neighbouring populations colonised by Britain.[71] These colonial powers' anxieties about the potential violence and loss of income brought on by decolonisation plans caused further instability within the central region of Africa once European mining companies began to react defensively to protect their access to African natural resources and labour.[72] Within the UN, Bunche was anxious about Lumumba's Soviet connections and the 'domino effect' too. He stressed to Hammarskjöld the need for the UN to prevent the crisis from becoming 'another Korea' and engulfing the Cold War superpowers.[73] Liu also shared these fears: 'The country had collapsed and if nothing was done, there would be a power vacuum which could very well lead to a major world crisis involving the direct involvement of the two major superpowers.'[74]

(Abingdon: Routledge, 2020); B. Marmon, 'Operation Refugee: The Congo Crisis and the End of Humanitarian Imperialism in Southern Rhodesia, 1960', *Cold War History*, 22:2 (2021), 131–152.

68 A. James, *Britain and the Congo Crisis, 1960–1963* (New York: Springer, 1996); R. Hyam, *Britain's Declining Empire: The Road to Decolonisation, 1918–1968* (Cambridge: Cambridge University Press, 2007).

69 R. Vitalis, *White World Order, Black Power Politics: The Birth of American International Relations* (Ithaca: Cornell University Press, 2015), p. 124.

70 R. F. Holland, *European Decolonization 1918–1981: An Introductory Survey* (London: Palgrave, 1985).

71 James, *Britain and the Congo Crisis*, p. 30.

72 F. Heinlein, *British Government Policy and Decolonisation, 1945–1963: Scrutinising the Official Mind* (London: Routledge, 2013), pp. 184–185.

73 UNA, S-0845-0001-03-00001, Cable from Ralph Bunche to Dag Hammarskjöld, 'Report from Elizabethville, Katanga, 4 August, 1960', p. 14.

74 F. T. Liu, 'Interview Transcript', *Yale-UN Oral History Project*, 23 March 1990, p. 57.

With violence escalating across the country in response to the Belgian intervention, the international media and member-state delegates put pressure on the UN to mount a peacekeeping operation.[75] Lumumba and Kasavubu also jointly requested a UN response in a letter to Hammarskjöld on 12 July, demanding the withdrawal of Belgian soldiers in order to re-stabilise the affected areas.[76] In this letter, the leaders were clear that the mission should challenge Belgian 'colonial machinations' in Katanga rather than negotiate the continued presence of Union Minière capitalists in the southern region.[77] The Belgian government's refusal to withdraw its troops during the Security Council debate on 13 July led to the rapid authorisation, construction, and deployment of the ONUC mission by Security Council vote on 14 July 1960. Unlike the UNEF mission, the Congo crisis did not directly involve any of the permanent members of the Security Council and so passed without the need for 'Uniting for Peace' legislation. The resolution mandated the mission to dissolve the Belgian's 'humanitarian intervention' and to re-establish law and order, but to limit military operations to self-defence. The first ONUC troops arrived in Congo on 15 July 1960, and by the end of September, large numbers of soldiers from Canada, Sweden, Ghana, Liberia, Ireland, Ethiopia, Mali, Morocco, Pakistan, Tunisia, and the UAR arrived in cities across Congo and began establishing themselves alongside the local communities.

Tshombe's demands for Katangan secession were a delicate area of the ONUC mission and required a diplomatic approach from the UN leadership in order to balance the context in Elizabethville (the capital of Katanga) with the politics of the central Congolese government based in Leopoldville. Tshombe insulated the Katangan region from much of the violence in the north and eastern regions within a *cordon sanitaire* and provided Belgians with a safe space in which to recalibrate before the deployment of ONUC. Although other Katangan politicians, such as Jason Sendwe, contested Katanga's secession, Tshombe retained control of most of the southernmost province with the aid of Belgian troops and financial support.[78] Tshombe's harbouring of many Belgian and European settlers and troops who fled Congo made waves internationally. The occupation was widely reported by global

[75] The New York Times Editorial Board, 'Caldron of the Congo', *The New York Times*, 13 July 1960.

[76] UN Doc, S/4382, 'Cable dated 12 July 1960 from the President of the Republic of the Congo and Supreme Commander of the National Army and the Prime Minister and Minister of National Defence Addressed to the Secretary-General of the United Nations'.

[77] UN Doc, S/4382, 'Cable dated 12 July 1960 from the President of the Republic of the Congo and Supreme Commander of the National Army and the Prime Minister and Minister of National Defence Addressed to the Secretary-General of the United Nations'.

[78] R. A. Loffman, '"My training is deeply Christian and I am against violence": Jason Sendwe, the Balubakat, and the Katangese Secession, 1957–1964', *The Journal of African History*, 61:2 (2020), pp. 270–273.

left-leaning newspapers, as well as the Soviet publication, *Pravda*: 'The whole world knows that Katanga is occupied by Belgian troops. And that [it] is far from being [a] domestic Congolese issue. It is an act of aggression threatening general peace.'[79] Tshombe's strategy for power complicated the UN's mission to Congo as his links with Belgium (and thus the credibility of the secessionist movement) remained in question by many.

However, Tshombe's relationship with the Belgians was dynamic and changeable. His relationship with Western Europeans evolved as he developed a state security system. He employed a wide range of mercenaries as well as consulting with transnational lobbying networks in the United States and France.[80] But Tshombe also sought to distance himself publicly from these relationships and to emphasise his independence. This changeable attitude was noted by Bunche:

> When asked about conditions in Katanga when the Belgian troops leave, [Tshombe] replied that 'the Belgian troops can go', 'we do not need them', 'they should leave quickly', and 'we are strong'. The Belgian officials said that this was the first time that M. Tshombe had spoken in this way about the Belgian troops.[81]

Making a similar argument, American Ambassador George McGhee, who was present during the early stages of ONUC, suggested that Tshombe 'was independent [of Union Minière]. I think he was basically a Katanga nationalist … Obviously, he was playing a game here, but I don't think he was under the control of Union Minière'.[82] Similarly, Guy Vanthemsche characterised Tshombe as a powerful nationalist actor with the 'ear and trust of many whites in central Africa', recognising that he could establish a *quid pro quo* relationship with the Belgians.[83] Tshombe also exhibited his personal devotion to Katangan independence and aspirations for the secession to be formalised within the international community when he wrote to the ICRC. He reported that he had taken steps to ensure that his country's *gendarmerie* aligned with the principles of the Geneva Conventions and used this compliance to exemplify Katanga's credible claim to statehood.[84]

[79] BNA, FO 371/146777, JB2251/186, 'Prime minister: gratitude for special correspondent's report from Moscow; official Soviet announcement', 8 August 1960.

[80] C. Hendrickx, 'Tshombe's Secessionist State of Katanga: Agency against the Odds', *Third World Quarterly* [OnlineFirst, 2021].

[81] UNA, S-0845-0001-03-00001, 'Cable from Bunche to Hammarskjöld, Report from Elizabethville, Katanga', 4 August 1960, p. 14.

[82] G. McGhee, 'Interview Transcript', *Yale-UN Oral History Project*, 9 May 1990, p. 20.

[83] Vanthemsche, *Belgium and the Congo, 1885–1980*, p. 210.

[84] International Committee of the Red Cross Archives (henceforth, CICR), 'Supplement Vol. XIV 1961', *Revue internationale de la Croix Rouge*, March 1961, pp. 44–45.

However, Belgium's material and financial support of Katanga undermined Tshombe's protests of autonomy. The Belgian government ordered the mobilisation of Belgian troops from neighbouring divisions in Ruanda-Urundi in August 1960, militarily asserting Katangese opposition to the central government.[85] UN official Ian Berendsen recalled witnessing multiple Belgian troops marching with the Katangese gendarmerie.[86] Belgian influence in Katanga also included professors from Liege and Ghent '[writing] the Katangan constitution', instructing the national intelligence service, and controlling the central bank.[87] This connection became so visible that the Tunisian representative in the Security Council argued, 'One cannot help thinking that there is a disturbing connexion between the intervention of Belgian paratroopers and the tendency, in Katanga, towards disunion [from the Republic of Congo central government].'[88] Tshombe maintained that without continued infrastructural assistance, Katanga would have collapsed during the July mutiny: '[the Belgian] presence has therefore been a factor making for peace and not for disorder.'[89] Tshombe's allegiances legitimised the continued presence of Belgians in Congo, challenging ONUC's mandate to force them to withdraw.

Belgium's allies were surprised by the Belgian military presence and their refusal to withdraw their troops and colonial staff following the June intervention. Officials within the British Foreign Office reported that comments had been made about the Belgian government losing diplomatic credibility due to its assumed complicity with the capitalists in Katanga and their refusal to comply with the UN Security Council request to withdraw their troops.[90] The Foreign Office reported 'a feeling that the Belgian Government could be playing a more active role in ensuring its compliance with the Security Council's resolutions'.[91] The French publicly offered their support to the Belgians in Katanga: '[the] French government feel[ing] strongly that Western Powers should do nothing which might impede [the] restoration of

85 BNA, FO 371/146779 JB2251/238, 'Text of an Appeal by Mwami of Ruanda to UN', 12 September 1960.

86 I. Berendsen, 'Interview Transcript', *Yale-UN Oral History Project*, 4 May 1990, p. 18.

87 van Reybrouck, *Congo*, pp. 311/312.

88 UN Doc, S/PV.878, 'United Nations Security Council Official Record, 878th Meeting', 21 July 1960, p. 7.

89 UN Doc, S/4451, 'Observations by the Special Representative of the Secretary-General in the Republic of the Congo on the Memorandum by Major General H. T. Alexander', p. 51.

90 Considering the poor reaction of the British government to the multiple Security Council resolutions following their invasion during the Suez crisis, these comments seem particularly evident of a hierarchy of behaviour within the international community whereby the permanent member-states were largely able to operate using a different set of rules than to – even – other European colonial powers, such as Belgium.

91 BNA, FO 371/146777, JB2251/180, 'Secretary of State: Incoming Telegrams for Perusal from New York and Brussels', 9 August 1960.

Belgian influence in the Congo if and when circumstances allow'.[92] However, the Belgian military leader General Roger A. Gheysen argued that Brussels's official position was far more aligned with ONUC's mandate of unifying Congo than supporting Katangan secession. Maintaining the argument that the June military intervention was motivated by humanitarian goals, he emphasised that Belgium was on the side of 'peace' in this crisis: 'Belgium did not want Katanga to secede from the rest of the Congo, and Belgium does not recognise Tshombe'.[93] This complex web of allegiances – international, domestic, private, and mercenary – and diplomatic pressures on the Belgian government and remaining Belgians in Katanga provides context for the Belgian government's refusal to formally recognise Katanga as an independent state in spite of a number of Belgian-nationals endorsing and financing the secession.[94]

For the ONUC leadership, the idea of a successful Katangan secession drove anxieties that Katanga could also trigger other secession movements in Congo, thus destabilising the national unit in Central Africa.[95] Other Congolese regions, such as in the Orientale Province, South Kasai region, and Kivu Province, were recorded by the ONUC leadership as unstable and vulnerable to secessionism. The borders determining the Congolese regional provinces were drawn by Belgian colonists during the so-called 'scramble for Africa' at the turn of the century and were cemented in the Berlin Act in 1885. These arbitrary borders demonstrated the colonists' lack of knowledge – or interest, if any – in constructing territorial units from existing tribal or ethnic communities.[96] Instead, driven by an imperialistic impulse to categorise and control, similar to British colonial efforts to survey populations via censuses and colour-coded maps,[97] the colonists prioritised drawing borders in areas that would best provide themselves with access to natural resources, populations to tax, and manual labour. However, these 'patchwork states' and the political identities that emerged from these new territorial communities) outlived the colonial era.[98] The nationalist policy of Congolese politicians, such as

[92] BNA, FO 371/146777, JB2251/192, 'Memorandum from Sir J Nicholls, FO Ambassador to Belgium', 18 August 1960.

[93] UNA, S-0845-0001-03-00001, 'Meeting between UN Military Representatives and Representative of the Belgian Army at 0930 hours. 13 August 1960 at Elizabethville', p. 59.

[94] van Reybrouck, *Congo*, p. 311.

[95] 'Interview with Ralph Bunche', *Jet Magazine*, 18 January 1962, vol 21, no 13, p. 26.

[96] S. Michalopoulos and E. Papaioannou, 'The Long-Run Effects of the Scramble for Africa', *The American Economic Review*, 106:7 (2016), pp. 1802–1848.

[97] B. Anderson, *Imagined Communities: Reflections on the Origin and Spread of Nationalism*, revised edition (London: Verso, 1991), pp. 163–185.

[98] A. Naseemullah, *Patchwork States: The Historical Roots of Subnational Conflict and Competition in South Asia* (Cambridge: Cambridge University Press, 2020); G. Mathys,

Lumumba, drove the Congolese government to protect the artificial borders of Belgian colonialism that had been in place for over sixty years and prevent the secession of these regions. For liberal internationalists, successful post-colonial nationalism required territorial unity in order for the state to be acceptably 'modern'.[99] As Mahmood Mamdani has argued, post-colonial elites 'modelled their political imagination on the modern European state, the result being that the nationalist dream was imposed on the reality of colonially imposed fragmentation. . .'[100]

The artificiality and coloniality of Congo's borders were perpetuated by ONUC through the mission's policy of protecting the 'unity' of the state above all other security concerns, such as withdrawing the remaining intervening Belgians. In an interview with *Jet* magazine, Bunche confirmed that 'The main problem [in Congo] is one of cementing unity and overcoming secessionist tendencies. The Congolese are forging unity slowly'.[101] Antony Gilpin, a UN Secretariat official serving as UN civilian officer for the Kasai Province was similarly convinced that 'intertribal' fighting presented an opportunity for the UN to remain on the ground for the long-term. He argued that

> Apart from the immediate problem of bring separatist elements, notably Katanga, into an integrated Congo, the main question marks are the reorganization of the Congolese army, the pacification of hostile tribes, and the desperate economic situation of the country. The need for substantial external help will remain for quite a long time.[102]

Bunche and his UN colleagues conceived of the 'secessionist tendencies' of the provincial leaders as illegitimate and part of a wider milieu of 'tribal warfare' in the post-colonial state,[103] rather than recognising that the secessions were political responses to these formative artificial borders and tribal units imposed by the colonial powers.[104]

'Questioning Territories and Identities in the Precolonial (Nineteenth-Century) Lake Kivu Region', *Africa*, 91:3 (2021), pp. 493–515; D. de Cunha, *The Invention of Rivers: Alexander's Eye and Ganga's Descent* (Philadelphia: University of Pennsylvania Press, 2018).

99 D. M. Ahmed, *Boundaries and Secession in Africa and International Law: Challenging* Uti Possidetis (Cambridge: Cambridge University Press, 2015), p. 64.

100 M. Mamdani, *Neither Settler nor Native: The Making and Unmaking of Permanent Minorities* (Cambridge, MA: Harvard University Press, 2020), p. 15.

101 'Interview with Ralph Bunche', p. 26.

102 G. M. Bradley, 'Antony Gilpin', *Friends Journal: Quaker Thought and Life Today*, 15 October 1961, vol 7, no 20, p. 423.

103 'Interview with Ralph Bunche', p. 26.

104 This organisational reluctance to support or engage with secessionist movements was confirmed during the Biafran conflict in the late 1960s. See E. Davey, *Idealism beyond Borders: The French Revolutionary Left and the Rise of Humanitarianism, 1954–1988* (Cambridge: Cambridge University Press, 2015), p. 30.

Meanwhile on the ground, the continued presence of the Belgian colonial staff became a useful source of staffing for the ONUC mission, supplementing the mission's shortfall of technical staff. Echoing Hammarskjöld's decision to preserve British technical and military staff during the UNEF mission, the ONUC mission also provided a conduit for colonial officials' presence and legitimised their authority as part of the stabilising process. Paradoxically, in their attempt to forge stability within Congo, the ONUC leadership requested the continued employment of 800 Belgian civil servants and technicians to help repair Congolese infrastructure despite recognising the ongoing tension provoked by their employment.[105] Following the creation of ONUC, there was a 'concerted influx of Belgians' to Congo from neighbouring Belgian bases in Ruanda-Urundi.[106] Hammarskjöld requested that the Belgian government make technicians trained in maintaining the military and administrative functions of the Kamina and Kitona army bases available to ONUC. ONUC leadership's decision to maintain a number of Belgians in their pre-independence roles in Congo meant that Belgian colonial officials had continued access to the Congolese population despite the violence of the June military intervention.

'Advisers, counsellors or executive officials . . . as well as civilian personnel', stayed or returned to mainland Congo as part of ONUC, many with the express intention of interfering in ONUC's operations.[107] Belgian technicians were also assigned to radio stations in Congolese cities where they instructed Congolese trainees. On occasion, this training led to the education of Congolese radio technicians in Brussels, who returned to Leopoldville to cease Congolese radio broadcasts in the four main indigenous languages.[108] Radio was the main mode of communication available, and its accessibility, especially during a conflict, was limited by Belgian interference. There were also reports of Belgian radio operators 'commit[ting] acts of physical sabotage of radio-electrical equipment'.[109] Official UN progress reports also noted the level of Belgian obstruction in the delivery of technical assistance reports and information to Congolese ministry officials.[110] UN reports highlighted the prevalence of Belgian interference and exhibited UN officials' naïve frustration that the Belgians were not taking their role in the mission seriously.

105 UN Doc, S/4475, 'Third Report by the Secretary-General on the Implementation of Security Council Resolutions S/4387 of 14 July 1960, S/4405 of 22 July 1960 and S/4426 of 9 August 1960', p. 2; 'Le Général Gheysen: Les troupes belges quitteront le Katanga à la fin du mois', *Le Monde*, 29 August 1960.

106 UN Doc, S/4475, 'Third Report by the Secretary-General', p. 2.

107 Special to the *New York Times*, 'Belgians Fill Key Congo Jobs and Cause Problems for U.N.', *The New York Times*, 5 January 1961.

108 UN Doc, S/4557, 'Second Progress Report to the Secretary-General', p. 18.

109 UN Doc, S/4557, 'Second Progress Report to the Secretary-General', p. 18.

110 UN Doc, S/4557, 'Second Progress Report to the Secretary-General', p. 17.

One report in particular emphasised its upset that the Belgians were acting against ONUC instructions as 'Non-Congolese advisers and experts could surely be of great value at this critical juncture'.[111] Rather than the Belgian ONUC staff helping to stabilise Congo, they actively *destabilised* the country and made the population increasingly vulnerable.

Belgian obstruction was not limited to infrastructural damage and misinformation, however. In meetings with Belgian capitalists in Katanga, ONUC administrator Linnér discovered that several Union Minière workers feared losing control over Congolese natural resources to the UN and so had adopted an anti-ONUC position. Linnér reported to Hammarskjöld that he had been told 'that the UN aimed at driving away all the Belgians so that they could take over the business in Katanga in the interest of some other western powers'.[112] Belgian ONUC workers had become conduits for anti-UN publicity within Congo and had been discovered encouraging Congolese colleagues to consider a return to Belgian administration.[113] Bunche believed that Belgian technicians also spread rumours that the UN was pro-Communist and that the organisation had purportedly condoned recent 'atrocities in Hungary and Tibet'.[114] Perhaps mostly importantly, ONUC's absorption of Belgian technicians invited disruption into the mission bureaucracy and provided legitimacy for the perpetuation of colonial personnel and knowledge in Congolese governance structures and society. As in the Gaza Strip and Sinai during UNEF, populations were forced to not only tolerate the continued presence of their occupiers, but to accept their armed authority.

Manufacturing a 'Civilising' Influence

Despite Belgian technical interference, ONUC established control over the Congolese infrastructure and civil service through their recruitment of international civil servants, technicians, and administrative staff from around the world.[115] In order to support the 'advancement' of Congo, the UN Secretariat leadership staffed the Congolese civil service and technical posts with international civil servants selected from various UN specialised agencies, to 'provide bone and sinew to the [Congolese] Administration', forging their own control over the post-colonial nation without consultation with

[111] UN Doc, S/4557, 'Second Progress Report to the Secretary-General', p. 35.

[112] UNA, S-0845-0001-03-00001, 'Incoming Code Cable: To Secretary-General from Bunche, Leopoldville, 7 August 1960, B-380', p. 5.

[113] Special to *The New York Times*, 'Belgians Fill Key Congo Jobs and Cause Problems for U.N.', p. 3.

[114] UNA, S-0845-0001-03-00001, 'Addendum to "Report from Elizabethville, Katanga, 4 August, 1960" (2). 5 August 1960, 11:30 A.M.', p. 18.

[115] R. O. Jackson, 'The Failure of Categories: Haitians in the United Nations Organization in the Congo, 1960–64', *Journal of Haitian Studies*, 20:1 (2014), pp. 34–64.

Congolese politicians or infrastructural personnel.[116] As Eva-Maria Muschik described in her work on the ONUC development projects, 'The [UN] Secretariat reasoned that there was no need for individual Congolese approval of staffing, if UN employees were dispatched who had served or were currently serving the organization to the satisfaction of member states'.[117] Building upon colonial legacies of development logic and racist hierarchies of 'expertise',[118] Hammarskjöld recruited hundreds of international staff from specialised agencies within the UN institutional bureaucracy for ONUC and planned to assign roles based on the expertise of their home agency. Initially designed as an 'all-United Nations show' with the 'Congolese government a more or less inactive free rider', ONUC leadership emphasised the calibre of international expertise being brought into the country from the offices of the UN.[119] Doctors and nurses from the World Health Organization (WHO) and the ICRC staffed the Health department and hospitals;[120] those from the UN Food and Agriculture Organization led agricultural and epidemic projects;[121] and UNESCO staff presided over the schools and Education department.[122] Focused on training a small percentage of the Congolese population,[123] the UN civilian mission sought to establish a technocratic elite or bourgeois professional class in Congo, not dissimilar to the Belgian *evolué* system.[124] UN special representative Rajeshwar Dayal declared it 'the largest civilian team they have ever had in one country at one time'.[125]

The UN peacekeeping staff sought to replace and perpetuate the systems of the evacuated Belgian administrators and technicians as part of their belief that Congolese instability in July was primarily due to 'intense inter-tribal conflict' rather than a legacy of exploitative colonial administration and racist oppression.[126] In doing so, the mission recruitment choices and practices on the ground revived colonial infrastructures and modes of governance, disconnecting the peacekeeping staff from the demands, aspirations, and experiences

[116] UN Doc, S/4531, 'First Progress Report to the Secretary General', p. 25.

[117] Muschik, *Building States*, pp. 226–227.

[118] J. M. Hodge, *Triumph of the Expert: Agrarian Doctrines of Development and the Legacies of British Colonialism* (Athens: Ohio University Press, 2007.

[119] Tanner, 'U.N. IN CONGO'.

[120] CICR, B AG 121 229-001, 'Letter from R. Gallopin to Pierre Gaillard', 29 July 1960.

[121] UN Doc, S/4531, 'First Progress Report to the Secretary General', p. 16.

[122] G. A. Fullerton, *UNESCO in the Congo* (Paris: UNESCO, 1964).

[123] UN Doc, S/4531, 'First Progress Report to the Secretary General'.

[124] D. Tödt, *The Lumumba Generation: African Bourgeoisie and Colonial Distinction in the Belgian Congo* (Berlin: De Gruyter, 2021); D. Tödt, '"Les Noirs Perfectionnés", Cultural Embourgeoisement in Belgian Congo during the 1940s and 1950s', Working Paper of the *Sonderforschungsbereich*, 640:4 (2012), pp. 1–23, available at: http://edoc.hu-berlin.de/series/sfb-640-papers/2012-4/PDF/4.pdf.

[125] UN Doc, S/4531, 'First Progress Report to the Secretary-General', p. 16.

[126] UN Doc, S/4557, 'Second Progress Report to the Secretary-General', p. 29.

of the local population. As reported in *The New York Times*, 'The reaction of the Congolese [to the arrival of the UN staff was] nascent resentment over not being masters in their own house any more than before the departure of the Belgians'.[127]

During the early weeks of the ONUC mission, Hammarskjöld inserted pro-Western personnel, often with personal ties to himself, in mid-level positions of power to choreograph the mission from the ground. Significantly, Hammarskjöld placed his family friend and mining expert Šture Linnér in the executive position of Chief of Civilian Operations (also referred to as Officer-in-Charge) to further extend his control over the delivery of technical assistance. Linnér had just left a job as Executive Vice-President and General Manager of the Liberian-American-Swedish Mining Company (LAMCO), which was chaired by Bo Hammarskjöld, the secretary-general's brother.[128] The breadth of sectors included as part of ONUC's civilian administration was vast. Linnér held executive authority over the following governmental departments: 'Agriculture, Communications, Education, Finance, Foreign Trade, Health, Labour, Magistracy, Military Instruction, Natural Resources and Public Administration.'[129] He believed that Hammarskjöld had hired him because of his previous experience as a businessman which had given him a unique ability to cut through red tape. However, his recruitment indicates a level of comfort with cronyism within the upper echelons of UN peacekeeping. Linnér's interpretation of the mission mandate was shaped by the political sensibilities and instruction of the secretary-general due to the unprecedented dual functions of the peacekeeping mission – civilian *and* military. Harold Beeley, Deputy Head of the British Mission to the UN, stated in his memo to the Foreign Office that 'The Congo debacle, indeed, is likely to turn out to be a growing point for the U.N. which is being forced to devise new techniques to deal with a situation without precedent'.[130] The motto 'let Dag do it' or 'leave it to Dag' had become common parlance within the international community[131] following the perceived success of Hammarskjöld during the later years of the Korean War and the construction of the UNEF mission.[132] Colleagues from other international humanitarian organisations spoke of the transnational networks accessible to Hammarskjöld for ONUC recruitment and

[127] Tanner, 'U.N. IN CONGO'.
[128] Linnér, 'Interview Transcript', p. 39.
[129] BNA, FO 371/146779, JB2251/243, 'UN and the Congo: Report of General Events', 31 August 1960.
[130] BNA, FO 371/146779, JB2251/243, 'UN and the Congo: Report of General Events', 31 August 1960.
[131] Lipsey, *Hammarskjöld*, p. 308.
[132] B. Urquhart, 'The Evolution of the Secretary-General', in S. Chesterman (ed.), *Secretary or General: The UN Secretary-General in World Politics* (Cambridge: Cambridge University Press, 2007), p. 20.

Figure 3.1 Congolese woman with baby, U1240454, 22 July 1960.
Reproduced with permission from Bettmann/Getty Images.

cooperation due to his reputation and connections. An ICRC official described the level of international organisational cooperation exercised at the beginning of the mission, commenting that 'exceptional circumstances ... necessitate exceptional measures'.[133] Thus, belief in the expertise and legitimacy of ONUC

[133] CICR, B AG 130-051.03, 'Letter from M. Thudichum to Š. Linnér', 4 November 1960.

was built upon Hammarskjöld's reputation in conflict response and international trust in his decision-making.[134]

The potential for ONUC staff's political instrumentalisation of the mission through technical infrastructure was highlighted by prominent Congolese voices. Lumumba had begun voicing concerns about ONUC staff's refusal to consult with him over their technical assistance plans following the mission's deployment in July.[135] He was particularly concerned that the ONUC leadership had taken on too much authority in the governance of the country during a period of political fragility.[136] This anxiety was also visible in cables sent to the secretary-general in July and August 1960. The *Association des étudiants congolais de Belgique* warned Hammarskjöld to enforce the boundaries of the mission's mandate as 'The UN cannot become a colonialist superstructure. Its Congo mission consists in safeguarding law and order and not in supplanting legal authorities'.[137] Dayal also noted in his first progress report to Hammarskjöld that there had been unspecified accusations that the mission was intending to replace the Belgians.[138] These accusations also charged the mission leadership with attempting to construct a UN trusteeship through its administrative control of the core state sectors.[139] That he chose to report this to headquarters colleagues suggests that the UN leadership recognised the negative implications of this perception of the mission and how destructive it could be to their efforts on the ground and their reputation globally. Congolese voices were not passive in this process of 'advancement', and Lumumba repeatedly reminded the ONUC leadership and Hammarskjöld that his request for their intervention was limited to removing the Belgian interveners and to support the reestablishment of law and order in the aftermath of the ANC mutiny.

Within ONUC civilian operations there emerged a fascinating paradox. The international actors intervened in the crisis, directed Congolese 'development' and 'advancement', and maintained law and order through technical, policing, and military activities. However, international staff like Linnér would simultaneously break the UN's own procedures and seemingly re-make the rules of 'civility' by violating the trust of allied parties in the conflict in the name of saving lives.[140] Linnér saw his contribution to the mission as the anti-

134 R. L. Duffus, 'Key Man in the U.N.'s New Test', *The New York Times*, 7 August 1960.

135 UNA, S-0845-0001-03-00001, 'Confidential: Notes on Conversation with Mr Lumumba, at 2.30p.m. on 12 August 1960', p. 63.

136 UNA, S-0845-0001-03-00001, 'Confidential: Notes on Conversation with Mr Lumumba, at 2.30p.m. on 12 August 1960', p. 63.

137 UNA, S-0845-0001-02-00001, 'Private Telegram from Association des étudiants congolais de Belgique to Dag Hammarskjöld', 9 September 1960, p. 51.

138 UN Doc, S/4531, 'First Progress Report to the Secretary General', p. 6.

139 UN Doc, S/4531, 'First Progress Report to the Secretary General', p. 6.

140 This has been termed the 'liberal peacebuilding paradox' in IR scholarship.

bureaucratic cog in the vast UN machine.[141] Recalling one incident in Kasai, Linnér suggested that his non-UN background allowed him to 'get the job done' as he admitted to stealing trucks from the ANC (supposedly ONUC's allies) and painting them with the UN emblem to deliver food aid.[142] This deviance from UN protocol and Congolese law illustrated a disconnect between ONUC field operations and the strict procedural environment of the New York and Geneva offices. His argument that the ANC used the trucks 'for mischief anyway' also illustrated the racialised dynamic between the mission officials and the Congolese army, showing the lack of respect he held for ANC troops.

Linnér's actions inspired similar illegal activities by his staff. ONUC staff, such as Antony Gilpin, UN representative in Kasai (a southern region in Congo) and assistant to the special representative of the secretary-general witnessed UN peacekeepers violating Congolese convicts. Gilpin, a devoted Quaker and career-bureaucrat within the UN Secretariat, took personal photographs during his repeated periods of service with the UN in Congo.[143] One of his photos captured his fellow UN peacekeeper, Colonel Thompson, disrespecting a Congolese convict (in a striped uniform) and being 'piggy-backed' across knee-high muddy water.[144] Another photo depicted the UN peacekeepers using Congolese convict labour to unload ONUC military equipment, including UN 'Ferret' armoured cars, from shipments.[145] Gilpin believed that his Quaker religion and the peacekeeping operations worked towards the same aims of a better world, but his capture and preservation of these instances of abuse indicate that he was content to benefit from the power dynamic not only between peacekeeper and civilian but also between peacekeeper and convict.[146] ONUC cultures of anti-bureaucratism entrenched cultures of racialised exceptionalism, humanitarian machismo, and impunity for international actors within the ONUC bureaucracy, shaping their relationships with civilians. It was clear that the UN staff did not hold themselves to the standards that they claimed to be instilling in the Congolese.

ONUC diplomats, civil servants, and experts saw the crisis as an opportunity to encourage the Congolese state to align itself with so-called Western principles and standards. Linnér's response to the calibre of UN staff joining the mission spoke to his desire for ONUC to exercise a 'civilising' influence on

141 Linnér, 'Interview Transcript', p. 39.
142 Linnér, 'Interview Transcript', p. 7.
143 Bradley, 'Antony Gilpin', pp. 422–423.
144 Bod, MS. Photograph c. 50, Antony Gilpin, fol 52.
145 Bodleian Library (henceforth, Bod), MS. Photograph c. 50, Special Collections United Nations Career Records Project, Antony Gilpin, fol 53.
146 Bradley, 'Antony Gilpin', p. 423.

the Congolese population and environment.[147] Ashamed of his 'primitive working conditions' in Leopoldville, Linnér hoped that the 'aristocratic' quality of these incoming civil servants would challenge the chaos he saw in Leopoldville, disregarding that he was observing the city for the first time in a context of war.[148] His delight in welcoming large numbers of international civil servants into roles vacated by Belgian colonists revealed that his conception of the ongoing instability in Congo was grounded in racism. As James Ferguson has highlighted in his work on international development officials, international staff viewed the Global South as a space in which they could interchangeably apply their 'expertise', steering the decolonising/post-colonial nation towards 'best practice'.[149] ONUC staff directly influenced the governance and future infrastructure of the nation and prioritised an international vision over consulting with Congolese experts. ONUC leadership dismissed most of the Congolese population as uneducated and untrained, thus perpetuating colonial prejudices, structures, and hierarchies within Congolese society.[150] The ONUC bureaucracy became a microcosm of Western-dominated international society; an experiment of liberal internationalist governance, rather than a mission acting in support of Congolese self-determination and political agency. In combination with 'progress' rhetoric or Modernization Theory, the influx of international UN staff indicated that ONUC was not, as advertised by Hammarskjöld in multiple public statements,[151] an impartial, apolitical mission.[152]

However, the vast number of positions vacated by Belgian colonists meant that in the early months of ONUC there were not enough international staff, and many were assigned managerial roles they had little experience in and no more training than their Congolese trainees or colleagues. As was common to the mindset of Western interveners, the ONUC staff's perception of post-colonial Congo as a 'blank slate' reinforced the belief within the international bureaucracy that any and every UN employee was more qualified than any and every Congolese citizen.[153] The restrictions placed on the Congolese population during colonial rule prevented most citizens from accessing education and skilled employment. This repression excluded Congolese citizens

[147] Linnér, 'Interview Transcript', p. 4.

[148] Linnér, 'Interview Transcript', p. 46.

[149] J. Ferguson, *The Anti-Politics Machine: 'Development', Depoliticisation, and Bureaucratic Power in Lesotho* (Minneapolis: University of Minnesota Press, 1998), p. 70.

[150] UN Doc, S/4531, 'First Progress Report to the Secretary-General', pp. 22–23.

[151] UNA, S-0845-0001-03-00001, 'Statement by Secretary-General on Entry of Troops into Katanga', 3 August 1960, p. 68.

[152] L. Parrott, 'U.N. Chief Offers Wide Aid to Congo: Would Lend Experts in Many Fields – Vows Neutrality', *The New York Times*, 13 August 1960.

[153] M. Sabaratnam, *Decolonising Intervention: International Statebuilding in Mozambique* (London: Rowman and Littlefield, 2018), p. 134.

from positions of power and thus institutionalised systems of structural marginalisation and exploitation. Despite the intention of Secretariat staff for the mission to produce a bureaucracy of international experts, Gilpin noted in a personal letter that because of the need for such a high number of staff, ONUC 'was quite evidently scraping the bottom of the barrel for some of its personnel'.[154] Gilpin had extensive experience of working internationally with different UN agencies, and his reflections indicated his surprise at the inappropriate appointments made for the mission. He even commented on his own lack of specialism in his role:

> Apparently my job is to assist in setting up the provincial government services – an assignment for which I've made it clear I have no technical qualifications whatsoever! Since it will be starting from scratch, perhaps that won't matter ... one can see the whole thing as a quite astonishing experiment which has somehow got to succeed.[155]

For Hammarskjöld, a key part of the ONUC mission was to ensure the future integration of Congo into the liberal internationalist system. ONUC leadership emphasised from the outset that the 'moral force' of the mission, as invoked to UNEF troops, was intended as the first step for the Congolese state to progress into political modernity; ONUC's liberal ideals were thus portrayed as technocratic, peacebuilding strategies.[156] Rather than delivering apolitical technical assistance, as described in Rajeshwar Dayal's ONUC progress reports, the ONUC mission was explicitly political in its aims for Congo's future geopolitical value.[157] Dayal had been a pivotal figure in the UN's mediation and operations in the United Nations Observer Group in Lebanon (UNOGIL) during 1958, and his core involvement in ONUC demonstrated India's expanding participation in UN peacekeeping since its initial hesitancy regarding UNEF.[158] His progress reports noted that the mission's work had 'gone well beyond the operative phase in the past month, to the point where it is having a wider and, if conditions permit, a long-term effect on the economic and social conditions of the country'.[159] Hammarskjöld announced to the Congolese government that their 'development' would be facilitated in alliance with the UN: 'We are at the start of a long road. The road

[154] Bod, MS.Eng.c. 4674 (fols 244–324), Special Collections United Nations Career Records Project, Antony Gilpin, fol 247.
[155] Bod, MS.Eng.c. 4674, Antony Gilpin, fol 256.
[156] UN Doc, S/4531, 'First Progress Report to the Secretary-General', p. 26.
[157] UN Doc, S/4531, 'First Progress Report to the Secretary-General', pp. 26–27.
[158] For more on Dayal and UNOGIL, see S. K. Nayudu, '"In the Very Eye of the Storm": India, the UN, and the Lebanon Crisis of 1958', *Cold War History*, 18:2 (2018), pp. 221–237.
[159] UN Doc, S/PV.873, United Nations Security Council Official Records, 13/14 July 1960, p. 32.

is your own. During the difficult first steps, we will be happy to accompany you, holding hands.'[160] This proposal of collaborative statecraft was emphasised in Hammarskjöld's speech to the Council of Ministers of the Republic of the Congo in Leopoldville:

> In view of the paramount importance of integrating the Republic [of Congo] into the great international family in a harmonious way, part of the great task which you have to face will be to explain to your people what the United Nations is, what are its ideals and goals, and that you can all find [within the UN] support in your difficulties.[161]

This phrasing exemplified the paternalistic dynamic between humanitarian donor and recipient – the liberal instruction of 'this is in your best interests; you'll see'.

In order to exert further control over Congolese politicians, the ONUC leadership established a UN monopoly over the delivery of military assistance to Congo. This allowed UN staff to gatekeep which Congolese politicians could access external material support, thus interfering in the strategic direction of the conflict and potentially impeding Congolese officials' efforts to defend themselves from attack. The official direction of member-state-supplied aid was unilaterally under the jurisdiction of the secretary-general, although the mission was supported multilaterally. This encouraged Congolese dependence on the organisation and cast suspicion on the motivations of member-states that tried to donate military support to the Congolese government.[162] In one example, Harold Beeley, Deputy-Head of the British Mission to the UN, reported to the Foreign Office that a Polish cargo ship of arms was en route along the Congo River. It had been requested by the Congolese government – likely by Lumumba – and the ONUC leadership was obstructing its delivery. The cable reported:

> ...Bunche has ordered a United Nations unit down to Matadi, and that Hammarskjöld has sent a message to Lumumba, saying that, while he acknowledges the right of the Congo Government to import arms, he hopes that in the present circumstances they will agree to this cargo being off-loaded and held by the United Nations.[163]

The secretary-general argued that the ONUC resolutions (S/4387, S/4405, S/4426) permitted UN staff with the access and authority necessary to police the

[160] UNA, S-0845-0001-03-00001, 'UN Speech to Congolese Government', 1 August 1960, p. 80.
[161] UNA, S-0845-0001-03-00001, 'UN Speech to Congolese Government', 1 August 1960, p. 79.
[162] UN Doc, A/RES/1474 (ES-IV), 'Question Considered by the Security Council at Its 906th Meeting on 16 September 1960'.
[163] BNA, FO 371/146770, JB 2251/33, 'Cable from Beeley to the FO', 17 July 1960.

Congolese government's private acquisition of 'materials of war and military personnel' from other countries during the 'temporary period of military assistance through the United Nations' on the grounds that it represented a threat to law and order.[164] This approach imposed harsh restrictions on the host country; anything that could be interpreted as material aid to the central government would have to go through the UN first, even if the sovereign state requested the aid. This monopoly on the delivery of military donations placed the ONUC leadership in a powerful gatekeeping role whereby they could control the military strength of different Congolese politicians to their advantage, and it was a technique peacekeeping leadership later applied to the Cyprus context.

International Development and Racialised Concepts of Progress

ONUC civilian administrators expanded their influence over the political life of the country through access to Congolese core infrastructural services, such as air traffic towers and communications systems, to control the direction of the conflict. The likelihood of UN interference in Congolese politics had been predicted: 'When the first planes had landed, UN troops at Ndjili [a municipality of capital city Leopoldville] in July 1960, a senior UN official watching them had been quoted as saying ironically: "Now the UN has its first colony".'[165] Gilpin commented that this was 'an unfortunate remark which turned out to be a warning', suggesting a level of cognisance regarding the UN's presence and mandate in Congo.[166] ONUC's approach to technical assistance and infrastructural aid was part of longer legacies of colonial power dynamics and conceptions of technocratic superiority, grounded in racialised post-Enlightenment, liberal ideas of 'modernity' and 'progress'. The US-supported Modernization Theory, pushed by President Kennedy as an anti-communism tool in the early 1960s, was also underpinned with paternalism.[167] The racial tropes and hierarchies of colonists' *mission civilisatrice* were built into the logic of post-war development operations and adopted by humanitarian organisations in the 1950s as NGOs expanded their practices from relief distribution to long-term development assistance.[168] British politicians used humanitarian and development rhetoric to justify maintaining

[164] UN Doc, S/4557, 'Second Progress Report to the Secretary-General', p. 47.

[165] Bod, MS.Eng.c. 4675, Antony Gilpin, fol 2.

[166] Bod, MS.Eng.c. 4675, Antony Gilpin, fol 2.

[167] For more on Modernization Theory, see D. B. Kunz, *Butter and Guns: America's Cold War Economic Diplomacy* (New York: Free Press, 1997), pp. 125–128.

[168] E. Davey, J. Borton, and M. Foley, 'A History of the Humanitarian System: Western Origins and Foundations', *HPG Working Paper* (2013), p. 10; U. Kothari, 'From Colonialism to Development: Reflections of former Colonial Officers', *Commonwealth and Comparative Politics*, 44:1 (2006), pp. 118–136.

colonial rule whilst making the same judgements about human capacity for progress as their Enlightenment ancestors.[169] The racialised rationale and hierarchies interwoven with post-war aid maintained that development rhetoric and power dynamics in Global South communities remained the same as during nineteenth-century colonial administrations; the dominant party determined who would receive the aid and the type of support that would be supplied.[170] This paternalistic dynamic manifested in peacekeeping operations. UN staff in the field shaped the 'development' or 'modernisation' of Congo in alignment with the organisation's political vision and felt entitled to dictate Congo's political evolution out of colonisation.

ONUC's civilian assistance relied upon the same technocratic justifications and aims as colonial state-led international development operations: the 'modernisation' or 'advance' of a nation and guidance on the necessary steps to meet an arbitrary standard of sufficient 'advancement'.[171] As Fred Cooper has argued in relation to French colonists in the 1940s, international administrators emphasised the 'technical' aspect of their assistance and asserted that it was 'in the name of general good' to evade criticism, and that this would be 'later assimilated into the development framework'.[172] Similarly, Ferguson's work in *The Anti-politics Machine* has also demonstrated this pattern of international staff deploying technical rhetoric to conceal political interference in the Global South. He argued that development workers in 1970s Lesotho justified the re-allocation of resources as 'technical solutions to technical problems', thus rendering political decisions apolitical.[173] This apolitical rhetoric entrenched a characterisation of the international development staff as unassailable experts, empowered with superior knowledge of the local environment and society than that of local populations. In the same way, ONUC leadership obscured their political decision-making and operations through mandated access to social and education departments and technical personnel in Congo. The 'anti-politics' of ONUC technical assistance rhetoric disguised

169 C. L. Riley, '"The Winds of Change are Blowing Economically": The Labour Party and British Overseas Development, 1940s–1960s', in Smith and Jeppesen, *Britain, France and the Decolonization of Africa*, p. 50.

170 A. Lester, 'Personifying Colonial Governance: George Arthur and the Transition from Humanitarian to Development Discourse', *Annals of the Association of American Geographers*, 102:6 (2012), p. 1482.

171 A. Escobar, *Encountering Development: The Making and Unmaking of the Third World* (Princeton: Princeton University Press, 1995); T. Mitchell, *Rule of Experts: Egypt, Techno-Politics, Modernity* (Berkeley: University of California Press, 2012).

172 F. Cooper, 'Modernizing Bureaucrats, Backward Africans, and the Development Concept', in F. Cooper and R. Packard (eds.), *International Development and the Social Sciences: Essays on the History and Politics of Knowledge* (Berkeley: University of California Press, 1997), p. 65.

173 Ferguson, *The Anti-Politics Machine*, p. 87.

the explicitly political aims of the peacekeeping leadership, as well as imbuing the poorly-assigned bureaucrats with technocratic authority.

In order to maintain this technocratic guise, the peacekeeping leadership attributed the mission's shortcomings or failings on Congolese ingratitude, blaming the newly independent population for any resistance to ONUC's widespread administration and criticising them for the socio-economic legacies of Belgian imperialism. Hints of anti-ONUC sentiment were included in an early progress report detailing an instance where Congolese 'diesel workers' refused to cooperate with the UNESCO experts sent to provide emergency support.[174] Dayal, the author of the report, was perplexed by this rejection and concerned that the Congolese had wasted the time of UNESCO's experts; he did not consider why the workers had declined this help.[175] Similarly, *The New York Times* reported how a 'quiet Congolese' interrupted an ONUC official who was giving a speech and 'broke in quietly: "Excuse me sir, may I ask you a question? Is this our country or yours?"'[176] ONUC leadership swept aside these examples and recorded only small examples of dissent, dismissing Congolese criticism of the UN's 'reservoir[s] of goodwill' (i.e. the public works, international staffing, and unemployment projects).[177] Instead, reports to Hammarskjöld's office in New York focused on how the mission was impeded by an ungrateful or unmotivated population.[178] For an organisation attuned to international criticism, the UN leadership's flippant approach to Congolese opinions helped shed light on the mission's culture of racial exceptionalism and technocracy.

Bunche rationalised these failures and the protests of local workers by infantilising the population, reporting to the Security Council that the mission 'has been dropped into the midst of a country and people who are totally unprepared by experience and psychology to understand it and to appreciate its function and real worth'.[179] These exasperated comments are analogous to the French colonial reports highlighted by Cooper in his study of post-war development in Equatorial Africa.[180] Reminiscent of the colonial trope of the 'ungrateful African',[181] ONUC leadership chose to shift the blame of failing or unwelcome or openly paternalistic projects onto the apparent refusal – or

174 UN Doc, S/4557, 'Second Progress Report to the Secretary-General', p. 34.
175 UN Doc, S/4557, 'Second Progress Report to the Secretary-General', p. 34.
176 Tanner, 'U.N. IN CONGO'.
177 UN Doc, S/4557, 'Second Progress Report to the Secretary-General', p. 34.
178 UN Doc, S/4557, 'Second Progress Report to the Secretary-General', p. 34.
179 UN Doc, S/4451, 'Observations by the Special Representative in the Republic of the Congo on the Memorandum by Major-General H. T. Alexander', 21 August 1960, p. 1.
180 Cooper, 'Modernising Bureaucrats, Backwards Africans, and the Development Concept', p. 73.
181 C. Prior, 'Writing Another Continent's History: The British and Pre-colonial Africa, 1880–1939', available at: www.gla.ac.uk/media/Media_64283_smxx.pdf, p. 13.

supposed mental incapacity – of some of the Congolese population to accept and appreciate assistance.[182] Bunche's conception of the population as being psychologically 'unprepared' for ONUC support also revealed his racist belief in African 'backwardness'. Although he was an important figure in the US civil rights movement, his conceptions of Black Africans were not dissimilar to those of the white UN officials he worked alongside. He may have written of his upset at the racist treatment of Congolese politicians by Belgian politicians, but he – and his fellow UN leadership – also maintained deeply racist beliefs about Congolese intellect and society. As Marie-Luce Desgrandchamps and Yolana Pringle have both demonstrated, a commonly held prejudice within Western liberal internationalist circles in the late 1950s was that Black Africans were too 'psychologically primitive' to understand 'the notions of charity and solidarity': that is, that they did not know how lucky they were.[183] Pringle has revealed how the ICRC used this racist justification to delay their response to the Mau Mau detention camps during the Kenyan counterinsurgency. Thus, Bunche's comments about an 'unprepared' people were symptomatic of an entrenched racism within the international humanitarian sector – for officials of any race and nationality – whereby international staff tempered organisational criticism by blaming Black populations' ingratitude, rather than the institutions' staff, (in)action, and lack of contextual understanding of post-colonial psychological trauma and societal legacies.

Importing international technicians as part of staffing the ONUC mission perpetuated racist and de-contextualised perceptions of Congo as a 'backward' country requiring expert advice.[184] Linnér infantilized the Congolese politicians he engaged with and emphasised their inexperience to justify taking control of the majority of governmental sectors, remarking on the extent of the 'undertaking' and 'patience' of ONUC administrators when working with Congolese ministers.[185] Linnér's policies in Congo demonstrated the vitality of the imperial trope of the 'white man's burden' within international humanitarian organisations.[186] His comments exposed the culture of intellectual superiority within the ranks of the ONUC bureaucrats over the Congolese

[182] UN Doc, S/4557, 'Second Progress Report to the Secretary-General', p. 1.

[183] M. Desgrandchamps, 'Entre ambitions universalistes et préjugés raciaux: La mission du Comité international de la Croix-Rouge en Afrique méridionale et centrale au début des années 1960', *Histoire@Politique*, 40 (2020), pp. 1–16; Y. Pringle, 'Humanitarianism, Race and Denial: The International Committee of the Red Cross and Kenya's Mau Mau Rebellion, 1952–1960', *History Workshop Journal*, 84 (2017), p. 93.

[184] T. F. Brady, 'Congo Lacking 1,500 Teachers and Aides in Secondary Schools', *The New York Times*, 27 August 1960, p. 2.

[185] Linnér, 'Interview Transcript', p. 12.

[186] For more on the 'white man's burden' as a humanitarian impulse, see W. Easterly, *The White Man's Burden: Why the West's Efforts to Aid the Rest Have Done So Much Ill and So Little Good* (London: Penguin Books, 2006).

politicians, civil servants, and local population. Again, this dynamic speaks to Cooper's work on late French colonial development administrators and their remarks about feeling like they were 'starting from zero' in colonised territories.[187] This paternalistic 'patience' required by international officials while attempting to 'act on the native' was deployed to excuse the failings or slowness of development projects in post-colonial Congo and the lack of consultation with Congolese officials and politicians.[188]

ONUC staff perceived widespread Congolese ignorance, disregarding not only the reality of educated Congolese in 1960, but also the context of colonial Belgium's restrictions on secular Congolese education and training institutions for the past eighty years.[189] In his progress reports, Dayal reiterated the myth that only seventeen Congolese had graduated university by the point of independence: 'not one doctor, no engineers, professors, architects, etc., and few, if any, qualified lawyers'.[190] Similarly, when the Director-General of UNESCO visited Leopoldville in August 1960 to scope the educational necessities of the country, he emphasised the emergency, arguing that 'these requirements are apparently the biggest and most difficult that have ever been submitted to UNESCO', with a preliminary survey suggesting that UNESCO may need to 'recruit something like 1,600 technicians' to support the new academic year.[191] The international belief in the incompetence of the Congolese was chronic within the ONUC leadership, and the implications of this myth are still visible in modern representations of post-independence Congo.[192] Herbert Weiss, among other historians of Congolese society, has argued that this perception was incorrect and based on a Western definition of educational qualifications. He pointed out that:

187 Cooper, 'Modernising Bureaucrats, Backwards Africans, and the Development Concept', p. 73.

188 Cooper, 'Modernising Bureaucrats, Backwards Africans, and the Development Concept', p. 73.

189 B. A. Yates, 'Educating Congolese Abroad: An Historical Note on African Elites', *The International Journal of African Historical Studies*, 14:1 (1981), p. 64.

190 UN Doc, S/4531, 'First Progress Report to the Secretary General', p. 22. This figure was also reproduced in U Thant's white paper on ONUC: UNA, S-0875-0005-01-00001, 'White Paper – The United Nations and the Congo', 1 March 1962, p. 2.

191 BNA, FO 371/146779, JB2251/243, 'UN and the Congo: Report of General Events', 31 August 1960.

192 Brian Urquhart, Personal Assistant to the Secretary-General, was recorded as part of the United Nations Intellectual History Project. He stated, 'The Congo was in the first place, a Belgian territory. It also had a very complex infrastructure, it was extremely rich, the Congolese had no training, there was nothing above a sergeant in the army, and there were only 17 Congolese with university degrees.' This myth of Congolese incompetence was discussed further in Wilson Centre, 'The Congo Crisis, 1960–1961: A Critical Oral History Conference', 28 November 2011.

> There were what one could call university level graduates from the seminaries or even MA level graduates if one compares them to Americans with secular education ... there were 3,000 Congolese alive at that time, who had reached the level of 'Grande Seminare' which, in our terms, can be compared to our MA level.[193]

Although Belgian restrictions on Congolese education were considerable within the secular state system, a significant percentage of the Congolese population received education from missionaries, with boys' and girls' Catholic schools established across the country in the late colonial state.[194] Weiss's argument contrasts with ONUC's reports from the ground in 1960 which highlighted the 'urgent' lack of educated Congolese and ignited calls for UN specialised agencies to devote their international staff to the state-building effort.[195]

Weaponising Infrastructure and Destabilising the Congolese Government

The political power vacuum of September 1960 further entrenched a culture of technocratic and racial paternalism into the ONUC bureaucracy and enabled the UN leadership to politically interfere in Congolese governance. Kasavubu and Lumumba's coalition had collapsed following rumours of Lumumba's correspondence with Khrushchev, despite the two politicians having initially united over their shared desire to bring about Congolese independence.[196] Kasavubu's decision to illegally remove the democratically elected Lumumba was rejected by the majority of both Congolese houses of Parliament, and Lumumba swiftly demanded Kasavubu's resignation. Despite the constitutional confusion, the secretary-general decided that, for the purposes of ONUC, Kasavubu was the Chief (or Head of State) and that he was therefore 'the only clear legal authority'.[197] This was contrasted by the decision of the Congolese Parliament whereby the members voted in a joint session to grant Lumumba emergency powers.[198] ONUC bureaucrats like Linnér proved to be crucial political tools during the crisis both for Kasavubu and his allies, using

[193] 'Wilson Centre: 'The Congo Crisis, 1960–1961', pp. 116–117.

[194] R. A. Loffman, *Church, State and Colonialism in Southeastern Congo, 1890–1962* (Berlin: Springer, 2019), pp. 191–192.

[195] BNA, FO 371/146779, JB2251/243, 'UN and the Congo: Report of General Events', 31 August 1960.

[196] N. Telepneva, 'Cold War on the Cheap: Soviet and Czechoslovak Intelligence in the Congo, 1960–1963', in P. E. Muehlenbeck and N. Telepneva, *Warsaw Pact Intervention in the Third World: Aid and Influence in the Cold War* (London: I. B. Tauris, 2018), p. 130.

[197] Bod, MS.Eng.c.6472 (fols 56–60), Catalogue of the Papers of George Ivan Smith, 1888–1995, 'Incoming Code from SecGen to Cordier, 6 September 1960, Number 1552'.

[198] Young, *Politics in Congo*, p. 329.

this political emergency to implement the anticommunist goals of the UN leadership who believed Kasavubu to be the preferable Congolese leader. Although the constitutional crisis and the anti-Lumumba bias of UN staff, in particular Hammarskjöld, has received a great deal of historical analysis,[199] little attention has been paid to the precise mechanisms put in place by the ONUC mission in the field to directly interfere with the Prime Minister's efforts to combat the *coup d'état* to remove him from power and to not directly challenge Lumumba's arrest, a decision that eventually contributed to – if not, enabled – his violent murder.

Hammarskjöld and ONUC staff were keen to ensure that the man he described as a 'Communist stooge' would not remain as Prime Minister, despite little evidence to support this characterisation of Lumumba.[200] He argued it would violate the impartiality principle in the mission's mandate.[201] As Anne-Sophie Gijs has argued that Lumumba's unpopularity within Western-allied circles was reinforced by Belgian rumours of his requests for Soviet aid during the summer of 1960 after Hammarskjöld refused to intervene militarily in Katanga.[202] In one of his July reports to Hammarskjöld, Bunche recalled discussing these rumours with the wife of an American Consulate official. She asked, '"Mr Bunche, are the *Reds* [underlining Bunche's own] really coming?" I replied, mischievously and not altogether untruthfully, "My dear lady, they are here".'[203] Later, while visiting Katangan President Tshombe in early August, Bunche wrote to Hammarskjöld, 'There was [in Elizabethville] egotism, arrogance and ignorance galore, but more evidence of graciousness than in Leopoldville.'[204] This conviction was later shared by many within the ONUC leadership who rallied against Lumumba during August and resented his criticisms of the peacekeeping mission.[205] Indeed, unbeknownst to UN officials, on 25 August 1960, President Eisenhower and CIA Director Allen Dulles agreed to cable Leopoldville and organise the murder of Lumumba. CIA Deputy Director Bronson Tweedy

[199] See M. G. Kalb, *The Congo Cables: The Cold War in Africa – From Eisenhower to Kennedy* (Basingstoke: Macmillan, 1982), pp. 50–58, P. Gendebien, *L'Intervention des Nations Unies au Congo, 1960–1964* (Berlin: Walter de Gruyter, 1967), pp. 64–65.

[200] BNA, FO 371/146779, JB2251/231 225, 'Lumumba: Secretary General's Consideration of Applying Pressure through Dr Nkrumah, President of Ghana', 31 August 1960.

[201] H. Melber, 'Mission Impossible: Hammarskjöld and the UN Mandate for the Congo (1960–1961)', *African Security*, 10:3–4 (2017), pp. 254–271.

[202] A. Gijs, 'Fighting the Red Peril in the Congo: Paradoxes and Perspectives on an Equivocal Challenge to Belgium and the West (1947–1960)', *Cold War History*, 16:3 (2016), p. 284.

[203] UNA, S-1069-0012-11, 'Letter-Report from Bunche to Hammarskjöld from Leopoldville', 4 July 1960.

[204] UNA, S-0845-0001-03-00001, 'Cable from Bunche to Hammarskjöld, 'Report from Elizabethville, Katanga, 4 August, 1960', p. 14.

[205] Liu, 'Interview Transcript', p. 19.

later testified that this cable was the '"most authoritative statement" on the "policy consensus in Washington about the need for the removal of Lumumba" by any means, including assassination'.[206]

Meanwhile, ONUC leadership, in particular Linnér, increasingly supported Kasavubu and his ally Joseph-Désiré Mobutu, closely working with the Congolese leader during August and September. In contrast with other UN officials, like Dayal, who struggled to get close to any Congolese figures, Linnér and Kasavubu developed a friendship as a result of Linnér's involvement in the reorganisation of the Congolese civil service. Linnér socialised frequently with Kasavubu and other central government politicians based in Leopoldville, remarking, 'We get along wonderfully well. I happen to like Africans.'[207] Although Kasavubu was frequently publicly critical of the mission, these insights into his personal interactions with the upper echelons of the UN mission indicate a political alliance that belied the impartiality of the mission mandate.[208] As a consequence of this collegiality, Linnér recalled how Kasavubu asked him for a map of Congo in August and instructed him to plan how the country would look with additional administrative units.[209] This plan matched Kasavubu's federal plan to create a seventh province in Congo – a key source of disagreement between the two Congolese leaders.[210] Liu argued that new UN special representative Andrew Cordier was also aware in August of Kasavubu's intentions to remove Lumumba, despite ONUC's mandate to stabilise the region.[211] Whilst looking over the map, Kasavubu asked Linnér how to 'make a *coup d'etat'* , and Linnér responded, 'that's easy, you avoid violence; you take over the radio station; you take away the man you want to replace, feed him well; you don't go into any excesses of any kind, no physical harm of any kind'.[212] However, Kasavubu did not need to take over the radio stations; the ONUC technicians were already in place.

Hammarskjöld's dislike of Lumumba was matched in Western diplomatic circles. Beeley encouraged the Foreign Office to support Hammarskjöld in his attempts to exclude Lumumba from all positions of power. Foreign Office notes state that 'Mr Hammarskjöld is clearly inclined to back [Kasavubu] and

[206] 'Alleged Assassination Plots Involving Foreign Leaders, an Interim Report of the Select Committee to Study Governmental Operations with Respect to Intelligence Activities', US Senate, 20 November 1975 (US Government Printing Office: Washington, DC, 1975), pp. 13–16, available at: www.intelligence.senate.gov/sites/default/files/94465.pdf.

[207] 'The Congo: A New Start', *TIME Magazine*, 30 June 1961.

[208] K. Teltsch, 'Kasavubu Scores UN on Lumumba: Notes Criticise World Body for Barring Arrest of Premier He Deposed', *The New York Times*, 5 November 1960.

[209] Linnér, 'Interview Transcript', p. 22.

[210] UNA, S-1069-0012-11, 'Letter from Ralph Bunche to Dag Hammarskjöld from Leopoldville', Monday, 27 June 1960.

[211] Liu, 'Interview Transcript', p. 29/30.

[212] Linnér, 'Interview Transcript', p. 22.

to treat his government as the only legal one' despite international outcry in support of Lumumba's democratic sovereignty following the coup.[213] British diplomats decided to treat the situation 'very carefully', as they recognised that vocal British support for Kasavubu would attract the attention of the USSR 'and defeat our own purpose by strengthening M. Lumumba's hand and encouraging his Soviet backers'.[214] Assistant Under-Secretary for Foreign Affairs Archibald Ross suggested 'that it was better not to applaud every time Kasavubu asserted himself against Lumumba'.[215] Western diplomats recognised that Hammarskjöld and ONUC staff on the ground were not only politically aligned to Kasavubu but also actively invested in the removal of his rival – the perceived 'source of instability'.[216]

The leadership wielded immense power over sectors such as communication and air travel which held particular strategic importance during the constitutional crisis. The mission's staffing of the radio and communications systems allowed them to control the dissemination of 'official' information across the country to Kasavubu's benefit. Additionally, the mission's operating of the air traffic control systems enabled the ONUC technical staff to restrict the movement of politicians and civilians across the country.[217] This control became a tool for political intervention throughout September as UN special representative Cordier repeatedly ordered the closure of Manono, Leopoldville, and Elizabethville airports as well as the local radio station, Radio Léopoldville.[218] His justification was that closing these facilities, as well as airfield resources, would prevent the spread of violence from city to city.[219] However, two small planes piloted by Belgians were able to take off from Elizabethville airport on 10 September during the ONUC ban on air traffic and refuel at an airfield in Kamina that was being held by an Ethiopian battalion of ONUC despite efforts to stop the Belgian fliers by UN official Ian Berendsen.[220] This act of defiance from Katangan Belgians ignited further anger from Lumumba and his supporters in response to the so-called travel 'ban'. On 12 September 1960, Lumumba instructed his followers to attempt to regain

[213] BNA, FO 371/146779, JB2251/247, 'Kasavubu's Government Delegation: Departure to New York', 12 September 1960.

[214] BNA, FO 371/146779, JB2251/247, 'Kasavubu's Government Delegation: Departure to New York', 12 September 1960.

[215] BNA, FO 371/146779, JB2251/247, 'Kasavubu's Government Delegation: Departure to New York', 12 September 1960.

[216] K. Dunn, *Imagining the Congo: The International Relations of Identity* (New York: Springer, 2003), p. 99.

[217] UN Doc, S/4531, 'First Progress Report to the Secretary General', p. 17.

[218] UNA, S-0845-0001-01-00001, 'Cable: CY 9 LEO SS 254 2 1325Z: P4', p. 40.

[219] UNA, S-0845-0001-01-00001, 'Cable: CY 9 LEO SS 254 2 1325Z: P4', p. 40.

[220] A. M. Rosenthal, 'Katanga Police Defy U.N. Use Airports It Occupied', *The New York Times*, 10 September 1960.

control of these spaces, triggering further tensions.[221] Despite his brief time on the ground, Cordier intensified the politically motivated violence during the constitutional crisis. Indeed, scholars such as Carole Collins have argued that his decision to close the airports produced wider ramifications for the future political turmoil in the country and the takeover of Mobutu's authoritarian regime in 1965.[222]

In response to the closure of airports and the radio station, many anti-colonial groups and diplomatic representatives from Ghana, Guinea, and Tunisia wrote to Hammarskjöld, reminding him of the mission's impartial mandate.[223] Dennis Phombeah, President of the Committee of African Organisations,[224] cabled that he was 'Convinced ONU taking sides in Congo [sic]. Demand you free radio and all airfields immediately repeat immediately'.[225] The Hungarian government also complained that the ONUC technicians' occupation of the national broadcasting station 'openly intervened in the internal affairs of the country'.[226] The use of military force to close Leopoldville airport was outrageous to Lumumba supporters considering Hammarskjöld's repeated refusal to use of force in Katanga for the same reason (interference in Congolese internal politics).[227] Additionally, activists such as *Le congrès d'Association des juristes démocrates*, a Paris-based group, telegrammed its shock,

> that today, following the intervention of UN forces, the Congolese government, which has never been put in the minority by the Congolese chambers, has been reduced to powerlessness by the authorities of the UN who deprived him of the use of national radio and airfields.[228]

In the midst of this political crisis, many groups sought to remind Hammarskjöld that Lumumba was the lawful Prime Minister of Congo and any attempt to

221 BNA, FO 371/146779, JB2257/239, 'Weekly Situation Report: UN Force', 12 September 1960.

222 C. J. L. Collins, 'The Cold War Comes to Africa: Cordier and the 1960 Congo Crisis', *Journal of International Affairs*, 47:1 (1993), p. 246.

223 Liu, 'Interview Transcript', p. 32.

224 For more on Phombeah and his career during decolonisation, see J. R. Brennan, 'The Secret Lives of Dennis Phombeah: Decolonization, the Cold War, and African Political Intelligence, 1953–1974', *The International History Review*, 43:1 (2020), pp. 153–169.

225 UNA, S-0845-0001-02-00001, 'Cable: UNATIONS RC19 UXS845 OPH3874', 7 September 1960, p. 53.

226 UNA, S-0845-0001-02-00001, 'Cable: UNATIONS DS41 T196 BUDAPEST 149 14 1102', 14 September 1960, p. 47.

227 UNA, S-0845-0001-03-00001, 'Statement by Secretary-General on Entry of Troops into Katanga', 3 August 1960, p. 2.

228 UNA, S-0845-0001-02-00001, 'Cable: UNATIONS NY, BUN ACR1/TG350/ST130', 17 October 1960, pp. 30–31.

prevent him accessing Congolese spaces was a direct breach of his sovereignty and contrary to ONUC's impartiality.

Although not officially in sovereign control of the country, Cordier's actions provoked international accusations that the UN had taken advantage of the power vacuum during the constitutional crisis to transform Congo into a UN trusteeship.[229] British MP Isaac James Pitman reported to the House of Commons that confusion surrounding UN sovereign control had led to the ONUC mission shouldering greater responsibilities for the safety and maintenance of facilities, such as the airports, that would typically be under the jurisdiction of the host government. He recalled how in 'late August the American Ambassador in Leopoldville, Mr. [Clare] Timberlake, was reported as, '"sharply protesting that US aircraft would not land any more at the Congo airports until ... the United Nations could guarantee adequate military protection for the aircraft and their crews"'. Timberlake's point prompted Pitman to ask the House: 'Who is responsible for the safety of aircraft landing? Is it really the United Nations and not the Government of the country concerned?'[230] Cordier's decision to close Leopoldville's airport and its radio station shook what had been virtually unanimous international support of the ONUC mission as seen in the passing of the initial resolution, prompting member-state representatives to question the independence and political motivations of Cordier's ruling. This incident recalibrated international perceptions of the UN leadership's intentions – and power – in Congo.[231]

The access provided to the ONUC technicians by infrastructural jobs in airports and broadcasting stations swiftly became a diplomatic issue for contributing nations. The United Arab Republic (UAR) deployed troops to the ONUC mission in August, but following the perceived failure of ONUC staff to accept Lumumba's legal standing as Prime Minister of Congo, the UAR leadership withdrew their troops from United Nations command. Egyptian leader, Nasser, and Syrian military commanders established the political union on 1 February 1958 as a demonstration of Pan-Arab unity. Although the UAR continued to host UNEF for another seven years, UAR leaders criticised ONUC's manipulation and instrumentalisation of Congolese infrastructure in support of Kasavubu and his main political ally, Mobutu. The British embassy in Cairo wrote to the Foreign Office to inform them that all their private documents relating to UAR's decision emphasised the role of ONUC's closure of Leopoldville airport and broadcasting station as the primary reasons for their withdrawal of support and troops from the ONUC

[229] Dunn, *Imagining the Congo*, p. 99.

[230] UNA, S-0845-0001-02-00001, I. J. Pitman, 'House of Commons Speech: United Nations, the Congo and a World Security Authority', Wednesday, 21 December 1960, p. 6.

[231] UN Doc, S/4387, '143 (1960). Resolution of 14 July 1960: The Congo Question'.

mission.[232] The UAR representative argued that Cordier's actions had created 'suspicion of bias against Lumumba'.[233] The UAR Minister of State, Abdul al-Qadir Hatim, publicly confirmed these motivations for the decision and described the UN technicians within the airport and radio stations as participating in an 'occupation ... [constituting] a grave menace to the independence and unity of the Congo'.[234]

The ONUC mission continued to attract international criticism and controversy following the constitutional crisis, damaging the UN's reputation (particularly with Afro-Asian nations) and spiralling into a financial crisis for the organisation.[235] In response to Cordier's closures of the airports and radio-stations, the Afro-Asian People's Solidarity Organisation (AAPSO) created a fund in November 1960 to counteract post-colonial states' economic dependence on the UN and ensure autonomy from the organisation.[236] Katherine McGregor and Vanessa Hearman have argued that this fund was set up 'because after the events of Congo [Afro-Asian nations] no longer trusted the UN'.[237]

The ONUC mission's approach to Lumumba was further criticised once the Prime Minister was first placed under house arrest and then later formally arrested by Kasavubu's ally, Mobutu and his soldiers on 1 December 1960.[238] In footage from the arrest, Mobutu tied up Lumumba and allowed one of his soldiers to try and force into Lumumba's mouth a crumpled speech asserting

232 BNA, FO 371/146779, JB2251/256, 'Statement by UAR Deputy Minister for Presidential Affairs: Announcement of the Withdrawal of UAR Troops from UN Command', 12 September 1960.

233 BNA, FO 371/146779, JB2251/256, 'Statement by UAR Deputy Minister for Presidential Affairs: Announcement of the Withdrawal of UAR Troops from UN Command', 12 September 1960.

234 BNA, FO 371/146779, JB2251/256, 'Statement by UAR Deputy Minister for Presidential Affairs: Announcement of the Withdrawal of UAR Troops from UN Command', 12 September 1960.

235 R. L. West, 'The United Nations and the Congo Financial Crisis: Lessons of the First Year', *International Organization*, 15:4 (1961), pp. 603–617; T. J. Hamilton, 'THE U.N.: Problems over Goa, Congo and Finances Create New Crisis for World Organization', *The New York Times*, 24 December 1961; T. J. Hamilton, 'U.N. Financial Troubles: Some Members' Failure to Pay Share Jeopardizes Future Operations', *The New York Times*, 3 December 1961.

236 K. McGregor and V. Hearman, 'Challenging the Lifeline of Imperialism: Reassessing Afro-Asian Solidarity and Related Activism in the Decade 1955–1965', in L. Eslava, M. Fakhri, and V. Nesiah (eds.), *Bandung, Global History, and International Law: Critical Pasts and Pending Futures* (Cambridge: Cambridge University Press, 2017), p. 171.

237 McGregor and Hearman, 'Challenging the Lifeline of Imperialism', p. 171.

238 G. Nzongola-Ntalaja, *The Congo from Leopold to Kabila: A People's History* (London: Bloomsbury, 2002), pp. 109–112.

his claim to power.[239] Mobutu flew Lumumba first to Leopoldville and then to Thysville to supposedly put the deposed Prime Minister on trial. The international reaction to his arrest was immediate: the Soviet Union demanded his release and drafted resolutions that instructed ONUC to put the Prime Minster back in power. National contingents from Yugoslavia, Ceylon, Indonesia, Morocco, and Guinea followed the UAR in withdrawing their troops in protest of the mission leadership's treatment of Lumumba, voicing concerns about the independence of the mission. The withdrawal of Morocco's troops was a heavy strategic blow for ONUC as the 3,300 troops were the largest national contingent in the UN mission.[240] Guinean President Touré emphasised in the Security Council that 'We denounce with profound indignation the complicit of the international organization with the usurpers of power in the Congo'.[241] Yugoslavian representative Dobrivoje Vidic questioned the 'unexplainably tolerant attitude' of the UN in response to Lumumba's arrest.[242] Ghanaian President Kwame Nkrumah also criticised the overt 'partisanship' of the mission against Lumumba but was conflicted as it had been Ghanaian troops that occupied Radio Léopoldville.[243] Tunisian representative Mongi Slim reminded Hammarskjöld of the large numbers of Belgian nationals remaining in Congo and the failure of ONUC to remove them despite their direct role in exacerbating conflict in Katanga.[244] ONUC's decision-making in during this period shifted international perceptions of the mission for the international community and, in particular, contributing nations. These events revealed the ONUC leadership's willingness to not only occupy but also to instrumentalise the governmental activities of another nation to suit their own political preferences. For an organisation that relied upon the operational donations of troops and funds from its member-states, criticism from contributing nations threatened the operational stability of not only ONUC but also future peacekeeping missions.

Whilst these political reactions destabilised ONUC's reputation, Lumumba and two of his political associates were moved by Mobutu and Tshombe to Katanga to prevent his escape. Once in Elisabethville, Katangan police officials (most of whom were Belgian) and Belgian mercenaries tortured and executed

[239] British Pathe, 'Congo: Premiere Lumumba Arrested', 1960, Film ID: 3000.07, available at: www.britishpathe.com/video/congo-premiere-lumumba-arrested-aka-lumumba-arrest.

[240] L. Parrott, 'Two Nations to Quit UN Force: Charter Violations Charged by Morocco and Guinea', *The New York Times*, 13 December 1960.

[241] Parrott, 'Two Nations to Quit UN Force'.

[242] J. Feron, 'Three Countries Quit UN Congo Force in Protest Move', *The New York Times*, 8 December 1960.

[243] J. Mohan, 'Ghana, the Congo, and the United Nations', *Journal of Modern African Studies*, 7:3 (1969), p. 390.

[244] Parrott, 'Two Nations to Quit UN Force'.

Lumumba and his colleagues on 17 January 1961. The Belgian government had ordered his assassination, and CIA officials oversaw the disposal of his body in a shallow grave and, the next day, disinterred and dissolved in sulfuric acid.[245] In an act of colonial violence, the Belgian mercenaries removed Lumumba's gold-capped tooth as a 'souvenir'.[246] Subsequently, the remains were transported to Belgium by Gérard Soete, a Belgian police officer, who had participated in the murder and described the tooth as 'a type of hunting trophy'.[247] Sixty-one years later, the Belgian government returned Lumumba's remains to his descendants in a ceremony on 20 June 2022.[248] No criminal investigation has been opened into his murder.

Once made aware of the murders, the UN leadership prepared for the shock Lumumba's death would have on the Congolese population. ONUC personnel worried that it would provoke instability and violence against international staff. Ludo de Witte has examined how Dayal 'informed diplomats in the Congo that "the United Nations is offering protection to everybody on Katangan soil", meaning of course, that every *foreigner* could take advantage of the organisation's benevolence'.[249] Although a UN Commission of Inquiry was set up to investigate the circumstances surrounding Lumumba's death, the Belgian government concealed their reports of the assassination, thus obstructing any meaningful investigation into the crime.[250] In establishing this Commission of Inquiry, the UN leadership obstructed the complicity of the ONUC staff and mission operations in facilitating the political conditions for Lumumba's murder. Georges Nzongola-Ntalaja has explored Bunche's anti-Lumumba position during his time as representative in Congo and has argued that Bunche's evident 'contempt' for the Congolese Prime Minister was a 'contributing factor to Lumumba's demise'.[251] Nzongola-Ntalaja's analysis of cables between Hammarskjöld and Bunche during Congo's early months has

245 For extensive detail on the actors involved in the assassination of Lumumba, see L. de Witte, *The Assassination of Lumumba* (London: Verso, 2001); E. Gerard, *Death in the Congo: Murdering Patrice Lumumba* (Cambridge, MA: Harvard University Press, 2015); L. Seilig, *Lumumba: Africa's Lost Leader* (London: Haus Publishing, 2015); G. Nzongola-Ntalaja, *Patrice Lumumba* (Athens: Ohio University Press, 2014); S. Kelly, *America's Tyrant: The CIA and Mobutu of Zaire* (New York: American University Press, 1993.

246 For more on 'trophy-taking' as an imperial practice, see K. Wagner, *The Skull of Alum Bheg: The Life and Death of a Rebel of 1857* (London: Hurst, 2017).

247 C. Gijs and S. Faris, 'Lumumba's Tooth: Belgium's Unfinished Reckoning with Its Colonial Past', *POLITICO*, 2 June 2022.

248 J. Flanagan and B. Waterfield, 'Belgium Says Sorry for Patrice Lumumba's Murder with Return of His Gold Tooth', *The Times*, 27 May 2022.

249 de Witte, *The Assassination of Lumumba*, p. 139.

250 UN Doc, S/3476, 'Report of the Commission of Investigation established under the terms of General Assembly resolution 1601 (XV) of 15 April 1961', 11 November 1961.

251 G. Nzongola-Ntalaja, 'Ralph Bunche, Patrice Lumumba, and the First Congo Crisis', in R. A. Hill and E. J. Keller (eds.), *Trustee for the Human Community: Ralph J Bunche, the*

further illuminated the internal racist logic of UN peacekeeping staff and demonstrated that it shaped ONUC's interference in Congolese politics, provoking ongoing violence and political instability.[252]

Once Lumumba's death was announced a month after his murder, the news further fuelled solidarity abroad and distrust from Afro-Asian nations, prompting international protests against the ONUC mission and the UN secretary-general as well as the Belgian government.[253] Outside the UN headquarters and Belgian Embassies in major cities, such as Cairo, Accra, Havana, Moscow, London, and Brussels, demonstrators blamed UN leadership for failing to protect the Prime Minister.[254] In New York, sixty men and women, mostly Black, interrupted the Security Council session on 16 February 1961 with signs such as 'Murder Inc., Hammarskjöld, Ralph Bunche, Kasavubu, Tshombe, Mobutu' and 'Imperialists – Lumumba's blood is on your hands'.[255] Later, three hundred protestors marched through midtown Manhattan.[256] Leftist student groups were particularly outraged by the execution, and Lumumba became a martyr for global national liberation and communist movements.[257] Women led the march in Accra, Ghana, on 17 February 1961 and held placards reading 'Down with Kasavubu the traitor', 'Africa holds Belgian responsible for Lumumba's death', and 'Hammarskjold must be sacked'. One woman held a sign which read, 'The evil that men do lives after them', lamenting the generational burden of patriarchal, imperialist violence.

In response to Lumumba's death, ONUC leadership reenergised their military operations in order to restore control over the political conflict in

United Nations, and the Decolonisation of Africa (Athens: Ohio University Press, 2010), p. 149

252 Nzongola-Ntalaja, 'Ralph Bunche, Patrice Lumumba, and the First Congo Crisis', p. 155.

253 S. Williams, *White Malice: The CIA and the Neocolonisation of Africa* (London: Hurst, 2021); P. Monaville, 'The Political Life of the Dead Lumumba: Cold War Histories and the Congolese Student Left', *Africa*, 89:S1 (2019), pp. S15–S39; C. Katsakioris, 'The Lumumba University in Moscow: Higher Education for a Soviet–Third World Alliance, 1960–91', *The Journal of Global History*, 14:2 (2019), pp. 281–300; S. Kendall, 'Postcolonial Hauntings and Cold War Continuities: Congolese Sovereignty and the Murder of Patrice Lumumba', in M. Craven et al. (eds.), *International Law and the Cold War* (Cambridge: Cambridge University Press, 2019).

254 'Riot in Gallery Halts U.N. Debate', *The New York Times*, 16 February 1961; J. Feron, 'U.N. Takes Steps to Prevent Riots: Guards Armed with Clubs – Arrests to Be Made in Future Demonstrations', *The New York Times*, 17 February 1961; 'Congo Issue Stirs Rioting in London: Police Halt Mob's Attempt to Rush Belgian Embassy in Lumumba Protest', *The New York Times*, 20 February 1961.

255 'Riot in Gallery Halts U.N. Debate'.

256 'Riot in Gallery Halts U.N. Debate'.

257 P. Monaville, *Students of the World: Global 1968 and Decolonization in the Congo* (Durham: Duke University Press, 2022).

Figure 3.2 Memorial Service for Patrice Lumumba in Accra: "Hammarskjold must be sacked" slogans, K036441.
Reproduced with permission from Keystone/Hulton Archive/Getty Images.

Congo, focusing on restoring law and order in Katanga as Belgian mercenaries continued to destabilise the region and promote anti-UN rhetoric.[258] In February 1961, the Security Council authorised the expansion of ONUC's military functions in Congo, and by September the mission leadership had launched Operation Morthor (Hindi for 'smash') to eliminate mercenaries from Katanga.[259] However, the violence swiftly escalated into open warfare with the Siege of Jadotville from 14 to 17 September 1961, resulting in the capture of a contingent of Irish peacekeepers by those fighting for the Katangan secession, including the Katangan army, Belgian mercenaries, and armed settlers.[260] The peacekeepers were caught in Katanga without knowledge of an incoming ONUC strike on Thursday, 13 September, and had only

[258] There is extensive literature on the role of mercenaries in Katanga, including memoirs and interviews. For a useful overview of their political contribution to the Congo crisis and the shift towards authoritarianism under Mobutu, see L. de Witte, 'The Suppression of the Congo Rebellions and the Rise of Mobutu, 1963–1965', *The International History Review*, 39:1 (2017), pp. 107–125.

[259] UN Doc, S/4741, S/RES/161, 'Security Council Resolution 161 (1961) [The Congo Question]', 21 February 1961.

[260] C. G. Thomas and T. Falola, *Secession and Separatist Conflicts in Postcolonial Africa* (Calgary: University of Calgary Press, 2020), pp. 48–49.

been told that the UN controlled the capital city in the southern region and that it was safe to enter. They were encircled by Katangan fighters within an hour of this communication, outnumbering the UN troops by almost 2,000 mercenaries.[261] During the four days of what one Irish peacekeeper described as 'sheer hell', the violent response of Belgian settlers and fighters further complicated the UN's attitude towards the question of Katanga.[262] In the beginning of the conflict, Hammarskjöld had determined that the violence in Katanga was an issue of Congolese internal affairs – despite Lumumba's pleas to intervene – and therefore outside of ONUC's military mandate. However, as reports of the siege of Jadotville emerged, it became clear that the UN and ONUC leadership had underestimated the military power in Katanga and had left the Irish troops in isolation. *The New York Times* reported that the Irish UN peacekeepers were 'bitter' that they had not been informed of the ONUC advance to capture Elizabethville earlier that week. They believed this was because the UN 'never really expected any serious Katangese resistance' in response to the September advance, suggesting that ONUC's military leadership was severely underprepared and disconnected from the security situation in Katanga, despite Lumumba's murder. This failure in communication also revealed the hierarchy in the field between mission staff and soldiers. After four days of fighting, the Katanganese fighters mutinied against their white Belgian officers and organised a ceasefire with the surrendering Irish peacekeepers.[263] The peacekeepers remained worried that their situation would be 'used by the United Nations as propaganda' and 'hurt their chances of freedom' before they could return to their barracks in Elizabethville.[264] This fear was correct. The Irish peacekeepers were held until the end of October, enabling the Katanganese leadership to negotiate the terms of the ceasefire and seek the release of Katangan prisoners held by the central Congolese government. This was a significant diplomatic failure for the ONUC mission.

Once the ONUC troops seized control of Elizabethville in Katanga and the Irish troops had surrendered, Hammarskjöld decided to personally mediate the situation and go to the region to establish a permanent ceasefire.[265] Whilst travelling to visit Katangan leader Tshombe in neutral territory, his plane was shot down near Ndola, Northern Rhodesia, on 18 September 1961, killing the secretary-general and sixteen other passengers. Although the crash was initially described as a tragic accident, rumours and conspiracies continued to

[261] 'Irish Troops' Four-Day Ordeal in Katanga Siege Is Described', *The New York Times*, 21 September 1961.
[262] 'Irish Troops' Four-Day Ordeal in Katanga Siege Is Described'.
[263] S. P. Brewer, 'UN Reports Irish Win a Cease-Fire at Katanga Base', 17 September 1961.
[264] 'Irish Troops' Four-Day Ordeal in Katanga Siege Is Described'.
[265] D. Halberstam, 'U.N. Takes Katanga', *The New York Times*, 14 September 1961.

question the events, and recent scholarship suggests that it was shot down by Belgian mercenaries from another plane or that South African mercenaries (potentially with CIA support) sabotaged the plane before take-off.[266] The resulting shock and fallout within the UN was felt on the ground within the ONUC bureaucracy as the ONUC troops struggled to contain the violence in Katanga, threatening the unity of the nation. The 'Siege of Jadotville' and Hammarskjöld's death brought further instability to the organisation and attracted greater international scrutiny to the peacekeeping practices and military presence in Congo. These crises shaped the future diplomatic discourses about the mission as a whole within the UN headquarters in New York; humiliating the UN, demonstrating its weakness in military operations, and exposing the political character of peacekeeping.[267]

The Security Council's temporary appointment of U Thant in November 1961 prompted a shift in ONUC's approach from defensive to offensive. The mission expanded its military functions once more, suggesting that Thant would be more reactive to the demands of the Afro-Asian bloc than Hammarskjöld. However, from December 1961, the expense of the mission in Congo became a source of criticism from multiple member-states, in particular the United States, as they criticised Thant for not being able to end the violence in Congo despite the expanded military mandate to combat Katanga.[268] As Operation UNOKAT escalated violence between ONUC troops and Katanganese fighters towards the close of 1961, it was clear that the mission would not be withdrawing soon. With a financial and reputational crisis on the horizon and continued bloodshed in Congo, the UN needed to swiftly demonstrate its value in international peace and security. Thant had been elected to the office of the secretary-general at a pivotal moment in UN history.

Conclusion

ONUC bureaucrats influenced the direction of the conflict and political future of Congo during the first phase of the mission, by supporting Kasavubu to remove Lumumba from power. Motivated by a paternalistic desire to educate

[266] For more on the conspiracies surrounding Hammarskjöld's crash, see S. Williams, *Who Killed Hammarskjöld?: The UN, the Cold War, and White Supremacy in Africa* (London: Hurst, 2011); S. Williams, *White Malice: The CIA and the Covert Recolonization of Africa* (London: Hurst, 2021); R. Somaiya, *Operation Morthor: The Death of Dag Hammarskjöld and the Last Great Mystery of the Cold War* (London: Penguin Books, 2020).

[267] For more detail on these diplomatic discourses and the fallout of ONUC in UN headquarters, see O'Malley, *The Diplomacy of Decolonisation.*

[268] Hamilton, 'THE U.N.: Problems over Goa, Congo and Finances Create New Crisis for World Organization'; Hamilton, 'U.N. Financial Troubles'.

Congolese elites, UN staff replaced Belgian administrators and technicians, believing that the Congo crisis and political emergency was largely due to 'intense inter-tribal conflict' rather than the ongoing presence of colonial staff and troops.[269] Mission leadership revived colonial infrastructures and modes of governance, disconnecting the peacekeeping staff from the aspirations and experiences of the local population and making them unable to recognise the psychological or political impact of peace operations, particularly their close resemblance to a foreign invasion or occupation. In attempting to orchestrate Congo's future, the ONUC leadership revealed a desire to paternalistically interfere in the politics and governance of the sovereign nation. The apolitical image of ONUC's technical aid quickly wore away to reveal that the mission was an experiment in non-governmental state-building.

The intervention of the UN in this crisis and the leadership's concerns with maintaining the unity of Congo corresponded to the secretary-general's vision of a post-colonial liberal member-state with an anti-Soviet stance. ONUC's political intervention in September 1960 was made controversial through comparison to Hammarskjöld's refusal to use force in response to the Katangan secession and continued Belgian presence in the south.[270] The secretary-general's efforts to recruit ONUC leadership with similar political visions to him led to a culture of paternalism and entitlement within the mission bureaucracy. This culture pushed the ONUC leadership to interfere in the political milieu in Congo, igniting domestic and international resentment towards the mission and, more broadly, the UN peacekeeping project. Thus, the mission perpetuated late imperialism in its delivery *and* rationalisation of its operations in Congo: the ONUC leadership characterised their presence as part of a benevolent strategy to forge a modern, progressive state that would be welcomed into the Western-aligned bloc of the General Assembly.

The Congo mission allowed UN peacekeeping staff to intervene in a newly independent nation and offered mid-level bureaucrats an environment in which to experiment with non-state governance and post-colonial international administration – experiences that UN staff, such as U Thant and Bunche, would then transport into the UNTEA mission in West Papua and UNFICYP in Cyprus. With financial, geopolitical, and military pressures mounting in early 1962 and the reputations of Thant and the organisation at risk, the UN Secretariat staff waited for a conflict that would provide the conditions in which the UN could demonstrate its expertise in peacekeeping and international diplomacy. In May 1962, Thant requested Hammarskjöld's files on the West Papua dispute following a series of violent skirmishes in the

[269] UN Doc, S/4557, 'Second Progress Report to the Secretary-General', p. 29.
[270] Brady, 'Lumumba Angered by Use of Whites as Katanga Force'.

Pacific between the Dutch and Indonesian armies.[271] The violence had already attracted the attention of the two Cold War superpowers. This was the organisation's opportunity. He decided to intervene in West Papuan to de-escalate and control the situation before it grew into an international emergency like the Congo crisis.[272]

[271] UNA, S-0876-0001-06-00001, 'Confidential Note on Hammarskjöld Files from Thant to Engers', 31 May 1962.
[272] 'Another Jungle War', *The New York Times*, 20 May 1962.

4

Obstructing Self-Determination, 1962–1963

Introduction: Racialised Knowledge Production in West Papua

As the military strategies and controversies of the peacekeeping mission in Congo attracted negative attention in UN forums and the global media, the UN fought to restore its reputation, in particular with the Afro-Asian bloc, as a guardian of international peace and conflict response. However, as Cold War rivalries increasingly threatened global security in the early 1960s, the UN Secretariat staff became further convinced that preventing instability within decolonising contexts presented the greatest defence against communist influence or aggression. It was in this atmosphere of institutional anxiety and escalating external pressure that the organisation intervened in the Pacific and deployed a peacekeeping mission to West Papua – the territory sharing the 'Papua' or 'New Guinea' island with Papua New Guinea – as an administrative and sovereign intermediary between Dutch colonisation and Indonesian re-colonisation.[1] This peacekeeping mission was the organisation's first international territorial administration since its forebear organisation, the League of Nations, occupied the Saar territory on the Franco-German border from 1920 to 1935.[2] The General Assembly resolution 1752 (XVII) authorised the United Nations Temporary Executive Authority (UNTEA), also referred to as 'Auntie',[3] in September 1962 following a bilateral agreement brokered between the Netherlands and Indonesia by the new secretary-general,

[1] The territory was also referred to as West New Guinea, West Irian ('Irian' is a Biak word meaning 'hot land'), or Irian Barat during the 1960s. However, West Papuan activists adopted the term in 1961, and so it will be used throughout this chapter outside of direct quotes or references.

[2] R. Wilde, *International Territorial Administration: How Trusteeship and the Civilising Mission Never Went Away* (Oxford: Oxford University Press, 2008), p. 60; N. Macqueen, 'Cold War Peacekeeping versus Humanitarian Intervention: Beyond the Hammarskjöldian Model', in F. Klose (ed.), *The Emergence of Humanitarian Intervention: Ideas and Practice from the Nineteenth Century to the Present* (Cambridge: Cambridge University Press, 2015)', p. 235.

[3] B. Grant, '"Auntie" Takes over Irian Gently', *The Washington Post*, 14 October 1962; 'As the Dutch Say a Hard Farewell', *The Straits Times*, 15 October 1962.

U Thant.[4] The parties to the Agreement permitted the UN to govern West Papua for seven months, with the hopes that the mission would maintain the law and order in the territory and ensure a smooth transition from Dutch to Indonesian sovereignty. However, once deployed to the region, UNTEA staff swiftly became aware of anti-Indonesian Papuan activism as well as repeated Indonesian abuses against West Papuans who rejected annexation. As Papuans urgently communicated their fears to UNTEA staff, the mission leadership prioritised the completion of the mission mandate, their anxieties of growing Soviet influence in the Pacific, and the perpetuation of a self-determination hierarchy over the civil rights of Papuan communities.

UNTEA differed from the UNEF mission, shifting from a military emphasis to an administrative mandate. The military activities were completed by Pakistani troops deployed to the sister mission, the United Nations Security Force (UNSF), which concentrated on policing and maintaining law and order rather than front line warfare as in UNEF and ONUC. The UNTEA mission also diverged from ONUC in its size and scale: the number of staff on the ground for UNTEA/UNSF was 10 per cent of those deployed to ONUC, with 1,500 Pakistani troops, a small contingent of Canadian air force officers,[5] and around 600 civilian staff.[6] *The Straits Times* reported that initially only twenty international staff arrived in October 1962, excluding Indonesian and Dutch UNTEA staff, to take over administration of the territory.[7] Despite these differences in the size and scope of UNTEA and ONUC, the UNTEA peacekeepers' perception of the Papuan population was underpinned by similar racial prejudices and beliefs in the superiority of certain ethnic groups over others and thus the validity of their claims to statehood.

The West Papua dispute demonstrated that the UN's international relations paradigm and legal norms were fundamentally challenged by decolonisation processes: the issue of the increasing 'territorialisation of political identity' and questions of indigenous nationalist or independence movements were uncomfortable geopolitical problems for the UN leadership.[8] As more colonised nations achieved independence, some dominant states attempted to expand

[4] UN Doc, A/RES/1752(XVII), '1752 (XVII) Agreement between the Republic of Indonesia and the Kingdom of the Netherlands Concerning West New Guinea (West Irian)', 1127th General Assembly Plenary Meeting, 21 September 1962.

[5] Library and Archives Canada (LAC), RG25 (External Affairs, 6150, 50409-A-40, 'Visit of Canadian UNTEA Personnel to Djakarta, signed by Ambassador, 30 November 1962'.

[6] 'West New Guinea – UNSF: Background', United Nations Peacekeeping, available at: https://peacekeeping.un.org/en/mission/past/unsfbackgr.html.

[7] 'As the Dutch Say a Hard Farewell'.

[8] J. MacArthur, 'Decolonizing Sovereignty: States of Exception along the Kenya–Somali Frontier', *The American Historical Review*, 124:1 (2019), p. 109; D. B. Carter and H. E. Goemans, 'The Making of the Territorial Order: New Borders and the Emergence of Interstate Conflict', *International Organization*, 65:2 (2011), pp. 275–309.

their artificial borders and make claims on neighbouring or proximate regions.[9] In the post-colonial international order, imperialist ambitions and military aggression were no longer restricted to the 'Great Powers'. Although there was vocal anti-colonial rhetoric in the General Assembly and its Committees during the 1950s and 1960s,[10] some of the most vocal 'anti-colonial' states – such as Indonesia and India – simultaneously repressed independence campaigns *and* pursued imperial expansion.[11] Following independence from the British Empire, India had annexed the Portuguese territories of Goa, Damao, and Diu in December 1961, resulting in heated debates in the UN Security Council.[12] India also annexed the Himalayan kingdom of Sikkim in the same year that Indonesia began its military campaign to colonise East Timor.[13] This hypocrisy muddied the waters of anti-colonial voting alliances in UN forums. It also resulted in a lack of legal agreement between UN member-state representatives, and UN staff on the question of self-determination or political enfranchisement for non-nationalist, secessionist, or indigenous independence movements.[14]

Post-colonial states' expansionist aspirations translated into protracted disputes and violent conflicts attracting the attention of the UN Secretariat. Conflicts such as the Eritrean separatist movement from Ethiopian rule in 1961, the Kenya-Somali frontier debates in 1963, the annexation of the Western Sahara by Morocco in the mid-1970s, and the Indonesian occupation of East Timor in 1975 repeatedly tested the UN leadership on the principles of their own Charter *and* its diplomatic agility as it negotiated with this new age of colonialism.[15] Building upon the legal traditions and systems of the League of Nations, the membership structure of the UN in the post-war context fostered an international order whereby only nation-state status could provide access to the forums of global decision-making and recourse for rights and

[9] P. H. Justin and L. De Vries, 'Governing Unclear Lines: Local Boundaries as a (Re)source of Conflict in South Sudan', *Journal of Borderlands Studies*, 34:1 (2019), pp. 31–46.

[10] S. L. B. Jensen, *The Making of International Human Rights: The 1960s, Decolonization, and the Reconstruction of Global Values* (Cambridge: Cambridge University Press, 2016); J. Pearson, 'Defending Empire at the United Nations: The Politics of International Colonial Oversight in the Era of Decolonisation', *Journal of Imperial and Commonwealth History*, 45:3 (2017), pp. 525–549.

[11] R. Strating and A. E. Davis, 'Bordering the Postcolonial State: The Relevance of Sikkim in India's Support for Indonesia's Occupation of East Timor', *Commonwealth & Comparative Politics*, 60:2 (2022), pp. 169–189.

[12] Q. Wright, 'The Goa Incident', *The American Journal of International Law*, 56:3 (1962), pp. 617–632.

[13] Strating and Davis, 'Bordering the Postcolonial State', pp. 169–189.

[14] Jensen, *The Making of International Human Rights*.

[15] UN Doc, A/PV.1016, 'General Assembly, Sixteenth Session, Plenary Meetings: Tuesday, 26 September 1961', p. 108.

justice.[16] For minority or indigenous groups within (post)colonial territories, the evolving international community required them to immediately develop a popular nationalist movement or be re-colonised. This demand re-constructed regional allegiances and presented only the protection of nationalisation for those who refused re-colonisation.

This international system encouraged UN peacekeepers to make decisions in the interests of the organisation's international reputation rather than taking steps to protect the rights of the indigenous Papuan population because they did not fit UNTEA staffs' particular – racially motivated – perception of a credibly politically active population. In September 1962, the UN General Assembly delegates feared that the organisation was under threat and emphasised the need to re-establish member-states' confidence in the UN's operational capabilities following the death of Dag Hammarskjöld in September 1961.[17] The new acting secretary-general, U Thant, immediately faced multiple complicated crises in addition to existing financial and operational dilemmas. This institutional pressure was compounded by the outpouring of criticism following a series of controversial military manoeuvres during the Congo mission. ONUC had marred the perceived capability and credibility of the organisation's decision-making in the field, and the UNTEA mission was an opportunity for the organisation to reassert its expertise in terms of conflict response.

Avoiding 'Another Congo'

West Papua has been historically understood as a terrain not easily aligned with traditional concepts of national land borders and sovereignty.[18] It is a landscape that includes highlands, lowlands, and multiple islands and is positioned at the meeting point of Southeast Asia and Melanesia cultures in the Pacific Ocean.[19] Due to this topography, seventeenth-century Dutch

[16] M. L. Siegelberg, *Statelessness: A Modern History* (Cambridge, MA: Harvard University Press, 2020), p. 8; E. O. Abuya, U. Krause, and M. Mayblin, 'The Neglected Colonial Legacy of the 1951 Refugee Convention', *International Migration*, 59:4 (2021), p. 265.

[17] UNA, S-0876-0001-06-00001, 'Internal Report from Engers to Thant', 17 August 1962, p. 8; T. J. Hamilton, 'U.N. under Pressure: Financial Crisis and Criticism of Policy Beset World Organization', *The New York Times*, 11 February 1962.

[18] P. van der Veur, *Search for New Guinea's Boundaries: From Torres Strait to the Pacific* (Canberra: ANU Press, 1966).

[19] R. Eves, 'Unsettling Settler Colonialism: Debates over Climate and Colonization in New Guinea, 1875–1914', *Ethnic and Racial Studies*, 28:2 (2005), pp. 304–330; R. J. May, 'On the Asia–Oceania Interface: The West Papua Issue in a Regional Context', *Outre-Terre*, 58–59:1 (2020), pp. 143–179.

imperialists struggled to travel across the territory and only meaningfully administrated small areas of the territory.[20] Dutch colonial administrators were unable to interact with most of the Papuan population in the years before Indonesian independence from the Dutch East Indies, limiting the imperialists to superficial control.[21] Dutch colonisation of West Papua differed from the Indonesian experience. For the Indonesians, especially those on the island of Java, Dutch colonial oppression pervaded daily life throughout the late nineteenth and early twentieth century.[22] In contrast, the majority of the West Papuan population lived independently of colonial structures and Christian missionaries, and saw Dutch imperialism as a nominal arrangement until the Second World War.[23] The territories' contrasting experiences of Dutch colonialism shaped different public memories of the period and forged separate motivations for independence despite being ruled by the same European power. As Vincent Bevins has argued, 'Nothing brought the [Dutch East Indies islands] together other than the artificial boundaries imposed by a racist foreign power'.[24]

Having achieved from the Dutch in 1949, Indonesian resentment towards their colonisers grew out of a Dutch refusal to withdraw from West Papua and consent to its independence as part of Indonesia.[25] In the post-war period, Indonesia used the forum of the UN Security Council to promote its national identity and shed light on the crimes of Dutch imperialism.[26] When Indonesian President Sukarno demanded Papuan liberation from the Dutch during negotiations over Indonesian independence in 1949, he claimed that the people of West Papua should become part of Indonesia due to their shared identity as the Dutch East Indies during colonisation.[27] However, the Indonesian leadership

[20] S. R. Jaarsma, '"Your Work Is of No Use to Us...": Administrative Interests in Ethnographic Research (West New Guinea, 1950–1962)', *The Journal of Pacific History*, 29:2 (1994), p. 154.

[21] Jaarsma, '"Your Work Is of No Use to Us..."', p. 128.

[22] H. S. Nordholt, 'The Jago in the Shadow: Crime and "Order" in the Colonial State in Java', *RIMA*, 25:1 (1991), p. 77.

[23] Jaarsma, '"Your Work Is of No Use to Us..."', p. 154.

[24] V. Bevins, *The Jakarta Method: Washington's Anticommunist Crusade and the Mass Murder Program that Shaped Our World* (New York: PublicAffairs, 2020), p. 51.

[25] R. Aldrich, 'The Decolonisation of the Pacific Islands', *Itinerario*, 24:3–4 (2000), pp. 173–191.

[26] J. L. Foray, 'The Republic at the Table, with Decolonisation on the Agenda: The United Nations Security Council and the Question of Indonesian Representation, 1946–1947', *Itinerario*, 45:1 (2021), pp. 124–151.

[27] R. Elson, 'Marginality, Morality, and the Nationalist Impulse: Papua, the Netherlands and Indonesia: A Review Article', *Bijdragen en Mededelingen betreffende de Geschiedenis der derlanden*, 122:1 (2006), p. 5; B. Anderson, *Imagined Communities: Reflections on the Origin and Spread of Nationalism* (London: Verso, 1991), pp. 177–178; O. Mote and

did not appreciate the diversity of Dutch imperial practices and experiences across the region and how deeply this had affected the different populations' conceptions of their independent political, cultural, and national identities.[28] The Dutch government's refusal to transfer the territory to Indonesia led to outrage in Djakarta, the Indonesian capital.[29] The aspiration of national unity – the entirety of the Dutch East Indies – under an Indonesian flag was developed from the Indonesian population's suffering during Dutch imperialism.[30] These scars ultimately served as the motivation for the emotionally charged Indonesian campaign to 'reclaim' West Papua, regardless of the opinions of the West Papuan population.[31] For Indonesian Foreign Minister Subandrio, 'The basic facts of the situation could not be altered. West Irian was an integral part of the political entity known as Indonesia . . . Indonesian unity was based not on racial or ethnic ties, but on centuries of living together, and had been strengthened by common experiences under foreign rule.'[32] Throughout the 1950s, both Indonesian and Dutch diplomats lobbied for the support and votes of Afro-Asian UN member-states and the international community by providing anti-colonial arguments to justify their sovereign claims to the territory, although neither achieved universal success within the General Assembly or privately through meetings with other state delegates.[33]

By the end of the 1950s, the diplomatic dispute shifted from debates in the UN forums to violence in the Pacific. Vincent Kuitenbrouwer has stressed the volatile nature of this context and has described the two nations as on 'the brink of war' with 'skirmishes [claiming] the lives of dozens of soldiers on both sides',[34] worrying Australian, British, and US governments who occupied

D. Rutherford, 'From Irian Jaya to Papua: The Limits of Primordialism in Indonesia's Troubled East', *Indonesia*, 72 (2001), pp. 115–140.

28 Contrary to this Indonesian view, the opinion of most Papuans on the northern island of Biak-Numfoor was: 'The Papuans are not Indonesians . . . the Papuan country and the Papuan people have their own personality and the Papuan people [have] the right to have its own country in the same way as all the other peoples and nations of the world.' UNA, S-0884-0023-01-00001, 'Telegram from Numfoor District Council to U Thant', 24 July 1962, p. 30.

29 A. Lijphart, 'The Indonesian Image of West Irian', *Asian Survey*, 1:5 (1961), p. 11.

30 H. S. Nordholt, 'Indonesia in the 1950s: Nation, Modernity, and the Post-colonial State', *Bijdragen tot de Taal-, Land- en Volkenkunde*, 167:4 (2011), p. 398.

31 UNA, S-0884-0023-01-00001, 'Telegram from Numfoor District Council to U Thant', 24 July 1962, p. 30.

32 UN Docs, A/C.1/SR.905, 'General Assembly: Summary Record of the 905th Meeting', 20 November 1957, p. 199, para. 2.

33 C. Brown, 'Indonesia's West Irian Case in the UN General Assembly, 1954', *Journal of Southeast Asian Studies*, 7:2 (1976), p. 261.

34 V. Kuitenbrouwer, 'Beyond the "Trauma of Decolonisation": Dutch Cultural Diplomacy during the West New Guinea Question (1950–62)', *Journal of Imperial and Commonwealth History*, 44:2 (2016), p. 310.

nearby territories and protectorates.[35] Indonesia's increasingly close relationship with the Soviet Union also began to concern Western-aligned states in the international community. The geopolitical implications of the conflict between the two nations distracted the UN debates from West Papuan independence and instead focused global attention on the threat of escalating violence in the Pacific region. This escalation revealed how far the emotional attachment of the Indonesians to their colonial past – and present – was mirrored, in type, by the Dutch government. The Dutch campaign to retain West Papua was motivated by national anxiety over a waning international relevance following Indonesian independence in 1949.[36] For the Dutch government, West Papua represented the legacy of their former imperial 'glory' in the region and on the international stage, legitimising its diplomatic position within the geopolitical hierarchy.[37]

Paradoxically, by the late 1950s the Dutch had promised self-determination for the Papuan population, following a long period of tutelage (at least a decade) if the government retained colonial oversight over the territory.[38] Papuan nationalists had lobbied the Dutch for independence but recognised that the recent Congo crisis had provided the international community with a negative example of decolonisation and European evacuation. They insisted that the territory would not become 'another Congo' and that they were amenable to an incremental decolonisation in order to placate the international community's fears of another chaotic civil war.[39] Similarly in Papua, 'Opposition [to overt nationalist campaigns] also came from more moderate West Papuans, who criticised Parna's [Papuan political party] "flaming nationalism" and pointed to the Congo crisis as a warning against radical nationalism. In response to this comparison, [Parna leader] Wajoi reportedly declared: "the leaders of Parna are not Lumumbas and Kasavubus"', referring to the two Congolese leaders.[40] Although some Afro-

[35] US DoS, 'Memorandum from Robert H. Johnson of the National Security Council Staff to President Kennedy', *Foreign Relations of the United States, 1961–1963, Volume XXIII, Southeast Asia*, 30 November 1961.

[36] Kuitenbrouwer, 'Beyond the "Trauma of Decolonisation"', p. 309.

[37] B. Moore, 'Dutch Decolonisation', in M. Thomas, B. Moore and L. J. Butler (eds.), *Crises of Empire: Decolonization and Europe's Imperial States* (London: Bloomsbury, 2015), p. 225.

[38] D. Webster, 'Race, Identity and Diplomacy in the Papuan Decolonisation Struggle, 1949–1962', in P. Muehlenbeck (ed.), *Race, Ethnicity and the Cold War: A Global Perspective* (Nashville: Vanderbilt University Press, 2012); A. Muhammed, 'The Historical Origins of Secessionist Movement in West Papua', *Journal of Asia Pacific Studies*, 3:1 (2013), pp. 1–13.

[39] D. Webster, *Fire and the Full Moon: Canada and Indonesia in a Decolonizing World* (Vancouver: UBC Press, 2010), p. 121.

[40] E. Kluge, 'Decolonisation Interrupted: The West Papuan Campaign for independence and the United Nations, 1961–1969', unpublished PhD thesis, Sydney, 2020, p. 47.

Asian bloc nations were persuaded by this promise for a smooth transition to independence, conflicted nations (such as Ghana) argued that they would be unable to support the Dutch in the General Assembly because they could not support a European colonial power and they were already politically aligned with Sukarno's Indonesia.[41]

The West Papua dispute highlighted the diplomatic, legal, and geopolitical complications of decolonisation for territories without a clear pathway to statehood. It also demonstrated the plurality of 'self-determination' definitions during this period of political transformation. Significantly, it ignited conflict within the Afro-Asian bloc over the West Papuans' best interests, complicating the bloc's claims to South-South solidarity, universal self-determination, and united post-colonial internationalism.[42] Despite the anti-colonial language of the UN's 'Declaration on the Granting of Independence to Colonial Countries and Peoples' in December 1960,[43] the declaration's protections were in tension with the diplomatic context of the Papua dispute and the UN's structural deference to the nation-state paradigm. As Jamie Trinidad has argued:

> If the language of 'peoples' and 'rights' was suggestive of a norm with the potential to subvert the statist underpinnings of the international system, the drafters of the Colonial Declaration left no doubt that self-determination as a legal norm would be administered so as to uphold an international order founded on sovereign States and respect for existing territorial boundaries.[44]

The so-called 'Brazzaville' resolution (led by Francophone nations Cameroon, Central African Republic, Chad, Congo-Brazzaville, Dahomey, Gabon, Ivory Coast, Madagascar, Mauritania, Niger, Senegal, Togo, and Upper Volta on 24 November 1961) requested that the 'secretary-general to use his good offices . . . decides to establish a commission . . . to carry out an investigation into the conditions prevailing in the territory' and adding that the findings of the commission with not 'prejudice the right of the population to decide, in the last resort, the status of the territory'.[45] In a telegram, US Ambassador

[41] D. Webster, 'Self-Determination Abandoned: The Road to the New York: Agreement on West Papua (Papua), 1960–62', *Indonesia*, 95 (2013), p. 15; Webster, *Fire and the Full Moon*, p. 121.

[42] C. Ewing, '"With a Minimum of Bitterness": Decolonization, the Right to Self-Determination, and the Arab-Asian Group', *Journal of Global History*, 17:2 (2022), pp. 254–271.

[43] UN Doc, A/RES/1514(XV), 'Declaration on the Granting of Independence to Colonial Countries and Peoples', 14 December 1960.

[44] J. Trinidad, *Self-Determination in Disputed Colonial Territories* (Cambridge: Cambridge University Press, 2018), p. 10.

[45] UN Doc, A/L.368, 'Sixteenth Session, Agenda Item 88: The Situation with Regard to the Implementation of the Declaration on the Granting of Independence to Colonial Countries and Peoples', 24 November 1961, pp. 1–2.

Adlai E. Stevenson wrote to Secretary of State Dean Rusk that the 'real heroes were French-Africans who took on ardous [sic] task out of belief in principle of self-determination … Netherlands Papuans obviously keen to get Dutch out but were even stronger in their opposition to possible Indonesian domination'.[46] During these debates the Indonesian government reasserted their belief that West Papua had already achieved 'independence' alongside the rest of the archipelago in 1949 and thus rejected the idea of Papuan self-determination beyond reunification.[47] Ultimately, the Brazzaville resolution failed to secure the sufficient two-thirds of the General Assembly votes – despite the support of the Afro-Asian bloc members and the United States. However, the resolution demonstrated the legal and political complexity of self-determination and the diplomatic crisis within the Afro-Asian bloc on the dispute.

Throughout these UN debates, the dispute forced the UN delegates in the General Assembly to contemplate a people's right to self-determination *beyond* the lens of nationhood,[48] and, simultaneously, to reflect on the legality – and morality – of a nation-state to annex another territory in order to preserve a shared, artificial colonial border. Many Afro-Asian bloc states, such as Pakistan and Ghana, eventually supported Indonesia in the General Assembly despite their earlier concerns about Papuan self-determination. India supported Indonesia, building upon a long history of South-South solidarity that had been solidified during Indonesia's campaign for independence and would continue with Indonesia's annexations of West Papua in 1963 and East Timor in 1975.[49] This success indicates the lobbying power of Indonesia within the Afro-Asian bloc during this period, in the aftermath of the Bandung Conference in 1955. However, this instance of South-South solidarity set a troubling precedent for the group; a minority or marginalised territory's right to self-determination was insignificant in the context of supporting a fellow Afro-Asian bloc member-state against a European colonial nation.[50]

[46] John F. Kennedy Library, National Security Files, 205, 'US Mission to United Nations Report', 30 November 1961.

[47] N. Viartasiwi, 'The Politics of History in West Papua – Indonesia Conflict', *Asian Journal of Political Science*, 26:1 (2018), pp. 142–143.

[48] Elisabeth Leake has also shown how Afghan elites promoted this conception of self-determination in the post-war era within the UN General Assembly and its subcommittees; see E. Leake, 'States, Nations, and Self-Determination: Afghanistan and Decolonization at the United Nations', *Journal of Global History*, 17:2 (2022), pp. 272–291.

[49] S. L. Jagtiani, '"Foreign Armies Are Functioning on Asian Soil": India, Indonesian Decolonisation and the Onset of the Cold War (1945–1949)', *Cold War History* (2022), pp. 1–22; Strating and Davis, 'Bordering the Postcolonial State', pp. 169–189.

[50] Kuitenbrouwer, 'Beyond the "Trauma of Decolonisation"', p. 318.

Geopolitical Anxieties in the Pacific

The concept of an international 'trusteeship' or 'protectorate' of West Papua had circulated for some time by 1962 but had remained an unlikely political reality. Indonesian diplomats based in the Dutch Embassy had initially suggested an international arrangement in 1959 but took no formal steps towards negotiations.[51] Later in March 1961, the Indonesian government communicated to the US embassy in Djakarta that it was prepared to accept a period of UN authority before it assumed sovereignty in West Papua. The government suggested this on the condition that the territory would not be put under 'trusteeship'.[52] However, they had yet to communicate their willingness to the secretary-general. These private statements stood in stark contrast with violence in the Pacific and the public diplomatic positions of the two nations within the UN General Assembly in 1961. For the international community, the Dutch and Indonesian governments showed no intention of compromising on their aims for the future of West Papua. Thus, the UN secretary-general's involvement in the negotiation process in mid-1962 and resolution of the dispute were hard-won victories for Thant.[53] When U Thant accepted the role of acting secretary-general in November 1961, he inherited Hammarskjöld's informal involvement in the West Papua dispute at a point when diplomatic relations between the Netherlands and Indonesia were on the verge of collapse.[54] However, he swiftly organised negotiations with the two states to settle the crisis, centring the UN in the resolution process. Once he established UNTEA, he also arranged that it would be financed equally by Indonesia and the Netherlands, providing the UN with some much-needed fiscal respite.[55] The success of the new secretary-general in unifying the two countries' outlook on the territory and avoiding the outbreak of war was enormously significant at a time when he was also mediating the missile crisis in Cuba.[56]

[51] US DoS, 'Despatch from the Embassy in the Netherlands to the Department of State', *Foreign Relations of the United States 1958–1960, Indonesia*, Volume XVII, Document 223, 3 September 1959.

[52] US DoS, 'Telegram from the Embassy in Indonesia to the Department of State', *Foreign Relations of the United States 1961–1963, Southeast Asia*, Volume XXIII, Document 150, 3 March 1961.

[53] U Thant, '3. From Transcript of Press Conference, Geneva, 3 May 1963', in A. Cordier and M. Harrelson (eds.), *Public Papers of the Secretaries-General of the United Nations: Volume VI, U Thant, 1961–1964* (New York: Cornell University Press, 1976), p. 337.

[54] UNA, S-0876-0001-06-00001, 'Confidential Note on Hammarskjöld Files from Thant to Engers', p. 6.

[55] Hamilton, 'U.N. under Pressure'.

[56] D. A. Walter and R. Pauk, 'Unsung Mediator: U Thant and the Cuban Missile Crisis', *Diplomatic History*, 33:2 (2009), pp. 261–292.

Thant's political upbringing and career experience within anti-colonial diplomatic circles prepared him for the neo-colonial violence in the Pacific. Thant had been raised in Pantanaw, British Burma, in a wealthy, highly educated family, where he engaged in local journalism and was politically moderate.[57] Although he remained moderate during clashes between Burmese nationalists and loyalists in the 1930s, his experiences during the Japanese occupation in the Second World War made him resistant to Japanese nationalism.[58] After the war, Thant worked in the Burmese civil service alongside the new Prime Minister of an independent Burma, U Nu, who was also an old school friend. Rising quickly through Burmese politics, Thant acted as secretary for the Bandung Conference in 1955, putting him at the centre of discussions on the advancements of anti-colonialism, self-determination, racial equality, Afro-Asian solidarity, and the Non-Aligned Movement.[59] His presence at the conference exposed him to pan-Afro-Asian unity and encouraged him to connect with other international diplomats. The Bandung Conference also introduced him to Indonesia's claim to West Papua as he heard Djakarta representatives describe the annexation as the final frontier of Indonesia's struggle for independence from Dutch imperialism.[60] His involvement at the Bandung Conference and conversations around Pan-Afro-Asian unity encouraged him to conceive of the annexation as part of Indonesia's post-colonial quest for unity, rather than the re-colonisation of a minority group.[61] Despite his experience with Japanese imperial occupation during the Second World War, Thant conceived of Indonesia's claim to West Papua as part of Indonesia's decolonisation process.

The UN Secretariat saw Thant's Afro-Asian diplomatic connections as desirable as they searched for Hammarskjöld's replacement. The recent transformations to the General Assembly membership strengthened demands for a secretary-general from the Global South. However, Cold War politics dictated the negotiations for selecting Hammarskjöld's successor.[62] Thant's

[57] A. Whitman, 'U Thant Is Dead of Cancer at 65', *The New York Times*, 26 November 1974.

[58] Whitman, 'U Thant Is Dead of Cancer at 65'.

[59] H. Weber and P. Winanti, 'The "Bandung Spirit" and Solidarist Internationalism', *Australian Journal of International Affairs*, 70:4 (2016), pp. 391–406; J. Dinkel, *The Non-aligned Movement: Genesis, Organization and Politics (1927–1992)* (Leiden: Brill, 2019), pp. 42–83.

[60] K. McGregor and V. Hearman, 'Challenging the Lifeline of Imperialism: Reassessing Afro-Asian Solidarity and Related Activism in the Decade 1955–1965', in L. Eslava, M. Fakhri, and V. Nesiah (eds.), *Bandung, Global History, and International Law: Critical Pasts and Pending Futures* (Cambridge: Cambridge University Press, 2017), p. 167.

[61] R. E. Elson, *The Idea of Indonesia: A History* (Cambridge: Cambridge University Press, 2008), p. 151.

[62] A. James, 'The Soviet Troika Proposals', *The World Today*, 17:9 (1961), pp. 368–376.

nomination to become the next UN secretary-general in 1961 was conditional on his nationality's non-aligned politics and his strong relationships with representatives from the Afro-Asian bloc. Anti-imperialist solidarity remained at the forefront of Thant's approach to global governance as he lobbied for (and undertook) the position of secretary-general.[63] The 'Spirit of Bandung' not only influenced Thant's appointment as secretary-general, but also guided his geopolitical allegiances once appointed, influencing his approach to experiences of colonialism and the threat of communism in Asia.[64] In the wake of the Congo mission controversies, Thant recognised that the UN leadership needed to improve Afro-Asian nations' trust in the organisation and the West Papua dispute provided an opportunity to align with the powerful nation that had hosted the Bandung Conference: Indonesia.

Following Hammarskjöld's death, Thant ordered a report on Hammarskjöld's existing files on West Papua.[65] These files showed that Hammarskjöld had initiated contact with the Dutch government through their UN Ambassador in early 1961 to discuss the possibility of UN-led mediation between the states.[66] Thant chose to continue these discussions in the hopes of a swift solution. He also learnt that Carl Schurmann, the Dutch Ambassador to the UN, had insinuated that the Dutch might grant permission for UN trusteeship in the territory.[67] Additionally, Thant discovered that Hammarskjöld had met with the Dutch Minister for Foreign Affairs, Joseph Luns, to advise him on a peaceful outcome.[68] Hammarskjöld had encouraged Luns to consider inviting UN observers to West Papua. However, Luns subsequently revealed these communications in a speech during Parliamentary proceedings in the Lower House of the Dutch Parliament, and Hammarskjöld rebuked him for his indiscretion.[69] This marked an end to their diplomatic dialogues and the topic of an international visit to West Papua until U Thant became secretary-general.[70]

Meanwhile, Dutch diplomat Theo Bot had invited two African representatives, Ambassador Maxime-Leopold Zollner from the Republic of Dahomey and Frédéric Guirma from the Upper Volta, to the territory through a UN

63 U Thant, 'A Burmese View of World Tensions', *The ANNALS of the American Academy of Political and Social Science*, 318:1 (1958), pp. 34–42.

64 L. Eslava, M. Fakhri, and V. Nesiah, 'The Spirit of Bandung', in Eslava, Fakhri, and Nesiah (eds.), *Bandung, Global History, and International Law: Critical Pasts and Pending Futures* (Cambridge: Cambridge University Press, 2017), pp. 3–32.

65 UNA, S-0876-0001-06-00001, 'Confidential Note on Hammarskjöld Files', 31 May 1962.

66 UNA, S-0876-0001-06-00001, 'Confidential Note on Hammarskjöld Files', 31 May 1962.

67 UNA, S-0876-0001-06-00001, 'Confidential Note on Hammarskjöld Files', 31 May 1962, p. 2.

68 UNA, S-0876-0001-06-00001, 'Confidential Note on Hammarskjöld Files', 31 May 1962, p. 2.

69 UNA, S-0876-0001-06-00001, 'Confidential Note on Hammarskjöld Files', 31 May 1962, p. 2.

70 UNA, S-0876-0001-06-00001, 'Confidential Note on Hammarskjöld Files', 31 May 1962, pp. 2–3.

goodwill mission in April 1962.[71] Their invitation was specifically to counteract the fears of 'Brazzaville group' nations, such as Dahomey and Upper Volta, that the Dutch were not sufficiently supportive of the West Papuan's right to self-determination. The visit was heavily choreographed in the Dutch's favour to build a picture of the Papuans as an underdeveloped population that were slowly being brought into modernity by the paternal hand of the Dutch administration.[72] Although Ambassador Zollner believed that the majority of the Papuan population was uneducated and disinterested in their territory's political future, he argued that many Papuans 'favour the creation of a Papuan national state and fear integration with Indonesia would threaten the legitimate aspirations of the Papuan peoples for their own development'.[73] Similarly, Ambassador Guirma found the idea of West Papuan independence preferable to the planned Indonesian takeover as he openly questioned the validity of Indonesia's claims to the territory and population. He was, reportedly,

> ...deeply impressed by the ethnical[sic] differences between Papuans and the inhabitants of Indonesia which led him to disregard Djakarta's contention that West Irians [West Papuans] are Indonesians. Moreover, Guirma rejected as spurious the Indonesian argument that Irian Barat [West Papua] had been considered as part of Indonesia from pre colonial days to the proclamation of Indonesian independence. In his opinion, the 800,000 Papuans could very well constitute in due course an independent national state...[74]

These reports were highly valuable for UN staff and member-state delegates whose opinion of the West Papuans was derived entirely from others' perspectives and recordings. Unfortunately, by the time that this report was available, Thant and his allies in the US government had already put his strategy for conflict resolution in the Pacific into action.

West Papua's re-colonisation was a shared calculation by parties – such as the UN and US leadership – interested in preventing further Soviet aggression in the Pacific and re-stabilising the region. In November 1961, the US National Security Council predicted that Indonesia's economic vulnerability might push the state further into collaboration with the Soviet Union if they were not able to annex West Papua:

[71] 'Africans in W. Papua', *South Pacific Post*, 17 April 1962, cited in E. Kluge, 'West Papua and the International History of Decolonization, 1961–69', *International History Review*, 42:6 (2020), pp. 1159.

[72] Kuitenbrouwer, 'Beyond the "Trauma of Decolonisation"', p. 320.

[73] 'Report on "The Impact of the West New Guinea Settlement" Canadian High Commission in Australia Report', 23 August 1962, available at: http://historybeyondborders.ca/?p=491.

[74] 'Report on "The Impact of the West New Guinea Settlement" Canadian High Commission in Australia Report', 23 August 1962, available at: http://historybeyondborders.ca/?p=491.

> The Indonesians are going through a foreign exchange crisis. This fact may restrain them from attacking West New Guinea. On the other hand, it might drive them only further into Soviet hands for economic aid, while the Soviets support and encourage an attack upon West New Guinea. In any event, the pressures upon Nasution [Indonesian Chief of Staff] are going to mount until they become irresistible unless there is real hope of progress through negotiations. An attack could so preoccupy the army as to open new opportunities to the Communists in Indonesia. The fact that the attack was launched with Soviet aid and support will also markedly strengthen the Communist position.[75]

By August 1962, US President Kennedy was highly concerned about the potential geopolitical damage of an escalation in the conflict over (what the US National Security Council termed) a 'bit of colonial debris'.[76] Kennedy hosted meetings with Dutch diplomats to encourage their quick withdrawal from the West Papua,[77] and emphasised the strategic value of the territory in the Cold War.[78] The Kennedy administration believed that negotiating Papuan self-determination would only serve to aggravate the Indonesian government and thus threaten 'the entire free world position in Asia'.[79] US National Security adviser, Robert Komer, argued, 'A pro-Indo policy on WNG [West Papua] won't solve all our problems. But it will at least keep our foot in the door so we can compete. Otherwise, we may be heading for a really major defeat in SEA [Southeast Asia] – one which would dwarf the loss of Laos.'[80] Similarly, President Kennedy insisted:

> US pressure on both sides for peaceful compromise not based on pros or cons of WNG issue or on supposed anti-colonial bias; it hinges rather on

[75] US DoS, 'Memorandum from Robert H. Johnson of the National Security Council Staff to President Kennedy', *Foreign Relations of the United States, 1961–1963, Volume XXIII, Southeast Asia*, 30 November 1961.

[76] John F. Kennedy Library, National Security Files, 'Memorandum from Robert W. Komer of the National Security Council Staff to Carl Kaysen', IN-WNG-1961–1963, 15 January 1962.

[77] Webster, 'Self-Determination Abandoned', p. 13.

[78] For more on the United States and Indonesia, see Bevins, *The Jakarta Method*; B. Simpson, *Economists with Guns: Authoritarian Development and U.S.-Indonesian Relations, 1960–1968* (Redwood City: Stanford University Press, 2008); B. Anderson, *Java in a Time of Revolution: Occupation and Resistance, 1944–1946* (Ithaca: Cornell University Press, 1972).

[79] Annex B, The Foreign Service of the United States of America, 'Letter from John F. Kennedy to the Prime Minister of the Netherlands, 2nd April 1962', available at: www.freewestpapua.org/documents/secret-letter-from-john-f-kennedy-to-the-prime-minister-of-the-netherlands-2nd-april-1962/, accessed on 29 December 2018.

[80] John F. Kennedy Library, National Security Files, 'Memorandum from Robert W. Komer of the National Security Council Staff to Carl Kaysen', IN-WNG-1961–1963, 15 January 1962.

> our acute concern over further undermining of Western position in Indonesia, which in turn could affect whole Free World strategic position in FE [Far East] ... We greatly disturbed by drift Indonesia into closer relations with [Soviet] bloc ... We also fearful WNG will escalate into another major crisis in SEA, at a time when we pre-occupied with Laos and South Vietnam.[81]

Therefore, despite the US's public anti-colonial rhetoric, in practice colonised populations' rights were secondary to the threat of potential Soviet interference and the economic loss of Indonesian oil.[82]

Thant shared the US government's anxieties over the threat of the Soviet Union in the Pacific and its ambiguous relationship with the Indonesian government.[83] The secretary-general's relationship with US actors has been over-simplified in the dominant historiographical narrative. Many have wrongly assumed that all decision-making in the UN was led by US manipulation and followed by a passive Thant, rather than considered how Thant's own politics and UN geopolitical pressures – as well as organisational cultures of anticommunism – may have encouraged an alignment with US interests on this issue.[84] The role of the US government in the construction and design of the UN entrenched a close relationship between the UN Secretariat and the US government, further compounded by the location of the UN headquarters.[85] However, Thant took over as secretary-general at a point when the Afro-Asian bloc had diluted the diplomatic weight of the US voting power within the General Assembly. Although the US veto was still a powerful tool within the UN, the superpower did not control the secretary-general's office. Indeed, Thant was frustrated that the UN and the United States' agreement on West Papua had ignited international suspicions that he was an American stooge; the American State Department recorded that Thant was 'miffed at us [the Americans] on several counts' during this period.[86]

[81] John F. Kennedy Library, National Security Files, 'Draft Presidential Letter from JFK to Robert F. Kennedy, Attorney General', IN-WNG-1961–1963, 22 February 1962.

[82] D. Faidiban, 'Accused of Being a Separatist', in L. Visser (ed.), *Governing New Guinea: An Oral History of Papuan Administrators, 1950–1990* (Leiden: KITLV Press, 2012), p. 71.

[83] US DoS, 'Telegram from the Embassy in Indonesia to the Department of State', *Foreign Relations of the United States 1961–1963, Southeast Asia, Volume XXIII, Document 218*, 27 December 1961.

[84] H. B. Schaffer, *Ellsworth Bunker: Global Troubleshooter, Vietnam Hawk* (Chapel Hill: UNC Books, 2004), p. 95; C. McMullen, *Mediation of the West New Guinea Dispute, 1962: A Case Study* (Washington, DC: Institute for the Study of Diplomacy, 1981).

[85] S. Wertheim, 'Instrumental Internationalism: The American Origins of the United Nations, 1940–1943', *Journal of Contemporary History*, 54:2 (2019), pp. 265–283.

[86] US DoS, 'Memorandum from Robert W. Komer of the National Security Council Staff to the President's Special Assistant for National Security Affairs (Bundy)', *Foreign Relations*

Thant focused on resolving the conflict quickly as he 'appealed' to the belligerent states, seeking to demonstrate personal and organisational expertise in conflict response.[87] Increasingly exasperated by interstate skirmishes in the Pacific throughout the late 1950s and early 1960s,[88] Thant considered using the judicial weight of the UN Security Council.[89] He suggested that using Article 40 of the UN Charter, he should send UN observers to West Papua with the intention of scoping the UN exercising authority over the territory. Thant hoped this suggestion would cease the continued 'aggravation of the situation'.[90] He had written to both state leaders on 19 December 1961, repeating his request for a peaceful solution to the territorial question.[91] However, a naval clash mid-January in 1962 between Indonesian and Dutch ships off the coast of West Papua had escalated the dispute and ignited fears of Soviet intervention. Thant solicited a 'humanitarian gesture' from Prime Minister de Quay of the Netherlands to release Indonesian prisoners captured during this naval skirmish and sent a UN representative to the territory to arrange the repatriation of these prisoners.[92] Thant seized upon this thaw in Dutch–Indonesian relations in early 1962 and coaxed the states towards a two-stage diplomatic solution; 'the first phase would be secret and informal, and the second stage would be formal'.[93]

In August 1962, Thant led the formal negotiations between Indonesia and the Netherlands, building upon the preliminary, 'exploratory', informal talks held by Thant's nominated representative, Ellsworth Bunker, in March of 1962.[94] Following the informal talks, Thant approved the creation of the 'Bunker Plan' which encouraged the parties to agree to a transitional UN authority in West Papua. Thant's personal endorsement of this plan, evident

for the United States, 1961–1963, Volume XVIII, Near East, 1962–1963, Document 151, 7 February 1963.

87 UNA, S-0876-0001-07-00001, 'Press Release: United Nations Administrator of West New Guinea Leaves for Djakarta', 7 November 1962, p. 20.

88 W. Platje, 'Dutch Sigint and the Conflict with Indonesia 1950–1962', *Intelligence & National Security*, 16:1 (2001), pp. 285–312.

89 UNA, S-0876-0001-06-00001, 'Confidential Note on Hammarskjöld Files', p. 6.

90 UNA, S-0876-0001-06-00001, 'Internal Report from Engers to Thant', 17 August 1962, p. 6.

91 U Thant, 'Text of Identical Cables to Jan de Quay, Prime Minister of the Netherlands, and Achmed Sukarno, President of Indonesia – New York, December 19 1961', in Cordier and Harrelson (eds.), *Public Papers*, p. 76.

92 U Thant, 'Exchange of Communications with Prime Minister de Quay – February 1, 1962', in Cordier and Harrelson (eds.), *Public Papers*, pp. 77–78.

93 U Thant, 'From Transcript of Press Conference – March 27 1962', p. 87.

94 U Thant, 'From Transcript of Press Conference – March 27 1962', p. 87.

in his private correspondence[95] and in press conferences,[96] guided his approach to the formal negotiations. His communication with President Sukarno and Prime Minister de Quay emphasised the UN's united front in solving the dispute.[97] Bunker was in regular contact with the secretary-general as he recognised that his role was 'under [Thant's] aegis' rather than that of the UN, or even the US; he was present 'at [Thant's] request and as [Thant's] representative'.[98] Thant argued that his involvement in the informal negotiations was his diplomatic pressure, keeping both states at the table in order to make progress towards the formal negotiations to settle the dispute.[99] Thus, although he was more involved with the second stage of the negotiations, Thant and his diplomatic weight as UN secretary-general were integral to the informal discussions held by Ellsworth Bunker and the formal talks held in August 1962.

Whilst the August negotiations were ongoing in New York, Papuan protestors used this time to demonstrate across their territory and communicate their desire to remain independent of Indonesia. During August 1962 there were five large protests held by nationalist activists across West Papua. *The Sydney Morning Herald* reported that in one of the rallies, approximately 1,000 people met to protest outside the New Guinea Council building in the capital city of Hollandia to contest the negotiations and reject the New York Agreement. Those protesting carried signs stating, 'Down with Soekarno', 'We are not merchandise' and 'How many Yankee dollars for selling Papua?'[100] Meanwhile, the success of formal talks in August 1962 resulted in the parties signing the New York Agreement on 15 August 1962 to authorise the transfer of West Papua from Dutch to Indonesia via a UN peacekeeping mission. The New York Agreement outlined the provisions and duties of the UN peacekeeping mission that would come into force on 21 September 1962. The prestige attached to the organisation's involvement in the negotiations was emphasised by the location of the New York Agreement's authorisation: the UN headquarters.[101]

95 UNA, S-0876-0001-06-00001, 'Confidential Note on Hammarskjöld Files', pp. 6–7; UNA, S-0884-0022-07-00001, 'Letter from Ellsworth Bunker to U Thant', 12 September 1962, p. 5. This also illustrates Thant's approval of Bunker's plan and strategy during negotiations.

96 U Thant, 'From Transcript of Press Conference – March 27 1962', p. 87.

97 Cordier and Harrelson (eds.), *Public Papers*, p. 127–132.

98 UNA, S-0884-0022-07-00001, 'Letter from Ellsworth Bunker to U Thant', 12 September 1962, p. 5.

99 U Thant, 'From Transcript of Press Luncheon Given by the United Nations Correspondents Association – New York, April 24 1962', in Cordier and Harrelson (eds.), *Public Papers*, p. 97.

100 'Mass Protest by Papuans', *The Sydney Morning Herald*, 12 August 1962, p. 5.

101 UN Doc, 'New York Agreement', 15 August 1962, available at: https://peacemaker.un.org/sites/peacemaker.un.org/files/ID%20NL_620815_AgreementConcerningWestNewGuinea.pdf, accessed on 3 June 2020.

However, in the UN New York headquarters, the West Papuan protests did not shift the negotiating parties or the UN leadership; the protests could not compete with the organisation's pride at having overcome – or, at least, lessened – a reputational crisis and reinserted itself on the ground of another international conflict. Thant's concern over the need for a quick win in the Indonesian–Dutch negotiations was motivated both by the threat of Cold War conflict in the Pacific but was also underwritten by the organisation's own state of crisis. The anxieties of UN staff were particularly pressing following the controversies of ONUC.[102] This damage was specifically due to the Afro-Asian bloc's complaints about the UN's incompetence and untrustworthiness following the death of Lumumba and violent chaos during Operation Morthor.[103] Indeed, these complaints did not cease despite the UN Advisory Board on the Congo's construction of an investigation commission, 'in order to ascertain the circumstances of the death of Mr. Lumumba and his colleagues' in February 1961.[104] The 'storm of criticism' grew over the later months of 1961 and into 1962, and was compounded by the 1962 financial crisis.[105] The expense of ONUC's operations, in addition to the Soviet Union, France, and the United States withdrawing agreed funding for peacekeeping operations, culminated in the UN incurring significant debt.[106] UN delegates disclosed hopes that the success of UNTEA and its lack of financial burden for the organisation would help to reduce some of the international criticism.[107] James F. Engers, executive assistant and under-secretary-general for special political affairs, reported to Thant that 'Some [delegates] believe that the recent agreement will open the way to solve other problems at the United Nations, and would restore its prestige to the United Nations'.[108] Fundamentally, the UN's reputation was bound up in member-states' perception of its reliability in upholding the interests of peace and security. The organisational and geopolitical stakes for the success of the UNTEA mission were elevated in October 1962.

The UN delegates and Secretariat personnel in the New York headquarters were not alone in appreciating the importance of the New York Agreement

[102] A. O'Malley, *The Diplomacy of Decolonisation: America, Britain and the United Nations During the Congo Crisis 1960–1964* (Manchester: Manchester University Press, 2018), pp. 98–101.

[103] O'Malley, *The Diplomacy of Decolonisation*, pp. 98–101.

[104] UNA, S-0875-0007-05-00001, 'A/4964 S//4976 Report of the Commission of the Investigation Established under the Terms of the General Assembly Resolution 1601 (XV)', 11 November 1961.

[105] Hamilton, 'U.N. under Pressure'.

[106] A. Yoder, *The Evolution of the United Nations System* (Oxford: Taylor and Francis, 1997), p. 186.

[107] UNA, S-0876-0001-06-00001, 'Internal Report from Engers to Thant', 17 August 1962, p. 8.

[108] UNA, S-0876-0001-06-00001, 'Internal Report from Engers to Thant', 17 August 1962, p. 8.

(and, therefore, the operations of the UNTEA mission) in serving the wider interests of the UN. The two UNTEA administrators were both diplomats with extensive experience with the UN. Crucially, they were 'acceptable to Indonesia and the Netherlands'.[109] The first 'temporary' UNTEA administrator, José Rolz-Bennett, was only in West Papua for a month at the beginning of the UNTEA mission as an interim authority before arrangements were made for a more permanent representative to take over the role in November 1962. Ultimately, Thant recruited Dr Djalal Abdoh, an Iranian politician with close ties to the Afro-Asian bloc,[110] to represent the secretary-general in West Papua as the permanent UNTEA administrator until the agreed date of transition to Indonesian sovereignty (1 May 1963). He was familiar with the conflict between Indonesia and the Netherlands over West Papua, and chaired General Assembly debates on 'The Question of West Irian [Papua]' in 1957.[111] Having met Thant in 1955 at the Bandung Conference as Head of the Iranian delegation, Abdoh was well known as an established and vocal delegate within the Afro-Asian bloc representatives. He was also present at Indonesia's speeches at Bandung and heard their justification for absorbing West Papua as a final step in their decolonisation process.[112] Like Thant, Abdoh's involvement in the Afro-Asian solidarity movement and elite position within international politics put him in a strong position for UN employment as non-aligned credentials increasingly became key aspect of the recruitment process for mid- to upper-level UN leadership. He built upon his international experience from 1956 to 1960 as Iranian Permanent-Representative to the UN, and in 1961, he was appointed UN Plebiscite Commissioner for the UN-organised referendum in the Southern Cameroons.[113] These roles helped to build his international reputations as a diplomat skilled in 'reconciling opposing factions'.[114] His previous employment within the UN and his shared experience with the 'spirit of Bandung' made him a reliable colleague whom Thant felt he could trust to protect the institution's reputation in West Papua.

[109] UNA, 0876-0001-07-00001, 'Press Release: Actin Secretary-General Appoints Administrator of West New Guinea (West Irian)', 22 October 1962, p. 18.

[110] R. Burke, '"The Compelling Dialogue of Freedom": Human Rights at the Bandung Conference', *Human Rights Quarterly*, 28:4 (2006), p. 956.

[111] UN Docs, A/C.1/SR.905, 'General Assembly: Summary Record of the 905th Meeting', 20 November 1957.

[112] McGregor and Hearman, 'Challenging the Lifeline of Imperialism', p. 167.

[113] For more about the plebiscite in the Cameroons, see B. Chem-Langhëë, *The Paradoxes of Self-Determination in the Cameroons under United Kingdom Administration: The Search for Identity, Well-Being, and Continuity* (Lanham: University Press of America, 2004); N. F. Awasom, 'Politics and Constitution-Making in Francophone Cameroon, 1959–1960', *Africa Today*, 49:4 (2002), pp. 3–30.

[114] UNA, S-0876-0001-07-00001, 'Dr Djalal Abdoh Newspaper Cuttings', p. 4.

Figure 4.1 Dr Djalal Abdoh arrives in West Papua on 14 November 1962.
Reproduced with permission from the UN Photo Library. UN7693809.

However, the temporary nature of the mission, constant staff turnover, and its fixed end-date of 1 May 1963 forged a disconnect between international peacekeeping staff and the Papuan population from the beginning; the international bureaucrats kept one foot out of the door for the duration of UNTEA. Wing Commander Herbert, a Canadian air force officer deployed as part of UNTEA/UNSF, reported that the

> U.N. administrators were not a coherent group (they were drawn from something like 30 different countries) and there was a rapid turn-over of personnel at most positions. Most U.N. appointees arrived late (not before October) and departed early after May 1st if not earlier. The transitional character of the U.N. tenure of office was thus emphasized and it is unlikely that it will have had any permanent effect over the territory.[115]

[115] Library and Archives Canada (LAC), RG25 (External Affairs, 6150, 50409-A-40, 'Canadian Officer's Report on West New Guinea, 28 May 1963'.

The priority for the UNTEA administration in the New York Agreement was to stabilise the region and prevent any immediate interstate violence. However, the mission did not have enough staff to govern all areas as thoroughly as initially planned. As the British Foreign Office recorded, '[UNTEA] has lacked adequate staff and have only been able to administer the more civilised fringes of this immense and jungly [sic] territory'.[116] In contrast to the administrative strategy in ONUC which staffed all governmental departments, the UNTEA staff neglected day-to-day administrative processes to focus on the surface-level transitions from Dutch to Indonesian authority, and getting out of the territory before the implications of the New York Agreement resulted in instability. One UNTEA divisional commissioner argued that international staff should prepare a swift exit from the island, perhaps even before the official end-date, warning 'That there will ultimately be quite serious resistance to the Indonesians is, I think, certain . . . it behoves the UNTEA to depart as soon as the Indonesians are thick enough on the ground. . .'[117]

Once deployed, the UNTEA staff were keen to wrap themselves in a familiar organisational and internationalist culture, even if the staff themselves were from a wide range of different countries. One Australian reporter commented that 'there [was] an air of fraternity among the headquarters staff members. Drawn from all countries, they have in common an intellectual smoothness that permits their conversation to move easily from New York gossip to Papuan mating habits'.[118] This social detachment between peacekeepers and Papuan civilians fed into pervasive cultures of racialism and intellectual supremacy within the UNTEA bureaucracy. International diplomats' and civil servants' career trajectories often placed them within, or proximate to, the same UN networks, regardless of political stance, national background, or job level; they spoke the same technocratic language and held similar paternalistic beliefs about host populations. This tourist lens – as in UNEF – served to 'other' the host population and thus create an intimacy and camaraderie between the peacekeeping bureaucrats: 'They are travellers. They haven't seen each other since the Congo, or a technical assistance conference in Bolivia, or drinks at some airport bar years ago.'[119] These temporary international networks and epistemic communities fostered a culture of paternalism, reifying colonial knowledge and legitimising prejudices against local populations – to each other and the international community – as peacebuilding strategies. Importantly, these insular communities also encouraged UN peacekeepers to stay confined to their 'bungalows overlooking Humboldt Bay . . . or at Government Hotel' or military quarters outside work hours, socialising only among one another,

[116] BNA, FO 371/169952, DJ 1019/7, 'Parliamentary Question', 2 February 1963.
[117] UNARMS, S-0876-0001-07-00001, 'Abdoh Report to Thant', 13 December 1962, p. 40.
[118] Grant, '"Auntie" Takes over Irian Gently'.
[119] Grant, '"Auntie" Takes over Irian Gently'.

much like how present-day peacekeepers create their own exclusive 'spaces of aid' in conflict zones within UN compounds and hotels.[120] For two Canadian UNTEA aircraft personnel, their position in West Papua was a tolerable job, reporting that '[they] have remained in good health and are reasonably contented if not actually enjoying their experience of serving in a primitive part of the world'.[121]

Denying West Papuan Political Enfranchisement

The New York Agreement precluded the UNTEA staff from debating the question of Papuan self-determination.[122] However, mid-level UN staff, particularly the UNTEA administrator Djalal Abdoh and his divisional commissioners, chose to acknowledge and stay updated on Papuan political activities in order to police their demonstrations and meetings, circulating their findings to the UN Secretariat in New York.[123] Weekly situational updates from each divisional commissioner to Abdoh also included analysis of political events in their area. Papuan nationalist activism made Abdoh uneasy as, within the norms of the UN, secessionist claims from (post)colonial territories – especially from minority or indigenous groups – were deemed not 'legitimately national' (just as with Katanga) and threatened the credibility of the New York Agreement.[124] For the leadership of UNTEA, it was more beneficial to legitimise and amplify racist perceptions of Papuans than to engage in diplomatically delicate and time-intensive discussions about post-colonial sovereignty and statehood. Breaching the New York Agreement and arguing that it had been negotiation on the basis of false information would not have been a popular diplomatic or legal decision. Thus, the UNTEA administration reproduced racist mischaracterisations of the Papuan population to Thant and his Secretariat colleagues to protect the New York Agreement and, more broadly, the reputation of the organisation by 'keeping the peace' and avoiding international controversy.

Abdoh's decision-making as UNTEA administrator sheds light on how anti-colonial diplomats conceived their own discretionary racial, political, and class standards of 'credible' anti-colonial activity. During the 1960s, racism existed

[120] For more, see L. Smirl, *Spaces of Aid: How Cars, Compounds and Hotels Shape Humanitarianism* (London: Zed Books, 2015).

[121] Library and Archives Canada (LAC), RG25 (External Affairs), 6150, 50409-A-40, 'Visit of Canadian UNTEA Personnel to Djakarta, signed by Ambassador, 30 November 1962'.

[122] UN Doc, 'New York Agreement', 15 August 1962.

[123] For more on the UNTEA efforts to restrict the human and civil rights of the Papuan population, see M. Tudor, 'Gatekeepers to Decolonisation: Recentring the UN Peacekeepers on the Frontline of West Papua's Re-colonisation, 1962–1963', *Journal of Contemporary History*, 57:2 (2022), pp. 293–316.

[124] L. Walker, 'Decolonisation in the 1960s: On Legitimate and Illegitimate Nationalist Claims-Making', *Past & Present*, 242:1 (2019), p. 228.

on a gradient, differentiating the perceived 'civilisation' of an African American lawyer or Iranian diplomat against the supposed 'primitivism' of a West Papuan. Elite bureaucrats in positions of power, like Abdoh, held the authority to prevent a population from achieving self-determination, reinforcing the existing power dynamic between UN officials and host populations. Peacekeeping missions provided fertile conditions for technocratic exceptionalism to thrive within international bureaucracies in foreign contexts. Although colonised populations deployed formal and informal strategies to attract the attention of UN officials, arbitrary and racialised standards of 'credibility' obstructed many 'peripheral' populations from access to international rights or legal protections.

UNTEA directors' and divisional commissioners' experiences, practices, and ideas amassed during colonial employment were integral to analysis and knowledge-production within the peacekeeping bureaucracy.[125] An undisclosed number of UNTEA's departmental directors and divisional commissioners were 'persons who have served in colonial territories for a considerable part of their career', influencing their analysis of the Papuan population.[126] For the UNTEA headquarters staff based in Hollandia, the weekly situational updates from the divisional commissioners provided their only insight into non-urban Papuan communities. Abdoh highlighted his colleagues' colonial experience and his concern about some of their 'observations and ideas' in his report to Thant, noting that he 'took exception' to some of their remarks.[127] However, he continued to use their updates to build his – and Thant's – conceptions of the territory. Thus, there was a tension between Abdoh's anti-colonial credentials and his practices as UNTEA administrator: in principle, he championed the right to self-determination, but on the ground his racialised perception of which populations should be afforded that right made him complicit in the re-colonisation of the territory.[128]

[125] For more on this dynamic of colonial officials in international civil service positions, see E. Muschik, 'The Art of Chameleon Politics : From Colonial Servant to International Development Expert', *Humanity*, 9:2 (2018), pp. 219–244; U. Kothari, 'From Colonialism to Development: Reflections of Former Colonial Officers', *Commonwealth & Comparative Politics*, 44:1 (2006), pp. 118–136; J. M. Hodge, *Triumph of the Expert: Agrarian Doctrines of Development and the Legacies of British Colonialism* (Athens: Ohio University Press, 2007); J. M. Hodge, 'British Colonial Expertise, Post-Colonial Careering and the Early History of International Development', *Journal of Modern European History*, 8:1 (2010), pp. 24–46; S. A. Wempe, 'From Unfit Imperialists to Fellow Civilizers: German Colonial Officials as Imperial Experts in the League of Nations, 1919–1933', *German History*, 34:1 (2016), pp. 21–48; R. Joy, 'Facing Decolonisation: British Agricultural Officers in Postcolonial East Africa', paper delivered at BIHG, 31 August 2018 in Exeter, Britain.

[126] UNA, S-0876-0001-07-00001, 'Abdoh Report to Thant', 13 December 1962, p. 40.

[127] UNA, S-0876-0001-07-00001, 'Abdoh Report to Thant', 13 December 1962, p. 40.

[128] R. Burke, *Decolonisation and the Evolution of International Human Rights* (Philadelphia: Philadelphia University Press, 2010), p. 45.

UNTEA's practices were driven by widespread racist rhetoric against the Papuans as can be seen within mission communications and reports. For example, Gordon S. Carter, Divisional Commissioner for the Central Highlands, complained in his November situational update to Abdoh that he was struggling to

> guide the faltering steps of stone-age man along the dimly lit paths of progress and enlightenment ... the obligation is of course a moral one towards some 200-300,000 extremely primitive peoples ... many of whom are still in the stone-age state of primitive savagery and tribal warfare.[129]

Divisional commissioners' racist comments and prejudicial asides were regularly woven into the 'technical' sections of their situational updates, whilst still asserting that their judgement of Papuan society was apolitical and based on development expertise. As Victor Ray has highlighted, international organisations' supposedly neutral, technocratic identities help to conceal international staff's complicity in social constructions of race.[130] He has argued that 'Organizations help launder racial domination by obscuring or legitimating unequal processes' through technocratic or supposedly impartial rhetoric.[131] Although Abdoh relied on divisional commissioners' updates to compile his reports about the rural regions of West Papua, he was aware of the diverse political activism across the region due to the police reports and Papuan petitions delivered to his office in Hollandia. He also witnessed protests in the city, as well as receiving letters directly. Anti-Indonesian petitions authored during the UNTEA period marked the beginning of a prolific West Papuan tradition of petitioning to the UN throughout the 1960s and beyond, using this technique to articulate their demands and their personal experiences of Indonesian abuses.[132] Despite this direct engagement with Papuan political activity, Abdoh picked out generalising and racialised comments from his divisional commissioners' reports to project a specific characterisation of the territory to the secretary-general. His curation of racialised and paternalistic 'evidence' in his reports to Thant legitimised the UN's perceptions of the population and reinforced the logic of the New York Agreement. By reproducing divisional commissioners' opinions to Thant, Abdoh encouraged an open culture of prejudice towards the Papuans and an 'us vs. them' mentality.

[129] BL, MS.Eng.c. 4713, Papers of D. Burnell Vickers, Sections 53–60, 'Central Highlands, Situation Report 7th November 1962', pp. 1–2 and 8.

[130] Ray, 'A Theory of Racialized Organizations', *American Sociological Review*, 84:1 (2019), pp. 26–29.

[131] Ray, 'A Theory of Racialized Organizations', p. 35.

[132] Kluge, 'Decolonisation Interrupted', pp. 19–20; Webster, 'Race, Identity and Diplomacy in the Papua Decolonization Struggle, 1949–1962'.

In his first month as administrator, Abdoh instructed the divisional commissioners to consult Papuans on their perceptions of self-determination to gauge their reception of the Indonesian takeover.[133] He then curated and compiled their responses in a long report that he later dispatched to the Secretariat in New York. Abdoh described the role of the divisional commissioners as 'eyes on the ground' for the administration to gather regional news and distribute updates to the more rural communities. Abdoh's report was written for Thant but was also received by C. V. Narasimhan, Chef de Cabinet of the UN Secretariat, and other UN officials within the inner circle at the headquarters, including Ralph Bunche.[134] This report detailed Abdoh's assessment of the population's general mood regarding two key topics 'based to some extent on discreet enquiries made through the divisional commissioners'.[135] First, Abdoh's report addressed the issue of potentially shortening the length of the UNTEA administration, and, second, it examined the question of Papuan self-determination and political life on the island. Quoting a breadth of UNTEA staff and Papuans, the discretion of these inquiries is questionable. Abdoh used this long report to reassure Thant that his efforts during the negotiations were supported by the situation on the ground and that the mission was fulfilling its mandate. His characterisation of the majority of the Papuan population as disengaged in international and domestic politics served to prolong understandings in the New York headquarters of a disinterested population who were unable to – through their geographic isolation or psychological incapacity (in a similar manner to Bunche's assessment of the Congolese population) – hold an opinion on whoever governed their territory.

In order to develop this assessment of Papuan political disengagement, Abdoh dismissed the petitions, letters, and direct claims made by Papuan activists to UN staff as anomalies against the general political apathy of the population.[136] In structuring his long report to Thant throughout the first phase of the mission, from October to December 1962, Abdoh introduced the three main strata of the Papuan population and, in turn, dismissed their political positions as unrepresentative and evidence of underdevelopment: elite, urban, and rural communities. He labelled any Papuan political engagement as illegitimate due to its unreliability or unrepresentative nature, in order to justify the mission's decision not to publicise the treatment of activists on the island and push for the plebiscite under UN jurisdiction. However, spiritual and cultural practices such as the 'Koreri' movement, as well as

[133] UNA, S-0703-0003-01, 'Private and Confidential Memo from Biak Divisional Commissioner Rawlings to Somerville, Director of Internal Affairs', 12 December 1962.

[134] UNA, S-0876-0001-07-00001, 'Abdoh Report to Thant', 13 December 1962.

[135] UNA, S-0876-0001-07-00001, 'Abdoh Report to Thant', 13 December 1962, p. 29.

[136] UNA, S-0876-0001-07-00001, 'Abdoh Report to Thant', 13 December 1962, p. 30.

experiences during the Second World War, helped to forge pan-Papuan solidarity between urban and rural communities during the post-war period, cultivating a sense of racial, 'ethnic and cultural distinctiveness in West Papuan nationalists'.[137] Furthermore, contemporaneous literature by Dutch scholars van der Kroef and van der Veur observed in the early 1960s that the vibrancy of youthful and rural Papuan nationalist engagement was visible across the territory throughout the 1950s and was formalised by the creation of several political parties and communal groups pre-UNTEA.[138] As has Emma Kluge explained in the context of the 1961 New Guinea Council elections,

> While the Dutch had planned for the affair to be understated, with the quiet election of a few local representatives, they were overwhelmed by the interest from West Papuans ... Local newspapers reported that on average 65 to 85 per cent of those eligible to vote showed up at the polls. Participation was higher in rural areas – some districts had up to 90 per cent voter turn out. Voters went to great lengths to exercise their right to vote. In the West-Nimboran voters had to traverse a flooded river to make it to the voting stations, while voters from Tegegapuh refused to let a flu epidemic deter them from making the three-day trek to cast their votes. Although the Dutch hadn't put much effort into promoting the elections, West Papuans spread the news amongst their families and communities. A young West Papuan staying on Numfoor island received a letter from his relatives urging him to return to participate in the elections. The letter was accompanied by a sum of money to help him make the trip back ... Illiterate voters were accommodated through the option of a 'whispering ballot,' in which voters would whisper the name of their chosen representative to the polling official.[139]

As Abdoh and his divisional commissioners were aware, West Papuans, especially the younger generations, were highly invested in their own politics, representation, and suffrage, and had been for several years before the arrival of UNTEA.

Abdoh generalised all elite Papuans as a tiny group that should be totally disregarded in the UNTEA decision-making process, noting that their opinions were likely to be unquestioningly pro-Indonesian and meaningless. He described elite or prominent Papuan individuals as selfish, disingenuous, and mercenary:

137 Kluge, 'Decolonisation Interrupted', pp. 31–33.

138 J. M. van der Kroef, 'Nationalism and Politics in West New Guinea', *Pacific Affairs*, 34:1 (1961), pp. 45; P. W. van der Veur, 'Political Awakening in West New Guinea', *Pacific Affairs*, 36:1(1963), pp. 59–60.

139 Kluge, 'Decolonisation Interrupted', pp. 55–57.

> Irrespective of their real feelings, they try to be on the right side of the Indonesians and thereby secure their future. No wonder that they should be prone to follow whatever lead comes from Indonesia and thereby remain in the forefront of public life.[140]

This disregard of the Papuan leadership and elite strata was also followed by other international actors. The British Foreign Office commented that 'The various [Papuan] leaders of opinion . . . had now virtually all gone over to the Indonesians with whom their bread would in future be buttered'.[141] Abdoh's belief that all Papuan leaders were 'mostly motivated by their own narrow self-interest rather than a genuine interest in a public cause' exposed an entrenched disregard for the diversity of opinion within the Papuan elite class and a contempt for the host population he was employed to protect.[142]

However, whilst complaining about elite Papuan's 'meaningless' opinions on Indonesian rule, Abdoh also ignored UNTEA's complicity in creating a hostile environment increasingly dominated by Indonesian soldiers, politicians, and administrators, many of whom were absorbed within the mission itself.[143] To be sure, some Papuan elites, including military 'heroes' Marthen Indey, Lukas Rumkorem, and Silas Papare, accepted the fait accompli of incoming Indonesian rule and supported the Indonesian unity project.[144] These elite Papuans used this transitional period to build goodwill with Indonesian politicians in order to maintain power through the changeover.[145] As the Divisional Commissioner of Merauke wrote to Abdoh, 'Already pressure from paratroopers on local residents has made some Papuans feel it would be good for the future health to favour Indonesia now.'[146] However, this was far from a widespread attitude, even within elite Papuan circles. Several Papuan leaders and important figures, such as Nicolaas Jouwe, Marcus Kaisiepo and Filiman Jufuway, adopted vocal anti-Indonesian positions and attempted to promote the population's right to self-determination to the international community.[147] By excluding this nuance, Abdoh's prejudice against Papuan self-determination manifested in his generalisation of the

[140] UNA, S-0876-0001-07-00001, 'Abdoh Report to Thant', 13 December 1962, p. 29.

[141] BNA, FO 371/169952, DJ 1019/4, 'Letter from Vines to A.S. Fair in the Commonwealth Relations Office', 14 January 1963.

[142] UNA, S-0876-0001-07-00001, 'Abdoh Report to Thant', 13 December 1962, p. 30.

[143] UNA, S-0701-0003-04, 'Report from Divisional Commissioner, Biak, to Director of Internal Affairs, Hollandia, 26 March 1963', p. 1.

[144] Van der Veur, 'Political Awakening in West New Guinea', p. 59.

[145] J. Saltford, *The United Nations and the Indonesian Takeover of West Papua, 1962–1969: The Anatomy of Betrayal* (London: Psychology Press, 2003), pp. 31–32.

[146] UNA, S-0876-0001-07-00001, 'Abdoh Report to Thant', 13 December 1962, p. 38.

[147] CICR, B AG 200 158-002 200 (96), 'Letter from New Guinea Council and Hollandia to President of ICRC in Geneva', 27 January 1963.

population's elite class despite evidence that this group held multiple political positions, including demanding self-determination.

In his next section, Abdoh dismissed the political activities and activism of urban Papuan communities, arguing that they were numerically insignificant. He suggested that their activism had been engineered by interested groups outside the territory as he believed it unfeasible for Papuans to demonstrate such political imagination and to organise marches.[148] Writing to Thant, Abdoh emphasised how unrepresentative the urban activists were within the vast territory, especially noting the protests in Hollandia. However, these protests were not isolated events. Anti-Indonesia demonstrations in the capital city took place *before*, *during*, and *after* the UNTEA mission, disrupting Abdoh's characterisation of a population predominantly in favour of annexation and disinterested politically. Despite these protests taking place in the same city as his UNTEA office, he argued that Papuans were unable to collect together and share national imaginaries for the territory: 'The normal media through which public opinion expresses itself are non-existent. Communications are incredibly poor; large areas are still inaccessible and lie outside the administrative control. The combined effect of all this is to make it a well-nigh impossible task.'[149]

There was also a prejudicial dynamic which advocated that communities living further away from urban centres were likely disinterested in the politics of their own territory. Abdoh asserted that the absence of a territory-wide communications network made the construction of a unified nationalist movement impossible. Thus, he understood the pockets of anti-Indonesian groups across the country as evidence of an isolated population of which it is impossible to gauge the opinion, rather than an indication of a widespread opinion held by multiple communities limited by colonial legacies of poor infrastructure. This was a common trope across colonial territories. The allegation of 'impossible' communications enabled the ruling power to delegitimise the political opinions of those living in rural communities. It excused their failed efforts – due to supposedly insufficient staffing or financing – to visit these spaces or to make meaningful connections with rural leadership. In his report, Abdoh noted his disregard of groups distant to Hollandia, such as the Biak-Numfoor Regional Council, and their interactions with their divisional commissioner despite these rural communities representing the majority of the Papuan population.[150] Criticising their agricultural lifestyle, he described them as 'politically inarticulate', unable to forge a public opinion 'even in a rudimentary form', and 'nothing to do with social life or political

148 UNA, S-0876-0001-07-00001, 'Abdoh Report to Thant', 13 December 1962, p. 30.
149 UNA, S-0876-0001-07-00001, 'Abdoh Report to Thant', 13 December 1962.
150 UNA, S-0876-0001-07-00001, 'Abdoh Report to Thant', 13 December 1962, pp. 39–40.

changes taking place in this territory'.[151] He maintained that the rural population's political opinion was so 'inarticulate' that most of them would not be intellectually capable of understanding alternative scenarios for the future direction of the territory, nor able to find a basis upon which to choose between them.[152] Through this prejudicial generalisation, Abdoh abdicated the mission from the UN's commitment to self-determination, as expressed in the UN Charter (Articles 1 and 55), as well as the organisation's recent declaration against colonialism in the December 1960 General Assembly resolution,[153] characterising the majority of the Papuan population as not just apolitical, but intellectually incapable of concerning themselves with the political processes in their own territory. Recognising the tension between the New York Agreement and the UN's foundational principles, Abdoh's report affirmed that there was nothing for Thant to be worried about. He falsely confirmed for the secretary-general that the Papuans would not have been interested in or capable of statehood, even if Papuan independence had been considered as an option during the August negotiations.

The Agreement's deferral of self-determination and UNTEA's disregard for the reality on the ground conflicted with the Papuan activists' understanding of the guiding principles of the UN. Whilst Abdoh curated his report during the first phase of the mission, Papuan activists promoted their situation in the hopes that the UN would support their claim to self-determination. Most Papuan anti-Indonesian groups were unified in their opinion that the plebiscite should take place under UNTEA administration no matter how long it took.[154] This demand was especially popular on the northern-most island of Biak-Numfoor where a movement for self-determination gained traction across the entire area.[155] The island's Regional Council wrote to the UNTEA mission announcing their faith in the administration to organise a plebiscite whilst still in authority over the territory.[156] When their initial appeal was unsuccessful, they escalated their anti-Indonesian statement to Thant via a cable. The Council reminded him of the applicability of the December 1960 General Assembly resolution (whereby self-determination was rendered an international norm) to their population. They argued that this resolution 'decided that the rights of small nations are the same as those of big nations'

[151] UNA, S-0876-0001-07-00001, 'Abdoh Report to Thant', 13 December 1962.
[152] UNA, S-0876-0001-07-00001, 'Abdoh Report to Thant', 13 December 1962.
[153] UN Doc, A/RES/1514(XV), 'Declaration on the Granting of Independence to Colonial Countries and Peoples', 947th Plenary Meeting, 14 December 1960.
[154] UNA, S-0876-0001-07-00001, 'Abdoh Report to Thant', 13 December 1962, p. 37; Kluge, 'Decolonisation Interrupted', p. 113.
[155] CICR, B AG 200 158-002 200 (96), 'Letter from New Guinea Council and Hollandia to President of ICRC in Geneva', 27 January 1963.
[156] UNA, S-0876-0001-07-00001, 'Abdoh Report to Thant', 13 December 1962, p. 34.

and therefore their right to an independent plebiscite was clear.[157] They also made note of the articles in the resolution that were particularly relevant to their cause for self-determination, exhibiting their legal fluency.[158] However, Thant relied upon Abdoh's knowledge and assessment of the region in his decision-making and thus these direct efforts to attract the secretary-general's attention failed to shift the UN strategy towards West Papua.

As Indonesian political and violent attempts to quash all Papuan activism increased towards the middle of the UNTEA mission,[159] Papuan pro-independence groups acknowledged that they needed to act quickly. Shrewdly, these groups attempted to negotiate their own independence through a policy of flattery towards the mission staff, accentuating the emotional importance of UNTEA's administration to the population. To emphasise the humanitarian power of the mission staff over the Papuans, they characterised this as being 'under [UNTEA] protection'.[160] They hoped to encourage the mission staff to amplify their requests to the international community and rectify the mischaracterisation of the population as apolitical or disengaged – something that had not taken place during the Bunker negotiations and New York Agreement drafting processes. The UNTEA divisional commissioner of Merauke, a southeast coastal district, argued that Papuans from his region had great confidence in the ability of the UNTEA mission to challenge the betrayal of Papuan self-determination. He reported to Abdoh that

> If, while UNTEA is still in control, a decision is made not to hold a plebiscite at some time in the future the Papuans will feel cheated by UNTEA. It will be no good saying that this is the result of an Agreement between the Dutch and Indonesian governments because the Papuans do not trust either of them anymore but they do have a pathetic trust in UNTEA who they regard as their last hope ... To many Papuans here the Agreement in practice means a guarantee by UN and UNTEA [to provide a plebiscite].[161]

157 UNA, S-0884-0023-01-00001, 'Cable from Party of Papuan Independence to U Thant', August 1962, pp. 16–17.

158 UNA, S-0884-0023-01-00001, 'Cable from Party of Papuan Independence to U Thant', August 1962, pp. 16–17.

159 Papuan Civil Servant Luther Saroy recalls that 'In November 1962 the Indonesian army forced 11 Papuan leaders to sign a document stating that they relinquished the right to self-determination. And in December came the arrest and persecution of Papuans who had stirred up a demonstration, declaring their desire for the election to be held under the protection of the UNTEA, that is, the UN.' See Visser (ed.), *Governing New Guinea*, p. 194.

160 UNA, S-0884-0023-01-00001, 'Cable from Party of Papuan Independence to U Thant', August 1962, pp. 16–17.

161 UNA, S-0876-0001-07-00001, 'Abdoh Report to Thant', 13 December 1962, p. 38.

The UNTEA divisional commissioner's description of the Papuans' 'pathetic trust' in the administration exposed the mission's dismissal of Papuan concerns. The administration was in no way planning on engaging with these protests or supporting the Papuans' right to a plebiscite during UNTEA. However, as phase one of UNTEA ended in December 1962, Papuan hopes for the mission to challenge the Indonesian government were waning in the northern region. The divisional commissioner for Manokwari wrote to Abdoh that 'there is a desire for a plebiscite but at the same time a growing fear that the United Nations may lack the means, and even the will to oppose Indonesia'.[162] These fears served only to exacerbate anxiety about the eventual Indonesian takeover. Papuan government workers in the Central Highlands described their 'gravest fears of their future under Indonesian control and that they would prefer to remain under the wing of UNTEA for as long as possible'.[163] The strategies employed by the Papuan regional groups to provoke an empathetic and humanitarian reaction from UNTEA staff, based on their knowledge of the founding principles of the UN, demonstrated the political sophistication and desperation of the groups within West Papua as well as the callous attitude of the UNTEA peacekeeping bureaucrats.

By the beginning of the second phase of the UNTEA mission on 1 January 1963, the New Guinea Council described itself as 'at its wits' end' in trying to persuade the UNTEA mission of the injustice of the New York Agreement and the impending authoritarianism of Indonesian annexation.[164] By 1963, most Papuan activists were aware that the UNTEA leadership had disqualified their situation from international oversight and reiterated the population's lack of preparedness for self-determination, just as the Dutch imperialists had before their exit.[165] In addition to claims made by the Council on Biak-Numfoor to Thant in 1962, the three Papuan leaders of the New Guinea Council, Nicolaas Jouwe, Marcus Kaisiepo, and Filiman Jufuway, appealed to the ICRC headquarters in Geneva in January 1963.[166] They wrote to the ICRC that 'we know that [our complaints of a series of attacks on Papuan nationalists by Indonesian soldiers] are not listened to or are qualified as not true'.[167] The councillors were politically informed and literate in the protections of

[162] UNA, S-0876-0001-07-00001, 'Abdoh Report to Thant', 13 December 1962, p. 36.

[163] UNA, S-0876-0001-07-00001, 'Abdoh Report to Thant', 13 December 1962, p. 35.

[164] CICR, B AG 200 158-002 200 (96), 'Letter from New Guinea Council and Hollandia to President of ICRC in Geneva', 27 January 1963.

[165] Most Dutch imperialists argued that the population required years of tutelage before self-determination could be considered: Webster, 'Race, Identity and Diplomacy in the Papuan Decolonisation Struggle, 1949–1962', p. 3.

[166] CICR, B AG 200 158-002 200 (96), 'Letter from New Guinea Council and Hollandia to President of ICRC in Geneva', 27 January 1963.

[167] CICR, B AG 200 158-002 200 (96), 'Letter from New Guinea Council and Hollandia to President of ICRC in Geneva', 27 January 1963.

international law. They used their elite position within Papuan society to internationalise the situation in their territory whilst the UNTEA administration was in sovereign authority as they recognised this period was a brief opportunity for the territory to resist re-colonisation. They reported multiple incidents of Indonesian violence against nationalist Papuans during the UNTEA administration. Attaching a statement by UNTEA physician R. Kummer, who had returned to the Netherlands, the Council leaders requested an independent investigation into the terms of the New York Agreement on humanitarian and human rights grounds.[168] Although many politically active Papuans had fled or been evacuated – effectively, exiled – from West Papua to Papua New Guinea or the Netherlands at the beginning of the UNTEA period, such as Jouwe, the displacement of activists had not limited diaspora West Papuan networks from transmitting and amplifying news of violence and authoritarianism.[169]

A week after receiving the petition, Roger Gallopin, the Executive Director of the ICRC, wrote to the Director General of the UN in Geneva Pier Spinelli, to alert him to the accusations made by the activists.[170] Gallopin suggested that Abdoh, as the administrator appointed by Thant, 'would be better than anyone able to rule on the merits of the complaints we received'.[171] He also argued that the administrator would be in the best position to take action to prevent violence, 'if [the abuses] have actually taken place', indicating that the ICRC leadership found it hard to believe accounts of violence under UN authority.[172] Returning the power of oversight to the UN officials on the ground, the ICRC's assumption of a UN senior official's independence and their preference to not interfere with the UN's area of jurisdiction prevented the Papuan activists from accessing international humanitarian recourse or any legal protections. Following communication between the UN Secretariat office in New York and the ICRC headquarters, the councillors received a short letter from an ICRC delegate – rather than Gallopin – stating that they believed any previous instances of violence between Indonesian officials and Papuan civilians were 'exceptional', and efforts had been made by the UNTEA mission to avoid 'a repetition' of 'any disagreement or tension'.[173]

[168] CICR, B AG 200 158-002 200 (96), 'Letter from New Guinea Council and Hollandia to President of ICRC in Geneva', 27 January 1963.

[169] Kluge, 'Decolonisation Interrupted', pp. 128–129.

[170] CICR, B AG 200 158-002 200 (96), 'Letter from R. Gallopin to P. Spinelli (Directeur général de l'Office européen des Nations Unies)', 8 February 1963.

[171] CICR, B AG 200 158-002 200 (96), 'Letter from R. Gallopin to P. Spinelli (Directeur général de l'Office européen des Nations Unies)', 8 February 1963.

[172] CICR, B AG 200 158-002 200 (96), 'Letter from R. Gallopin to P. Spinelli (Directeur général de l'Office européen des Nations Unies)', 8 February 1963.

[173] CICR B AG 200 158-002 200 (96), 'Letter from ICRC Delgate to Mr. N. Jouwe', 11 March 1963.

Humanitarian organisations such as the ICRC thus contributed to the delegitimisation of reported instances of serious violence in West Papua by characterising them as exaggerations or misunderstandings, grounding their logic in the independence and expertise of the UN peacekeeping bureaucrats.

These international perceptions of the UN's humanitarian principles and assumptions of the mission's inherent benevolence also prevented Papuans from internationalising their claims of political asylum to nation-states. Papuans who lost all hope in the UNTEA attempted to seek asylum across the border in Australian-mandated Papua New Guinea before the Indonesian takeover.[174] Following the New York Agreement, 8,000 Papuans from the Sentani district near Hollandia requested political asylum in Papua New Guinea.[175] Further waves of asylum claims followed throughout the UNTEA period.[176] However, the Australian government argued that a basis for political asylum could not be made from civilians leaving a UN-administered territory. They stated that UNTEA should be responsible for these asylum requests rather than a national government, 'bearing in mind the humanitarian principles to which the United Nations subscribe'.[177] Without the support of the UNTEA or the recourse to apply for political asylum, the Papuan population was unable to internationalise their demand for an immediate plebiscite under UNTEA jurisdiction. The UNTEA administration's prioritisation of diplomatic stability between the UNTEA mission staff and the increasing numbers of Indonesian soldiers during the second phase of the mission,[178] as planned in the Agreement, manifested in Papuan activists' feelings of impotence, anxiety, and a loss of trust in the UN.[179]

The lack of an international platform for Papuan activists, following their failed experiences with the ICRC and the Australian government, meant that their efforts to popularise anti-Indonesian feeling were limited to the information disseminated, formally and informally, by current and former UNTEA

[174] For more on the Papua New Guinean experience of Australian colonial rule, see N. Ferns, *Australia in the Age of International Development, 1945–1975: Colonial and Foreign Aid Policy in Papua New Guinea and Southeast Asia* (London: Springer, 2020); T. Moss, *Guarding the Periphery: The Australian Army in Papua New Guinea, 1951–1975* (Cambridge: Cambridge University Press, 2017).

[175] 'Natives Fear Indonesian Rule', *Sydney Morning Herald*, 18 August 1962.

[176] UNA, S-0703-0001-02, 'Memorandum on Some Points of Interest Regarding West New Guinea – From Abdoh's Visit to the Netherlands', p. 3.

[177] UNA, S-0703-0001-02, 'Memorandum on Some Points of Interest Regarding West New Guinea – From Abdoh's Visit to the Netherlands', p. 3.

[178] UNA, S-0701-0003-04, 'Report from Divisional Commissioner, Biak, to Director of Internal Affairs, Hollandia, 26 March 1963', p. 1.

[179] Grant, '"Auntie" Takes over Irian Gently'.

mission staff. On 2 April 1963, the British Foreign Office South-East Asia Department received a confidential report from Mr Broome, a senior Foreign Office delegate, reporting a conversation he had had with Mr Harold Arthur Lee Luckham. Luckham had

> recently returned from being the UNTEA Administrator [Divisional Commissioner] at FakFak. With thirty years' experience of administration in Malaya he is well qualified to judge local feeling … As a source of information his name should not be revealed since he is still technically employed by the UN.[180]

Luckham had divulged to Broome that he was anxious to prevent a misunderstanding of popular Papuan political feeling in the territory. He argued that the influence of small pro-Indonesian faction had dominated all other examples of anti-Indonesian feeling and that reports of pro-Indonesian feeling among locals were utterly 'unrepresentative'.[181] Luckham's conversations with the British Foreign Office suggested that there were internal tensions within the UNTEA bureaucracy regarding the organisation's treatment of Papuan activists and acceptance of Indonesian annexation and that Abdoh's delegitimisation strategy had not been accepted by all UNTEA officials on the ground.

In violation of the chain of command within UNTEA and Abdoh's direction, Luckham impressed upon Broome the pressure he felt to educate the international community on the reality of political engagement on the ground. He stated that 'educated Papuans as a whole are anti-Indonesian and apprehensive. They look forward with misgiving to the future after May 1, and cling – somewhat naively, I fear – to the hope of protection afforded by the prospect of the ultimate plebiscite'.[182] Similarly, to the divisional commissioner who described the 'pathetic trust' of the Papuans towards the UNTEA mission, Luckham shared the same condescending pity whilst reporting on what the commissioner saw as the naïve wishes of those living in the territory.[183] He argued that the naivety of the Papuan population was the cause of the population's political misrepresentation; in his eyes, Papuan preconceptions of the rights-based principles of the UN made them vulnerable and 'amenable to peaceful persuasion by the UNTEA officials, and this

[180] BNA, FO 371/169951, DJ1013/15, 'Confidential Letter from Mr. Broome to the Foreign Office Southeast Asia Department', 8 April 1963.

[181] BNA, FO 371/169951, DJ1013/15, 'Confidential Letter from Mr. Broome to the Foreign Office Southeast Asia Department', 8 April 1963.

[182] BNA, FO 371/169951, DJ1013/15, 'Confidential Letter from Mr. Broome to the Foreign Office Southeast Asia Department', 8 April 1963.

[183] UNA, S-0876-0001-07-00001, 'Abdoh Report to Thant', 13 December 1962, p. 38.

may give a false impression that they are less anti-Indonesian than they really are'.[184]

Additionally, the UNTEA leadership distributed a memo within the mission bureaucracy in December 1962 that revealed that a number of the pro-Indonesian Papuan petitions contained coerced signatures from local civilians and should, therefore, be regarded with suspicion, corroborating Luckham's report of 'unrepresentative' pro-Indonesian support.[185] This early knowledge of pro-Indonesian activism being encouraged – and even fabricated – by the Indonesian government employees in West Papua did not affect the divisional commissioners or Abdoh's position. The memo and Luckham's complaint suggested that the divisional commissioners once on the ground encountered widespread anti-Indonesian feeling within the Papuan population. These officials were also aware that the mission had no intention of supporting anti-Indonesian groups to gain an independent plebiscite, despite knowledge of Indonesian coercion and corruption efforts. In response to UNTEA mischaracterisation of Papuan political life, Luckham used his connections within the British Foreign Office to divulge the situation in West Papua that he felt the UNTEA mission had concealed from the international community.

The overwhelming dominant opinion at all levels of the UNTEA bureaucracy was that a realistic or meaningful assessment of the political opinions of the Papuan population was impossible during their period of authority. David A. Sommerville, in his capacity as Director of Internal Affairs for UNTEA, argued that the isolation of the different regions and a range of different political opinions meant that 'the idea of a Papuan national feeling is novel and largely artificial'.[186] However, the diversity of political beliefs within a territory does not negate the existence a shared, national identity. Abdoh believed Papuans' political activity was either not representative or not the job of the UN to disentangle (and often both).[187] In order to placate the population and avert protests across the territory, the UNTEA divisional commissioners sought to 'let [the Papuans] down gently if they are not to explode'.[188] By infantilising the population, the peacekeeping staff persuaded

[184] BNA, FO 371/169951, DJ1013/15, 'Confidential Letter from Mr. Broome to the Foreign Office Southeast Asia Department', 8 April 1963.

[185] UNA, S-0075-0002-04, 'Re-assessment of the Situation, Merauke, Annex C.5, 8 December 1962', p. 1.

[186] UNA, S-0876-0001-07-00001, 'Abdoh Report to Thant', 13 December 1962, p. 36.

[187] UNA, S-0876-0001-07-00001, 'Press Release WNG/54: United Nations Administrator Leaves Djakarta for West New Guinea', 13 November 1962, p. 25.

[188] UNA, S-0876-0001-07-00001, 'Abdoh Report to Thant', 13 December 1962, pp. 39–40.

themselves that their only duty towards the Papuans was quashing protests, rather than publicising violations of their civil rights. In order to obstruct protests, processions, and meetings, UNTEA staff bureaucratised the process of organising by extending the time required for permission to be considered.[189] The divisional commissioners held the power over which groups could meet and which could result in a 'breach of the peace', further disempowering the population and threatening their civil rights.[190] Despite Papuan use of human rights rhetoric in their demands to the secretary-general, the ICRC, and their direct interactions with UNTEA staff on the ground in Regional Councils and demonstrations, their political agency was judged as unrepresentative and therefore legitimately ignored.

The success of Abdoh's delegitimisation strategy sheds light on the power dynamics between peacekeepers and citizens during decolonisation and highlights the pervasive cultures of exclusion and elitism interwoven with UN field-based practices. The UNTEA mission represented a final opportunity for the international recognition of Papuan rights before Indonesian annexation. However, the mission's focus on the completion of a smooth transfer drove the procedurally violent choice to actively misrepresent political feeling in West Papua and suffocate international knowledge of Indonesian abuses.[191] This misrepresentation served to legitimise Indonesia's occupation and nullified any attempt to amplify Papuan activists' demands to the wider international community. In effect, the mission's administrative staff constructed an image of a population that supposedly *consented* to, or were intellectually *incapable of rejecting*, Indonesian sovereignty. Rather than a passive, impartial administration that quietly 'did its job' and maintained law and order, the UNTEA mission staff made an active decision to communicate a misrepresentation of the Papuan context with full knowledge of the political activism in West Papua as well as the authoritarianism of the incoming Indonesian administration.

Iconographies of Statehood and Performative Militarism

To placate the population and assert control during the second phase of the mission, Abdoh orchestrated UNTEA performances of statehood. In response

[189] UNA, S-0700-0003-05, 'Draft Explanatory Note Concerning Public Processions', 19 January 1963; UNA, S-0700-0003-05, 'Decree Concerning Public Processions', 18 February 1963.

[190] UNA, S-0700-0003-05, 'Draft Explanatory Note Concerning Public Processions', 19 January 1963; UNA, S-0700-0003-05, 'Decree Concerning Public Processions', 18 February 1963.

[191] For more on Indonesian abuses during the mission and UNTEA staff complicity, see Tudor, 'Gatekeepers to Decolonisation'.

to repeated attacks, the UNTEA leadership used symbols of statehood as a means of asserting and communicating authority, such as public ceremonies, postage stamps, and pamphlets in order to express the independence of the mission to the Dutch and Indonesians obstructionists. In the aftermath of the mission, the UN awarded UNTEA medals to those who were deployed with a ribbon detailing central dark green, white, light green stripes and the phrase 'in the service of peace' in relief on the back. Jessica Gienow-Hecht has termed this marketing process as 'nation branding', emphasising how the ruling power focuses on national representations and perceptions rather than on meaningful nation *building* through the centring of host communities and traditions.[192] These visual and performative strategies sought to assert the UN's parity in authority with the Indonesians and Dutch in this conflict and also revealed the UN bureaucracy's aspirational performance of statehood and military authority.

The UNTEA leadership created tension on the ground by maintaining Dutch staff and introducing Indonesian personnel at the same time in October 1962. Although most of the Dutch administration left following news of the New York Agreement and Indonesian takeover,[193] just as Belgian administrators had fled Congo at the moment of decolonisation, of the 3,000 Dutch government staff in West Papua in 1962, 500 remained as part of UNTEA.[194] However, those who remained in the territory did not always favour the UNTEA administration. *The Straits Times* recounted that the Dutch are 'angry, disappointed and – a few of them – are suddenly aware that this strange land is home'.[195] This emotional transfer resulted in UNTEA reports of Dutch efforts to obstruct the new administration by taking supplies with them and leaving behind a 'burnt land', in order to hinder the newly arrived UNTEA bureaucrats.[196] In January 1963, reports emerged of

> scores of Dutch henchmen spread out in various localities of West Irian, bent on creating trouble and sabotage. The loss of maps and other important equipment at major installations served as an example of the fact that the Dutch planned to paralyse efforts for the realisation of development projects in that territory.[197]

[192] J. Gienow-Hecht, 'Nation Branding: A Useful Category for International History', *Diplomacy & Statecraft*, 30:4 (2019), p. 756.

[193] Grant, '"Auntie" Takes over Irian Gently'.

[194] 'As the Dutch Say a Hard Farewell'.

[195] 'As the Dutch Say a Hard Farewell'.

[196] UNA, S-0876-0001-04-00001, 'Press Conferences given by Brigadier General Rikhye at Djakarta on 27 August, at 5pm', p. 11.

[197] BNA, FO 371/169951, DJ1013, 'Selby (Djakarta Embassy) to Warner (FCO)', 25 January 1963.

This Dutch 'mischief-making', echoing the obstruction tactics of evacuating Belgian colonists in Congo, also involved inventing rumours of inbound Indonesian military aggression to provoke conflict between the Indonesian government and the UN.[198] One of the more dangerous plots revolved around their reporting of an uninsured Indonesian ship heading from Singapore to West Papua.[199] These false reports also encouraged anxieties within vulnerable sections of the Papuan population, such as schoolchildren. A British High Commission reported to the Commonwealth Office in London that 'the origin of [Papuan] refugees' decision to go to Australian New Guinea came from their Dutch Head Teacher who warned them of an awful fate when the Indonesians took over'.[200]

In contrast to the overt obstructionism employed by the remaining Dutch officials, Indonesian obstructionism was more covert. By the second phase of UNTEA, there was a significant influx of Indonesian personnel into West Papua, many of whom were described by the Biak divisional commissioner as 'younger people whose educational training appears to have been more political than practical'.[201] In November 1962, Canadian UNTEA officials reported that 'there were at least 200 [Indonesians] already installed and that 300 or 400 more were expected in December'.[202] The Indonesian personnel harnessed their authority as the incoming sovereign power over the local populations and used Papuans as proxies to challenge the length of UNTEA's administration. They cultivated and funded pro-Indonesian groups of Papuans, many of whom were coerced or misinformed,[203] to send petitions demanding the mission be cut short.[204] The Biak divisional commissioner reported that his local representatives told him that, on at least one occasion, a Papuan pro-Indonesian petition had euphemistically 'fallen into Indonesian hands' during its production.[205] Most of these pro-Indonesian obstruction and propaganda

198 BNA, FO 371/169951, DJ1013, 'Selby (Djakarta Embassy) to Warner (FCO)', 25 January 1963.

199 BNA, FO 371/169952, DJ1019/8, 'Transfer of West New Guinea to Indonesia: Papuan Self-Determination', 15 February 1963.

200 BNA, FO 371/169952, DJ1019/2, 'Confidential letter from E.V. Vines (British High Commission, Canberra) to A. S. Fair (Commonwealth Relations Office, London)', 25 January 1963.

201 UNA, S-0701-0003-04, 'Report from Divisional Commissioner, Biak, to Director of Internal Affairs, Hollandia, 26 March 1963', p. 1.

202 Library and Archives Canada (LAC), RG25 (External Affairs), 6150, 50409-A-40, 'Visit of Canadian UNTEA Personnel to Djakarta, signed by Ambassador, 30 November 1962'.

203 UNA, S-0075-0002-04, 'Re-assessment of the Situation, Merauke, Annex C.5, 8 December 1962', p. 1.

204 UNA, S-0701-0003-04, 'Report from Divisional Commissioner, Biak, to Director of Internal Affairs, Hollandia, 26 March 1963', p. 1.

205 UNA, S-0701-0003-04, 'Report from Divisional Commissioner, Biak, to Director of Internal Affairs, Hollandia, 26 March 1963', p. 1.

attempts, such as anti-UNTEA pamphlets and communications, were obvious to the majority of Papuans who, 'even in the far-off villages, they [have] begun to realise what is happening. Indonesian propaganda by radio mostly has a reverse result: people discovered that this propaganda consists of lies because they can locally verify what is being said'.[206] The most significant effect of Indonesian obstruction efforts was anxiety and instability for UNTEA, rather than the encouragement of Papuans to accept the Indonesian takeover.

Moreover, pro-Indonesian groups orchestrated demonstrations in the hopes that the UNTEA administration would have to call for the military reinforcement of UNSF and thus ignite the international media.[207] On 17 January 1963, the UN Department of Information broadcast reports of a 'spontaneous mass demonstration which had apparently been staged by some 2,000 West Irianese [Papuans] before the UNTEA office at Kotabaru'.[208] Indonesian troops employed *within* the UNSF also created disruption through a similar strategy. Abdoh wrote in his December progress report to Thant that he believed,

> There is also the risk that the Indonesians who are already in this Territory, might encourage, or engineer, incidents involving Indonesian troops in order to achieve their objectives. Incidents of this nature, which have already occurred sporadically, leave UNTEA with no other alternative than to use the UNSF to confine the Indonesian troops to their barracks, and should they resist, serious clashes will ensue.[209]

The Indonesian personnel within UNTEA recognised that damaging the UN's reputation was key to terminating the mission. These protests also attracted international interest. Some supported pro-Indonesian calls for the UNTEA period of authority to be shortened as it was an obstacle to Papuan self-determination and unity with Indonesia.[210] Thant, however, was unconvinced of the motivations behind the protests, believing that the Indonesians wielded influence over all young and elite sections of the population. The secretary-general 'had no doubt at all those demonstrations or representations by Papuans were Indonesian-inspired and were not spontaneous'.[211] UNTEA

206 UNA, S-0703-0016-01, 'Explanatory Memorandum of the Government in Southern New Guinea, Eibrink Jensen, 17 September 1962'.

207 For more on UNSF's mandate and operations, see N. Macqueen, 'United Nations Security Force in West New Guinea (UNSF)', in J. A. Koops, T. Tardy, N. Macqueen, and P. D. Williams (eds.), *The Oxford Handbook of United Nations Peacekeeping Operations* (Oxford: Oxford University Press, 2015).

208 BNA FO 371/169951, DJ1013/8, 'Restricted Letter from Selby to Warner', 25 January 1963.

209 UNA, S-0876-0001-07-00001, 'Abdoh Report to Thant', 13 December 1962, p. 29.

210 BNA FO 371/169951 DJ1013/8, 'Restricted Letter from Selby to Warner', 25 January 1963.

211 BNA, FO 371/169952, DJ1019/5, 'Priority Telegram from Australian Mission to the United Nations in New York to Canberra', 23 January 1963.

leadership prioritised the delegitimisation of Papuan demands for an UNTEA-led plebiscite over concerns about the incoming Indonesian authority and the absence of a meaningful survey of Papuan feeling by 1 May 1963.

Although the relationships between the UNTEA staff and the leadership of the Indonesian Liaison Mission seemed friendly on the surface,[212] cracks had started to appear in the regional districts by November 1962 as UNTEA staff became suspicious of their Indonesian colleagues.[213] Biak's divisional commissioner reported that 'Although outwardly polite and co-operative, the Indonesian Mission here is doing all possible to wrest the initiative from me'.[214] UNTEA staff pushed back against efforts to position the mission as a cover for an Indonesian takeover, insisting that the mission was independent. However, some staff were concerned about how the Indonesian Liaison Mission personnel interacted with Papuan civilians and what this indicated about the Papuans' future. The Biak divisional commissioner wrote to Abdoh:

> [Papuans on the Regional Council] think it likely that many of them will be ousted or imprisoned once the Indonesians have taken over. After the behaviour of the Indonesians towards Papuan leaders . . . and the activity and attitude of the Indonesian Mission as observed by me in Biak (e.g. their going round and significantly taking the names of the few who flew the Papuan flag on December 1st) I personally would place little reliance on Indonesian assurances to the contrary. And in so far as we offer Papuans assurances obviously based on Indonesian promises we must not expect to convince anybody in this country henceforth.[215]

Additionally, one of Abdoh's last progress reports to Thant mentions that the Indonesian Army Intelligence had scanned the island's communications for anti-Indonesian groups and petitions in order to threaten Papuan civilians in retaliation for their politics.[216] He also reported that he was aware of the Indonesian government's intention of setting up a military government in the territory and questioned, 'whether or not [a military government] is another way of bestowing further honours on the "liberators" of West Irian, to keep them somehow occupied. . .'.[217] His flippant tone indicated that although he did not support of the Indonesian government's plans for the island and how they

212 UNA, S-0682-0003-04, 'Letter from Sudjarwo Tjondronegoro, Head of Indonesian Mission, to Rolz-Bennett, 22 October 1962'.

213 UNA, S-0862-0003-04, 'Aide Memoire: Attitude of the Indonesian Staff Members of UNTEA, 20 November 1962'.

214 UNA, S-0701-0003-04, 'Report from Divisional Commissioner, Biak, to Director of Internal Affairs, Hollandia, 4 January 1963'.

215 UNA, S-0075-0002-04, 'Memorandum from Divisional Commissioner, Biak, to Dr. Abdoh, 4 December 1962'.

216 UNA, S-0075-0004-02, 'Progress Report from Abdoh, April 1963', pp. 8–9.

217 UNA, S-0075-0004-02, 'Progress Report from Abdoh, April 1963', pp. 9–10.

would threaten Papuans' future human and civil rights, he had no intention of 'rocking the boat'.[218]

Abdoh's response to ongoing anti-UNTEA obstruction was to project UN and mission symbols across West Papua to visibly demonstrate their authority to the Papuan population, the Dutch and Indonesian governments, and the international community. The performances of 'UN statehood' during UNTEA allowed Abdoh to experiment with methods of nationalism, communicating to the international community that the liberal internationalist organisation had managed to bring 'welfare and progress to the people of this territory' and, despite being an international organisation, reinforcing the liberal idea that the nation-state paradigm was the most peaceable political unit.[219] In the domestic sphere, UNTEA's symbols across the territory allowed the UN to assert power to Papuan communities outside Hollandia. For instance, UNTEA's name and authority was communicated around the territory via new postage stamps. UN stamps in West Papua physically asserted the authority of the mission across the region, from business to business, house to house, civilian to civilian. Alvita Akiboh's work on colonial currencies has revealed how states distributed stamps as symbolic performances of statehood to encourage populations to perceive them as politically legitimate.[220] Stamps functioned like currency in their mobility and movement across the territory; binding transactors to the same political economy or national identity represented in the art of the banknote or postage stamp and thus to the designing governing power.[221] Similarly, Roland Burke's scholarship on UN commemorative stamps has highlighted the power of stamps in organisational self-fashioning of national image and memory.[222] For the first UNTEA stamp, the UN administration overprinted the word 'UNTEA' on existing Dutch 'Nieuw Guinea' stamps, suggesting a functional – rather than commemorative – choice. Overprinting was an efficient method of 'replacing' the Dutch administration without great expense or effort. Despite the limited creativity of this decision, it was a significant choice to deface the Dutch stamps with a bold assertion of 'UNTEA', especially for a seven-month mission. The first UNTEA stamp

[218] For more on Indonesian abuses in West Papua and UNTEA efforts to quash Papuan nationalist activism, see Tudor, 'Gatekeepers to Decolonisation'.

[219] UNA, S-0876-0001-07-00001, 'Address by the United Nations Administrator of West Irian (West New Guinea), Djalal Abdoh', Press Release WNG/110, 29 April 1963, p. 52.

[220] A. Akiboh, 'Pocket-Sized Imperialism: US Designs on Colonial Currency', *Diplomatic History*, 41:5 (2017), pp. 874–902.

[221] W. Mwangi, 'The Lion, the Native and the Coffee Plant: Political Imagery and the Ambiguous Art of Currency Design in Colonial Kenya', *Geopolitics*, 7:1 (2002), p. 35; E. E. Inyang, 'Biafran Postage Stamps (1967–1970) and the Rhetoric of Sovereign Promise', *Nations and Nationalism*, 27:4 (2021), pp. 1213–1230.

[222] R. Burke, 'Premature Memorials to the United Nations Human Rights Program: International Postage Stamps and the Commemoration of the 1948 Universal Declaration of Human Rights', *History and Memory*, 28:2 (2016), p. 156.

Figure 4.2 United Nations Temporary Executive Authority stamps, 1962–1963. From author's own collection.

Reproduced with permission from the UN.

Figure 4.3 UN-printed First Anniversary United Nations Temporary Executive Authority stamp, 1963. From author's own collection.
Reproduced with permission from the UN.

conveyed a usurpation of the Dutch colonial administration, acting as a 'carrier' for the message of the UNTEA nationalism and territorial inheritance.[223]

The overprinted Dutch stamps communicated the institution's sovereign authority to both domestic and international audiences, allowing the mission to make an impact across the vast territory and connect with civilians beyond the reach of typical UNTEA activities. Most of these stamps were overprinted in Hollandia for domestic use, but a 'mint' batch was overprinted in the Netherlands and sold directly to the UN headquarters in New York, where it was sold on to visitors as a novelty item. Selling these stamps in the UN headquarters indicated that the organisation leadership saw benefits to projecting the mission as a way of performing statehood practices, as well as stabilising the region; it was part of a broader process of expanding the governing functions of the organisation during decolonisation. The UNTEA stamps were displayed and sold alongside other numerous commemorative stamps, many of which represented milestones in the organisation's international human rights project. These stamps provided 'static' memorialisation of institutional 'successes', collectable for only a small price.[224] Sales of the

[223] H. Hoyo, 'Posting Nationalism Postage Stamps as Carriers of Nationalist Messages', in J. Burbick and W. Glass (eds.), *Beyond Imagined Uniqueness: Nationalisms in Contemporary Perspectives* (Cambridge: Cambridge University Press, 2010), p. 68.

[224] Burke, 'Premature Memorials to the United Nations Human Rights Program', p. 153.

'mint' UNTEA stamps ceased on 31 May once Indonesian stamps for the territory became valid.[225] A year after the end of the mission, the UN Secretariat created a commemorative postage stamp to be sold from the UN headquarters, signifying the institution's decision to entrench the mission in the official history of the organisation's successes. On the stamp UNTEA is symbolised as a bridge between the two dates – the origin and conclusion of the mission – emphasising its 'bridging' transitional role and suggesting its solidity.

During the mission, Abdoh made a concerted effort to increase the media coverage given to UNTEA and 'make available to the people of the territory and the peoples of the world at large, factual information about what UNTEA has achieved', in order to publicise its operations to the international media.[226] He argued that the administrative nature of the mission had failed to capture the interest the global community once the UN staff had arrived. In the aftermath of the Cuban missile crisis and the ongoing armed conflict between India and China, Abdoh felt UNTEA was the UN's underdog operation and argued that the 'UNTEA task, being at present in its most part one of an economic and social character has – as usual in the case of UN work in similar fields – attracted less attention than it deserves'.[227] To challenge this lack of media interest and 'work against [the] odds', Abdoh established a public information campaign to increase the number of press releases issued by the mission from a maximum of ten a month under the Dutch administration to sixty.[228] The Popular Information Service (also referred to as the UNTEA Department for Information) organised a 'special information programme' to expand interest in the UN administration.[229] This publicity strategy demonstrated an evolution from the UNEF mission, which focused energy on building a mission identity internally, to the UNTEA mission which was about projecting an identity outwards beyond the boundaries of the mission headquarters, capital city, and even the host territory.

Abdoh encouraged the publicisation of the UN mission and its benevolent practices in West Papua but continued to silence the voices of Papuan activists and political activities within these publications. The Service disseminated positive reports of UNTEA's activities through multiple cultural routes, such as 'films, film strips, newspapers, books and pamphlets'.[230] They spread these

[225] F. Bruns Jr, 'U.N. Will Feature New UNTEA Stamp', *The Washington Post*, 14 July 1963.

[226] UNA, S-0703-0001-05, 'Meeting of Directors: Saturday, 1 December 1962, at 8am', p. 2.

[227] UNA, S-0703-0001-05, 'Meeting of Directors: Saturday, 1 December 1962, at 8am', p. 2.

[228] UNA, S-0703-0001-05, 'Meeting of Directors: Saturday, 1 December 1962, at 8am', p. 2.

[229] UNA, S-0703-0001-05, 'Meeting of Directors: Saturday, 1 December 1962, at 8am', p. 3.

[230] UNA, S-0876-0001-03-00001, 'Rolz-Bennett Report to Secretary General', 15 November 1962, p. 34.

throughout West Papua and arranged for them to be 'read in Schools and the posters were put up in public places'.[231] The UNTEA officers involved Papuans in the distribution of this information to more rural regions: 'throughout the territory there are about thirty bodies which could be described as study groups to help disseminate information, hold seminars and also to sell the books sent from the central office on a commission basis'.[232] Abdoh had the advantage of regional information distribution through his new public information campaign in his propaganda battle with obstructive activities.

Abdoh took advantage of any event that could be construed as a celebration of the UN and the mission. Using the UNTEA budget, the Popular Information Service disseminated 'a UN Day leaflet, the secretary-general's message with his photograph, a special talk prepared by the Press Bureau, the Temporary Administrator's speech, all in [Malay]'.[233] Additionally, UN Human Rights Day was observed in the territory and the Popular Information Service recorded celebrations in the regions and Hollandia.[234] A recent special issue, edited by Paul van Trigt, has drawn attention to UN observances (such as days, weeks, years, decades) as integral to the UN's 'institutional identity' and 'how the organization tries to connect the role of the various stakeholders with public opinion'.[235] The dissemination of this educational material performed an interactive function between the Papuan population and the UNTEA administration in a similar way to the postage stamps. These cultural media served a crucial purpose for publicising the identity of the institution internationally, as they related the activities of the mission to the core purpose of the organisation and linking it with past operations and future organisational strategies.

The mission also held flag ceremonies in which UN troops hoisted the UN flag in alignment with, first, the Dutch flag and, later, the Indonesian flag on 31 December 1962. The administration saw this as a method of ensuring recognition of the role played by the UN as a sovereign party within the history of the dispute.[236] Additionally, Abdoh used this visual event to 'psychologically prepare' the population for the changes of authority within the seven months of the

[231] UNA, S-0876-0001-03-00001, 'Rolz-Bennett Report to Secretary General', 15 November 1962, p. 35.

[232] UNA, S-0876-0001-03-00001, 'Rolz-Bennett Report to Secretary General', 15 November 1962, p. 34.

[233] UNA, S-0876-0001-03-00001, 'Rolz-Bennett Report to Secretary General', 15 November 1962, p. 35.

[234] UNA, S-0703-0001-05, 'Meeting of Directors: Saturday, 1 December 1962, at 8am: Human Rights Day'.

[235] P. van Trigt, 'Scripts for a New Stage: United Nations' Observances and New Perspectives on Diplomatic History', *Diplomatica*, 1:2 (2019), p. 146.

[236] UNA, S-0876-0001-07-00001, 'Press Release WNG/55: United Nations Administrator Arrives in West New Guinea', 14 November 1962, p. 26.

mission.[237] These ceremonies were often followed by 'a guard of honour, composed of detachments of the Pakistani contingent of the United Nations Security Force and a unit of the Indonesian army, [that] presented arms'.[238] The armed guards of honour projected the performance of statehood and militaristic nationalism within the UN mission, ritualising their governance of West Papua.[239] The scheduled presentations of military power indicated that those within the UNTEA administration were influenced by colonial military traditions, such as the guard of honour, as powerful displays of sovereign authority. The 1,500 'politically acceptable' Pakistani peacekeeping troops were trained alongside the rituals and practices enforced by the colonial British administration until independence in 1947.[240] The ceremonies blurred the lines between the separate military and administrative mandates and suggested an ingrained militarism in UN peacebuilding. The creation of military medals for the UNTEA peacekeepers in the aftermath of the mission further confirmed the entanglement of militarism and peacebuilding in UN peacekeeping, confirming that understandings – and projections of – international power remained confined to militaristic rituals and assertions of imperial dominance. As Marsha Henry has shown in her work on UN peacekeeping in Liberia, 'The medal ceremonies provide an opportunity for peacekeepers to perform military masculinity (mostly) and display their martial capital through nationalist performance, by exhibiting a form of national and embodied competence. . .'[241] Abdoh orchestrated the colonial spectacles of military guards and flag ceremonies to project the image of a peacekeeping administration in complete control.

By the date of Indonesian takeover, 1 May 1963, Abdoh and his staff were aware that the Indonesian annexation was grounded in misinformation and that the New York Agreement was contrary to the demands – and benefit – of much of the Papuan population. The divisional commissioner for Biak wrote to Abdoh to highlight the opportunity of the mission authority to encourage Thant to reassess the terms of the Agreement based on the overwhelming evidence on the ground. He argued,

[237] UNA, S-0876-0001-07-00001, 'Address by the United Nations Administrator of West Irian (West New Guinea), Djalal Abdoh', Press Release WNG/110, 29 April 1963, p. 53.

[238] BNA, FO 371/169952, DJ1019/3, 'United Nations Information Centre: Flag-Hoisting Ceremony in West New Guinea (West Irian)', 2 January 1963.

[239] For more on the colonial legacies of military nationalist performance, see S. A. Reily and K. Brucher (eds.), *Brass Bands of the World: Militarism, Colonial Legacies, and Local Music Making* (Abingdon: Routledge, 2016).

[240] N. Islam, 'Colonial Legacy, Administrative Reform and Politics: Pakistan 1947–1987', *Public Administration and Development*, 9 (1989), pp. 271–285; K. Imy, *Faithful Fighters: Identity and Power in the British-Indian Army* (Palo Alto: Stanford University Press, 2019).

[241] M. Henry, 'Parades, Parties and Pests: Contradictions of Everyday Life in Peacekeeping Economies', *Journal of Intervention and Statebuilding*, 9:3 (2015), pp. 378–379.

> The simple issue is whether largely fabricated evidence is to be discounted and a bona fide attempt made in time by the UN to ascertain Papuan feeling, with the assurance convincingly given in advance that if the vote goes in favour of Papuan separation from Indonesia it can and will be effectively supported.[242]

Any effort by UNTEA leadership to reflect on the situation was rejected. Ultimately, internal perceptions of the population, geopolitical and regional pressures, and Abdoh's political beliefs in support of the Indonesian takeover manifested in the peacekeepers dismissing and mischaracterising the political reality. The UNTEA staff deemed the voices of pro-independence Papuan activists as both unrepresentative *and* illegitimate. The brief opportunity for UNTEA staff to publicise the reality of the political conditions in the territory to the international community was lost. The reputational boon of successfully administrating a post-colonial territorial transfer remained unsullied for UN leadership in New York, and Thant characterised the transfer as a victory for peace.[243]

However, the prospect of Papuan civil rights and self-determination was bleak under Indonesian authority. During the mid-1960s, nationalist belief surged in West Papua resulting in several 'uprisings' across the territory, prompting Indonesian military interference and the exile of more Papuan activists.[244] Additionally, the UN was severely restricted in its ability to oversee the annexation process during these years. Post-UNTEA, the Indonesian government communicated to Thant that the UN's involvement in the future plebiscite would be, at best, limited. Although the New York Agreement (Article XVI) outlined that UN officials should remain in West Papua until the agreed plebiscite, Indonesia delayed this arrangement 'so that after May 1963 there were no UN officials in West Papua'.[245] The British Foreign Office saw this withdrawal as a minor humiliation for the UN and commented that 'The best that the United Nations has been able to arrange is for periodic visits by experts. We appreciate the difficulties under which the secretary-general is operating and would not care to embarrass him by asking him to do more'.[246] This lack of continued information and involvement in the annexation of West Papua post-UNTEA made the organisation's leadership significantly underprepared and ill-informed by the time the agreed plebiscite was arranged.

[242] UNA, S-0075-0002-04, 'Memorandum from Divisional Commissioner, Biak, to Dr. Abdoh, 4 December 1962', pp. 1–2.

[243] U Thant, '3. From Transcript of Press Conference, Geneva, 3 May 1963', p. 337.

[244] Kluge, 'Decolonisation Interrupted'.

[245] Kluge, 'Decolonisation Interrupted', p. 145.

[246] BNA, FO 371/169952, DJ1019/13, 'Parliamentary Question in House of Lords', 3 May 1963.

The eventual organisation and acceptance of the fraudulent plebiscite in West Papua in 1969 verified the inability of the UN to challenge or meaningfully react to the authoritarian threat of Indonesian annexation.[247] The 1969 plebiscite, also known as the 'Act of Free Choice', was originally mandated in the 1962 New York Agreement but had been delayed as the Indonesian government sought to find a loophole to avoid implementing the vote. In 1969, the two voting options offered were for the territory to remain part of Indonesia – having officially been annexed in May 1963 – or to become an independent nation and to, as one UN official put it, 'open a new chapter'.[248] The UN had agreed to 'advise, assist, and participate in arrangements' of the plebiscite.[249] Thant sent Fernando Ortiz-Sanz, the Bolivian Ambassador to the United Nations, to resume the organisation's relationship with the territory and provide a guise of democratic legitimacy to the proceedings. Simultaneously, Papuan activists sent Herman Womsiwor, Papuan businessman and politician, to the UN Headquarters in New York to lobby diplomats and international officials for an independent West Papua.[250] However, the 1969 vote was not designed to meaningfully collect a democratic consensus, but instead to force through a vote that protected Indonesian interests and confirmed the stabilisation of the territory for international observers. Despite Ortiz-Sanz's role as UN secretary-general special representative and a team of eighteen UN observers, the Papuan population was restricted from voting to ensure a pro-Indonesia vote.[251] Only a small number of Papuans representatives were permitted to vote (approximately 1,000 of the 800,000 population), and allegations of abuse and pressure on the chosen voters were rife. One Indonesian member of the Indonesian government admitted that they were just 'going through the motions'.[252] Many observers, including journalists and Ortiz-Sanz himself, highlighted the severe limits on freedom of speech and 'tight political control' over the Papuans.[253]

247 For a more in depth investigation into the 1969 plebiscite, see Kluge, 'Decolonisation Interrupted'; G. Cheng, 'The United Nations and West Papuan Self-Determination: Lingering Conceptions of "Civilization" in the Decolonization Process', in N. Eggers, J. L. Pearson, and A. Almada e Santos (eds.), *The United Nations and Decolonization* (Abingdon: Routledge, 2020); T. D. Musgrave, 'An Analysis of the 1969 Act of Free Choice in West Papua', in C. Chinkin and F. Baetens (eds.), *Sovereignty, Statehood and State Responsibility* (Cambridge: Cambridge University Press, 2015); Viartasiwi, 'The Politics of History in West Papua – Indonesia Conflict', pp. 141–159.

248 K. Teltsch, 'UN Team Arranging Vote', *The New York Times*, 7 May 1969.

249 UN Doc, 'New York Agreement', 15 August 1962.

250 Teltsch, 'UN Team Arranging Vote'.

251 Teltsch, 'UN Team Arranging Vote'.

252 P. Shabecoff, 'Irianese Begin "Act of Free Choice" on Whether to Remain Part of Indonesia', *The New York Times*, 7 July 1969.

253 UN Doc, A/7723, 'Report of the Secretary-General regarding the Act of Self-Determination in West Irian', 6 November 1969, p. 73.

In spite of these political restrictions and the threat of state violence, Papuan protestors collected across the territory to challenge the pro-Indonesia vote. Mirroring the West Papuan efforts to interfere in the New York Agreement negotiations in August 1962, a group of protestors stood together and held a sign stating, 'UNO Don't sell us like animals', directly calling on Ortiz-Sanz and his observer team to intervene in the illegitimate plebiscite.[254] The terms of the plebiscite had been made explicit in the 1962 New York Agreement: according to Article XVIII, the plebiscite or 'act of self-determination' must be 'carried out in accordance with *international practice*' – that is, universal suffrage – rather than the Indonesian practice of *musyawarah* (an Indonesian form of consensus building), which relied upon the votes of a few representatives.[255] The corruption and coercion of Papuan representatives violated both this traditional Indonesian practice and the international practice.[256] However, Ortiz-Sanz sanctioned the corrupted, unanimous results. He reported to Thant that 'an act of free choice has taken place in West Irian in accordance with Indonesian practice' and formally affirmed that the population wished to remain in Indonesia, in spite of his observations.[257] The UN General Assembly voted 84-0 in favour of accepting Ortiz-Sanz's report and the results of the plebiscite on 19 November 1969. Ortiz-Sanz's analysis of the Act was indispensable for those voting on the topic halfway across the world in New York.[258] Most Western and Asian nations voted to endorse the plebiscite, but thirty African and South American member-states abstained from the vote, suggesting that the Afro-Asian bloc remained as conflicted about the sovereignty of West Papua and the Indonesia's colonialism as they were in 1962. The parallel circumstances of the 1969 vote reemphasised the UN leadership's prioritisation of large state power over the self-determination of a marginalised population, just as they had previous to and during the UNTEA mission.

The UN decision-making during the UNTEA mission also shaped Indonesian foreign policy in the 1960s. Indonesia's experience with the UN over the West Papua dispute emboldened Sukarno to use the same aggressive approach to attempt to annex Malaysia in 1963, this time rejecting the need to include the UN secretary-general for meetings in New York or a formal agreement. The Indonesian government resisted the creation of an independent nation of Malaysia from a merger of the British crown colonies of North Borneo

[254] 'History of West Papua', available at: www.freewestpapua.org/info/history-of-west-papua/, accessed on 22 April 2022.

[255] UN Doc, 'New York Agreement', 15 August 1962, [emphasis is author's own].

[256] Musgrave, 'An Analysis of the 1969 Act of Free Choice in West Papua', p. 226.

[257] UN Doc, A/7723, 'Report of the Secretary-General regarding the Act of Self-Determination in West Irian', 6 November 1969, p. 73.

[258] UN Doc, A/PV.1813, 'Agreement between the Republic of Indonesia and the Kingdom of the Netherlands concerning West New Guinea (West Irian): Resolution / Adopted by the General Assembly', 19 November 1969.

and Sarawak, Singapore, and the Federation of Malaya (which had previously been British Malaya) and sought to colonise the region. Fighting between Malaysia and Indonesia was confined to the island of Borneo, although both parties were supported militarily by their Cold War allies (Malaysia received support from the UK, Australia, and New Zealand and Indonesia accepted Soviet military aid).[259] It was not until 1966 that the violence between the two states de-escalated and the leaders reached a peace agreement. Following President Sukarno's loss of power to Suharto in the wake of the failed 30 September 1965 coup, Indonesia's foreign policy strategy shifted from overt aggression and domination in the South East Asia region to the emergence of a 'New Order'.[260] Under Suharto's dictatorship, the Indonesian government favoured exerting authority through regional organisations, such as the Association of Southeast Asian Nations (ASEAN), rather than through costly military operations, as in West Papua and Malaysia. UN and US leaderships' anxieties about communist infiltration in Indonesia were exacerbated by the West Papuan dispute and Indonesian acquisition of Soviet weapons during the Indonesia–Malaysia conflict, and subsequently fed into the CIA's violent efforts to destroy all traces of the PKI (the Communist Party of Indonesia) and incite anticommunist massacres during 1965–1966.[261] This authoritarian anticommunist policy was escalated by Western-aligned states and diplomats post-UNTEA, eventually generating the political conditions for – as well as arming – the Army-led anti-Left massacres and forced disappearances across the Indonesian archipelago in 1965–1966.[262]

Conclusion

At the height of ONUC controversy, the UN leadership sought to demonstrate the expertise and value of the UN by peacefully stabilising a region in the midst of conflict. The UN leadership chose to prioritise the reputation of the organisation over the rights of the Papuan population, despite the moment of opportunity presented by UNTEA and the knowledge of the UN bureaucrats on the ground. The reputational damage of the Congo mission had catalysed a shift in the decision-making of UN staff that now prioritised organisational prestige and stability. UN personnel saw their institution in crisis and deployed the field operation to recover credibility, blinding the mission staff

[259] R. Boden, 'Cold War Economics: Soviet Aid to Indonesia', *Journal of Cold War Studies*, 10:3 (2008), pp. 110–128.

[260] For more on the transfer of power between Sukarno and Suharto, see Bevins, *The Jakarto Method*.

[261] G. B. Robinson, *The Killing Season: A History of the Indonesian Massacres, 1965–1966* (Princeton: Princeton University Press, 2019).

[262] Bevins, *The Jakarta Method*, pp. 137–158.

to rights abuses and credible nationalist claims-making in West Papua. This context of organisational turmoil and Abdoh's feelings of solidarity with his fellow Bandung representatives from Indonesia drove UNTEA staff to focus on smoothly completing the mission rather than examining the territory's political context. The UNTEA administration staff focused on the short-term nature of the mission and the institutional demand for a 'job well done' in spite of Papuan activists' efforts. The bureaucrats thrived on an organisational culture that made them feel superior to the local population, limiting any sympathy or solidarity with the Papuan activists and their ongoing colonial experience.

As the mission concluded, UNTEA staff were relieved to leave the isolated territory. In his last administrative report to the UN headquarters, George Janecek, UNTEA Chief Administrative Officer and Czech national, wrote to his UN colleagues in the New York offices, stating,

> I am sure that over these past seven or so months many of you have approached your 'UNTEA' desks in fear and trepidation and some of your exclamations have even reverberated throughout Hollandia/Kotabaru. You have, perhaps, heard our slogan which we ourselves use to each other in time of stress and pain in Hollandia/Kotabaru, West Papua/West Irian/ Irian Barat – 'You never had it so good'. Well, today, it almost is true.[263]

This report provides a vital glimpse into the insular peacekeeping cliques and officials' efforts to detach their duty to the mission from the rights-based principles of the organisation. The UN staff forged an identity built upon their shared conception of the post as unexciting and remote, positioning themselves on as intellectually and developmentally superior to the Papuans. This perceived supremacy facilitated the attitude that the Papuans did not yet 'deserve' self-determination and, therefore, were not worth the potential reputational damage or a resurgence of violence in the Pacific. This idea of territories, especially those in the Pacific, being deemed as 'not yet ready' for independence by international actors had its roots in the League's 1919 Mandate system which had later been transposed into Article 73 of the UN Charter.[264] As Kluge has argued, 'The Charter outlined the responsibilities of governing powers who were members of the United Nations, *rather* than the rights of indigenous peoples within the territory.'[265]

The UNTEA mission demonstrated the UN leadership's ability to construct a field operation as a means of reputational repair, rather than as an opportunity to support vulnerable populations with no other source of international

[263] UNA, S-0075-0003-05, 'Administrative Report No. 18, 30 April 1963'.

[264] L. V. Smith, *Sovereignty at the Paris Peace Conference of 1919* (Oxford: Oxford University Press, 2018).

[265] Kluge, 'Decolonisation Interrupted', p. 76, [emphasis is author's own].

recourse. However, despite significant efforts at 'repairing' the image of the UN in the aftermath of the Congo crisis, the UN leadership were consistent in seeing local challenges through the prism of racial hierarchy and colonial forms of knowledge, even though the ONUC and UNTEA missions were created for different purposes. Despite divergent mandates, racialised conceptions of the host population continued to pervade and underpin peacekeeping practices and decision-making in the field. Denying the diversity and vibrancy of Papuan nationalist politics in 1962–1963, the mid-rank UNTEA staff legitimised the colonial takeover, authorised Papuan dispossession, and paved the way for the fraudulent 'Act of Free Choice' plebiscite in 1969.

5

From Stagnation to Insignificance, 1964–1971

Introduction: The Consequences of Ceasefires in Cyprus

In the same year that UNTEA ceased operations, another post-colonial dispute erupted onto the international stage, this time in Cyprus. On 30 November 1963, the precarious post-independence peace between the island's Greek-Cypriot and Turkish-Cypriot communities fractured. Greek-Cypriot complaints about the protections afforded to Turkish-Cypriots within the constitution, such as quotas for government roles and veto powers within the Cypriot House of Representatives, ignited inter-communal violence.[1] Post-colonial deliberations had provoked feelings of political entitlement in both ethno-national identities, resulting in a violent struggle for sovereign authority and prompting the establishment of another armed peacekeeping mission. The UN Cyprus mission (UNFICYP)'s military and mediatory mandates – whilst distinct but related – both contributed in various ways to the stagnation of the island's conflict, in terms of facilitating the collapse of UN's peace-making efforts and the redirection by mainland nations towards superpower mediation. Consequently, the political mediatory role of the UN became irrelevant by 1971, whereas the military presence of the force on the ground proved useful and valuable to interested parties in unanticipated – and even undesirable – ways for the UN Secretariat and the contributing nations. Although the conflict and UNFICYP was not itself a direct consequence of decolonisation, the mission was driven by the ethno-nationalist divisions between Greek-Cypriots and Turkish-Cypriots that were themselves products of British colonial rule and the Cyprus insurgency of the 1950s. In essence, the UN picked up the pieces of decolonisation in the 1964 conflict but did so by freezing rather than resolving the conflict.

Although the UN member-states had discussed concerns about the inter-communal violence and colonial instability of Cyprus on and off throughout the 1950s, it was not until the bloodshed in winter 1963–1964 that the island

[1] 'Cyprus Problem = Makarios Problem', *The New York Times*, 18 October 1964.

became the focus of global attention.[2] Following independence from Britain in 1960, each community had characterised the other as obstructive to their administrative or municipal goals. However, these disputes had not ignited concerns for international peace and security until President of Cyprus and Greek-Cypriot leader, Archbishop Makarios III, announced his '13 Points' for the functional and political improvement of the constitution on 30 November 1963 and undermined the bi-communal character of the state.[3]

However, although Makarios's announcement provoked violence and displacement in December 1963, the conflict was rooted in decades of colonisation, international interference, and mainland state instrumentalisation. Cypriot anti-colonial insurgency against the British colonial administration during the 1950s had forged a highly militarised population: both Cypriot communities were trained, armed, and prepared to fight for their liberation. However, the power structures and ethno-nationalist divisions of this colonial, militarised society were not fully erased following decolonisation. The legacies of British colonial rule were evident in Greek-Cypriot strategies used against Turkish-Cypriot citizens during the outbreak of conflict in late 1963. For instance, in December 1963, Greek-Cypriot police rounded up hundreds of Turkish-Cypriot civilians and held them hostage in the same detention camps employed five years earlier by the British to hold Greek-Cypriot resistance fighters.[4] Turkish-Cypriot paramilitary groups were comparatively ill-resourced and were unable to defend their community and places of worship from desecration.[5] Red Cross relief trucks began to distribute emergency food supplies and kerosene in January 1964 as displaced Turkish-Cypriots fled to Nicosia, the capital city, to escape violence in the villages.[6] Faced with these worsening conditions, the Security Council unanimously adopted Resolution

[2] E. Johnson, 'Britain and the Cyprus Problem at the United Nations, 1954–58', *The Journal of Imperial and Commonwealth History*, 28:3 (2000), pp. 113–130; E. Johnson, 'Keeping Cyprus off the agenda: British and American Relations at the United Nations, 1954–58', *Diplomacy and Statecraft*, 11:3 (2000), pp. 227–255; S. G. Xydis, *Cyprus: Conflict and Conciliation, 1954–1958* (Columbus: Ohio University Press, 1967); S. G. Xydis, 'The UN General Assembly as an Instrument of Greek Policy: Cyprus, 1954–58', *The Journal of Conflict Resolution*, 12:2 (1968), pp. 141–158; D. W. Markides, 'Britain's "New Look" Policy for Cyprus and the Makarios-Harding Talks, January 1955–March 1956'; H. Faustmann, 'The UN and the Internationalization of the Cyprus Conflict, 1949–58', in O. Richmond and J. Ker-Lindsay (eds.), *The Work of the UN in Cyprus: Promoting Peace and Development* (London: Palgrave Macmillan, 2001).

[3] 'Cyprus Problem = Makarios Problem'.

[4] 'Cyprus Violence Goes on as Isle Unifies Forces', *The Washington Post*, 26 December 1963.

[5] 'Turk Cyprus Shrine Damaged by Bomb; Tension Runs High', *The Washington Post*, 24 January 1964.

[6] L. Fellows, 'New Cyprus Tension Imperils Reopening of Roads', *The New York Times*, 9 January 1964.

186 on 4 March 1964,[7] following a general consensus to formally recommend the construction of a UN peacekeeping force in Cyprus (UNFICYP).[8] The UN leadership designed the Force in the hope that it would de-escalate the inter-communal violence on the island between Greek- and Turkish-Cypriots before the guarantor states (Britain, Turkey, and Greece) – and potentially the Cold War superpowers – became militarily engaged.

The island swiftly became a site of Cold War anxieties. Crucially, Cyprus provided NATO countries a direct non-Arctic route to the Soviet Union and was proximate to the Black Sea.[9] The island also represented a geographic meeting point between Europe and the Middle East, providing access to NATO-aligned nations, especially those within the newly constructed 'Southern Flank'.[10] Post-Suez, Britain was increasingly protective of the island as a symbol of its global imperial standing, and the UN leadership grew concerned about the lengths that NATO-aligned nations would go to protect their strategic access to the island. In a Security Council meeting in February 1964, Thant emphasised the danger of the conflict to international peace and security.[11] Similarly, the UN mediator for Cyprus, Galo Plaza, characterised UNFICYP as integral not only to the restoration of peace in the 'eastern Mediterranean area [but] possibly the world as a whole'.[12] The Greek-Cypriot leadership also recognised the international dimensions of the conflict and the opportunity to seize sole authority of the island. As Greek-Cypriot General Georgios Grivas stated, 'Of course we all realise Cyprus can never become a world power. All the same we can certainly do our best to go on being a world problem'.[13] However, by keeping the island a 'world problem', the Cypriot population remained vulnerable to ever-shifting geopolitical interests and pressures, and the Cypriot leadership remained disinclined to meaningfully resolve the conflict; for those in power, promoting the protracted nature of the conflict helped to maintain that power.

[7] UN Doc, S/PV.1099, 'Security Council Official Records, 19th year, 1099th Meeting, 28 February 1964, New York'.

[8] UN Doc, S/RES/186, S/5575, 'Resolution adopted by the Security Council at Its Meeting on 4 March 1964'.

[9] J. Ker-Lindsay, *Britain and the Cyprus Crisis, 1963–1964* (Berkeley: Bibliopolis, 2009), p. 9.

[10] For more on the development of NATO's 'Southern Flank', see D. Chourchoulis, *The Southern Flank of NATO, 1951–1959: Military Strategy or Political Stabilization* (Lanham: Lexington Books, 2014); T. Balci, 'The Cyprus Crisis and the Southern Flank of NATO (1960–1975)', *International Review of Turkish Studies*, 2:3 (2012), pp. 30–55.

[11] 'Cyprus Crisis Goes to U.N. Today', *The Times*, 17 February 1964; 'Makarios Backed in Cyprus: Deepening of Conflict Feared if His Proposals Are Rejected', *The New York Times*, 2 January 1964.

[12] UNA, S-0869-0001-10-00001, 'Report of the United Nations Mediator on Cyprus to the Secretary-General, 26 March 1965', p. 49.

[13] Bod, Special Collections United Nations Career Records Project, Papers of Charles Harris concerning his work in Cyprus, fols 185–336. Lt.-Gen. Sir James Wilson 1964–1966, 'Memoir: Chapter 17, The U.N. Force Commander', pp. 11–12.

Designing a Mission to Resolve Divergent Sovereign Imaginaries

Hostilities between the Greek- and Turkish-Cypriots emerged during Ottoman rule. Religious divisions between Greek (or largely Christian) and Turkish (or largely Muslim) Cypriots were fundamental to the evolution of ethno-nationalist feeling on the island. Under Ottoman authority, the Turkish-Cypriot minority was the dominant political group with Muslim religious leaders and institutions at the centre of Cypriot governance. However, these divisions remained fluid as co-habitation and inter-mingling remained common across the island.[14] In 1878, the Ottoman leadership granted Britain suzerainty of the island, causing a seismic shift in ethno-religious power relations between the communities. Once the dominant group in religious and political authority, the Turkish-Cypriots were now categorised and marginalised by the British colonists, causing less of a threat to their Christian authority.[15] Seeking to placate the majority population group of Greek-Cypriots, the British neglected Turkish-Cypriots' civil rights and political demands.[16] The British colonial administration exaggerated and entrenched the Ottoman *millet* system (of inter-communal religious divisions) into Cypriot governance, dividing the communities and over-emphasising the geographic distribution of the groups as immutable.[17] Once it had formalised Cyprus as a Crown colony, the British administration cemented these ethno-nationalist identities within Cypriot society and defined the groups as binaries, each characterised by its opposition of the other, thus accelerating inter-communal hostility, resentment, and nationalism on the island.[18]

Although the coloniality of the island has been neglected in historiography, works by Maria Chatzicharalampous and Carolien Stolte, Brian Drohan, and Victoria Nolan have recently connected the colonial and counter-insurgency practices in Cyprus to that of other British colonies across the globe, tracing common patterns and 'technologies of emergency'.[19] British demarcations, administrative categories, and territorial separation of communities were all

[14] M. Given, 'Maps, Fields, and Boundary Cairns: Demarcation and Resistance in Colonial Cyprus', *International Journal of Historical Archaeology*, 6:1 (2002), p. 20.

[15] E. Bouleti, 'Early Years of British Administration in Cyprus: The Rise of Anti-Colonialism in the Ottoman Muslim Community of Cyprus, 1878–1922', *Journal of Muslims in Europe*, 4:1 (2015), pp. 75–76.

[16] Bouleti, 'Early Years of British Administration in Cyprus', p. 75.

[17] Given, 'Maps, Fields, and Boundary Cairns', p. 4.

[18] A. Pollis, 'The Social Construction of Ethnicity and Nationality: The Case of Cyprus', *Nationalism and Ethnic Politics*, 2:1 (1996), pp. 67–90.

[19] B. Drohan, *Brutality in an Age of Human Rights: Activism and Counterinsurgency at the End of the British Empire* (Ithaca: Cornell University Press, 2017); M. Chatzicharalampous and C. Stolte, 'Technologies of Emergency: Cyprus at the Intersection of Decolonisation and the Cold War', *Contemporary European History* (2022), pp. 1–17; V. Nolan, *Military Leadership and Counterinsurgency: The British Army and Small War Strategy since World War II* (London: Bloomsbury, 2011).

part of the British colonial strategy of dividing – or diluting, as in the case of Malaysia – ethnic groups within the same state.[20] Through these colonial divisions, the power dynamics and historical grievances bound up in Cypriot ethno-religious identities were inflated and entrenched during the post-war period as a tool for British control, with both groups policing the other rather than uniting against their shared colonial power. Swiftly the 'majority/minority' articulation of ethnic separatism became linked to community claims for self-determination (or, as demanded by the Greek-Cypriot community, *enosis*).[21] As Mahmood Mamdani has argued, 'By identifying distinctive local customs and histories and incorporating these in the imperial historical narrative, census, and law, the British transformed existing cultural differences into boundaries of political identity that fragmented and fractured those they governed'.[22] Arie Dubnov and Laura Robson have offered a similar argument in their transnational history of partitionism.[23] They situated the experience and interests of the British colonial administration at the centre of post-colonial partitionism in Ireland, Pakistan, and Israel, arguing that 'Partition, then, belonged firmly within the imperial realm; it was less a vehicle for national liberation than a novel, sophisticated *dīvide et imperā* tactic that sought to co-opt the new global tilt toward the ethnic nation-state'.[24] Victor Kattan has also demonstrated how partitions in colonial settings constructed an 'imposed boundary, in which the negotiators, to the extent they were consulted, were not presented with a free choice'.[25] This dynamic can be best demonstrated by the origin story of the British 'Green Line' across the centre of Cypriot territory (just as was established in Palestine). In December 1963, in response to the outbreak of inter-communal violence, Major-General Peter Young, Commander of the British Joint Force, drew the ceasefire line on a

[20] T. Stockwell, 'Forging Malaysia and Singapore: Colonialism, Decolonization and Nation-Building', in G. Wang (ed.), *Nation Building: Five Southeast Asian Histories* (Singapore: ISEAS–Yusof Ishak Institute, 2005), pp. 191–200.

[21] A. Alecou, *Communism and Nationalism in Postwar Cyprus, 1945–1955: Politics and Ideologies under British Rule* (New York: Springer, 2016); C. Kaufmann, 'When All Else Fails: Ethnic Population Transfers and Partitions in the Twentieth Century', *International Security*, 23:2 (1998), pp. 120–156.

[22] M. Mamdani, *Neither Settler Nor Native: The Making and Unmaking of Permanent Minorities* (Cambridge, MA: Harvard University Press, 2020), p. 12.

[23] A. Dubnov and L. Robson, 'Introduction: Drawing the Line, Writing beyond It: Toward a Transnational History of Partitions', in A. Dubnov and L. Robson (eds.), *Partitions: A Transnational History of Twentieth-Century Territorial Separatism* (Palo Alto: Stanford University Press, 2019), pp. 1–3.

[24] Dubnov and Robson, 'Introduction', pp. 1–3; C. Demetriou, 'Divide and Rule Cyprus? Decolonisation as Process', *Commonwealth & Comparative Politics*, 57:4 (2019), pp. 403–420.

[25] V. Kattan, 'The Persistence of Partition: Boundary-Making, Imperialism, and International Law', *Political Geography*, 94 (2022), pp. 1–16.

map of the island with a green chinagraph pencil as an improvised solution to the conflict.[26] This Green Line – the product of 'imperial cartopolitical puppeteering', to use Rodrigo Bueno-Lacy and Henk van Houtum's term – had transformative implications for Cypriot society despite their lack of consultation. The sketched line formed the basis for the nation's partition: it outlined the UNFICYP buffer zone in 1964 and still today serves as the sovereign demarcations between the Republic of Cyprus and the Turkish Republic of Northern Cyprus.[27] Thus, Britain's colonial strategies not only entrenched ethno-national divisions into Cypriot governance structures but also provided the conditions for the mainland countries (Turkey and Greece) to make sovereign claims on the island to protect 'their' communities.

Following a decade of political debates and violent counter-insurgency, Cyprus achieved independence from Britain on 6 August 1960. However, the inter-communal divisions were not resolved by decolonisation as Britain sought to retain control over the strategic island, just as Belgium had with Congo. The British government orchestrated a constitutional drafting process and used the negotiations to prioritise the preservation of British military bases on the island.[28] The London-Zurich Agreements (or Accords) were signed by representatives of Britain, Greece, Turkey, and both Cypriot communities in February 1959, establishing Cyprus's constitution and road to independence. However, with the colonial administration no longer in power by August 1960, the communities characterised each other as the political obstacle to their ultimate goals: *enosis* (union with Greece) for Greek-Cypriots or *taksim* (partition of the island into Greek and Turkish sides) for Turkish-Cypriots. The majority of the drafting parties had failed to consider the practicalities of governing a sectarian society and instead prioritised the maintenance of guarantor interests and economic ties.[29]

The historical legacies of inter-communal tensions and brutal colonial counter-insurgency strategies created a highly volatile and militarised context in Cyprus by December 1963. In the 1950s, the Greek-Cypriot movement for *enosis* had instigated widespread violence against the British, supported by their mainland Greek allies.[30] British counter-insurgency techniques were not restricted to combatants, and many Cypriot civilians acquired arms to defend

[26] R. Bueno-Lacy and H. van Houtum, 'The Glocal Green Line: The Imperial Cartopolitical Puppeteering of Cyprus', *Geopolitics*, 24:3 (2019), p. 596.

[27] Bueno-Lacy and van Houtum, 'The Glocal Green Line', p. 614.

[28] R. Holland, *Britain and the Revolt in Cyprus 1954–1959* (Oxford: Clarendon Press, 2002), pp. 330–331.

[29] N. Salem, *Cyprus: A Regional Conflict and Its Resolution* (London: Palgrave Macmillan, 1992), p. 118.

[30] M. Hadjiathanasiou, *Propaganda and the Cyprus Revolt: Rebellion, Counter-Insurgency and the Media, 1955–1959* (London: Bloomsbury, 2020), p. 35/36.

themselves and their families.[31] This mobilised the population as Turkish-Cypriots fought to resist *enosis* whilst Greek-Cypriots fought against the island's colonial administration.[32] British counter-insurgency in Cyprus exacerbated inter-communal tensions, particularly during the last two years of the war, further compounding existing socio-political hostilities with a militarist binary logic – 'you're with us or against us'.[33] Following independence, political tensions between Greece and Turkey infected the island as both mainland nations transported propaganda, troops, and arms to Cyprus. With the two communities holding vastly different views of the future for the island, all issues of governance rapidly acquired sectarian meaning.[34]

The terms of the newly drafted constitution of the Republic of Cyprus became the crux of the post-colonial conflict between the two communities. The new constitution mandated that the Cypriot President must be Greek-Cypriot and Vice-President Turkish-Cypriot, and that they should be independently elected by their own communities. However, the 1963 crisis exposed Greek-Cypriot resentment of Turkish-Cypriot constitutional protections: why should the minority population have a representative with veto power? President of Cyprus and Greek-Cypriot leader, Archbishop Makarios III, announced his '13 Points' for the 'improvement' of the constitution on 30 November 1963, seeking to dilute the constitutional protections for Turkish-Cypriots and install Greek-Cypriot authority over the entirety of the island.[35] Makarios's announcement destabilised the bi-communal society and legitimised the militant sections of the Greek-Cypriot community. Starting with a small incident over a group of Turkish-Cypriots and their papers in Nicosia on 21 December 1964, the conflict grew into a Turkish-Cypriot protest in the city the next day that was aggressively policed by the Greek-Cypriot

[31] D. French, *Fighting EOKA: The British Counter-Insurgency Campaign on Cyprus, 1955–1959* (Oxford: Oxford University Press, 2015), p. 305.

[32] J. Stubbs and B. Taseli, 'Newspapers, Nationalism and Empire: The Turkish Cypriot Press in the British Colonial Period and Its Aftermath', *Media History*, 20:3 (2014), pp. 284–301; R. Bryant, *Imagining the Modern: The Cultures of Nationalism in Cyprus* (London: I. B. Tauris, 2004); C. H. Dodd, *The History and Politics of the Cyprus Conflict* (London: Palgrave Macmillan, 2010); G. H. Kelling, *Countdown to Rebellion: British Policy in Cyprus 1939–1955* (New York: Greenwood Press, 1990); I. D. Stefandis, *Isle of Discord: Nationalism, Imperialism and the Making of the Cyprus Problem* (New York: New York University, 1999); A. Rappas, *Cyprus in the 1930s: British Colonial Rule and the Roots of the Cyprus Conflict* (London: I. B. Tauris, 2014); E. Hatzivassiliou, 'Cold War Pressures, Regional Strategies, and Relative Decline: British Military and Strategic Planning for Cyprus, 1950–1960', *The Journal of Military History*, 73:4 (2009), pp. 1143–1166.

[33] Drohan, *Brutality in an Age of Human Rights*, pp. 69–70.

[34] 'Greeks and Turks in Street Battles', *The Times*, 23 December 1963.

[35] 'Cyprus Problem = Makarios Problem'.

army.[36] By 23 December, the Greek-Cypriot military and paramilitary forces had escalated the violence into a civil war with thousands of Turkish-Cypriots displaced and trapped in enclaves across the island.[37] This event was described by the Turkish Foreign Minister in 1963 as a 'genocide' and has since been referred to as 'Bloody Christmas' by Turkish-Cypriots.[38] As the conflict escalated, the British army established Truce Force on 26 December 1963 to impose a ceasefire. The Truce Force constructed roadblocks between the two communities (the Green Line) positioning the Greek-Cypriots alongside the national governance buildings.[39] The experience of the minority Turkish-Cypriot community during this period further entrenched their identity as a persecuted group.[40] In an echo of the British counter-insurgency characterisation of Greek-Cypriots as 'terrorists',[41] the Greek-Cypriots characterised all Turkish-Cypriot political activism as part of a 'rebellion' that sought to destroy the Republic.[42]

The scale of violence across the country in December 1963 and early 1964 alarmed the international community. British, Turkish, and Greek governments agreed that an international peacekeeping force would be the most effective way to de-escalate the crisis and prevent its expansion to mainland – or superpower – involvement.[43] However, *who* would lead this peacekeeping force remained contentious. During this period, the British had stepped into an intermediary role on a temporary basis with the Truce Force and had hoped that they would lead a NATO mission in Cyprus alongside the United States.[44] The Turkish government also supported a NATO-based solution (particularly one that would include the United States) as a preferable alternative to invading

[36] A. Efty, 'Two Cypriots Slain, Nine Hurt in Clashes: Greeks and Turks Fight over Planned Changes in Laws', *The Washington Post*, 22 December 1963; 'One More Slain in Cyprus Strife', *The New York Times*, 23 December 1963.

[37] For more detail on the escalation of the civil war in December 1963, see Ker-Lindsay, *Britain and the Cyprus Crisis, 1963–1964.*

[38] 'Violence Called "Genocide"', *The New York Times*, 25 December 1963.

[39] 'Eleven Cypriots Slain; Burn Turk Village', *Chicago Tribune*, 7 February 1964.

[40] UNA, S-0869-0001-02-00001, 'Urquhart's Confidential Notes on Meeting held in the Secretary-General's Conference Room at 11am on Thursday, 23 July 1964', p. 3.

[41] French, *Fighting EOKA*, p. 305.

[42] UNA, S-0870-0001-04-00001, 'Notes: Meeting between Archbishop Makarios and Ralph Bunche: Meeting held at the Presidential Palace, Nicosia, on Thursday 9 April 1964 from 11.10am to 12.50pm', pp. 5–7.

[43] J. Ker-Lindsay, 'The Joint Truce Force in Cyprus, December 1963–March 1964', in H. Faustmann and N. Peristianis (eds.), *Britain in Cyprus: Colonialism and Post-Colonialism 1878–2006* (Germany: Bibliopolis, 2006).

[44] A. Aksu, *The United Nations, Intra-State Peacekeeping and Normative Change* (Manchester: Manchester University Press, 2003), pp. 131–133.

the island.[45] However, the Greek government forcefully rejected the option of a NATO force as they were already concerned about Britain's involvement. Instead, Greece insisted that the UN Security Council was the only acceptable operator.[46] Even for a member of NATO like Greece, the UN was the superior 'non-aligned' option to lead an international mission due to its breadth of state-membership and past multilateral operations.

In addition to fears about continued British involvement, the Greek government recognised the vulnerability of the island to Cold War instrumentalisation. The Athens correspondent reported in *The Economist*, 'This eagerness to take cover under the so-called UN "umbrella" may not be unconnected with the Russians' keen display of interest in the Cyprus problem.'[47] The Soviet Union had used the post-colonial period in Cyprus to assert their support for a unified, demilitarised island, seeking to prevent NATO expansion through *enosis* and to disconnect Turkey from the 'Southern Flank'.[48] For the Greek government, the UN mission in Cyprus was understood as a means of staving off Soviet influence from the 'vulnerable' host population. Britain reluctantly deferred to the UN and agreed to the Force as a workable option. The Foreign Office made plans to comply with the UN's Force to retain their Sovereign Base Areas (SBAs).[49] The British government had justified their continued occupation of Egyptian territory in 1956 under a similar pretext, but due to heightened Cold War anxieties during the Cyprus conflict and the absence of Nasser's nationalist demands, the US government and UN leadership were more supportive of the British maintaining their military presence in the host territory in 1964 than they were in 1956. The SBAs contained the two main British bases: Akrotiri, a south-eastern coastal port, and Dhekelia, a south-western coastal port, totalling 3 per cent of the island.[50] These ports were not only of strategic benefit to the British government. The island also had recently become a crucial military base for NATO's Middle-Eastern and anti-Soviet operations due to the Suez crisis.[51] As James Ker-Lindsay has argued, 'Turkey,

45 N. Uslu, *The Cyprus Question as an Issue of Turkish Foreign Policy and Turkish-American Relations, 1959–2003* (New York: Nova Publishers, 2003), pp. 28–29.

46 Ker-Lindsay, *Britain and the Cyprus Crisis*, pp. 48–49.

47 'When Pride Simmers', *The Economist*, 210:6285, 8 February 1964, p. 498.

48 J. Sakkas and N. Zhukova, 'The Soviet Union, Turkey and the Cyprus Problem, 1967–1974', *Les cahiers Irice*, 1:1 (2013), p. 125.

49 BNA, FO 371/174763, C1201/59/G, 'Directive for UN Force in Cyprus, 23 March 1964'.

50 British SBA Administration website, 'Background', available at www.sbaadministration.org/index.php/background.

51 Chourchoulis, *The Southern Flank of NATO, 1951–1959*; Sakkas and Zhukova, 'The Soviet Union, Turkey and the Cyprus Problem, 1967–1974'; M. Agmon, 'Defending the Upper Gulf: Turkey's Forgotten Partnership', *Journal of Contemporary History*, 21:1 (1986), pp. 81–97; A. Stergiou, 'Les Russes à Chypre dans l'après-guerre froide', *Outre-Terre*, 1:27 (2011), p. 121.

in particular, was regarded as a vital component of NATO's security against the Soviet Union as it was the West's only direct non-arctic [maritime] route into the USSR'.[52] Much to the concern of Thant, Cyprus held a unique position in Anglo-American Cold War interests in 1964, following the loss of the Suez Canal Company, thus enticing superpower involvement in the Cyprus conflict.

During the construction of UNFICYP it became increasingly apparent that member-state participation in a peacekeeping mission was significantly less attractive to contributing nations if the mission was likely to experience criticism or failure. The operational and financial controversies of the Congo mission had damaged the willingness of member-states to contribute troops and fiscal support to the Cyprus mission, in contrast with the popularity of the UNEF mission, despite the perceived success of UNTEA. A *New York Times* article reported Thant's difficulties, 'in trying to recruit the new force [indicating] the mounting problems such operations face'.[53] ONUC put the organisation in significant debt and the UN's financial precarity demanded the Secretariat's attention throughout 1964.[54] Member-states were particularly reluctant to participate in the mission due to the risk that it might be accused of partiality, as in Congo. In response to Thant's letters to member-states requesting donations, some nations, such as Denmark, cautiously made offers.[55] Denmark proposed to donate forty police officers to UNFICYP on the condition that the mission was 'to refrain from any notion designed to influence the political solution in Cyprus except through contributing to a restoration of quiet'.[56] Nations negotiated their contributions on the condition that they would not become embroiled in the same 'storm of criticism' as had surrounded ONUC.[57] The UNFICYP leadership officially took-over from the British-led Truce Force in March 1964, but Thant was forced to gradually deploy contingents as member-states were still reluctant to join UNFICYP. Eventually, he was able to recruit and dispatch 6,411 personnel to Cyprus by 8 June 1964.[58]

The military contingents were donated by Austria, Canada, Denmark, Finland, Ireland, and Sweden, shifting the battalion nationalities from Global South-dominated during UNEF to Global North exclusivity during

[52] Ker-Lindsay, *Britain and the Cyprus Crisis, 1963–1964*, p. 9.
[53] 'Cyprus: Test for the UN', *The New York Times*, 8 March 1964.
[54] S. Pope, 'Finances Imperil UN Cyprus Force', *The New York Times*, 21 August 1964.
[55] UNA, S-0869-0001-01-00001, 'Letter from Hans Tabor, Danish Permanent Representative to the UN, to U Thant, 4 May 1964', p. 106.
[56] UNA, S-0869-0001-01-00001, 'Letter from Hans Tabor, Danish Permanent Representative to the UN, to U Thant, 4 May 1964', p. 106.
[57] Hamilton, 'U. N. Under Pressure', *The New York Times*, 11 February 1962.
[58] UN Publication, 'Establishment of UNFICYP', *The Blue Helmets – A Review of United Nations Peace-Keeping* (New York: UN Department of Public Information, 1985).

UNFICYP.[59] A British contingent was also included in UNFICYP, breaching Hammarskjöld's rule of excluding permanent-members from participating militarily in UN peacekeeping missions. Although a British contingent had been explicitly excluded from the UNEF mission, it became integral to UNFICYP. This inclusion suggested that by 1964, the UN leadership had become more concerned with thwarting Cold War threats from the Soviet Union than policing the military interventions of colonial regimes. The UNFICYP leadership attempted to make the transfer from the British Truce Force to the UN mission as overt as possible so as to avoid any confusion between the two Forces. Echoing the UNTEA flag ceremonies, 'The British flag was lowered at sundown of 26 March and the United Nations flag was hoisted at sunup of 27 March and the members of the United Kingdom contingent of UNFICYP donned blue berets, blue scarves and United Nations shoulder emblems'.[60] Dressed in recently dispatched ONUC uniforms, almost seven thousand troops arrived into Cyprus in March 1964, many directly from active duty as part of Congo or UNEF missions.[61] This inheritance of other mission uniforms and personnel – as well as organisational, financial, and resource constraints – illustrated the rapid transition from the end of the Congo mission in June 1964 to the new geopolitical context of the Cyprus conflict.

UNFICYP troops were deployed into a highly volatile environment where bomb attacks, heavily armed civilians, and a lack of logistics regularly threatened the Cypriot population's safety, as well as their own. The Cyprus conflict had been going for over four months by the time the first UNFICYP staff arrived on the island at the end of March 1964, and so the leadership had to begin tackling the situation on the back foot. However, as in all previous UN missions, the secretary-general had authorised the deployment of the UN mission before comprehensively staffing and resourcing it, therefore forcing field-based peacekeepers to rely upon the available technical and materiel support from nation-states already on the ground – in this case Britain – to launch peacekeeping operations. For UNFICYP, just as in UNEF, British military and technical support was instrumental during the early months.[62] Army officials based at SBAs made vehicles and materiel available to the UN troops to supplement the UNFICYP shortage.[63] SBA influence extended to the command structure of UNFICYP as the 'existing

[59] UN Publication, 'Establishment of UNFICYP'.

[60] UNA, S-0869-0003-14-00001, 'Press Release CYP/21: Lieutenant-General P.S. Gyani Assumes Command of United Nations Peacekeeping Force in Cyprus, 27 March 1964', p. 38.

[61] UNA, S-0869-0001-01-00001, 'Communique Issued by the Swedish Government in Stockholm on 10 April 1964', p. 61; UNA, S-0869-0002-09-00001, 'Note RE Initial Group for Administrative Arrangements for Cyprus (UNFICYP), 5 March 1964', p. 29.

[62] BNA, FO 371/174764, C/1201 183, 'Memo from Foreign Office to Ministry of Defence, 25 May 1964'.

[63] UNA, S-0869-0002-09-00001, 'Note RE Initial Group for Administrative Arrangements for Cyprus (UNFICYP), 5 March 1964', p. 29.

British command structure [was] used as a framework'.[64] The UNFICYP leadership cloned their administrative and logistical procedures from British colonial command structures. Therefore, the British troops not only helped to restore law and order across the island but also inspired the UNFICYP command pattern for the mission.

Additionally, British troops were seconded into UNFICYP and provided with UN peacekeeping uniforms. The 'seconded personnel would be considered as members of UNFICYP',[65] indicating the formalisation of this relationship.[66] This secondment was a technical addition to the permanent British contingent of over three thousand troops who were already participating.[67] These British troops joined the UNFICYP mission a month before other nationalities arrived on the island, provoking criticism from the Greek-Cypriot community about the unilateral character of the mission (especially as the Greek government had emphasised the benefits of the UN's multilateral missions).[68] Without the British, UNFICYP would have been unable to begin in March, but the decision indicated that the UN leadership were, once again, prioritising the swift operationality of the UN mission over both the complete recruitment and resourcing of the mission *and* a judicious disconnect from the (ex-)occupying colonial power.

In addition to materiel and logistical assistance, the relationship with the British troops in SBAs was more than just a professional collaboration. Deputy Force Commander A. J. Wilson, a British officer, reflected in his memoir that many of the UNFICYP troops regularly used the SBA buildings as a 'splendid escape' and 'relaxation from the stresses and strains of the Cyprus problem', building friendships and taking time away from the pressures of peacekeeping.[69] He suggested that the collaboration improved the reputation of the British army for those who served in Cyprus, although other reports – especially from Greek-Cypriots – suggested that the collaboration damaged the reputation of UNFICYP.[70] Friendships between British troops and their

[64] BNA, FO 371/174763, C1201/45, 'Military Plan for Establishing the UN force in Cyprus', 19 March 1964.

[65] UNA, S-0869-0002-09-00001, 'Note RE Initial Group for Administrative Arrangements for Cyprus (UNFICYP), 5 March 1964', p. 29.

[66] Neil Briscoe has argued that many of the British troops found it difficult to adjust to the 'spirit' of peacekeeping, despite the blue berets: N. Briscoe, *Britain and UN Peacekeeping, 1948–1967* (London: Palgrave Macmillan, 2003), pp. 186–187.

[67] BNA, FO 371/174763, C1201/59/G, 'Directive for UN Force in Cyprus, 23 March 1964'.

[68] L. Fellows, 'British U.N. Units Return Fire of Greek Cypriotes', *The New York Times*, 31 March 1964.

[69] Bod, Papers of Charles Harris; fols 185–336, Lt.-Gen. Sir James Wilson 1964–1966, 'Memoir: Chapter 16: The Blue Berets', p, 38.

[70] Bod, Papers of Charles Harris; fols 185–336, Lt.-Gen. Sir James Wilson 1964–1966, 'Memoir: Chapter 16: The Blue Berets', p, 38.

peacekeeping colleagues encouraged mixing between the two forces and blurred the distinction between UN and British military spaces, challenging UNFICYP's image of impartiality.

At first, the UN leadership in New York was supportive of the collaborative relationship but increasingly aware of how this partnership could affect diplomatic relations with the Greek-Cypriots and the Greek government.[71] A series of attacks by Greek-Cypriots aimed at British UN troops prompted concerns that the involvement of British troops in UNFICYP could potentially threaten the host population's trust in the UN mission and jeopardise law and order.[72] In spite of Thant's communications with the British government emphasising his gratitude for their support in Cyprus,[73] Bunche privately cabled temporary UNFICYP Force Commander General Prem Singh Gyani, an Indian national, to caution him about accusations of 'inheriting' the British colonial authority in Cyprus.[74] Gyani's role as Force Commander in UNEF from 1959–1963 and head of the UN Yemen Observation Mission (UNYOM) in 1963 had given him extensive experience in the Middle East as well as protracted ethnonationalist conflicts.[75] Although acknowledging that 'most of our administrative support will be from SBAs', the UN leadership in New York were keen to avoid any perception of 'relieving' or replacing the British as they had experienced in Congo.[76] Bunche encouraged Gyani to recognise that despite the 'excellent' role played by the British in supporting UNFICYP operations in the early months, 'it is equally to our interest that the predominance of British troops [be] reduced as soon as possible to give the Force an international look'.[77]

These fears were beginning to manifest on the ground as the 'inheritance' of responsibilities threatened the delicate diplomatic balance that UNFICYP had established with the Greek-Cypriot government. General Carver, Commander of the British UNFICYP troops, commented that many Greek-Cypriots remained suspicious of the British troops due to the recent period of counter-insurgency despite their UN uniform. He commented, 'As might be expected, the Greek-Cypriots did not regard British troops, who donned UN

[71] UNA, S-0869-0001-15-00001, 'Confidential Letter from Ralph Bunche to General Gyani, 30 March 1964', p. 12.

[72] Fellows, 'British U.N. Units Return Fire of Greek Cypriotes'.

[73] UNA, S-0869-0001-01-00001, 'Cable from U Thant to Permanent Representative of the United Kingdom of Great British and Northern Ireland to the UN, 29 October 1964', p. 200.

[74] UNA, S-0869-0001-15-00001, 'Confidential Letter from Ralph Bunche to General Gyani, 30 March 1964', p. 12.

[75] 'Indian Gen. Gyani Replaces von Horn', *The Jerusalem Post*, 12 September 1963.

[76] 'Indian Gen. Gyani Replaces von Horn'.

[77] 'Indian Gen. Gyani Replaces von Horn', pp. 12–15.

insignia, as the genuine article.'[78] Indeed, Neil Briscoe has cited the kidnap and murder of two British servicemen by the local population as evidence of growing hostility towards the British troops, despite their UN uniform.[79] The neo-colonial implications of the relationship between the British troops and the UN mission became increasingly concerning for contributing nations too, especially once the UNFICYP's logistical capacities improved and additional contingents arrived on the island. Wearing a UN uniform made the national battalions largely indistinguishable from one another – by design – but in this context it concerned contributing nations that their troops may be mistaken or targeted for being British. In a meeting with the Secretariat leadership and UNFICYP contributing governments, the Swedish and Danish Ambassadors, already reluctant to participate in the mission,[80] emphasised their hesitance in accepting the British troops into UNFICYP.[81] Ultimately, the UN leadership made a calculated assessment of the situation in Cyprus: they had accepted the neo-colonial character of the relationship (without considering the security risks) as long as it benefitted their operations, but as soon as the mission was sufficiently resourced, they sought to distance UN operations from the British SBAs and to emphasise their independence from the British military.

However, collaboration between the UN mission and the British was not the only source of anti-UN controversy in UNFICYP's first months. Violence between Greek-Cypriot fighters and Turkish-Cypriots also provoked anti-UN feeling among the Turkish-Cypriot community who felt the mission was inadequate and failing to protect them from attack. As the Greek-Cypriot troops targeted posts held by British UN troops in the village of Ayios Theodoros, they also fought with Turkish-Cypriots in the northeast of the island at Saint Hilarion Castle in April 1964.[82] Turkish-Cypriot fighters and civilians had taken shelter in the castle and the surrounding hills as they tried to defend their position from machine gun and mortar siege from Greek-Cypriot fighters. This ongoing attack, in addition to other recent violent clashes between the communities, prompted 150 Turkish-Cypriot women to demonstrate outside the home of their leader, Vice-President Fazıl Küçük whilst UNFICYP Commander Gyani was visiting in the late afternoon of 26 April 1964.[83] *The Washington Post* reported that up to 500 onlookers witnessed the Turkish-Cypriot

[78] Bod, Papers of Charles Harris; fols 1–115. Field Marshall Lord Carver, 1964, 'Lecture', p. 5.

[79] Briscoe, *Britain and UN Peacekeeping 1948–67*, p. 186.

[80] UNA, S-0869-0001-01-00001, 'Letter from Hans Tabor, Danish Permanent Representative to the UN, to U Thant, 4 May 1964', p. 106.

[81] UNA, S-0869-0001-02-00001, 'Notes on the Meeting held in the Secretary-General's Conference Room at 4.30pm on 12 June 1964 to discuss the future of UNFICYP', p. 18.

[82] 'The Attack on St Hilarion', *The Guardian*, 29 April 1964.

[83] 'Turks Mob U.N. Chief on Cyprus: 150 Women Hurl Rocks and Shout "Death to Gyani, Death to Gyani"', *The Washington Post*, 27 April 1964.

protestors shout 'Death to Gyani' and 'Gyani, butcher of Moslems [sic]'.[84] Some threw stones at the Vice-President's house, forcing Gyani to leave through a back door.[85] On the same day, 5,000 Turkish-Cypriot women and children demonstrated against the UN mission headquarters in Nicosia, 'accusing it of doing nothing to prevent "massacres" of civilians'.[86] UNFICYP mediator Sakari Tuomioja travelled to Athens and Cyprus to talk to Cypriot leaders about the violence against UNFCYP troops and the escalating violence on the island.[87]

After ordering a ceasefire on the Saint Hilarion Castle siege, Thant responded to Turkish-Cypriot criticisms of the failure of the UNFICYP in preventing the killings, arguing that 'It would be incongruous, even a little insane, for that force [UNFICYP] to set about killing Cypriots, whether Greek or Turkish, to prevent them from killing each other'.[88] However, much like the criticism faced by the ONUC leadership for the mission's lack of intervention in the nation's 'internal affairs' (during the Katanga secession),[89] voices within the international communist and global media insisted that responding to this kind of context militarily was the *very purpose* of the peacekeeping function of the UN – that is, intervening in violent attacks to save civilian lives – and called on the UNFICYP to 'get tough'.[90] The mission leadership's hesitation to use force in the aftermath of Congo operations in Katanga, despite the violence against Turkish-Cypriots, negatively affected the mission's international reputation and the UN leadership's decision to collaborate with – and second – British troops into UNFICYP harmed its relationship with both Turkish-Cypriots and Greek-Cypriots. The first few months of the mission had failed to implement a confident start, but now that all UNFICYP troops had arrived on the ground, the mission leadership could begin to re-stabilise the island.

84 'Turks Mob U.N. Chief on Cyprus: 150 Women Hurl Rocks and Shout "Death to Gyani, Death to Gyani"'.

85 'Turks Mob U.N. Chief on Cyprus: 150 Women Hurl Rocks and Shout "Death to Gyani, Death to Gyani"'; 'Nicosia Mob Stones Auto of UN Chief', *Chicago Tribune*, 27 April 1964.

86 'Nicosia Mob Stones Auto of UN Chief'.

87 'The Attack on St Hilarion'; Fellows, 'British U.N. Units Return Fire of Greek Cypriotes'; S. Pope, 'UN Chief Offers New Cyprus Plan to Bar "Disaster"', *The New York Times*, 30 April 1964.

88 'Greeks End Assaults on Castle', *The Baltimore Sun*, 30 April 1964.

89 L. Parrott, 'U.N. Urged to Use Force to Prevent War in Congo', *The New York Times*, 18 February 1961; T. F. Brady, 'Lumumba Angered by Use of Whites as Katanga Force: Assails Hammarskjöld Stand that U.N. Will Not Help to Subdue Secessionists', *The New York Times*, 14 August 1960.

90 '"Get Tough" in Cyprus, U.N. Troops Ordered: Sterner Attitude Results From Worldwide Criticism of Inability to Halt Island War', *Los Angeles Times*, 2 May 1964.

Military Humanitarianism and Palliative Relief

The implications of the escalating violence became evident as the UN mission struggled to respond to the Turkish-Cypriot displacement crisis. UNFICYP arrived four months into the ongoing forced displacement of thousands of Turkish-Cypriot refugees into improvised refugee camps, as the UN staff referred to them, largely in the western region of Kokkina and areas north of Nicosia.[91] In response to the Turkish-Cypriot community's rejection of the Greek-Cypriot government's authority, the Turkish-Cypriot leadership reinforced the 'Green Line' partition between the groups, beginning with mixed villages across the island. Widespread reports, beginning in January 1964, recorded humanitarian and human rights abuses of the Turkish-Cypriot community by their own (para) military forces as they executed this separation. For example, a UN Press Release described Turkish-Cypriot civilians' resistance to violent displacement or resettlement to demarcated Turkish-Cypriot regions and many begged to remain with their Greek-Cypriot neighbours.[92] The de facto partition between the two communities was criticised by the Greek-Cypriot leadership, who saw it as a step closer to a Turkish invasion and the implementation of *taksim*. This displacement crisis prompted the UNFICYP staff to establish palliative humanitarian solutions using military equipment or military supplies. However, these acts of military humanitarianism enabled the stagnation of the conflict, taking the political pressure off leadership to negotiate an immediate solution to the displacement emergency. Polly Pallister-Wilkins has similarly argued that humanitarian solutions depoliticise uneven mobility and its structural causes, and instead 'present them as natural rather than a product of human decisions and actions' or, as in this case, inactions.[93]

The displacement crisis may have been escalated by the Turkish-Cypriot paramilitary leadership, but the economic hardships imposed on the displaced communities in their regions were orchestrated by the Greek-Cypriot government. Makarios strategically benefitted from having the Turkish-Cypriots confined to villages across the island. The Cypriot military repeatedly cut off the Turkish-Cypriot refugees' water and food supplies, provoking violence between the communities.[94] Thant announced in his Security Council report that

[91] UN Doc, S/5950, 'Report on the United Nations Operations in Cyprus by the Secretary-General, 10 September 1964: Addendum covering the developments from 10 to 15 September 1964', p. 23.

[92] UNA, S-0869-0003-14-00001, 'Press Release: Permanent Mission of Cyprus to the United Nations, 24 January 1964', p. 11.

[93] P. Pallister-Wilkins, *Humanitarian Borders: Unequal Mobility and Saving Lives* (London: Verso Books, 2022), p. 17.

[94] UNA, S-0870-0001-04-00001, 'Meeting Held at Dr Kucuk's Residence, Nicosia on Thursday 9 April 1964 from 1735 to 2010 hours', p. 15.

> the economic restrictions being imposed against the Turkish communities in Cyprus, which in some instances have been so severe as to amount to veritable siege, indicate that the Government of Cyprus seeks to force a potential solution by economic pressure as a substitute for military action.[95]

Similarly concerned by the crisis, the new UNFICYP Force Commander, Indian-national, General Kodandera Thimayya, described the

> 1,000 Turks remaining in the Kokkina beachhead as 'starving' and . . . [Thimayya] expected new fighting to break out between Greek and Turkish-Cypriots. 'The Turks cannot go on living much longer' He said. There was only a week's supply of food in Kokkina and no water or cooking oil. He said that the Turkish-Cypriots were getting 'worked up' and unless the economic squeeze being increased was stopped, they would begin to feel it.[96]

The Turkish-Cypriot leadership would not let civilians leave, and the Greek-Cypriot leaders were blockading the camps to force them to break the partition, putting the vulnerable population on the front line and disrupting peoples' livelihoods to antagonise the other belligerent party.[97]

Despite a lack of humanitarian mandate, training, or resources, the armed UNFICYP troops assumed a humanitarian role and adopted responsibility for the delivery of relief to Cypriot internally displaced persons. Michael Harbottle, Chief of Staff for the Cyprus Force 1966–1968, argued that the mission's contribution to the conflict diversified during the economic blockade as 'The military therefore were very much involved and more often than not had to play the roles of adjudicator, appeaser, and provider'.[98] Troops improvised and built temporary housing in the displacement camps near Nicosia, housing approximately 1,500 Turkish-Cypriots in tents in June 1964, over half of whom were children.[99] The troops built 'provisional sub-shaded bamboo roofs which will be used as shelters during the hottest period of the day'.[100] The bamboo roofs prevented dehydration and provided shade for the families during the hot Cypriot summer. Concern for the health and well-being of displaced children also led to the construction of 'a provisional classroom' by

95 UN Doc, S/5950, 'Report on the United Nations Operations in Cyprus by the Secretary-General, 10 September 1964: Addendum covering the Developments from 10 to 15 September 1964', p. 66.

96 UNA, S-0869-0001-17-00001, 'Telegram: Reuters, 13 August 1964', p. 29.

97 UNA, S-0869-0001-17-00001, 'Telegram: Reuters, 13 August 1964', p. 28.

98 M. Harbottle, *The Impartial Soldier* (Oxford: Oxford University Press, 1970), p. 29.

99 UN Doc, S/5764, 'Report to the Security Council on the United Nations Operation in Cyprus, for the Period 26 April to 8 June 1964 / By the Secretary-General', p. 29.

100 UN Doc, S/5764, 'Report to the Security Council on the United Nations Operation in Cyprus, for the Period 26 April to 8 June 1964 / By the Secretary-General', p. 29.

UNFICYP engineering corps in order to 'encourage the continuation of school classes, using a provisional construction of cables and bamboo mats . . . some open-air showers are also being installed where at certain times of the day water could be sprayed over the children'.[101] Thant reported this to the Security Council but did not consult with the population regarding their needs. He followed up on this in his next report in September 1964 to assert that the survival of many of the refugee children in this region was directly attributable to the actions of the UN troops.[102] These activities blurred the mission's mandate as a military force and falsely cast the UN troops as humanitarians to the host population.

The lack of resources or training for the troops meant that their improvised humanitarian efforts were rarely effective or useful in the long-term, especially in responding to the housing crisis in refugee camps. Over the winter months in 1964, the refugee camps near Nicosia – with improvised bamboo roofs – were devastated by very heavy rainfall and severe flooding. These roofs became damaged and useable, decaying in the rain, as no provision had been for the change in season. Turkish-Cypriots were particularly affected as 'many houses . . . are not very solidly built of mud bricks . . . [which caused families] to be rendered homeless by bad weather'.[103] Unable to provide a solution for the homeless families, the troops donated 'four small tents' to the villagers and extended 'its good offices' to the Government of Cyprus to try and bring political attention to the situation.[104] Rather than finding a long-term, meaningful solution to the displacement and housing crisis, the mission leadership organised palliative, short-term, improvised solutions for a refugee population of thousands.

UNFICYP officials also organised relief donations to the refugees during the summer of 1964 in collaboration with the ICRC. Humanitarian efforts were shared between the UNFICYP staff and the Joint Relief Commission – acting under the auspices of the ICRC – and Turkish Red Crescent in Turkish-Cypriot controlled areas.[105] UNFICYP staff coordinated relief supplies from the Red Crescent which were then distributed by the Joint Relief Commission, a small organisation established by the ICRC but entirely staffed with British

[101] UN Doc, S/5764, 'Report to the Security Council on the United Nations Operation in Cyprus, for the Period 26 April to 8 June 1964 / By the Secretary-General', p. 29.

[102] UN Doc, S/5950, 'Report on the United Nations Operations in Cyprus by the Secretary-General, 10 September 1964: Addendum covering the Developments from 10 to 15 September 1964', p. 51.

[103] UN Doc, S/7969, 'Report by the Secretary-General on the United Nations Operation in Cyprus: (For the Period from 6 December 1966 to 12 June 1967)', pp. 58–59.

[104] UN Doc, S/7969, 'Report by the Secretary-General on the United Nations Operation in Cyprus: (For the Period from 6 December 1966 to 12 June 1967)', p. 59.

[105] UN, 'The Blue Beret - UNFICYP Edition, 27 April, 1964', p. 3, available at: https://unficyp.unmissions.org/sites/default/files/27_april_1964.pdf.

nationals,[106] with consent from the Greek-Cypriot government.[107] The Turkish Red Crescent provided 'food and medical supplies, tents, clothing, etc' in regular shipments and were the primary donors of relief to the Turkish-Cypriot population.[108] However, burdened by the relief efforts as a financial and operational inconvenience, the UN leadership were keen to push responsibility for the relief operations onto the ICRC as soon as possible.[109] In response, the ICRC leadership voiced concerns about the political nature of the displacement crisis in Cyprus, especially as almost all displaced persons were Turkish-Cypriot. ICRC delegates had been on the island since 1 January 1964, and they had hoped that the UN Force would assume responsibility for the organisation of relief once it was established.[110] In May 1964, the ICRC leadership sent a cable to Thant, arguing,

> The United Nations having now assumed responsibility for the maintenance of order and peace in Cyprus, the ICRC is of the opinion that the United Nations Forces political adviser, [Flores] in cooperation with all those concerned, should deal with relief . . . The main problem facing any relief agency in Cyprus today is basically of a political nature, and as such it cannot be dealt with by the Red Cross.[111]

ICRC practices were guided by principles of neutrality and impartiality, and the organisation felt that continuing to provide humanitarian aid to the Turkish-Cypriot refugees would potentially threaten their reputation and offend the Greek-Cypriot and Greek governments. This reluctance to take responsibility for the displacement crisis from both the UN and ICRC during this period demonstrated just how constrained these organisations were by reputational anxieties; both were paralysed by the idea that they would face criticism. In short, the ICRC leadership saw the situation as too political for them, while the UN leadership saw it as too humanitarian.

However, the potential optics of a famine during a UN mission motivated the UN leadership to compromise with the ICRC.[112] The mission leadership rejected the ICRC's reports that the UN had 'assumed the running of relief

[106] UNA, S-0079-0005-06, 'Inter-Office Memo from UNFICYP Senior Political Adviser, Flores, to Rolz-Bennett', 9 May 1964.

[107] UNA, S-0869-0003-14-00001, 'Press Release CYP/154: Statement by General K.S. Thimayya, Commander of UNFICYP, 12 September 1964', p. 158.

[108] UNA, S-0079-0005-06, 'Inter-Office Memo from UNFICYP Senior Political Adviser, Flores, to Rolz-Bennett', 9 May 1964.

[109] UNA, S-0079-0005-06, 'Memo between Deputy Director of European Office of the UN, Palthey, and Bunche', 3 June 1964.

[110] UNA, S-0079-0005-06, 'Topical Red Cross News: Cyprus, Six Months of ICRC Activity', Geneva, 7 July 1964, p. 2.

[111] UNA, S-0079-0005-06, 'Cable from ICRC to Secretary-General', May 1964.

[112] UNA, S-0079-0005-06, 'Memo between Deputy Director of European Office of the UN, Palthey, and Bunche', 3 June 1964.

operations' and insisted that it just assisted in 'their smooth running'.[113] The UNFICYP remained reluctant to take official responsibility for what they deemed a 'very difficult task, if not an impossible one', complicated by political dynamics and operational shortcomings.[114] Despite these protests, the unofficial mandate of Cyprus relief work from July 1964 onwards was held by the UN Force with the ICRC providing additional support and personnel; the ICRC preferred to take ownership of 'technical' operations such as distribution of aid, which they deemed 'neutral'.[115] The negotiation of humanitarian responsibility in Cyprus delayed relief agencies from consulting the population about long-term solutions to the displacement crisis and further contributed to the stagnation of the mission operations.

The month-to-month delivery of relief to displacement camps throughout the mid-1960s engrained dependency and left the refugees in a precarious position.[116] This precarity threatened the supply of relief to the displacement camps and made the refugees vulnerable to Greek-Cypriot instrumentalisation. In September 1964, Red Crescent supplies were denied entry to the country by the Greek-Cypriot police.[117] Thant authorised Thimayya to

> send emergency supplies to Kokkina as soon as possible. Accordingly, on 13th September, 4,000 lbs of food from UNFICYP's own stores were flown to Kokkina by two UNFICYP helicopters. Blankets and clothing were sent to Kokkina by lorry, under UNFICYP and Cyprus police escort.[118]

The mission's own limited stores were used to improvise a humanitarian solution; the peacekeepers effectively worked as part of a palliative relief agency.[119] Relying on regular deliveries from the Turkish Red Crescent every three months, in addition to the logistical and materiel assistance from the SBAs, UNFICYP's operational capacity was constantly vulnerable to political interference or bureaucratic delays.[120] For example, in November 1965, the

[113] UNA, S-0079-0005-06, 'Inter-Office Memo from Flores to Rolz-Bennett, JBR/djh', 28 July 1964.

[114] UNA, S-0079-0005-06, 'Inter-Office Memo from Flores to Rolz-Bennett, JBR/djh', 28 July 1964.

[115] UNA, S-0079-0005-06, 'Cable from ICRC to Secretary-General', May 1964.

[116] UN Doc, S/5764, 'Report to the Security Council on the United Nations Operation in Cyprus, for the period 26 April to 8 June 1964 / By the Secretary-General', pp. 28–29.

[117] UN Doc, S/5950/Add.2, 'Report on the United Nations Operations in Cyprus by the Secretary-General, 10 September 1964', p. 2.

[118] UN Doc, S/5950/Add.2, 'Report on the United Nations Operations in Cyprus by the Secretary-General, 10 September 1964', p. 2.

[119] 'UN Airlifts Food to Cyprus Village', *The New York Times*, 14 September 1964.

[120] UN Doc, S/5950, 'Report on the United Nations Operations in Cyprus by the Secretary-General, 10 September 1964: Addendum covering the developments from 10 to 15 September 1964', p. 55.

Greek-Cypriot government refused to let a Turkish Red Crescent ship unload the food and clothing destined for Turkish-Cypriot refugees due to an outstanding customs charge.[121] This improvised humanitarian effort led to disorganisation as the UNFICYP's 'fire-fighting' troops could only experiment with improvised solutions before turning to the next emergency, avoiding sustainable assistance and putting vulnerable sections of the population at risk.

Once it was clear that UNFICYP was unable – or politically unwilling – to establish stable or long-term solutions to the displacement crisis, tensions within the refugee camps rose. For those who had lived in the camps for almost a year, there appeared no recourse other than military action to encourage a political solution; the stagnation of the conflict left the displaced Turkish-Cypriots behind. The mission's failure to resolve the Turkish-Cypriot displacement issue resulted in the perpetuation of structures of inequalities within the two communities. These geographic and identity-based patterns of displacement were repeated in future peaks of violence on the island.[122] Intercommunal tensions incubated within the displacement camps as Turkish-Cypriot civilians and combatants waited for the opportunity to reclaim their political representation, their jobs, and their homes.[123] More broadly, this early period of UNFICYP demonstrated how each party to the conflict (international organisation or nation-state) had a different set of expectations for Cyprus: the UNFICYP leadership expected to conduct a relatively short-term, military 'interposition'-focused mission;[124] the ICRC wanted to remain 'neutral' and technically focused in its provision of aid; both Cypriot communities expected different kinds of political solutions or results from the UN mission. The ambiguity of these interests, the variety of expectations, and the political power of the group informed the manner in which on-ground considerations could shift and transform the mission's power dynamics and operational priorities.

[121] 'Turkish Aid Stirs Dispute in Cyprus', *The New York Times*, 16 November 1965.

[122] For more on post-1974 Turkish Cypriot displacement, see P. Loizos, *The Heart Grown Bitter: A Chronicle of Cypriot War Refugees* (Cambridge: Cambridge University Press, 1981); Bryant, *Imagining the Modern*; P. Gatrell, '"Some Kind of Freedom" Refugees, Homecoming, and Refugee Voices in Contemporary History', in P. Gatrell, *The Making of the Modern Refugee* (Oxford: Oxford University Press, 2013); L. Dikomitis, *Cyprus and Its Places of Desire: Cultures of Displacement among Greek and Turkish Cypriot Refugees* (London: I. B. Tauris, 2012).

[123] R. J. Fisher, 'Cyprus: The Failure of Mediation and the Escalation of an Identity-Based Conflict to an Adversarial Impasse', *Journal of Peace Research*, 38:3 (2001), p. 314.

[124] R. Hatto, 'From Peacekeeping to Peacebuilding: The Evolution of the Role of the United Nations in Peace Operations', *International Review of the Red Cross*, 95:891–892 (2013), pp. 495–515.

The 'Plaza Moment': Negotiating Geopolitical Stakes

A year after the initial deployment of the Force to Cyprus, the leadership's attention shifted to the impending publication of the UN mediator Galo Plaza and his report on the conflict. After fire-fighting violent outbreaks and humanitarian crises throughout 1964, UNFICYP troops had managed to install a fragile ceasefire by December 1964, although the underlying inter-communal tensions remained unresolved.[125] The mission leadership were now able to focus on the political dimensions of the crisis and its settlement. The 1964 UN Security Council resolution authorised the UN mediator as an addition to the UNFICYP mission although Thant emphasised the distinction between the two mandates.[126] The military activities of UNFICYP and the diplomatic purpose of the mediator were to be 'separate and distinct operations and are to be kept so in every respect' despite practical recognition that the conditions for the withdrawal of the force were in the hands of the mediator.[127] The political activities of the UN mediator directly influenced the future of UNFICYP and the scale of its military operations.[128] Despite this, Thant characterised the military wing of UNFICYP as impartial and apolitical. The force was deployed to establish a ceasefire along the 'Green Line' and to reinforce law and order across the island; the political roots of the crisis were not its domain, nor were they within the oversight of the mandate.[129] However, the conflict required a political solution, and Thant had to recruit a UN mediator that would work in parallel with the military force, recognising that the military stabilisation of the nation would not resolve the roots of the conflict. Thus, the military mission was inextricably linked to the explicitly political aims of the mediator, despite the UN leadership emphasis on the separation between the two mandates.

Previous UN peacekeeping pursuits in formal mediation had been led exclusively by the secretary-general or those within the UN Secretariat inner circle based in the New York headquarters. Count Bernadotte's experience as UN mediator in Palestine in 1948 was a formative innovation for the organisation, but the UN's involvement in the Arab-Israeli conflict was entirely unarmed and

[125] UN Doc, S/6102, 'Report by the Secretary-General on the United Nations Operation in Cyprus: (For the Period 10 September to 12 December 1964)', 12 December 1964, p. 4.

[126] UN Doc, S/5575, 'Resolution Adopted by the Security Council at Its Meeting on 4 March 1964', p. 2.

[127] UNA, S-0869-0003-04-00001, 'Confidential: General Directive no. 1 – 1964: From U Thant to General Gyani, 27 March 1964', p. 13.

[128] For greater detail about this period of the UNFICYP mission and the activities of the UN Mediator in Cyprus, see M. Tudor, 'Reputation on the (Green) Line: Revisiting the "Plaza Moment" in United Nations Peacekeeping Practice, 1964–1966', *Journal of Global History*, 16:2 (2021), pp. 227–245.

[129] Tudor, 'Reputation on the (Green) Line', pp. 227–245.

staffed by military observers, creating a different dynamic between the UN field-based staff and the belligerent parties than in Cyprus.[130] Dag Hammarskjöld was successful in mediating the release of eleven kidnapped American B-29 pilots during the Korean War,[131] attracting international confidence in his personal diplomatic skills.[132] Similarly, U Thant was a key mediatory figure in negotiations between Washington and Moscow during the Cuban missile crisis in 1962.[133] Therefore, before UNFICYP, UN mediation efforts were highly dependent on the popular personality, international respect, and professional weight of the person leading the negotiations. The UN secretary-general's rank as the Head of the UN Secretariat and representative of the UN offered significant political and diplomatic authority as an independent political figure. As the military functions of the organisation expanded, the UN leadership invested in the development of the organisation's field-based diplomatic expertise, going beyond the secretary-general. By 1964, Thant could not afford to devote himself to protracted negotiations requiring extensive consultations in several countries. Recognising that UNFICYP's military operations and mediatory activities could work in tandem to produce a peaceful settlement,[134] the secretary-general saw the activities of the UN mediator as integral to the successful completion of UNFICYP's mandate, to 'seek out a durable solution' to the Cyprus question, and critical for his plans to broaden peacekeeping practices to include international diplomacy.[135]

The designation of a diplomat whose role was solely to focus on the mediation of the conflict was an innovation for the Cyprus mission. It divorced mediatory processes from the political weight available to a secretary-general or

130 UN Doc, S/RES/57, '57 (1948). Resolution of 18 September 1948'.

131 Brian Urquhart's description of the crisis places Hammarskjold's diplomatic weight as the primary reason for the successful release: 'In Deputy Prime Minister and Foreign Minister Zhou Enlai, Hammarskjöld was dealing with a fellow intellectual. In an epic negotiation over the six following months, first the four fighter pilots were released. The crew of a B-29, with much intelligence equipment on board the plane, took longer, but on Hammarskjöld's fiftieth birthday, at a remote fishing village in southern Sweden, he received Zhou's telegram. The eleven B-29 crew members were on their way out of China and the Chinese government sent its best wishes on Hammarskjöld's fiftieth birthday.' B. Urquhart, 'The Evolution of the Secretary-General', in S. Chesterman (ed.), *Secretary or General: The UN Secretary-General in World Politics* (Cambridge: Cambridge University Press, 2007), p. 20.

132 R. Lipsey, *Hammarskjöld: A Life* (Ann Arbor: University of Michigan Press, 2013), p. 308.

133 A. O'Malley, *The Diplomacy of Decolonisation: America, Britain and the United Nations during the Congo Crisis 1960–1964* (Manchester: Manchester University Press, 2018), p. 148.

134 UNA, S-0869-0003-04-00001, 'General Directive No 1 – 1964, from the Secretary-General to General Gyani', 27 March 1964.

135 UN Doc., S/5575, 'The Cyprus Question: 186 (1964). Resolution of 4 March 1964', p. 2.

inner circle diplomat, requiring greater focus on the negotiations producing solutions in and of themselves. Yet, finding an adequate, experienced mediator proved tricky. Thant first searched within the UN Secretariat. Initially, he suggested his colleague Jose Rolz-Bennett, a senior-ranked UN Secretariat civil servant, in March 1964.[136] However, Rolz-Bennett was swiftly rejected by the Turkish government, which believed him to be unqualified and unfamiliar with the region.[137] Turkey's veto put Thant under pressure. He struggled to find a mediator acceptable to all the parties who would also refrain from 'prima donna' behaviour.[138] Although Thant had intimated that he was hoping to have close oversight of the mediation process, Anglo-American diplomats expressed concern, both to him and each other, and reminded him to avoid too great an involvement in this 'controversial and time-consuming assignment'.[139] Reacting to the time-pressure presented by the emergency on the ground, Thant shifted his hiring practices to search externally from the New York headquarters inner circle.[140]

Thant's decision in September 1964 to promote the Ecuadorian politician Galo Plaza to the role of mediator in Cyprus stemmed from the unexpected passing of the previous mediator, Finnish diplomat Sakari Tuomioja, who had collapsed from a stroke whilst negotiating with the interested parties in Geneva and in the midst of drafting his report for the Security Council.[141] Tuomioja's mediatory approach had been to prioritise contact with all the guarantor states (Britain, Greece, and Turkey), and he spent most of his mediation period in talks in Geneva. During the few months he was investigating, he 'made [himself] available for consultations, as appropriate, with the diplomatic representatives of other States'.[142] Plaza's appointment as his replacement was unsurprising, and *The New York Times* reported that he had been 'thought of immediately' for the role due to his existing position in

136 UNA, S-0079-0007-10, 'CYE 26 Galo Plaza I – Draft of Section of Report to the Security Council on Question of Mediator', 11 March 1964.

137 'Turks Reject U. N. Mediator', *The New York Times*, 10 March 1964.

138 US Department of State, '479. Telegram from the Mission to the United Nations to the Department of State', *Foreign Relations of the United States, 1964–1968, Vol. XXXIII*, Organization and Management of Foreign Policy; United Nations, 5 March 1964.

139 US Department of State, '479. Telegram from the Mission to the United Nations to the Department of State', *Foreign Relations of the United States, 1964–1968, Vol. XXXIII*, Organization and Management of Foreign Policy; United Nations, 5 March 1964.

140 S. P. Brewer, 'U.N. Is Assured on Force to Keep Peace in Cyprus: Finland, Ireland and Sweden Confirm Commitment on Troops', *The New York Times*, 15 March 1964.

141 Tuomioja's meditator's report was compiled by his legal and political advisers from his notes after he became ill: UNA, S-0870-0001-01, 'Letter from Robert T Miller to U Thant', 28 August 1964.

142 UNA, S-0870-0001-01-00001, 'Outline Organisation of an International Force for Cyprus by Major General Rikhye, 21 February 1964', p. 5.

the field with UNFICYP as Thant's special representative.[143] Plaza had been on the ground in previous peacekeeping missions such as the observation mission to Lebanon (UNOGIL) in 1958,[144] and had replaced Bunche as special representative in ONUC.[145] His successful efforts during UNOGIL in uniting religious leaders drew praise from Dag Hammarskjöld, and he attracted the attention of Thant, who was searching for a special representative to monitor the efforts of the UNFICYP mission in May 1964.[146] On accepting his promotion to UN mediator in September 1964, Plaza remarked in a press conference that 'as a Latin American he felt he had a special understanding of Mediterranean problems'.[147] In an interview with the UNFICYP *Blue Beret* magazine, he clarified that 'he was of Spanish origin and by ancestry a Mediterranean himself. This made it possible, he said, not to believe in extreme positions'.[148] Plaza was dedicated politician and international diplomat, and he perceived the UN as functionally imperative for peaceful international communication between nation-states.[149] Recognising the restrictions placed on a peacekeeping mission such as UNFICYP, staffed entirely by troops and military staff but only mandated to defend, he described the mission at a UN press conference as 'the most unmilitary military activity' he had ever known.[150] He sympathised with the trained soldiers and officers within UNFICYP who had spent their lives training to *fight* a war, now employed in ways that meant their battalion 'could never win a battle, whilst on the other [hand] it could never be defeated'.[151]

Plaza's rejection of the London-Zurich Agreement in his 1965 report was a much more radical stance than Tuomioja.[152] The previous mediator had accepted the terms of the London-Zurich Agreement and had attempted to build upon the guarantor states' interests, as protected in the Agreement, before he became ill. Plaza's decision to immediately change tack and announce that 'the very fact that a mediator had been appointed was proof that a new solution had to be found' concerned the state actors who signed the

[143] S. Pope, 'Problem for Thant', *The New York Times*, 18 August 1964.

[144] K. Teltsch, 'Ecuadorian Given UN Cyprus Role', *The New York Times*, 12 May 1964.

[145] UN Doc, S/5691, 'Report by the Secretary-General to the Security Council on the Operations of the United Nations Peacekeeping Force in Cyprus', 11 May 1964', p. 2.

[146] G. Plaza, Interviewed by Diego Cordovez, 28 March 1984, pp. 2–3.

[147] UNA, S-0869-0003-14-00001, 'Press Release CYP/110: Secretary-General's Special Representative Returns to Cyprus, 15 August 1964', p. 104.

[148] 'Galo Plaza Returns to Cyprus', *The Blue Beret UNFICYP Edition*, 18 August 1964, p. 3.

[149] Plaza, Interviewed by Diego Cordovez, UN Interview, 28 March 1984, pp. 15–16.

[150] UNA, S-0869-0003-14-00001, 'Press Release CYP/110: Secretary-General's Special Representative Returns to Cyprus, 15 August 1964', p. 103.

[151] UNA, S-0869-0003-14-00001, 'Press Release CYP/110: Secretary-General's Special Representative Returns to Cyprus, 15 August 1964', p. 103.

[152] UN Doc, S/5691, 'Report by the Secretary-General to the Security Council on the Operations of the United Nations Peacekeeping Force in Cyprus', 11 May 1964', p. 1.

Agreement, especially the Turkish government.[153] Plaza argued that the guarantor states should no longer be prioritised over the Cypriot population.[154] A *Washington Post* article interpreted this to mean that 'the best way for solving the bitter Cyprus impasse is to abandon the old concept that Greece and Turkey must come together and instead let the talking begin with the two factions most immediately involved, the Greek and Turkish residents of Cyprus itself'.[155] Pre-Plaza, the UNFICYP mediator's policy was to rely on Turkey and Greece to negotiate the territory's future. Plaza changed this: 'My first concern,' he argued, 'was to return the scene of mediation to the island of Cyprus'.[156]

Invalidating Greece's claim to the island further, Plaza claimed in his report that, based upon his consultation of the Greek-Cypriot community, the desire for *enosis* was waning in favour of a more traditional form of Cypriot independence.[157] In a private letter to Thant, Plaza noted

> something [Makarios] does not want and a growing number of people in Cyprus agree with him [upon], is *Enosis* although he must pay lip service to this vague and never clearly defined aspiration which still has its followers in rural areas and among those that do not realise that their country in many ways, is drifting away from *Enosis* in the direction of unfettered independence.[158]

Despite the Greek-Cypriot community's demands for *enosis* throughout the 1950s, by 1965 many within the community had begun to question whether moving from one colonial power to the annexation of another would be the correct choice for the Greek-Cypriot population.

Following months of meetings, travelling, and negotiations between 28 September 1964 and 22 March 1965, Plaza's sixty-six-page report was finally delivered to the Secretariat on 26 March 1965. Thant received the report only a week after the UN Security Council authorised a three-month extension to the mission on 19 March 1965, securing UNFICYP's position on the ground during the potentially incendiary period immediately following the report's

[153] UNA, S-0869-0001-09-00001, 'Notes on Galo Plaza Conference, 25 September 1964', p. 17.
[154] UNA, S-0869-0001-09-00001, 'Notes on Galo Plaza Conference, 25 September 1964', p. 17.
[155] UNA, S-0869-0001-10-00001, 'Clipping: The Washington Post, "The UN and Cyprus", Wednesday, 7 April 1965', p. 77.
[156] UNA, S-0869-0001-10-00001, 'Report of the United Nations Mediator on Cyprus to the Secretary-General, 26 March 1965', p. 38.
[157] UNA, S-0869-0001-10-00001, 'Report of the United Nations Mediator on Cyprus to the Secretary-General, 26 March 1965', p. 41.
[158] UNA, S-0869-0001-09-00001, 'Confidential Letter from Plaza to U Thant, 11 March 1966', p. 32.

distribution.[159] UNFICYP Force Commander Thimayya took military precautions to anticipate any negative reactions on the ground, and expectations were heightened as Cypriots awaited the responses of the Turkish, Greek, and British governments.[160] Describing the vitality and hope of Plaza's report, a *New York Times* article on 1 April 1965 promoted it as injecting 'a new factor that [could] serve as a basis for another state towards quenching one of the most dangerous fires in the world'.[161] Thant attached an endorsement of the report to the Security Council document before he published it to the member-states and reminded the interested parties that the mediator would return to Cyprus in a month's time to put 'himself at the disposal of the parties in any way he may usefully serve'.[162] Plaza's report presented a moment for the country to pull away from the guarantor state interests that had historically *increased* inter-communal divisions rather than worked to remedy them. Unsurprisingly, senior UN officials pronounced the report 'brilliant' to *Guardian* reporter Hella Pick.[163] However, they acknowledged that the complicated political context in Cyprus might prevent any real change and were reportedly 'sanguine' about the implementation of Plaza's recommendations.[164]

International responses to the report varied and ignited tensions between the UN Force and the Turkish government. The Greek-Cypriot representative, President of the Cypriot Parliament, or House of Representatives, and close advisor to Makarios, Glafcos Clerides was the first politician to make an official comment on the report.[165] *The Cyprus Mail* recorded him describing it as a 'bold and welcome' report.[166] A *New York Times* article published in April 1965 reported that the Greek government antagonised the Turks by stating that 'the continuation of Mr Plaza as mediator would be an essential condition for the solution of the Cyprus problem'.[167] In stark contrast, the Turkish government

[159] UN Information Office 'Security Council Adopts Resolution on Fourth UNFICYP Extension', The Blue Berets, 24 March 1965, pp. 1, 8.

[160] UNA, S-0869-0001-10-00001, 'Suggested Action for the Transmission of the Mediator's Report', 22nd March 1965', p. 4.

[161] UNA, S-0869-0001-10-00001, 'Clipping: *New York Times*, "A Chance for Cyprus", Thursday, 1 April 1965', p. 75.

[162] UNA, S-0869-0001-10-00001, 'Draft Letter from the Secretary-General to the Parties Concerned', n. d., p. 4.

[163] H. Pick, 'Two Sides Urged to Meet in Cyprus: Senor Galo Plaza's Report', *The Guardian*, 31 March 1965.

[164] Pick, 'Two Sides Urged to Meet in Cyprus'.

[165] These positive comments about the Plaza report were expanded on in the following document: UNA, S-0079-0007-11, 'Communication Addressed to the Mediator from President Makarios', 25 May 1965.

[166] 'Clerides Calls for 'Careful Thought': "End to Wishful Thinking", Cyprus 'at Threshold of Momentous Decisions', *Cyprus Mail*, 1 April 1965.

[167] UNA, S-0869-0001-10-00001, 'Clipping: *New York Times*, "Turkish Cypriots Cool to UN Plan", Friday, 2 April 1965', p. 76.

and Turkish-Cypriot leadership accused Plaza of abusing of his mediatory jurisdiction and producing a pro-Greek-Cypriot document.[168] Turkish Ambassador Orhan Erlap called for Plaza's resignation, suggesting that he had gone 'beyond [the] terms of reference specified in the 4 March 1964 resolution of the Security Council'.[169] Turkish-Cypriot representative Rauf Denktash made a speech to the Security Council in August 1965, describing Plaza's report as 'a shield for the [Greek] ulterior motives'.[170] Meanwhile, although the Greek government complained that the report did not see *enosis* as the solution to the conflict, broadly they accepted Plaza's recommendations as a positive result for their demands.

Thant promptly defended Plaza's report in a letter to Erlap, but the damage to Plaza's reputation was permanent for the Turkish government in Ankara.[171] Turkey's allies within NATO were upset by its reaction to the report and critical of their dismissal of the UN mediator's recommendations. A *Washington Post* article reported that 'if the Cypriot situation defied solution at least it should not be deprived of a UN mediation effort to keep it from worsening. That is why Turkey's call for Plaza's dismissal seems disappointing to Turkey's friends'.[172] The dispute over the mediator provided guarantor states, particularly Turkey, with an opportunity to stall any attempt at a political solution to the Cyprus conflict and continue to make claims on the island.[173] The shock of the Turkish government's 'prompt and unexpected rejection of Mr Plaza's report' reverberated around the globe.[174] Rolz-Bennett wrote to Plaza in April to applaud the report and the responses it had provoked:

> Your report has dramatized the need and urgency of such negotiations and, by the impact [...] has improved the prospect of bringing them about. In this respect, it has achieved its primary objective of dislodging

[168] V. K. Fouskas and A. O. Tackie, *Cyprus: The Post-imperial Constitution* (London: Pluto Press, 2009), p. 43; 'Turkish Cypriots Cool to UN Plan', *The New York Times*, 2 April 1965.

[169] UNA, S-0869-0002-04-00001, 'Letter from Erlap, Turkish Permanent Mission to the UN to U Thant, 31 March 1965', p. 10.

[170] R. Denktash, 'Speech Two: 5 August 1965', in M. Moran, *Rauf Denktash at the United Nations: Speeches on Cyprus* (Huntingdon: Eothen Press, 1997), p. 142.

[171] S. Pope, 'Cyprus Mediator Backed by Thant: UN Leader Says Turkey's Move against Plaza Could Wreck Settlement Hopes', *The New York Times*, 3 April 1965.

[172] UNA, S-0869-0001-10-00001, 'Clipping: *The Washington Post*, "The UN and Cyprus", Wednesday, 7 April 1965', p. 77.

[173] At one point in the aftermath of Turkey's rejection of the report, they were threatening to invade Cyprus. A dispatch from *The Times* in London reported, 'In the last few days since Turkey's abrupt rejection of a report submitted by the United Nations mediator for Cyprus, Galo Plaza Lasso, there has been rising anti-Western feeling in Turkey combined with bitter criticism of Greece. The Turks feel let down by the West over Cyprus'. See 'Turks' Intervention in Cyrus Is Hinted', *The New York Times*, 9 April 1965.

[174] 'Greeks Will Confer on Report by Plaza', *The New York Times*, 4 April 1965.

> the Cyprus problem from its 'dead centre'. We all believe that the momentum created by your report should not be wasted through prolonged inaction and that an attempt should be made soon to bring about the proposed direct negotiations, but the question is, what is the best way of doing so in the present?[175]

Plaza resigned on 22 December 1965, accepting that he would not be able to continue his negotiations following the Turkish government's reaction.[176] He remained involved in the conflict and continued to privately consult with Thant on 'the Cyprus question' despite the end of his formal role as UNFICYP mediator.[177] Initially he was not replaced. Michael Harbottle, Chief of Staff for the Cyprus Force 1966–1968, recalled that this period was hopeless for the UNFICYP mission. He commented that 'On the political side, matters were at an even greater standstill and no glimmer of light was visible; if anything the political scene by the middle of 1965 was probably as gloomy as it could be'.[178] In February 1966, Thant sent Rolz-Bennett to Cyprus to explore the possibility of a new mediator and to keep the channels of negotiation open while UNFICYP was still on the ground.[179] Rolz-Bennett took advantage of his visits to Ankara and Athens to meet face-to-face with the mainland countries' leaders.[180] Confirming suspicions in the New York headquarters, Rolz-Bennett wrote a memo to Thant to record that 'the prospects of appointing a new Mediator are very dim, to say the least'.[181] Harbottle similarly noted that 'mediation had gone out of the window, at least for the time being, and both Governments of Cyprus and Turkey, for very different reasons, opposed the appointment of a new Mediator'.[182] The damage to the UN's reputation was done, and for the UN leadership, the immediate concern was regaining the trust of the mainland states in order to restore the UN's reputation on the ground for conflict response.

In the years following Plaza's report, UN mediation efforts in Cyprus devolved from being an important, complementary wing of the mission to a curtailed role, limited to an additional duty for an existing mid-ranking UN official in the field. On 2 March 1966, Thant extended Carlos Bernardes's

175 UNA, S-0079-0007-10, 'Confidential Letter from Rolz-Bennett to Galo Plaza', 14 April 1965.

176 'Plaza Resigns UN Post as Mediator in Cyprus', *The New York Times*, 10 January 1966.

177 UNA, S-0309-0037-19, 'Letter from Plaza to Thant, 11 March 1966'.

178 Harbottle, *The Impartial Soldier*, p. 55.

179 UNA, S-0869-0001-11-00001, 'UN Internal Memo, Cyprus Mediation, 2 February 1966', p. 3.

180 UNA, S-0869-0001-11-00001, 'UN Internal Memo, Cyprus Mediation, 2 February 1966', pp. 1–3.

181 UNA, S-0869-0001-11-00001, 'Cable from Rolz-Bennett to U Thant, Report of Talks in Ankara and Athens on Cyprus, 24 February 1966', p. 8.

182 Harbottle, *The Impartial Soldier*, p. 56.

duties as his special representative in Cyprus to include the employment of UN 'good offices'.[183] Bernardes was a Brazilian career diplomat who had been President of the Security Council in February 1964. However, Thant wrote to Plaza of his reluctance to move 'too quickly in the direction of new political initiatives' following the 'impact caused by [Plaza]', suggesting that Bernardes's policy of passivity was not unwelcome to the UN leadership in the post-Plaza era.[184]

Whilst the UN special representatives and the UN leadership placed their hopes on an external solution to the Cyprus conflict, President Makarios benefitted from the stagnant political environment on the island. Makarios's political position as President of the Republic had long been associated with the pursuit of *enosis*, due to his support of the policy throughout the 1940s and 1950s.[185] However, following independence, Makarios recognised that his power base was in Cyprus, not Greece; the implementation of *enosis* would likely dilute – if not erase – his authority. Equally, a referendum, plebiscite, or any other formal process of self-determination would provide no clarification on what *enosis* would practically entail. Plaza found evidence of this confusion during his consultations. He wrote,

> As a practical step [*enosis*] in the political evolution of Cyprus it has struck me, in discussions with a wide range of Greek-Cypriot opinion, as having a much less united and imperative driving force behind it. I understand *Enosis* to mean in its literal sense the complete absorption of Cyprus into Greece, but I would hesitate to say that this is what every Greek-Cypriot favouring it intends it to mean.[186]

Makarios knew this too and recognised that if the population were asked to vote for *enosis*, there was no guarantee that they would share an understanding of what annexation would mean for Cyprus. For Makarios, this could lead to political fracturing within the Greek-Cypriot community and a fatal crumbling of his political base.

Makarios's alternative was to promote political stagnation and emphasise the impossibility of a settlement in Cyprus. His inactivity was preferable to a painful process of outlining a practicable vision of *enosis* – a vision that had yet to be

183 UN Doc, S/7180, 'Note by the Secretary-General', 4 March 1966.

184 UNA, S-0309-0037-19, 'Thant Letter to Plaza, 6 April 1966'.

185 M. Hadjiathanasiou, 'Colonial Rule, Cultural Relations and the British Council in Cyprus, 1935–1955', *The Journal of Imperial and Commonwealth History*, 46:6 (2018), pp. 1096–1124; A. Yiangou, *Cyprus in World War II: Politics and Conflict in the Eastern Mediterranean* (London: Bloomsbury, 2012); D. W. Markides, *Cyprus 1957–1963 from Colonial Conflict to Constitutional Crisis: The Key Role of the Municipal Issue* (Minneapolis: University of Minnesota, 2001).

186 UNA, S-0869-0001-10-00001, 'Report of the United Nations Mediator on Cyprus to the Secretary-General, 26 March 1965', p. 60.

determined within his own community, let alone agreed with the increasingly unstable Greek government.[187] Movement towards *enosis* would also further alienate the Turkish-Cypriot community, thousands of whom remained displaced. Wilson, Deputy UNFICYP Commander, recollected that

> Makarios later remarked to me that he always worried if he saw two [Greek] Cypriots in conversation at a party or social occasion. The 'outcome', he remarked, 'will almost certainly be another three parties' . . . Though most Greek-Cypriots were still reluctant to admit it, none of them by now, except for a few extremists, still wanted a genuine *Enosis*.[188]

In response, Makarios used the military stability of UNFICYP as a crutch for his lack of political impetus. Whilst the Greek-Cypriots were at war with the Turkish-Cypriots, they each remained – to a large extent – united within their communities and politically powerful. Describing the UNFICYP as 'insurance' against any violence, Wilson believed that Makarios wished to prolong the conflict until Cyprus could announce independence and confirm Greek-Cypriot hegemony, thus, avoiding 'the need to make unpleasant decisions'.[189] The palliative operations of the Force, in the absence of an effective mediatory policy, provided space for Makarios to protect his position rather than acknowledge the colonial legacies underpinning Cypriot divisions and ultimately threaten his political authority.

That Makarios and other parties to the conflict benefitted from the stagnation of the conflict was not a secret within the UNFICYP bureaucracy. The UN leadership and UNFICYP contributing nations' representatives identified the instrumentalisation of the mission as early as November 1966. An internal document drafted by Rolz-Bennett revealed organisational anxieties about the continuing damage being done by the mission to the conflict and a growing lack of belief in the mission's ability to resolve the crisis. He stated that contributing:

> [g]overnments are disturbed by the impression given over the last several months, which the Secretary-General also shares, that the presence and activity of the peace-keeping force has tended to relieve the parties in dispute from the necessary sense of urgency in making a serious effort at finding the basis for a settlement. These misgivings have been aggravated by the well-known experience of the Mediator, and more profoundly, by its significance for the generally accepted principles of United Nations mediation. The mediation process has been proved capable of being stultified by the particular attitude of a single party to the dispute.[190]

187 D. F. Schmitz, *The United States and Right-Wing Dictatorships, 1965–1989* (Cambridge: Cambridge University Press, 2006), p. 62.

188 Bod, Papers of Charles Harris; fols 185–336. Lt.-Gen. Sir James Wilson 1964–1966, 'Memoir: Chapter 17, The U.N. Force Commander', p. 11.

189 Bod, Papers of Charles Harris; fols 185–336. Lt.-Gen. Sir James Wilson 1964–1966, 'Memoir: Chapter 17, The U.N. Force Commander', p. 10.

190 UNA, S-0079-0007-09, 'Draft Aide-Memoire', 5 November 1966.

In the meantime, Alain L. Dangeard, Assistant in the Secretariat, wrote an internal report to emphasise these issues:

> It may be argued that the presence of UNFICYP is still useful inasmuch as it limits the scope of unnecessary bloodshed on the island and also prevents the precipitation of an international crisis. In view, however, of the risks of UN's deeper involvement in internal disputes, and the precariousness of the financial support to be given to the UNFICYP operation, before suggesting to the Council the extension of the UNFICYP for three more months, the Secretary-General may attempt to gain firm assurances from the parties that they will work towards a settlement.[191]

These financial and diplomatic anxieties illustrated the significance of the Plaza report in disrupting the UN leadership's perception of the Cyprus conflict. After the Turkish government's reaction to the report, those within the Secretariat began to reconsider UNFICYP's contribution. However, instead of considering how the continued presence of the mission was extending the conflict and damaging the population, discussions focused on how a continued presence would *appear* to contributing nations and other member-states, potentially harming the UN's reputation.

Rolz-Bennett's attempts to undo the mistrust between the guarantor states and UNFICYP through his visits in 1966 did little to re-centre Cypriot politicians in discussions and instead re-focused the international community on the guarantor states as the solution to the conflict. The UN leadership was fixated on the potential political solutions offered by the mainland countries, such as double *enosis* or unification of the divided Cypriot communities with their respective mainland countries, rather than on encouraging political solutions to arise from the Cypriot population.[192] Rolz-Bennett and Thant's journeys to the Mediterranean demonstrated their pursuit of a mainland state-led approach as they spent most of their time in Ankara and Athens.[193] Meanwhile, Greece and Turkey announced that they had begun a private 'dialogue' following the Plaza report and that these talks would not include a UN mediator.[194] Plaza wrote to his assistant F. T. Liu to communicate his shock that the British were involved in the dialogue: 'It is surprising that they should pin such high hopes on the bilateral Greek-Turkish talks',

[191] UNA, S-1070-0030-01, 'Confidential: Forthcoming Review by the Secretary-General of the Situation in Cyprus, Dangeard's draft', n.d.

[192] For more on 'double enosis', see Ş. Kıralp, 'Cyprus between Enosis, Partition and Independence: Domestic Politics, Diplomacy and External Interventions (1967–1974)', *Journal of Balkan and Near Eastern Studies*, 19:6 (2017), pp. 591–609.

[193] UNA, S-0869-0001-12-00001, 'Text of Instructions to Be Cabled by Secretary-General to Bernardes, 1 March 1966', p. 10.

[194] C. Goktepe, *British Foreign Policy toward Turkey, 1959–1965* (Abingdon: Routledge, 2013), p. 179.

indicating that he did not have faith in the mainland discussions.[195] Similarly, Harbottle argued that the Greek and Turkish governments used the existence of this 'dialogue' to phase out UN involvement in the political settlement in the Cyprus conflict, post-Plaza.[196] Bernardes's resignation on 5 January 1967 confirmed his lack of progress with the Greek and Turkish governments. The Director General of the United Nations Office in Geneva, Pier Spinelli, took on the role after Bernardes but emphasised it would only be a temporary position, thus perpetuating the inertia of the UN's mediation efforts after Plaza.[197]

Canadian Ambassadors to the UN – Beaulne, Hearn, and Colonel Newlands – were also concerned about the role that the Force played in the political stagnation in Cyprus. They drew it to the attention of the secretary-general in a meeting of the UNFICYP contributing countries and the UN Secretariat on 7 December 1971, arguing that 'UNFICYP . . . has come to be regarded as a permanent feature in absence of progress on the political front. Unfortunately, this had tended to create the impression in some quarters that the presence of UNFICYP has itself contributed to the lack of political progress'.[198] The Ambassadors emphasised that

> It would be regrettable if the UNFICYP experience were to have the result of undermining confidence in the effectiveness of peacekeeping operations as a useful tool in dealing with the problems of international conflict. The importance of making progress towards a political settlement in Cyprus thus has relevance beyond the confines of the Cyprus dispute itself.[199]

Highlighting how stagnation could lead to UNFICYP's instrumentalisation and further harm, one of the Canadian Ambassadors highlighted how the mission was likely to induce complacency within the Greek-Cypriot government, acting as an instrument to increase inter-communal tensions on the island and therefore bolster ethno-nationalist politics on the island:

[195] UNA, S-0309-0037-19, 'Letter from Plaza to F. T. Liu, 12 July 1965'.

[196] Harbottle, *The Impartial Soldier*, p. 38.

[197] UNA, S-0869-0001-12-00001, 'S/7642: Note by the Secretary-General, 20 December 1966', p. 25.

[198] UNA, S-0869-0001-02-00001, 'Meeting of Countries contributing to UNFICYP to be held on Tuesday, 7 December 1971 at 4pm in the Secretary-General's Conference Room', p. 67.

[199] UNA, S-0869-0001-02-00001, 'Meeting of Countries contributing to UNFICYP to be held on Tuesday, 7 December 1971 at 4pm in the Secretary-General's Conference Room', p. 67.

> The longer UNFICYP lasts, the greater is the risk that the presence of United Nations contingents [in Cyprus] will be taken for granted and will become such a part of the landscape in Cyprus that the parties to the dispute are tempted to use UNFICYP for their own advantage.[200]

Rising Violence and Contributory Peacekeeper Criminality

The period of precarious stability and political stagnation following Plaza's report from 1965 to 1967 was disrupted by an increase in inter-communal violence in villages across the country, further exacerbated by the April 1967 military coup on mainland Greece. Thant had reduced the numbers of UNFICYP troops due to a deescalation in violence and organisational financial constraints, from 6,275 personnel in December 1964 to 4,610 in December 1966, making the mission ill-equipped to respond to the rapid surge in violence in mid-1967.[201] Distracted by the conflict in Indo-Pakistan and the operations of the United Nations India-Pakistan Observation Mission (UNIPOM) in 1965–1966,[202] many of the UN Secretariat staff became disengaged from the situation in Cyprus, contributing to the political stagnation on the island.[203] However, the outbreak of violence in mainland Greek and Cyprus in 1967 re-focused organisational attention to the Mediterranean. The mission's efforts were hampered, however, by repeated instances of peacekeepers involving themselves in smuggling and the Cypriot black market which further obstructed the UNFICYP's demilitarisation and stabilisation mandate. As a depleted UNFICYP faced shooting and bombing across the island and stagnated hostilities erupted into civil war once again, the UN leadership were anxious to de escalate the conflict before it provoked a Cold War superpower response.

Arms and people smuggling were central to the militarised environment of Cyprus in the 1960s, fostering a civilian stockpiling issue. Thant had argued that civilian arms stockpiling was one of the greatest risks to the success of the UN mission in 1964.[204] Beginning in early 1964, soldiers from Turkey and Greece arrived in ports across the country with large deliveries of weapons to

200 UNA, S-0869-0001-02-00001, 'Meeting of Countries contributing to UNFICYP to be held on Tuesday, 7 December 1971 at 4pm in the Secretary-General's Conference Room', p. 67.

201 UN Publication, *The Blue Helmets – A Review of United Nations Peace-Keeping* (New York: UN Department of Public Information, 1985).

202 P. Dimitrakis, *Failed Alliances of the Cold War: Britain's Strategy and Ambitions in Asia and the Middle East* (London: Bloomsbury, 2011), p. 58.

203 For more on the Indo-Pakistan conflict in 1965–1966, see F. Bajwa, *From Kutch to Tashkent: The Indo-Pakistan War of 1965* (London: Hurst, 2013).

204 UN Doc, S/5764, Report to the Security Council on the United Nations Operation in Cyprus, for the Period 26 April to 8 June 1964 / By the Secretary-General', p. 37.

distribute among their communities and paramilitary groups.[205] Incoming soldiers had been a regular occurrence since July 1964 when it was reported that

> 600 Greek-Cypriot servicemen return[ed] from [. . .] service in the Greek army, and some 2,000 Greek-Cypriot students together with a few volunteers returning from study abroad, of whom some few may have been non-Greek-Cypriot. It would appear that a proportion of these students had, to some extent, organised themselves while abroad and, many may have had military training while in Greece.[206]

Comparatively fewer Turkish-Cypriot troops had reached the coastline, but those who did also brought imported arms and ammunition.[207] These reports incited fear in several contributing governments with troops on the ground and created a security risk for UN officials on the ground. Thant cabled the President of Cyprus and Prime Ministers of Greece and Turkey in an attempt to cease arms smuggling from the mainland and emphasised that any 'party tending to increase the tension and the danger of armed clashes in Cyprus at this time falls squarely within the terms of the resolution of the Security Council of 4 March 1964'.[208] However, despite Thant's threats, the international influx of smuggled arms entering the island, especially from Greece and Turkey, continued.

Following initial concerns about civilian smuggling and stockpiling during the first months of the mission, the Cyprus National Guard increased searches and patrols along the Green Line. Expecting to find civilian criminality, the Guard were surprised to discover two UNFICYP officers and three UNFICYP troops of other ranks, all members of the Swedish UNFICYP contingent, on 24 September 1964, conducting 'illicit carriage of arms' in UN armoured cars.[209] Many of the arms found in the armoured car, particularly stocks of ammunition, were concealed in wheat sacks 'donated by the people of the United States of America', suggesting these peacekeepers' comfort with the instrumentalisation and exploitation of the mission's adopted humanitarian responsibility.[210] The arrest report by the UNFICYP military police unit

[205] UNA, S-0869-0003-08-00001, 'Background Notes on Reports of Build-up of Arms and Troops in Cyprus, 14 July 1964', p. 2.

[206] UNA, S-0869-0003-08-00001, 'Background Notes on Reports of Build-up of Arms and Troops in Cyprus, 14 July 1964', p. 2.

[207] UNA, S-0869-0003-08-00001, 'Background Notes on Reports of Build-up of Arms and Troops in Cyprus, 14 July 1964', p. 2.

[208] UNA, S-0869-0002-11-00001, 'Cable from Thant, 16 July 1964', p. 5/6.

[209] UNA, S-0869-0003-15-00001, 'Press Release CYP/164: Statement by United Nations Spokesman in Nicosia on 24 September 1964', p. 2.

[210] UNA, S-0869-0003-15-00001, 'Press Release CYP/164: Statement by United Nations Spokesman in Nicosia on 24 September 1964', p. 2.

Figure 5.1 Photograph taken by the Cyprus police during the arrest of UN troops, September, 1964. Report of inquiry in arms smuggling by Swedes, Cyprus, September 1964. UNA, S-1070-0026-18.
Reproduced with permission from the UN Archives.

Figure 5.2 Photograph taken by the Cyprus police during the arrest of UN troops, September 1964. Report of inquiry in arms smuggling by Swedes, Cyprus, September 1964. UNA, S-1070-0026-18.
Reproduced with permission from the UN Archives.

Figure 5.3 Photograph taken by the Cyprus police during the arrest of UN troops, September 1964. Report of inquiry in arms smuggling by Swedes, Cyprus, September 1964. UNA, S-1070-0026-18.
Reproduced with permission from the UN Archives.

Figure 5.4 Photograph taken by the Cyprus police during the arrest of UN troops, September 1964 of American wheat sack used to hold smuggled weapons. Report of board of inquiry in arms smuggling by Swedes, Cyprus', September 1964. UNA, S-1070-0026-18.
Reproduced with permission from the UN Archives.

revealed that Cypriot police stopped the tank because they suspected smuggling, indicating that this was not a unique occurrence.[211]

Peacekeepers' freedom of movement, as well as their permission to be armed, was repeatedly exploited for financial gain in Cyprus. The Cyprus police representative reported the notorious '"practice" of Swedish UNFICYP vehicles being used, by reason of their immunity from search by the Police, to transport Turkish Cypriots from one Turkish Cypriot village to another'.[212] A UNFICYP Board of Inquiry investigation headed by the Force Commander led to the return of the two officers to Sweden as the UN did not have its own criminal judicial process.[213] The inquiry revealed that one was a member of a right-wing party in Sweden and had initially not been allowed to join the mission.[214] Coincidentally, as part of the preliminary UNFICYP plans, Rolz-Bennett had specifically complimented the Swedish as 'an ideal nationality [for peacekeeping] and wonderful people'.[215]

The Swedish battalion was not the only contingent caught committing criminal acts in Cyprus, and as the conflict progressed, other UN troops profited from the Cypriot war economy and the peacekeepers' freedom of movement across the island. The Cyprus police caught Finnish and Danish peacekeepers smuggling and selling their weapons (two sub-machine guns and one automatic rifle) to Cypriot fighters 'on both sides', contributing directly to the black market and their own risk as peacekeeping troops in the conflict.[216] Five Austrian peacekeepers were repatriated after smuggling of explosives to Turkish-Cypriot fighters.[217] Four British troops were court martialled by the Commander of the British Contingent for attempting to transport ammunition and weapons, cement, uniforms, and other 'prohibited items' for Turkish-Cypriots.[218] In their sworn statements to the Special Investigation Unit for UNFICYP, the convicted troops confessed that they had been paid 'five pounds

211 UNA, S-1070-0026-17, 'Arms Smuggling by Swedes – September 1964: Press Release CYP/171', 30 September 1964.

212 UNA, S-1070-0026-18, 'Report of Board of Inquiry in Arms Smuggling by Swedes – Cyprus', September 1964, p. 35.

213 UNA, S-0869-0003-15-00001, 'Press Release CYP/175: Statement by United Nations Spokesman on 24 September Incident', 8 October 1964, p. 6.

214 UNA, S-1070-0026-18, 'Report of Board of Inquiry in Arms Smuggling by Swedes – Cyprus', September 1964, p. 8.

215 UNA, S-0869-0001-01-00001, 'Rolz-Bennett Note for Secretary-General, 21 February 1964', p. 1.

216 UNA, S-1070-0029-10, 'Finnish Weapons Through Black Markets to Cypriot Fighters on Both Sides', 31 October 1965.

217 UNA, S-1070-0029-12, 'Inter-Office Memo from Force Commander Martola to Bunche and Rolz-Bennett', 22 November 1966.

218 UNA, S-1070-0037-10, 'Press Release CYP/362: UNFICYP Issues Further Statement on Court Martial of Four Soldiers', 24 March 1966; 'Press Release CYP/364', 24 March 1966; 'Press Release CYP/365', 26 March 1966.

of Cyprus currency', following the delivery of 'military type jackets' by a UN Land Rover, and 'eight pounds' for the transport of cement.[219] Penalties for the British troops ranged from nine months detention to eighteen months in prison and an 'ignominious discharge'.[220] These were not petty crimes.

In another instance of British peacekeeper abuses, the Cypriot police caught two British UNFICYP troops smuggling weapons, having been 'suborned' by Turkish-Cypriots in January 1968.[221] Thant made an official statement describing how these troops were 'involved in transporting materials and, on one occasion, in transporting a Turkish-Cypriot [dressed in a UNFICYP uniform] . . . The UNFICYP soldiers involved undertook over 20 journeys, [and] for each one they were paid £25 between them by the Turkish-Cypriots'.[222] Thant's statement described the situation of the UNFICYP soldiers being 'suborned' or corrupted by Turkish-Cypriots, thus blaming the Turkish-Cypriots and making them responsible for the peacekeepers' crimes. In the same statement, Thant revealed that the Turkish-Cypriots used 'British-type military vehicles' with painted UN signs on the side, and he noted that this was a 'disturbing aspect' of the case.[223] 'Furthermore', he notes, 'these vehicles were driven to rendezvous with UNFICYP soldiers by Turkish-Cypriots dressed in UNFICYP uniforms.'[224] Despite their fellow troops' repatriation and dismissal, UN peacekeepers continued to smuggle and sell arms to fighters under the guise of UNFICYP operations; their operational freedom and uniform permitted the illegal movement of weapons and fighters. However, UNFICYP's moral authority encouraged the police to give peacekeepers the 'benefit of the doubt'. Peacekeeper participation in the arms smuggling trade on the island fed into the militarisation of the population, supplying the militias that they were explicitly mandated to demilitarise.

Whilst a number of UN peacekeepers profited from the conflict context, the increasing violence on the mainland began to threaten the solidity of the UNFICYP-implemented ceasefire in Cyprus. The Greek military coup in the spring of 1967, following a three-year power struggle between the monarchy and the left-wing and right-wing parties, ignited inter-communal violence in Cyprus.[225] The 'Generals' Coup' was characterised by tanks entering Athens and a large-scale operation to arrest opposing politicians and journalists,

219 UNA, S-1070-0037-10, 'Special Investigation Unit: United Nations Force in Cyprus, SIU/UNFICYP/23/66, 11 Mar 1966'.
220 UNA, S-1070-0037-10, 'Press Release CYP/362', 24 March 1966.
221 UNA, S-0869-0002-04-00001, 'Operation Files, 31st January 1968'.
222 UNA, S-0869-0002-04-00001, 'Secretary-General Cable Text, 31 January 1968', p. 81.
223 UNA, S-0869-0002-04-00001, 'Secretary-General Cable Text, 31 January 1968', p. 81.
224 UNA, S-0869-0002-04-00001, 'Secretary-General Cable Text, 31 January 1968', p. 81.
225 I. Tzortzis, *Greek Democracy and the Junta: Regime Crisis and the Failed Transition of 1973* (London: Bloomsbury, 2020), p. 29.

eventually numbering up to approximately 10,000 people.[226] This political 'victory' was unstable and contested by left-wing political groups on the mainland.[227] This context of political transgression and transformation led to outbreaks of violence in Cyprus that had not been experienced since 1964.[228]

International anxiety over the Generals' Coup challenged the stability and power that Makarios had enjoyed since independence from Britain as the policy of *enosis* returned to political importance. The new leadership in Athens were pro-United States and right-wing (with a long-term alliance with the CIA), and they sought to not only install *enosis* in Cyprus but remove all the politicians they believed to be left-leaning from power on the island, just as they had in Athens.[229] Plans to annex Cyprus were popular with right-wing Greek-Cypriots on the island who used the mainland coup as an opportunity to rebuild previously waning support for *enosis*. Makarios's fears of internal factions within the Greek-Cypriot community became a reality, and he worried about a coup in Cyprus, especially as the Greek-Cypriot National Guard employed a significant number of Greek soldiers.[230] In 1966, *The Economist* reported that there were around 8,500 to 10,000 'volunteer' troops from mainland Greece in Cyprus, in addition to the 'Greek army "training" officers in the 11,000-strong Cypriot national guard'.[231]

Meanwhile, Makarios's ideological position became a security problem for the UNFICYP mission. The new UNFICYP Force Commander, General Armas-Eino Martola (a Finnish-national), received intelligence that Makarios had repeatedly smuggled arms from Czechoslovakia throughout 1967, and possibly earlier, despite the Archbishop's public non-aligned position.[232] A *Washington Post* article argued that 'aggravating all this [the conflict with Turkish-Cypriots] has been Makarios' recent acquisition of Soviet military equipment via Cairo, including the construction of ground-to-air missile sites'.[233] Makarios used the imported Czech weapons to strengthen Greek-Cypriot paramilitary groups across the island that he then deployed into

[226] D. Ganser, *NATO's Secret Armies: Operation GLADIO and Terrorism in Western Europe* (London: Frank Cass, 2005), p. 221.

[227] 'More Militant than the Colonels', *The Economist*, 225:6485, 9 December 1967, p. 1046.

[228] Kıralp, 'Cyprus between Enosis, Partition and Independence', p. 593.

[229] Ganser, *NATO's Secret Armies*, p. 222.

[230] UNA, S-0869-0002-10-00001, 'Note for the Record by Jose Rolz-Bennett', 15 January 1968, pp. 3–4; 'CYPRUS STUDYING JUNTA'S INTENTION: Rumors of a Greek-Led Coup Cause Concern in Nicosia', *The New York Times*, 20 May 1967.

[231] 'Priest and Soldier', *The Economist*, 218:6396 (26 March 1966), p. 1220.

[232] UNA, S-0869-0001-03-00001, 'Notes on Meeting in the Secretary-General's Office at 11.30am on 18 November 1967', p. 3.

[233] UNA, S-0869-0001-10-00001, 'Clipping: *The Washington Post*, "The UN and Cyprus", Wednesday, 7 April 1965', p. 77.

Turkish-Cypriot regions throughout the summer 1967 as he attempted to shore up his position.[234] UNFICYP attempted to confiscate the Czech weapons as further deliveries arrived over the next months, just as it had attempted to obstruct deliveries to the Congolese government during ONUC.[235] In a private UN meeting in November 1967, the Greek Ambassador to the UN, Dimitrios Bitsios, commented that he 'had had no information at all about this situation and manifested surprise about it'.[236] The exclusion of the UNFICYP staff from important intelligence until the materiel was already distributed operationally stymied their ability to confiscate weapons but also indicated their disconnect from activities on the island. Additionally, the UNFICYP troops now had to prepare to combat parties supported by new Soviet-standard weaponry, rather than the colonial era leftovers.

A series of outbursts of serious violent attacks on both communities in November 1967 demonstrated to the UN leadership how geopolitically fragile the region had become. Two large-scale battles erupted in Kophinou, a village in the central-southern region, and Ayios Theodoros, a village in the central-western region. The battle of Kophinou, in particular, became a significant embarrassment to UNFICYP as Greek-Cypriot troops assaulted and stole weapons and ammunition from peacekeepers.[237] The UNFICYP Commander, General Robert Pascoe, argued that UN peacekeepers were targeted in the bomb attacks.[238] Violence in Turkish-Cypriot regions put vulnerable civilians and UNFICYP troops on the front line of the conflict, provoking the attention and condemnation of the Turkish government.[239] The conflict in Ayios Theodoros on 16 November 1967 was so violent that Thant argued in his report to the Security Council that the Greek-Cypriot-led Cyprus National Guard had used 'disproportionate force' against Turkish-Cypriot civilians.[240] The Guard's escalation in force prompted threats of invasion from the

[234] E. Hatzivassiliou, *Greece and the Cold War: Front Line State, 1952–1967* (Abington: Routledge, 2006), p. 173.

[235] UNA, S-0869-0001-03-00001, 'Notes on Meeting in the Secretary-General's Office at 11.30am on 18 November 1967', p. 3.

[236] UNA, S-0869-0001-03-00001, 'Notes on Meeting with Greek Ambassador to the UN', 18 November 1967, p. 4.

[237] Bod, MS. Eng. c. 4731 (fols 161–184) Papers of Gen. Sir Robert Pascoe, 'Official Report on Kophinou by UN Company Commander, R. A. Pascoe, 15 November 1967'.

[238] Bod, MS. Eng. c. 4731 (fols 161–184) Papers of Gen. Sir Robert Pascoe, 'Official Report on Kophinou by UN Company Commander, R. A. Pascoe, 15 November 1967'.

[239] UN Doc, S/8286, 'Report by the Secretary General on the United Nations Operation in Cyprus: For the Period 13 June to 8 December 1967'; UN Doc, S/8248, 'Special Report of the Secretary General on Recent Developments in Cyprus', 18 November 1967.

[240] D. Middleton, 'Thant Bids the U.N. Keep Cyprus Force: Thant Asks U.N. Council to Extend Cyprus Force Comment Is Repeated His Language Is Terse Major Element in Guard', *The New York Times*, 12 December 1967.

Turkish government if the attacks continued.[241] Subsequently, *Reuters* reported Greek-Cypriots evacuating Nicosia to the mountains in preparation for a Turkish intervention.[242]

Following the Plaza fallout, Greece and Turkey increasingly sought advice from state diplomats, particularly from the United States, in how to navigate the conflict in Cyprus, sidelining the UN and UNFICYP leadership.[243] The violence in mainland Greece had drawn the international community's attention on the situation in the Mediterranean. As a result, the Cold War superpowers grew increasingly invested in the politics of the conflict as they sought to exploit this resurgence in fighting on the island for their own strategic goals. Whilst the UNFICYP mission staff focused on stabilising the island, the US government expanded their mediation efforts with the Turkish government, anxious to prevent Soviet involvement.[244] The arrival of US special envoy Cyrus Vance in Ankara, sent by President Johnson,[245] dissuaded the Turkish government from intervention and calmed the anxious Greek government.[246] A month later, Thant published a press release calling for the withdrawal of all Greek and Turkish troops and requesting an expansion of UNFICYP pacification functions, including the supervised disarmament of all forces constituted after 1963.[247] Both Turkish and Greek governments responded positively to Thant's request in December 1967 with a joint agreement and implementation plan for the withdrawal of their materiel, personnel, and equipment.[248] However, the parties agreed to Thant's request weeks after Vance's mediation had already diminished the threat of mainland intervention. The UN mission, previously at the forefront of the mediation process in Cyprus, had been circumvented in high-diplomatic

[241] The UNFICYP's military operations and attitude towards the Turkish threat of invasion as a response to the conflict in Ayios Theodhoros can be found in Harbottle, *The Impartial Soldier*.

[242] 'Hope Voiced in Ankara: Would Safeguard Minority Invasion Forces Poised', *The New York Times*, 25 November 1967; J. Feron, 'Makarios Asserts That Turkey May Force a War', *The New York Times*, 25 November 1967; J. Feron, 'ROADBLOCKS SET ON TENSE CYPRUS: Some Residents Said to Flee Nicosia for Mountains 2 Envoys Cancel Visits Cypriotes Still Concerned Blacks Rock Island', *The New York Times*, 26 November 1967.

[243] US DoS, '257. Telegram from the Embassy in Greece to the Department of State: Athens, February 16, 1967', *Foreign Relations of the United States, 1964–1968, Volume XVI, Cyprus; Greece; Turkey.*

[244] A. Guney, 'The USA's Role in Mediating the Cyprus Conflict: A Story of Success or Failure?', *Security Dialogue*, 35:1 (2004), p. 32.

[245] M. Berger, 'Cyrus R. Vance, a Confidant of Presidents, Is Dead at 84', *The New York Times*, 13 January 2002.

[246] Guney, 'The USA's Role in Mediating the Cyprus Conflict', p. 32.

[247] UNA, S-0079-0006-20, 'Press Release CYP/492: Replies from Cyprus, Greece and Turkey to Secretary-General's Appeal', 3 December 1967.

[248] UNA, S-0079-0006-20, 'Press Release CYP/492: Replies from Cyprus, Greece and Turkey to Secretary-General's Appeal', 3 December 1967.

discussions, demonstrating a growing preference for mediators from their shared NATO ally.[249] As the Turkish Foreign Minister, Zeki Kuneralp, stated, 'The UN could not solve the conflicts. It was seen in the last crises of Cyprus that it was solved especially by American influence'.[250] This sidelining of the UN and acceptance of help from the United States was especially infuriating for Thant, who, by 1971, had suffered through years of failed negotiations with US politicians over the superpower's violent invasion and occupation of Vietnam, seeking to undermine the US government's persistent – and, seemingly, bipartisan – belief in a military solution to the war.[251]

Emphasising this failure in UN mediation in Cyprus, the secretary-general's invitation was, initially, omitted from inter-communal talks that were to be held at NATO Council meetings in Lisbon and Paris in November 1971.[252] Christos Xanthopoulos-Palamas and Osman Olcay, Greek and Turkish Foreign Ministers, had initially suggested only a four-party negotiation conference (Greece, Turkey, Britain, and Cyprus) at the NATO meeting.[253] Subsequently, Palamas and Olcay offered the secretary-general an opportunity to announce the agreement to pursue these talks. Rather than accepting this deal and tolerating the UN's limited role, Thant rejected the proposal. Acknowledging the agreement as a draft, he told Palamas and Olcay that 'he would submit a different proposal' as he 'had in mind a five-party conference with participation of a UN representative instead of four-party talks'.[254] Announcing this change to the interested parties in an official memo, before waiting for rebuttal from Palamas and Olcay, had offered Thant a degree of power, but in the grander scheme of the conflict, the guarantor states and Cypriot politicians no longer saw the UN as worth inviting to the negotiating table.

Conclusion

Thant retired as secretary-general in December 1971, concluding his premiership on a negative note. Having been sidelined and replaced by superpower

[249] L. Klarevas, 'Were the Eagle and the Phoenix Birds of a Feather? The United States and the Greek Coup of 1967', *Diplomatic History*, 30:3 (2006), pp. 471–508; C. Göktepe, 'The Cyprus Crisis of 1967 and Its Effects on Turkey Foreign Relations', *Middle Eastern Studies*, 41:3 (2005), p. 440.

[250] Z. Kuneralp, *Sadece Diplomat* (İstanbul: ISIS, 1999), p. 346.

[251] B. J. Firestone, 'Failed Mediation: U Thant, the Johnson Administration, and the Vietnam War', *Diplomatic History*, 37:5 (2013), pp. 1060–1089.

[252] A. Constandinos, *America, Britain and the Cyprus Crisis of 1974: Calculated Conspiracy or Foreign Policy Failure?* (Bloomington: AuthorHouse, 2009), p. 82; M. Stearns, *Entangled Allies: U.S. Policy toward Greece, Turkey, and Cyprus* (New York: Council on Foreign Relations, 1992), pp. 113–114.

[253] UNA, S-0869-0002-04-00001, 'Turkish Newspaper Extracts, 15 November 1971', p. 128.

[254] UNA, S-0869-0002-04-00001, 'Turkish Newspaper Extracts, 15 November 1971', p. 128.

and guarantor state representatives, UNFICYP maintained its military mandate on the ground, but the mission staff became increasingly pessimistic about a political resolution to the Cyprus conflict as talks were repeatedly delayed by the Turkish government.[255] With a dwindling budget and fewer troops on the ground, UNFICYP's involvement was always too tentative and limited to make a long-term contribution to the resolution of the conflict. Some commentators argue that this is the purpose of peacekeeping – to stabilise the region and provide space for political reconciliation – but the international response to the UN's inability to resolve the crisis suggests that global imaginaries (and organisational projections) of UN peacekeeping missions were misaligned from UN officials' operational and diplomatic strategies on the ground. The separation of inter-communal interactions and subsequent displacement crisis served to isolate and distort the two communities' national imaginaries, seemingly beyond the point of reconciliation. This mission demonstrated the incompatibility of functioning as an active military participant on the ground whilst simultaneously leading diplomatic negotiations for the resolution of the conflict; the UN could not expand into all areas of conflict response at the same time without sacrificing operational capacity and influencing belligerents' perceptions of the organisation.

During ONUC the mission leadership received criticism, but it was not the concept of peacekeeping that was targeted; rather, it was the strategic 'failure' of the personnel involved that was identified. Peacekeeping as a concept itself remained viable; it was the UN's ability to manage a peacekeeping mission that was brought into question. However, with UNFICYP, the powerful colonial legacies underpinning 1964 Cypriot society as well as the constant oversight of the guarantor states undermined the peacekeeping project and the diplomatic credentials of the organisation. Although the procedural processes of decolonisation had not directly sparked violence, the 1964 conflict emerged from the ethno-nationalist divisions between Greek-Cypriots and Turkish-Cypriots. These were products of British colonial rule and the Cyprus insurgency of the 1950s, thus drawing the UNFICYP mission into the longer history of colonial violence and community antagonism on the island. However, by isolating the fighting groups from one another, the UN directly engaged with the issue of decolonisation in Cyprus but did so by freezing rather than resolving the conflict.

The antagonism between both conflict parties questioned the efficacy of the core UN peacekeeping strategy of ceasefires, challenging the organisation's ability to compete in the expanding international marketplace of international peace and security services. The discovery of peacekeeper criminality also

[255] BNA, FCO 9/1501, 'Relations between Cyprus and Turkey: Letter from British Embassy in Ankara to Foreign Office', 16 May 1972.

further undermined the legitimacy of the mission and its impact on the stabilisation of the island population. However, despite recognition within the mission bureaucracy of the ongoing stagnation caused by keeping the mission on the ground, the UN leadership determined that the possibility of preventing further bloodshed through the permanence of a UN-patrolled buffer zone was sufficient to extend the mission indefinitely. This decision was undertaken despite the UN leadership's knowledge that a formal partition would cement the inter-communal hostilities into Cypriot politics and geography. Significantly, the permanence of the buffer zone has enabled UNFICYP to 'keep the peace' for almost sixty years, employ thousands of UN officials and soldiers, and construct generations of peacekeeping elites on the island.

Conclusion

The period of UN functional expansion and peacekeeping innovation from 1956 to 1971 ended on the eve of détente as the central figures of the original Secretariat inner circle left the organisation or became ill and died. Thant refused to stand for re-election as UN secretary-general for a third term and ended his era of premiership in December 1971. Ralph Bunche and his Secretariat colleague José Rolz-Bennett both passed away in December 1971 and December 1972, respectively. Reporting Thant's resignation, *The New York Times* commented that 'It is no fault of his that he leaves the world organization in worse shape than he found it, close to bankruptcy – fiscal, political and moral', signifying that the secretary-general retained his personal reputation even if the organisation's standing was precarious in 1971.[1] Ultimately this period represented distinctly transformative era in thc longer history of internationalism as UN officials weathered the 'poisoned international atmosphere of the sixties' whilst attempting to reconfigure the structures of sovereignty and global governance.[2]

By the late 1960s and the beginning of the 1970s, the 'spirit of Bandung' or 'Third World movement' had largely evaporated as the complexities of self-determination and nationalism conflicted with bloc voting unity and many original leaders of the movement had died or left power. Nehru's passing in 1964 and the coup in Indonesia in 1965 had removed the two key leaders of the Non-Aligned Movement from international politics. As Vincent Bevins noted, 'The "Bandung Spirit" had become a ghost'.[3] However, the lasting legacies of this period reach far beyond the 'UN Development Decade' of the 1960s. Virulent campaigns against communist activists and union members across the Global South, armed and funded by the United States, also helped to eradicate the forms of cross-class solidarity, economic revolution, and equality that had been so integral to the political platform at Bandung. Military regimes, as in Indonesia, Greece, and in Central and Southern America, 'rejected the

1 'The Liberation of U Thant', *The New York Times*, 29 December 1971.

2 'The Liberation of U Thant'.

3 V. Bevins, *The Jakarta Method: Washington's Anticommunist Crusade and the Mass Murder Program that Shaped Our World* (New York: PublicAffairs, 2020), p. 170.

ecumenical anticolonial nationalism of the Left and the liberals for a cruel cultural nationalism that emphasized racialism, religion, and hierarchy'.[4] Détente may have thawed the relationship between Moscow and Washington in the 1970s, but anticommunist leadership, continued to build upon the militarism and ideological propaganda fostered by Cold War politics and CIA agents during the 1950s and 1960s. Indeed, as Molly Avery has shown with the Chilean case, the Pinochet dictatorship went beyond the anticommunist strategy of the United States once the US government adopted a formal human rights policy during the presidency of Jimmy Carter. Avery notes, 'Despite US complicity in the overthrow of the government of [Left-leaning President] Salvador Allende, from as early as the first months of 1974 the Chilean junta made clear their conviction that it was they, not the United States, who were "the ones stopping communism".'[5] Although the UN deliberative forums and staff were largely independent of the United States, and frequently critical of US civil rights and foreign policy, the organisation took the same approach to anticommunism as a threat to international security and, therefore, worked in alignment with the United States in attempting to limit Soviet interference across the decolonising world through political interference. The foundational anticommunist strategies and political preferences imposed by UN peacekeepers on decolonising or newly independent territories, such as Congo and West Papua during the early Cold War, fed into the well-funded US propaganda war. They helped fuel the intra-state political violence and an eradication of the anticolonial, radical nationalist politics that set the Bandung group apart as the 'Third World'. UN missions during decolonisation undermined alternative forms of worldmaking and internationalism, thus contributing to the slide to the right as post-colonial authoritarianism, 'junta' politics, and US neocolonialism engulfed large swathes of the Global South in the 1970s.

UN peacekeeping practices in post-colonial contexts intervened in and shaped ongoing processes of decolonisation. In tandem, UN peacekeeping evolved out of the demands and constraints of decolonisation. This book has unearthed the colonial continuities perpetuated throughout the first armed UN peacekeeping missions and unpacked how these continuities influenced understandings amongst UN officials of the conflicts and the local populations caught up in them. Rather than inviting an uncomplicated 'moment of opportunity' for populations trapped by imperial rule, decolonisation processes provoked complex territorial, political, and national questions without

[4] V. Prashad, *The Darker Nations: A People's History of the Third World* (New York: The New Press, 2008), p. 164.

[5] M. Avery, 'Promoting a "Pinochetazo": The Chilean Dictatorship's Foreign Policy in El Salvador during the Carter Years, 1977–1981', *Journal of Latin American Studies*, 52:4 (2020), p. 763.

precedent,[6] troubling the UN Secretariat and peacekeeping staff on the ground. As Fred Cooper has argued, 'The triumph of independence movements over colonial rule in Asia and Africa is another of those metanarratives that needs to be rethought'.[7] The norms, hierarchies, and relationships established at the Bandung Conference in 1955 between Afro-Asian nations conflicted with the rights of internal or annexed populations.[8] The Afro-Asian bloc's efforts to defend the inviolability of a state's internal affairs were as rooted in colonial memory as they were in post-colonial imperialist aspirations. Vulnerable populations, non-elite classes, activist movements, and minority groups struggled to achieve self-determination, resulting in civil war, internal displacement, and re-colonisation. Using their field-based access and diplomatic authority, UN peacekeepers helped to entrench an uneven distribution of sovereignty in post-colonial contexts and legitimised hierarchies of power between stronger and weaker, larger and smaller, well-resourced and poorly resourced nations through their own prejudices, ideological pursuits, and diplomatic alignments. The innovation of peacekeeping missions in the UN organisational machinery remade sovereignty for the post-colonial international order; UN peacekeepers exploited the permissions afforded to the mission to violate the non-interventionist principle and paved the way for further international interference, especially from ex-colonial powers, and hierarchies of inequality in post-colonial host nations.

Peacekeeping practices reinforced the nation-state as the hegemonic unit of governance delivery and geopolitical legitimacy during a period in which ideas about sovereignty were being renegotiated by a range of older and emerging global powers.[9] Peacekeeping missions provided a humanitarian guise for the emerging industry of perpetual war and political stagnation, enabling the profit of extractive state and non-state sectors in the mid-twentieth century – such as (neo) colonial powers, defence contractors, military consulting firms, and natural resource mining companies. Ostensibly providing stability, peacekeeping practices produced a wide range of unequal political outcomes, characterised by corruption, inequality, ethno-nationalist divisions, and the denial of meaningful self-determination and enfranchisement. Alternative worldmaking plans during decolonisation, such as transnational or political federations, were constrained and, ultimately, eradicated through the statist focus of the peacekeepers and their

[6] M. Collins, 'Nation, State and Agency: Evolving Historiographies of African Nationalism', in Smith and Jeppesen, *Britain, France and the Decolonization of Africa*, p. 26.

[7] F. Cooper, 'The Dialectics of Decolonization: Nationalism and Labor Movements in Post-War Africa', *CSST Working Paper #84*, May 1992, p. 2.

[8] C. A. Choudhury, 'From Bandung 1955 to Bangladesh 1971', in Elseva, Fakhri, and Nesiah, *Bandung, Global History, and International Law*, pp. 322–336.

[9] A. Phillips, 'Beyond Bandung: The 1955 Asian-African Conference and Its Legacies for International Order', *Australian Journal of International Affairs*, 70:4 (2016), pp. 329–341.

efforts to protect the liberal internationalist paradigm. Peacekeepers' attempts to politically interfere and impose liberal internationalism – to limited success – in these spaces destabilised local forms of activism, entrenching hierarchies (racial, ethnic, or elite) and asymmetric military power between belligerents. Ultimately, the practice of peacekeeping legitimised and sanitised international interventions into post-colonial populations and politics, reinventing forms of colonialism into a necessary and, indeed, desirable solution to conflict and international security threats across the Global South.

By bringing together histories of peacekeeping and decolonisation, each chapter in this book has shed new light on the mechanisms through which sovereignty was negotiated and renegotiated from the mid-1950s onwards. It has challenged the state-actor focus of diplomatic and military narratives of UN operations and demonstrated how pivotal mid-level peacekeepers were in curating the norms and structures of the post-colonial international order, contrary to dominant scholarly focuses on New York or Geneva-based internationalism. However, as Pierre-Yves Saunier suggested, rather than substituting 'a history of the nation-state with a history without or against the nation-state', this book has examined how political power flowed between national and international actors, regional and global networks, and headquarters- and field-based levels, thus, discovering a 'way to study how nation-states and flows of all sorts are entangled components of the modern age'.[10] It has illuminated the patterns, continuities, and ruptures in peacekeeping operations and examined the variations in the political power of field-based personalities and mid-level bureaucrats throughout each mission. It has also explored how the UN Secretariat and mission staff related to geopolitical pressures in a myriad of ways and with differing levels of influence; as perceptions of the UN shifted from UNEF to UNFICYP, especially for the United States and Afro-Asian bloc, the UN leadership were less able to intervene in the direction of the conflict. From 1956 to 1971, the mid-level peacekeepers functioned as knowledge producers for the UN Secretariat staff, diplomats for regional and international belligerents, and international regulators for nationalist activists. They legitimised post-colonial territories and borders and intervened in the ideological alliances of the host state and were influenced by broader political concerns. Crucially, they helped to shape post-colonial sovereignty as a tool through which international actors attempted to maintain influence over post-colonial spaces during a period of Cold War anxiety and worldwide geopolitical transformation.

Deployed to disputed territories at this moment of geopolitical transformation, mid-level peacekeeping staff became central figures in wide-ranging debates about the collapse of European imperialism, the military threat of the

[10] P. Saunier, 'Learning by Doing: Notes about the Making of the *Palgrave Dictionary of Transnational History*', *Journal of Modern European History*, 6:2 (2008), p. 170.

Cold War, and the future of the nation-state system across the Global South. Their approach to peace operations were driven by personal views and political motivations, but also by escalating anxieties about the role that the UN should play in the world. They sought to reassure member-states that the organisation remained the gold standard for conflict response, both at the diplomatic level and in the field. However, this international focus continually prioritised geopolitical anxieties, distracting UN staff from implementing long-term solutions to conflicts for the regional populations. Performing from a defensive position in the wake of the Congo criticism left the UN staff vulnerable to further attack but eager to prove their worth. Through further expansions, with the development of the first UN territorial administration and the creation of a dedicated UN mediator, Thant granted greater powers to the mid-level peacekeepers in post-Congo missions. However, this devolution enabled the development of technocratic and racialised organisational patterns in the field and compounded peacekeeper exceptionalism during a period of institutional pressure. Rather than focusing on local populations, mid-level diplomats fixated on providing a 'win' for the organisation which, ultimately, protracted conflicts and inter-communal tensions further. They attempted to repair the UN's reputation through the pursuit of short-term stability in host territories, neglecting long-term issues, such as human rights, re-colonisation, or conflict stagnation.

By challenging claims that Cold War peacekeeping missions were impartial, simple, and apolitical,[11] this book has revealed how mid-level peacekeepers interfered in post-colonial states' political processes and negotiated the political interference of other nations, especially former or emerging colonial powers. Decolonisation across the Global South ignited Western fears that formerly colonised populations would shift from European control to agents of Soviet aggression.[12] Imperial proxies had allowed Washington and the UN Secretariat leadership to relax, to a degree, as these colonised Global South territories remained invulnerable to Soviet intervention. However, decolonisation altered global priorities, and throughout the 1950s, the UN Secretariat prioritised anticommunist operations in Korea, and Washington funded British and French colonial administrations.[13] The UN leadership – in particular, secretaries-general Dag Hammarskjöld and U Thant – conceived Soviet interference as a threat to law and order, not only in the host country but also to neighbouring populations. They installed an anti-Soviet approach to international security practices in the field, encouraging mid-level staff to implement

[11] A. J. Bellamy, P. D. Williams, and S. Griffin, *Understanding Peacekeeping* (Cambridge: Polity, 2010), p. 175; M. Goulding, 'The Evolution of United Nations Peacekeeping', *International Affairs*, 69:3 (1993), pp. 454–455.

[12] W. M. Roger Louis and R. Robinson, 'The Imperialism of Decolonisation', *The Journal of Imperial and Commonwealth History*, 22:3 (1994), p. 472.

[13] Roger Louis and Robinson, 'The Imperialism of Decolonisation', pp. 467–468.

anticommunist policies and practices within the peacekeeping bureaucracy under a guise of peacebuilding. This ideological bias manifested, for instance, in peacekeepers' efforts in Congo to restrict international imports, control communications and transport, and align with anti-Lumumba politicians in violation of the host country's sovereignty. Although other scholarship has examined the anticommunist leanings of UN Secretariat staff, this is the first history to explore the ideological leanings of mid-level bureaucrats, such as Šture Linnér, Galo Plaza, and Djalal Abdoh, and to trace the practical manifestations of their political interference on the ground.

This book has also situated peacekeeping missions as part of the longer historical legacies of nineteenth-century interventionism and colonialism. UN leadership recruited mid-level officials from a variety of past positions, from managing mining corporations to leading anti-colonial debates within the General Assembly, but they were integrated within the UN international civil service and, thus, driven by the same political preferences for liberal internationalism and the nation-state system. Grounded in racist and technocratic exceptionalism, mid-level peacekeeping personnel took inspiration, often instinctively, from previous career experiences and imperial administrations to establish stability in their host countries and assert military authority over the restive population. The peacekeeping staff were gatekeepers to the global community and held substantial power over local populations' political futures by perpetuating hierarchies of inequality in the peacebuilding territory through administrative staffing and racialised rhetoric. Formative missions entrenched existing racialised structures of unequal power dynamics, cultural hierarchies, and Western exceptionalism inherited from colonial administrations and Western networks into peacekeeping contexts and entrenched these practices into future peacekeeping processes.[14]

It is crucial to reflect on an important question that emerges from this history: how does bringing international organisations into histories of decolonisation and the Cold War change how we conceive diplomatic power during this period? Traditional scholarly examinations of diplomatic power have typically concentrated on interstate negotiations, conflicts, and personal alliances between governmental representatives and leaders, relying on state documents and interviews.[15] Reflecting the dominant international relations paradigm, diplomatic power during the Cold War and decolonisation has,

[14] S. Razack, *Dark Threats and White Knights: The Somalia Affair, Peacekeeping, and the New Imperialism* (Toronto: University of Toronto Press, 2004); A. M. Angathangelou and L. H. M. Ling, 'Desire Industries: Sex Trafficking, UN Peacekeeping, and the Neo-Liberal World Order', *The Brown Journal of World Affairs*, 10:1 (2003), pp. 133–148.

[15] For instance, K. Larres, *Churchill's Cold War: The Politics of Personal Diplomacy* (New Haven: Yale University Press, 2002); R. H. Immerman, *John Foster Dulles and the Diplomacy of the Cold War* (Princeton: Princeton University Press, 1992).

traditionally, been conceived by international historians as national.[16] Power has been categorised through a figure's proximity to an electoral mandate or authoritarian position, thus, providing them with mediatory or coercive power during international negotiations.[17] For example, within Cold War diplomacy, the personal diplomacy between superpower leaders John F. Kennedy and Nikita Khrushchev to avert the Cuban missile crisis in 1962 has remained a crucial moment in international history.[18] Similarly, when bureaucratic diplomacy is considered, examination has been often limited to governmental networks and involvement of state figures.[19] Indeed, the diplomatic strength of the UN Security Council and General Assembly has been assumed to be predominantly through the presence of state representatives within the forums, rather than through the UN administrators, bureaucrats, and officials behind the scenes and in the field.[20] Although this scholarship has unearthed significant diplomatic relationships and activities through the recently declassified Cold War and decolonisation documents,[21] these works reinforce a restrictive conception of political diplomacy and diplomatic power that centres on those employed by or representative of a nation-state.[22]

16 M. L. Ghettas, *Algeria and the Cold War: International Relations and the Struggle for Autonomy* (London: Bloomsbury, 2017); J. Darwin, 'Diplomacy and Decolonization', *The Journal of Imperial and Commonwealth History*, 28:3 (2000), pp. 5–24; P. M. McGarr, *The Cold War in South Asia: Britain, the United States and the Indian Subcontinent, 1945–1965* (Cambridge: Cambridge University Press, 2013); S. K. Nayudu, '"India Looks at the World": Nehru, the Indian Foreign Service & World Diplomacy', *Diplomatica*, 2:1 (2020), pp. 100–117.

17 K. M. Lascurettes, *Orders of Exclusion: Great Powers and the Strategic Sources of Foundational Rules in International Relations* (Oxford: Oxford University Press, 2020).

18 S. M. Stern, *Averting 'the Final Failure': John F. Kennedy and the Secret Cuban Missile Crisis Meetings* (Palo Alto: Stanford University Press, 2003); R. Keller, 'The Latin American Missile Crisis', *Diplomatic History*, 39:2 (2015), pp. 195–222.

19 J. Greenstock, 'The Bureaucracy: Ministry of Foreign Affairs, Foreign Service, and Other Government Departments', in A. F. Cooper, J. Heine, and R. Thakur (eds.), *The Oxford Handbook of Modern Diplomacy* (Oxford: Oxford University Press, 2013).

20 M. A. Heiss, 'Exposing "Red Colonialism": U.S. Propaganda at the United Nations, 1953–1963', *Journal of Cold War Studies*, 17:3 (2015), pp. 82–115; I. V. Gaiduk, *Divided Together: The United States and the Soviet Union in the United Nations, 1945–1965* (Palo Alto: Stanford University Press, 2012); W. R. Feeney, 'Sino-Soviet Competition in the United Nations', *Asian Survey*, 17:9 (1977), pp. 809–829.

21 E. Calandri, D. Caviglia, and A. Varsori, *Détente in Cold War Europe: Politics and Diplomacy in the Mediterranean and the Middle East* (London: Bloomsbury, 2015); S. Williams, *Who Killed Hammarskjöld?: The UN, the Cold War, and White Supremacy in Africa* (Oxford: Oxford University Press, 2014).

22 R. Pastor-Castro and M. Thomas (eds.), *Embassies in Crisis: Studies of Diplomatic Missions in Testing Situations* (Abingdon: Routledge, 2020).

However, recently historians have begun to challenge this narrow conception of political diplomacy during decolonisation.[23] They have posited the impact of international civil servants and non-state actors in navigating and shaping international diplomacy during the twentieth century and diversified conceptions of 'diplomatic' power during this period.[24] Scholars have revealed U Thant's important role during the Cuban missile crisis – for instance, benefitting from the opening of Cold War archives to the public, transforming the traditional superpower narrative, and nuancing understandings of diplomatic power within the international sphere.[25] Non-state actors, particularly UN secretaries-general, have been increasingly acknowledged for their diplomacy and mediation during the Cold War and decolonisation, with scholars drawing attention to the shift towards global governance following the Second World War. Whilst retaining a focus on 'great men' who, such as Hammarskjöld, works on non-state spaces and networks have also helped to illuminate the contributions of women to major diplomatic developments of the twentieth century.[26]

This book has examined the diplomatic activities and influence of mid-level international staff and those deployed to the field to reveal the internal

[23] Cultural diplomacy, or soft power, during the twentieth century has also been an increasingly popular area of study as institutes, such as the British Council, built transnational connections through music, art, sport, religion, and theatre. For more, see M. Hadjiathanasiou, 'Colonial Rule, Cultural Relations and the British Council in Cyprus, 1935–55', *The Journal of Imperial and Commonwealth History*, 46:6 (2018), pp. 1096–1124; N. Prevots, *Dance for Export: Cultural Diplomacy and the Cold War* (Middletown: Wesleyan University Press, 2012).

[24] G. Sluga and C. James (eds.), *Women, Diplomacy and International Politics since 1500* (Abingdon: Routledge, 2016); S. Pedersen, *The Guardians: The League of Nations and the Crisis of Empire* (Oxford: Oxford University Press, 2015); D. Maul, *Human Rights, Development and Decolonization: The International Labour Organisation, 1950–1970* (Basingstoke: Palgrave Macmillan, 2012); S. Jackson and A. O'Malley (eds.), *The Institution of International Order: From the League of Nations to the United Nations* (Abingdon: Routledge, 2018).

[25] A. W. Dorn and R. Pauk, 'Unsung Mediator: U Thant and the Cuban Missile Crisis', *Diplomatic History*, 33:2 (2009), pp. 261–292.

[26] See K. Aggestam and A. Towns, 'The Gender Turn in Diplomacy: A New Research Agenda', *International Feminist Journal of Politics*, 21:1 (2019), pp. 9–28; M. Terretta, *Petitioning for Our Rights, Fighting for Our Nation: The History of the Democratic Union of Cameroonian Women, 1949–1960* (Oxford: African Books Collective, 2013); Sluga and James, *Women, Diplomacy and International Politics*. This is not to say there has been no important works examining the role of women within national service. For example, H. McCarthy, 'Petticoat Diplomacy: The Admission of Women to the British Foreign Service, c.1919–1946', *Twentieth Century British History*, 20:3 (2009), pp. 285–321; H. McCarthy, 'Women, Marriage and Work in the British Diplomatic Service', *Women's History Review*, 23:6 (2014), pp. 853–873; K. A. M. Wright, M. Hurley, and J. I. G. Ruiz, *NATO, Gender and the Military: Women Organising from Within* (Abingdon: Routledge, 2019).

decision-making and practices concealed with the UN bureaucracy. It has charted the organisation's operational innovations and experiments during decolonisation and argued that many were developed by mid-level staff rather than by the UN leadership in New York, such as the impulsive decision of Linnér to co-opt ANC trucks for the ONUC mission, or Cordier's decision to close the Leopoldville airports and radio stations. Events in Congo provoked the UAR to withdraw their troops and prompted protests from Afro-Asian representatives, paving the way for further outrage following the murder of Lumumba only months later. Rather than passive intermediaries, mid-level peacekeepers sought to 'cut through red tape' and exploit their power to shape the political future of the host territory and the post-colonial international order. Additionally, each chapter has also reflected on the state-building impulse within UN peacekeeping staff towards performative and identity-building practices, such as stamps, newsletters, flags, and military ceremonies, whilst on the ground. Mid-level UN officials used their access to belligerents and political activists to negotiate political and governance structures, such as national unity, a non-aligned ideology, and democratic processes, that benefitted the organisation's nation-state system, in exchange for support and legitimacy from the UN officials. Thus, as peacekeepers experimented with non-state diplomacy in the field and bargained with the warring parties, they reinforced a post-colonial world vision with the UN at the centre of state regulation and the international security paradigm.

In sum, peacekeeping missions and staff were integral to the reshaping and remaking of the international community during and following decolonisation during the 1950s and 1960s. Uniquely placed and protected within the conflict context, UN officials should be better recognised in decolonisation historiography for their contribution and interventions, particularly in the literature of twentieth-century sovereignty. Rather than being peripheral to spaces of diplomatic innovation, peacekeepers' field-based decision-making, prejudices, and politics entrenched the norms and standards of the nation-state system that remain hegemonic today. As the current secretary-general, António Guterres, noted in 2018, 'A peacekeeping operation is not an army, or a counter-terrorist force, or a humanitarian agency. It is a tool to create the space for a nationally-owned political solution'.[27] Decolonisation was not a discrete process with a predictable outcome; UN peacekeepers played an integral role in translating liberal internationalism onto post-colonial territorial disputes as a peacebuilding policy whilst characterising alternative global or national visions

[27] A. Guterres, 'Remarks to Security Council High-Level Debate on Collective Action to Improve UN Peacekeeping Operations', 28 March 2018, available at: www.un.org/sg/en/content/sg/speeches/2018-03-28/collective-action-improve-un-peacekeeping-operations-remarks, accessed on 18 June 2020.

as threats to international security. Across the Global South, UN peacekeepers reinvented international interventionism as a post-colonial function whilst using their field-based access and privileges to preserve and entrench uneven hierarchies of race, expertise, and diplomatic power within newly independent populations and nations.

REFERENCES

Archives

Amnesty International

EUR 25/007/1977, 'Torture in Greece: The First Torturers' Trial 1975', available at www.amnesty.org/en/documents/eur25/007/1977/en/, accessed on 21 May 2019.

Bodleian Library, Oxford

MS.Eng.c. 4713 (fols 1–248), Papers of D. Burnell Vickers.
MS.Eng.c. 4674 (fols 244–324), Papers of Antony Gilpin.
MS.Eng.c. 4675 (fols 1–65, 73–95, 100–101, 107–108), Papers of Antony Gilpin.
MS.Eng.c. 4704 (fols 123–313), Papers of Winifred Tickner.
MS.Eng.c. 4731 (fols 1–336), Papers of Charles Harris.
MS.Eng.c. 4743 (fols 118–158, 218–249), Papers of Charles Harris.
MS.Eng.c. 6472 (fols 56–60), Papers of George Ivan Smith.
MS.Eng.c. 6488 (fols 201–219), Papers of George Ivan Smith.
MS. Photogr. c. 50. Photographs by Antony Gilpin.

British Library, London

U.N.A.466, UN Public Information Office, *Sand Dune: The UNEF Weekly*, Editions 2-33, BLL01003710404.

British National Archives, London

FO 371/72676, FO 371/118873, FO 371/118874, FO 371/118876, FO 371/118878, FO 371/118879, FO 371/118880, FO 371/118884, FO 371/118885, FO 371/125551, FO 371/129792, FO 371/134302, FO 371/146770, FO 371/146776, FO 371/146777, FO 371/146779, FO 371/160007, FO 371/169951, FO 371/169952, FO 371/174763, FO 371/174764, FO 371/174765, FCO 9/1501, DEFE 24/1473, DEFE 25/354, DO 220/85.

International Committee of the Red Cross Archives, Geneva

B AG 121 229 – Zaïre – 1959–1967.
B AG 130 – Relations avec l'Organisation des Nations Unies (ONU) et ses institutions spécialisées – 1950–1970.
B AG 141 053 – Congo – 1960–1962.
B AG 200 158 – Papouasie-Nouvelle-Guinée – 1958–1965.
B AG 200 229 – Zaïre – 1960–1960.
B AG 201 049 – Chypre – 1963–1963.
B AG 202 049 – Chypre – 1955–1965.
B AG 202 229 – Zaïre – 1960–1966.
B AG 210 158 – Papouasie-Nouvelle-Guinée – 1962–1963.

Library and Archives Canada, Ottawa

RG25 (External Affairs), 6150, 50409-A-40.

University of Massachusetts Amherst Libraries

Special Collections and University Archives, W. E. B. Du Bois Papers (MS 312).

United Nations Archives, New York

S-0472-0098-04-00001, S-0472-0103-25-00001, S-0309-0037-19, S-0313-0001-01, S-0313-0002-07, S-0313-0002-12, S-0313-0003-06, S-0313-0005-06, S-0316-0010-01, S-0316-0012-06, S-0370-0028-08, S-0370-0051-05, S-1069-0012-11, S-1070-0026-17, S-1070-0026-18, S-1070-0029-10, S-1070-0029-12, S-1070-0030-01, S-1070-0037-10, S-0530-0011-0011, S-0845-0001-01, S-0845-0001-02, S-0845-0001-03, S-0862-0003-04, S-0869-0001-01, S-0869-0001-02, S-0869-0001-03, S-0869-0001-09, S-0869-0001-10, S-0869-0001-11, S-0869-0001-12, S-0869-0001-13, S-0869-0001-15, S-0869-0001-17, S-0869-0002-04, S-0869-0002-09, S-0869-0002-10, S-0869-0002-11, S-0869-0003-04, S-0869-0003-08, S-0869-0003-13, S-0869-0003-14, S-0869-0003-15, S-0870-0001-01, S-0870-0001-04, S-0870-0001-14, S-0875-0005-01, S-0875-0007-05, S-0876-0001-03, S-0876-0001-04, S-0876-0001-06, S-0876-0001-07, S-0884-0022-07, S-0884-0023-01, S-0075-0002-04, S-0075-0003-05, S-0075-0004-02, S-0079-0005-06, S-0079-0006-20, S-0079-0007-09, S-0079-0007-10, S-0079-0007-11, S-0682-0003-11, S-0701-0003-04, S-0703-0001-02, S-0703-0016-01, S-0703-0001-05.

United States Government

Department of State: Office of the Historian – Foreign Relations of the United States

1952–1954, Volume III.
1955–1957, Suez Crisis, 26 July–31 December 1956, Volume XVI.

1958–1960, Indonesia, Volume XVII.
1961–1963, Southeast Asia, Volume XXIII.
1961–1963, Volume XVIII, Near East, 1962–1963.
1964–1968, Volume XXXIII, Organization and Management of Foreign Policy; United Nations.
1964–1968, Volume XVI, Cyprus, Greece, Turkey.

Office of Archives and History, US National Security Agency/ Central Security Service

'The Suez Crisis: A Brief Comint History (U)', United States Cryptologic History, Special Series, Crisis Collection, Volume 2, 1988, available at www.archives.gov/files/declassification/iscap/pdf/2013-117-doc01.pdf, accessed on 2 June 2020.

United States Mission to the United Nations

Press Release No. 4374, 'Dag Hammarskjöld Memorial Lecture by Ambassador Adlai E. Stevenson. "From Containment to Cease-Fire and Peaceful Change"', 23 March 1964.

Other

'Letter from John F. Kennedy to the Prime Minister of the Netherlands, 2nd April 1962', available at www.freewestpapua.org/documents/secret-letter-from-john-f-kennedy-to-the-prime-minister-of-the-netherlands-2nd-april-1962/, accessed on 29 December 2018.
'United States Proposal for Temporary United Nations Trusteeship for Palestine: Statement by President Truman, March 25, 1948', available at https://unispal.un.org/UNISPAL.NSF/0/C3AFF48D711D26158525715400730A30.

Published Sources

British Pathe

British Pathe, 'Congo: Premiere Lumumba Arrested', 1960, Film ID: 3000.07, available at www.britishpathe.com/video/congo-premiere-lumumba-arrested-aka-lumumba-arrest.

Digitised Speeches

Baruch, B., 'The Baruch Plan, presented to the United Nations Atomic Energy Commission, June 14 1946', available at www.atomicarchive.com/resources/documents/deterrence/baruch-plan.html, accessed on 8 April 2020.

Baudouin, 'King Baudouin Declares Congo Independent (1960)', British Pathé, available at www.youtube.com/watch?v=TjCgC64odYw, accessed on 18 March 2020.

Bunche, R., 'Acceptance Speech, 10 December 1950', available at www.nobelprize.org/prizes/peace/1950/bunche/acceptance-speech/, accessed on 7 April 2020.

'Declaration of Establishment of State of Israel', 14 May 1948, available at www.mfa.gov.il/mfa/foreignpolicy/peace/guide/pages/declaration%20of%20establishment%20of%20state%20of%20israel.aspx, accessed on 9 April 2020.

Guterres, A., 'Remarks to Security Council High-Level Debate on Collective Action to Improve UN Peacekeeping Operations', 28 March 2018, available at www.un.org/sg/en/content/sg/speeches/2018-03-28/collective-action-improve-un-peacekeeping-operations-remarks, accessed on 18 June 2020.

Lie, T., 'Trygve Lie, Secretary-General of the United Nations, announces his resignation', *British Pathe*, Film ID: 2636.23, 10 November 1952, available at www.britishpathe.com/video/trygve-lie-resigns, accessed on 9 April 2020.

Lumumba, P., 'Statement at the Closing Session of the Belgo-Congolese Round Table Conference', 20 February 1960, available at www.marxists.org/subject/africa/lumumba/1960/02/statement.htm, accessed on 18 March 2020.

International Committee of the Red Cross

La Ligue des Sociétés de la Croix-Rouge, 'Assistance médicale au Congo: Rapport sur l'action de la Croix-Rouge internationale chargée de pourvoir en personnel quelque trente hôpitaux abandonnés dans la République du Congo nouvellement indépendante pour une période d'urgence de 12 mois (juillet 1960–juin 1961)', 1961.

'Supplement Vol. XIV 1961', *Revue internationale de la Croix Rouge*, March 1961.

International Court of Justice

'Reparations for Injuries Suffered in the Service of the United Nations', Advisory Opinion of 11 April 1949.

Lyndon B. Johnson Library

'Secretary Cyrus R. Vance', Interviewed by Paige E. Mulhollan, 3 November 1969, available at www.adst.org/OH%20TOCs/Vance,%20Cyrus%20R.pdf, accessed on 21 May 2019.

Newspaper Articles

Los Angeles Times

'"Get Tough" in Cyprus, U.N. Troops Ordered: Sterner Attitude Results from Worldwide Criticism of Inability to Halt Island War', *Los Angeles Times*, 2 May 1964.

The Atlantic

Einstein, A., 'Atomic War or Peace', *The Atlantic*, November 1947.

The Baltimore Sun

'Greeks End Assaults on Castle', *The Baltimore Sun*, 30 April 1964.

The Chicago Tribune

'Eleven Cypriots Slain; Burn Turk Village', *Chicago Tribune*, 7 February 1964.
'Nicosia Mob Stones Auto of UN Chief', *Chicago Tribune*, 27 April 1964.

Cyprus Mail

'Clerides Calls for "Careful Thought": "End to Wishful Thinking", Cyprus "at Threshold of Momentous Decisions', *Cyprus Mail*, 1 April 1965, available at https://cyprus-mail.com/wp-content/uploads/2015/07/April-1-1965.jpg, accessed on 21 May 2019.

The Economist

'When Pride Simmers', *The Economist*, 210:6285, 8 February 1964.
'Priest and Soldier', *The Economist*, 218:6396, 26 March 1966.
'More Militant than the Colonels', *The Economist*, 225:6485, 9 December 1967.

The Guardian

Unattributed

'Marred: M. Lumumba's Offensive Speech in King's Presence', *The Guardian*, 1 June 1960.
'The Attack on St Hilarion', *The Guardian*, 29 April 1964.

Attributed

Pick, H., 'Two Sides Urged to Meet in Cyprus: Senor Galo Plaza's Report', *The Guardian*, 31 March 1965.

The Jerusalem Post

'Indian Gen. Gyani Replaces von Horn', *The Jerusalem Post*, 12 September 1963.

Life Magazine

Cloete, S. and Spencer, T., 'White Men Flee in Terror from Chaos of the Congo: Fear, Sorrow and Farewells and End of Era with Threat of the Jungle Taking Over, But from U.N. Resolute Step', *Life Magazine*, 49:5, 1 August 1960.

Le Monde

'Le Général Gheysen: Les troupes belges quitteront le Katanga à la fin du mois', *Le Monde*, 29 August 1960.

The New York Times

Unattributed

'Austria Sends Force to Bar Nazi Rioting', *The New York Times*, 12 January 1935.

'Refugees Shot at from Saar Side', *The New York Times*, 17 January 1935.

'U.N. and It's Police Force', *The New York Times*, 21 April 1947.

'Ban on the Veto Favored by Taft', *The New York Times*, 16 September 1947.

'Liberals Urge End of the Veto in UN: Party Gives Stand on World Issues and Its U.S. Goals in National Platform', *The New York Times*, 31 October 1949.

'Baruch Urges Curb on Veto Powers in U.N. with World Force to Halt Aggression', *The New York Times*, 15 February 1950.

'War Is Declared by North Koreans', *The New York Times*, 25 June 1950.

'Moscow Charges US Plot in Korea: Says Dulles Gave Signal for Hostilities There with View to Launching World War III', *The New York Times*, 2 July 1950.

'For a UN Army', *The New York Times*, 7 July 1950.

'Hammarskjoeld [sic] Elected Successor to Lie as U. N. Secretary General: Swede Gets 57 of 60 Votes and Will Take Oath on Friday', *The New York Times*, 8 April 1953.

'Finletter Urges Full Disarmament', *The New York Times*, 28 June 1955.

'Concert Will Mark United Nations Day', *The New York Times*, 24 October 1956.

'Blue Helmets at Abu Suweir', *The New York Times*, 16 November 1956.

'24 Killed in Riot in Belgian Congo: Troops Sent to Stanleyville to Quell Outbreak Laid to African Nationalists', *The New York Times*, 1 November 1959.

'Belgium's Forces Fight Congolese to Quell Risings', *The New York Times*, 11 July 1960.

'Belgians Fill Key Congo Jobs and Cause Problems for U.N.', *The New York Times*, 5 January 1961.

'Riot in Gallery Halts U.N. Debate', *The New York Times*, 16 February 1961.

'Congo Issue Stirs Rioting in London: Police Halt Mob's Attempt to Rush Belgian Embassy in Lumumba Protest', *The New York Times*, 20 February 1961.

'Irish Troops' Four-Day Ordeal in Katanga Siege Is Described', *The New York Times*, 21 September 1961.

'Another Jungle War', *The New York Times*, 20 May 1962.

'One More Slain in Cyprus Strife', *The New York Times*, 23 December 1963.

'Violence Called "Genocide"', *The New York Times*, 25 December 1963.

'Makarios Backed in Cyprus: Deepening of Conflict Feared If His Proposals Are Rejected', *The New York Times*, 2 January 1964.

'Cyprus: Test for the UN', *The New York Times*, 8 March 1964.

'UN Airlifts Food to Cyprus Village', *The New York Times*, 14 September 1964.

'Turkish Cypriots Cool to UN Plan', *The New York Times*, 2 April 1965.

'Greeks Will Confer on Report by Plaza', *The New York Times*, 4 April 1965.

'Turks' Intervention in Cyrus Is Hinted', *The New York Times*, 9 April 1965.
'Turkish Aid Stirs Dispute in Cyprus', *The New York Times*, 16 November 1965.
'Plaza Resigns UN Post as Mediator in Cyprus', *The New York Times*, 10 January 1966.
'Czech Arms for Makarios Stir Athens-Nicosia Rift: Under Control of Athens', *The New York Times*, 5 December 1966.
'Makarios Agrees Not to Use Czech Arms "for Time Being"', *The New York Times*, 7 December 1966.
'Cyprus Studying Junta's Intention: Rumors of a Greek-Led Coup Cause Concern in Nicosia', *The New York Times*, 20 May 1967.
'Hope Voiced in Ankara: Would Safeguard Minority Invasion Forces Poised', *The New York Times*, 25 November 1967.
'The Liberation of U Thant', *The New York Times*, 29 December 1971.
'Greece Disavows Force on Cyprus: But Declares That Makarios Should Obey Athens', *The New York Times*, 5 March 1972.
'Greece – Cyprus Crisis: A Complex Mosaic', *The New York Times*, 18 March 1972.

Attributed

Baldwin, H. W., 'Armed Forces for UN Still a Remote Idea', *The New York Times*, 27 October 1946.
'U.N. vs. the Congo: World Body Faces Its Severest Test As Tragicomic Struggle Still Goes On', *The New York Times*, 8 November 1960.
Barrett, G., 'Position of UN Chief Aide Is Thrust into Uncertainty: Council Tells Assembly of Failure to Agree on a Secretary General', *The New York Times*, 13 October 1950.
Berger, M., 'Cyrus R. Vance, a Confidant of Presidents, Is Dead at 84', *The New York Times*, 13 January 2002.
Bigart, H., 'Coalition Urged in Belgian Congo', *The New York Times*, 29 May 1960.
Brady, T. F., 'Lumumba Angered by Use of Whites as Katanga Force: Assails Hammarskjöld Stand that U.N. Will Not Help to Subdue Secessionists', *The New York Times*, 14 August 1960.
'Congo Lacking 1,500 Teachers and Aides in Secondary Schools', *The New York Times*, 27 August 1960.
Brewer, S. P., 'UN Reports Irish Win a Cease-Fire at Katanga Base', 17 September 1961.
Brown, M., 'Jews, Arabs Adopt Jerusalem Truce in Old Walled City', *The New York Times*, 29 April 1948.
Callender, H., 'In the Saar History Writes a Chapter', *The New York Times*, 13 January 1935.
Duffus, R. L., 'Key Man in the U.N.'s New Test', *The New York Times*, 7 August 1960.
Fellows, L., 'New Cyprus Tension Imperils Reopening of Roads', *The New York Times*, 9 January 1964.

'British U.N. Units Return Fire of Greek Cypriotes [sic]', *The New York Times*, 31 March 1964.

Feron, J., 'Three Countries Quit UN Congo Force in Protest Move', *The New York Times*, 8 December 1960.

'U.N. Takes Steps to Prevent Riots: Guards Armed with Clubs – Arrests to Be Made in Future Demonstrations', *The New York Times*, 17 February 1961.

'Kosygin, in Ankara, Regrets Czecks' [sic] Arms Sale to Cyprus', *The New York Times*, 22 December 1966.

'Makarios Asserts That Turkey May Force a War', *The New York Times*, 25 November 1967.

'Roadblocks Set on Tense Cyprus: Some Residents Said to Flee Nicosia for Mountains 2 Envoys Cancel Visits Cypriotes Still Concerned Blacks Rock Island', *The New York Times*, 26 November 1967.

Gardner, R. N., 'Needed: A Stand-by UN Force: In Cyprus, the U.N. Has Been Called upon for the Fourth Time on a Large Scale to Keep Peace by Military Means. Here Is the Case for Institutionalizing that Capacity', *The New York Times*, 26 April 1964.

Gilroy, H., 'Jailed Congolese Freed for Talks: Lumumba Expected Today at Meeting in Brussels – Kasavubu Walks Out', *The New York Times*, 26 January 1960.

'The Congo: From Colony to Independence: Belgium's Preserve in Africa Gets Promise of Early Sovereignty', *The New York Times*, 21 February 1960.

'The Congo: Problems of Independence: Struggle for Control of Belgian Colony Grows Amid Regional and Tribal Controversy', *The New York Times*, 19 June 1960.

'Lumumba Assails Colonialism as Congo Is Freed', *The New York Times*, 1 July 1960.

'Belgium Ignores Congo on Troops', *The New York Times*, 14 July 1960.

'The Congo Crisis as the Belgians See It', *The New York Times*, 17 July 1960.

Halberstam, D., 'U.N. Takes Katanga', *The New York Times*, 14 September 1961.

Hamilton, T. J., 'Tight Plan Sought: Bernadotte for Controls that Will Make Truce in Holy Land Work', *The New York Times*, 3 June 1948.

'Russia Insists UN Send Soviet Group to Palestine: US and Canada in Security Unit Oppose Moscow Military Observers', *The New York Times*, 11 June 1948.

'UN Rejects Move to Send Soviet Observers to Palestine', *The New York Times*, 16 June 1948.

'Riley Carries Plan', *The New York Times*, 2 June 1949.

'Bunche Ends Task as UN Mediator', *The New York Times*, 28 July 1949.

'Most UN Delegates Favor Use of Land Force in Korea', *The New York Times*, 1 July 1950.

'Action by Council: American Troops on Their Way to the Front in Korea', *The New York Times*, 8 July 1950.

'UN Council Meets Today on Lie Term: Takes Lead in Proposed 2 or 3 Year Extension but Soviet Stand Is Unknown', *The New York Times*, 9 October 1950.

'Lie Term Extended as US Secretary for 3 Years', *The New York Times*, 2 November 1950.

'Soviet Veto Blocks Pearson UN Boom', *The New York Times*, 14 March 1953.

'U.N. Financial Troubles: Some Members' Failure to Pay Share Jeopardizes Future Operations', *The New York Times*, 3 December 1961.

'The U.N.: Problems Over Goa, Congo and Finances Create New Crisis for World Organization', *The New York Times*, 24 December 1961.

'U.N. under Pressure: Financial Crisis and Criticism of Policy Beset World Organization', *The New York Times*, 11 February 1962.

Middleton, D., 'Thant Bids the U.N. Keep Cyprus Force: Thant Asks U.N. Council to Extend Cyprus Force Comment Is Repeated His Language Is Terse Major Element in Guard', *The New York Times*, 12 December 1967.

Parrott, L., 'U.N. CHIEF OFFERS WIDE AID TO CONGO: Would Lend Experts in Many Fields – Vows Neutrality', *The New York Times*, 13 August 1960.

'Two Nations to Quit UN Force: Charter Violations Charged by Morocco and Guinea', *The New York Times*, 13 December 1960.

'U.N. Urged to Use Force to Prevent War in Congo', *The New York Times*, 18 February 1961.

Pope, S., 'UN Chief Offers New Cyprus Plan to Bar "Disaster"', *The New York Times*, 30 April 1964.

'Problem for Thant', *The New York Times*, 18 August 1964.

'Cyprus Mediator Backed by Thant: UN Leader Says Turkey's Move against Plaza Could Wreck Settlement Hopes', *The New York Times*, 3 April 1965.

Reston, J. B., 'Fifty-One Nations in Search of Unity', *The New York Times*, 27 January 1946.

Rosenthal, A. M., 'New UN Secretary Cautious on Issues', *The New York Times*, 10 April 1953.

'Katanga Police Defy U.N. Use Airports It Occupied', *The New York Times*, 10 September 1960.

Streit, C. K., 'Saar and League Face Tense Period', *The New York Times*, 20 January 1935.

Tanner, H., 'U.N. IN CONGO: Some Resentment Found among Congolese at World Agency's Large Role', *The New York Times*, 31 July 1960.

Teltsch, K., 'Kasavubu Scores UN on Lumumba: Notes Criticise World Body for Barring Arrest of Premier He Deposed', *The New York Times*, 5 November 1960.

'Ecuadorian Given UN Cyprus Role', *The New York Times*, 12 May 1964.

'UN Team Arranging Vote', *The New York Times*, 7 May 1969.

The New York Times Editorial Board, 'Caldron of the Congo', *The New York Times*, 13 July 1960.

Whitman, A., 'U Thant Is Dead of Cancer at 65', *The New York Times*, 26 November 1974.

The Observer

Graham-Harrison, E., Rocksen, A., and Brügger, M., 'Man Accused of Shooting Down UN Chief: "Sometimes you have to do things you don't want to..."', *The Observer*, 12 January 2019.

POLITICO

Gijs, C. and Faris, S., 'Lumumba's Tooth: Belgium's Unfinished Reckoning with Its Colonial Past', *POLITICO*, 2 June 2022.

TIME Magazine

'The Congo: A New Start', *TIME Magazine*, 30 June 1961.

South Pacific Post

'Africans in W. Papua', *South Pacific Post*, 17 April 1962.

Survey Graphic

Shotwell, J. T., 'Control of Atomic Energy', *Survey Graphic* 34 (October 1945).

The Straits Times

'As the Dutch Say a Hard Farewell', *The Straits Times*, 15 October 1962.

The Sydney Morning Herald

'Mass Protest by Papuans', *The Sydney Morning Herald*, 12 August 1962.
'Natives Fear Indonesian Rule', *The Sydney Morning Herald*, 18 August 1962.

The Times (London)

'Plan to Drop Partition of Palestine', *The Times*, 20 March 1948.
'Cyprus Crisis Goes to U.N. Today', *The Times*, 17 February 1964.
Flanagan, J. and Waterfield, B., 'Belgium Says Sorry for Patrice Lumumba's Murder with Return of His Gold Tooth', *The Times*, 27 May 2022.

The Washington Post

Unattributed

'Dispute over Lumumba's Insult to Belgium Shakes Congo Cabinet', *The Washington Post*, 2 July 1960.
'Cyprus Violence Goes on as Isle Unifies Forces', *The Washington Post*, 26 December 1963.
'Turk Cyprus Shrine Damaged by Bomb; Tension Runs High', *The Washington Post*, 24 January 1964.

'Turks Mob U.N. Chief on Cyprus: 150 Women Hurl Rocks and Shout "Death to Gyani, Death to Gyani"', *The Washington Post*, 27 April 1964.

Attributed

Bruns Jr, F., 'U.N. Will Feature New UNTEA Stamp', *The Washington Post*, 14 July 1963.

Efty, A., '2 Cypriots Slain, 9 Hurt in Clashes: Greeks and Turks Fight over Planned Changes in Laws', *The Washington Post*, 22 December 1963.

Grant, B., "Auntie' Takes over Irian Gently', *The Washington Post*, 14 October 1962.

Quaker Publications

Friends Journal: Quaker Thought and Life Today, 7:20, 15 October 1961.

UN Blue Beret: UNFICYP Edition

'The Blue Beret – UNFICYP Edition, 27 April 1964', available at https://unficyp.unmissions.org/sites/default/files/27_april_1964.pdf, accessed on 22 April 2020.

'The Blue Beret – UNFICYP Edition, 18 May 1964', UN Public Information Office.

United Nations Public Documents

General

UN Charter, 24 October 1945, available at www.un.org/en/sections/uncharter/index.html, accessed on 14 May 2018.

'New York Agreement', 15 August 1962, available at https://treaties.un.org/doc/Publication/UNTS/Volume%20437/volume-437-I-6311-English.pdf.

'Dag Hammarskjöld, Second Secretary-General of the United Nations', available at www.un.org/en/sections/nobel-peace-prize/dag-hammarskjold-second-secretary-general-united-nations/index.html.

'West New Guinea – UNSF: Background', United Nations Peacekeeping, available at https://peacekeeping.un.org/en/mission/past/unsfbackgr.html.

Yearbook of the United Nations, 1956 (New York: United Nations Public Information Office, 1956), available at https://unispal.un.org/DPA/DPR/unispal.nsf/0/07B20C5327E7A152852562CE0075C0B0.

General Assembly Records

A/364, A/553, A/656, A/689, A/819, A/2380, A/3289, A/3302, A/3354, A/3385, A/L.368

A/7723, A/47/277

A/PV.591, A/PV.592, A/PV.594, A/PV.600, A/PV.703, A/PV.1016, A/PV.1209, A/PV.1813

A/C.1/SR.905
A/AC.24/SR.30, A/AC.24/SR.31, A/AC.24/SR.32, A/AC.24/45,
A/RES/106 (S-1), A/RES/112(II), A/RES/167, A/RES/181 (II), A/RES/186 (S-2), A/RES/195(III), A/RES/273 (III), A/RES/293 (IV), A/RES/297 (IV), A/RES/376 (V), A/RES/377(V), A/RES/997 (ES-I), A/RES/1000 (ES – 1), A/RES/1001 (ES-1), A/RES/1120 (XI), A/RES/1474 (ES-IV), A/RES/1514(XV), A/RES/1752 (XVII)

Public Information

PAL/189, PAL/208, PAL/210, PAL/290

Security Council Records

S/727, S/743, S/801, S/1018, S/1376 (II), S/1501, S/1506, S/1511, S/1588, S/3476, S/3671, S/4382, S/4387, S/4389, S/4426, S/4451, S/4475, S/4531, S/4557, S/4741, S/5575, S/5691, S/5764, S/5950, S/5950/Add.2, S/6102, S/7969, S/8248, S/8286
S/PV.317, S/PV.320, S/PV.749, S/PV.751, S/PV.873, S/PV.877, S/PV.878, S/PV.886, S/PV.1099

United Nations Publications

To Live Together in Peace with One Another as Good Neighbors: For United Nations Day, Questions and Answers, 24 October 1956 (New York: United Nations Department of Public Information, 1956).

Yearbook of the United Nations, 1956 (New York: United Nations Public Information Office, 1956), available at https://unispal.un.org/DPA/DPR/unispal.nsf/0/07B20C5327E7A152852562CE0075C0B0, accessed on 2 June 2020.

The Blue Helmets – A Review of United Nations Peace-Keeping (New York: UN Department of Public Information, 1985), available at https://unficyp.unmissions.org/1967-crisis, accessed on 23 April 2020.

Yale-UN Oral History Project

All interviews available via the United Nations Digital Library (https://digitallibrary.un.org/).

Beeley, W., 'Interview by James Sutterlin', 20 June 1990.
Berendsen, I., 'Interview by Jean Krasno', 4 May 1990.
Guillion, E., 'Interview by Jean Krasno', 8 May 1990.
Kidron, M., 'Interview by James Sutterlin', 17 April 1991.
Lall, A., 'Interview by Jean Krasno', 27 June 1990.
Linnér, Š., 'Interview by Jean Krasno', 8 November 1990.
Liu, F. T., 'Interview by James Sutterlin', 23 March 1990.
McGhee, G., 'Interview by James Sutterlin', 9 May 1990.
Murray, G., 'Interview by James Sutterlin', 10 January 1991.

Plaza, G., 'Interview by Diego Cordovez', 28 March 1984.
Urquhart, B., 'Interview by Leon Gordenker', 15 October 1984.

US Government Printing Office

Alleged Assassination Plots Involving Foreign Leaders, an Interim Report of the Select Committee to Study Governmental Operations with Respect to Intelligence Activities, US Senate, November 20th 1975 (Washington, DC: US Government Printing Office, 1975), pp. 13–16, available at www.intelligence.senate.gov/sites/default/files/94465.pdf.
Revision of the United Nations Charter: Hearings before the United States Senate Committee on Foreign Relations, Subcommittee on Revision of the United Nations Charter, Eighty-First Congress, Second Session, on Feb. 2, 3, 6, 8, 9, 13, 15, 17, 20, 1950 (Washington: US Government Printing Office, 1950).
United States Policy in the Korean Crisis (US Department of State Pub. 3922, Far Eastern Series 34).
United States Senate, *Revision of the United Nations Charter*, Report No. 2501 (Washington: US Government Printing Office, 1950).

Secondary Literature

PhD Theses

Frielingsdorf, P., '"Machiavelli of Peace": Dag Hammarskjöld and the Political Role of the Secretary-General of the United Nations', unpublished PhD thesis, London School of Economics and Political Science, 2016.
Kluge, E., 'Decolonisation Interrupted: The West Papuan Campaign for Independence and the United Nations, 1961–1969', unpublished PhD thesis, The University of Sydney, 2020.
Pearson, J., 'From the Civilizing Mission to International Development: France, the United Nations, and the Politics of Family Health in Postwar Africa, 1940–1960', unpublished PhD thesis, New York University, 2013.
Riley, C. L., 'Monstrous Predatory Vampire and Beneficent Fairy-Godmothers: British Post-war Colonial Development in Africa', unpublished PhD thesis, University College London, 2013.
Wagner, F., 'Colonial Internationalism: How Cooperation among Experts Reshaped Colonialism (1830s–1950s)', unpublished PhD thesis, European University Institute, 2016.

Books and Articles

Abrahamsen, R., 'Internationalists, Sovereigntists, Nativists: Contending Visions of World Order in Pan-Africanism', *Review of International Studies*, 46:1 (2020), pp. 56–74.

Abuya, E. O., Krause, U., and Mayblin, M., 'The Neglected Colonial Legacy of the 1951 Refugee Convention', *International Migration*, 59:4 (2021), pp. 265–267.

Aggestam, K. and Towns, A., 'The Gender Turn in Diplomacy: A New Research Agenda', *International Feminist Journal of Politics*, 21:1 (2019), pp. 9–28.

Agmon, M., 'Defending the Upper Gulf: Turkey's Forgotten Partnership', *Journal of Contemporary History*, 21:1 (1986), pp. 81–97.

Ahmed, D. M., *Boundaries and Secession in Africa and International Law: Challenging* Uti Possidetis (Cambridge: Cambridge University Press, 2015).

Akande, D., 'The Diversity of Rules on the Use of Force: Implications for the Evolution of the Law', *EJIL: Talk!*, 11 November 2019, available at www.ejiltalk.org/the-diversity-of-rules-on-the-use-of-force-implications-for-the-evolution-of-the-law/, accessed on 3 June 2019.

Akiboh, A., 'Pocket-Sized Imperialism: US Designs on Colonial Currency', *Diplomatic History*, 41:5 (2017), pp. 874–902.

Aldrich, R., 'The Decolonisation of the Pacific Islands', *Itinerario*, 24:3–4 (2000), pp. 173–191.

Alecou, A., *Communism and Nationalism in Postwar Cyprus, 1945–1955: Politics and Ideologies under British Rule* (New York: Springer, 2016).

Alleyne, M., *Global Lies? Propaganda, the UN and World Order* (New York: Springer, 2003).

Altman, D., 'The Evolution of Territorial Conquest after 1945 and the Limits of the Territorial Integrity Norm', *International Organization*, 74:3 (2020), pp. 490–522.

Amrith, S., *Decolonizing International Health: India and Southeast Asia, 1930–65* (New York: Springer, 2006).

Unruly Waters: How Mountain Rivers and Monsoons Have Shaped South Asia's History (London: Allen Lane, 2018).

Anderson, B., *Java in a Time of Revolution: Occupation and Resistance, 1944–1946* (Ithaca: Cornell University Press, 1972).

Imagined Communities: Reflections on the Origin and Spread of Nationalism, revised edition (London: Verso, 1991).

Anderson, C., *Eyes off the Prize: The United Nations and the African American Struggle for Human Rights, 1944–1955* (Cambridge: Cambridge University Press, 2003).

Angathangelou, A. M. and Ling, L. H. M., 'Desire Industries: Sex Trafficking, UN Peacekeeping, and the Neo-Liberal World Order', *The Brown Journal of World Affairs*, 10:1 (2003), pp. 133–148.

Anghie, A., 'The Evolution of International Law: Colonial and Postcolonial Realities', *Third World Quarterly*, 27:5 (2006), pp. 739–753.

Imperialism, Sovereignty, and the Making of International Law (Cambridge: Cambridge University Press, 2007).

Anievas, A. (ed.), *Race and Racism in International Relations: Confronting the Global Colour Line* (Abingdon: Routledge, 2014).

Arendt, H., 'Peace or Armistice in the Near East?', *The Review of Politics*, 12:1 (1950), pp. 56–82.

Armitage, D., 'The Contagion of Sovereignty: Declarations of Independence since 1776', *South African Historical Journal*, 52:1 (2005), pp. 1–18.

Asante, C., 'Ghana and the United Nations' 1960s Mission in the Congo: A Pan-African Explanation', *Third World Quarterly*, 41:3 (2020), pp. 470–486.

Awasom, N. F., 'Politics and Constitution-Making in Francophone Cameroon, 1959–1960', *Africa Today*, 49:4 (2002), pp. 3–30.

Bajwa, F., *From Kutch to Tashkent: The Indo-Pakistan War of 1965* (London: Hurst, 2013).

Balci, T., 'The Cyprus Crisis and the Southern Flank of NATO (1960–1975)', *International Review of Turkish Studies*, 2:3 (2012), pp. 30–55.

Balibar, É., *We, the People of Europe? Reflections on Transnational Citizenship* (Princeton: Princeton University Press, 2004).

Banivanua Mar, T., *Decolonisation and the Pacific: Indigenous Globalisation and the Ends of Empire* (Cambridge: Cambridge University Press, 2016).

Barkawi, T., 'From Law to History: The Politics of War and Empire', *Global Constitutionalism*, 7:3 (2018), pp. 315–329.

Barnes, R., 'Chief Administrator or Political "Moderator"? Dumbarton Oaks, the Secretary-General and the Korean War', *Journal of Contemporary History*, 54:2 (2019), pp. 347–367.

Barnett, M., 'International Paternalism and Humanitarian Governance', *Global Constitutionalism*, 1:3 (2012), pp. 485–521.

Barros, J., 'Pearson or Lie: The Politics of the Secretary-General's Selection, 1946', *Canadian Journal of Political Science*, 10:1 (1977), pp. 65–92.

Baughan, E., *Saving the Children: Humanitarianism, Internationalism, and Empire* (Oakland: University of California Press, 2021).

Bayley, C. A. et al., 'AHR Conversation: On Transnational History', *The American Historical Review*, 111:5 (2006), pp. 1441–1464.

Beckerman, C., *Unexpected State: British Politics and the Creation of Israel* (Bloomington: Indiana University Press, 2020).

Behdad, A., *Belated Travelers: Orientalism in in the Age of Colonial Dissolution* (Durham: Duke University Press, 1994).

Bell, D., 'What Is Liberalism?', *Political Theory*, 42:6 (2014), pp. 682–715.

Empire, Race and Global Justice (Cambridge: Cambridge University Press, 2019).

Dreamworlds of Race: Empire and the Utopian Destiny of Anglo-America (Princeton: Princeton University Press, 2020).

Bellamy, A. J. and Williams, P. (eds.), *Peace Operations and Global Order* (Abingdon: Routledge, 2014).

Bellamy, A. J., Williams, P. D., and Griffin, S., *Understanding Peacekeeping* (Cambridge: Polity, 2010).

Ben-Dror, E., *Ralph Bunche and the Arab–Israeli Conflict: Mediation and the UN, 1947–1949* (Abingdon: Routledge, 2015).

'Ralph Bunche and the 1949 Armistice Agreements Revisited', *Middle Eastern Studies*, 56:2 (2019), pp. 274–289.

Benton, L., *A Search for Sovereignty: Law and Geography in European Empires, 1400–1900* (Cambridge: Cambridge University Press, 2010).

Bereketeab, R., *Self-Determination and Secession in Africa: The Post-Colonial State* (Abingdon: Taylor and Francis, 2014).

Berger, S. and Scalmer, S. (eds.), *The Transnational Activist: Transformations and Comparisons from the Anglo-World since the Nineteenth Century* (New York: Springer, 2017).

Bevins, V., *The Jakarta Method: Washington's Anticommunist Crusade and the Mass Murder Program that Shaped Our World* (New York: PublicAffairs, 2020).

Biddiscombe, P., 'Branding the United Nations: The Adoption of the UN Insignia and Flag, 1941–1950', *The International History Review*, 42:1 (2020), pp. 19–41.

Bildt, C., 'Dag Hammarskjöld and United Nations Peacekeeping', *UN Chronicle*, 2 (2011), available at https://peacekeeping.un.org/sites/default/files/un_chronicle_carl_bildt_article.pdf, accessed on 3 June 2018.

Blaxland, J., Kelly, M., and Higgins, L. B. (eds.), *In from the Cold: Reflections on Australia's Korean War* (Canberra: ANU Press, 2020).

Boden, R., 'Cold War Economics: Soviet Aid to Indonesia', *Journal of Cold War Studies*, 10:3 (2008), pp. 110–128.

Boose, D. W. and Matray, J. I. (eds.), *The Ashgate Research Companion to the Korean War* (Abingdon: Taylor and Francis, 2016)

Booth, A., 'The Economic Development of Southeast Asia: 1870–1985', *Australian Economic History Review*, 31:1 (1991), pp. 20–52.

Borgwardt, E., *A New Deal for the World: America's Vision for Human Rights* (Cambridge, MA: Harvard University Press, 2005).

Bouleti, E., 'Early Years of British Administration in Cyprus: The Rise of Anti-Colonialism in the Ottoman Muslim Community of Cyprus, 1878–1922', *Journal of Muslims in Europe*, 4 (2015), pp. 70–89.

Bourneuf, P., 'La Société des Nations et la force internationale à Vilna (1920–1921): Un projet précurseur pour le maintien de la paix?', *Relations Internationales*, 166:2 (2016), pp. 87–102.

Brantlinger, P., *Taming Cannibals: Race and the Victorians* (Ithaca: Cornell University Press, 2011).

Brennan, J., *Taifa: Making Nation and Race in Urban Tanzania* (Athens: Ohio University Press, 2012).

'The Secret Lives of Dennis Phombeah: Decolonization, the Cold War, and African Political Intelligence, 1953–1974', *The International History Review*, 43:1 (2020), pp. 153–169.

Briscoe, N., *Britain and UN Peacekeeping 1948–1967* (London: Palgrave Macmillan, 2003).

Brown, C., 'Indonesia's West Irian Case in the UN General Assembly, 1954', *Journal of Southeast Asian Studies*, 7:2 (1976), pp. 260–274.

Bryant, R., *Imagining the Modern: The Cultures of Nationalism in Cyprus* (London: I. B. Tauris, 2004).

Bueno-Lacy, R. and van Houtum, H., 'The Glocal Green Line: The Imperial Cartopolitical Puppeteering of Cyprus', *Geopolitics*, 24:3 (2019), pp. 586–624.

Bulfin, A., 'The Fiction of Gothic Egypt and British Imperial Paranoia: The Curse of the Suez Canal', *English Literature in Transition, 1880–1920*, 54:4 (2011), pp. 411–443.

Burbick, J. and Glass, W. (eds.), *Beyond Imagined Uniqueness: Nationalisms in Contemporary Perspectives* (Cambridge: Cambridge University Press, 2010).

Burke, R., '"The Compelling Dialogue of Freedom": Human Rights at the Bandung Conference', *Human Rights Quarterly*, 28:4 (2006), pp. 947–965.

Decolonization and the Evolution of International Human Rights (Philadelphia: Philadelphia University Press, 2010).

'Premature Memorials to the United Nations Human Rights Program: International Postage Stamps and the Commemoration of the 1948 Universal Declaration of Human Rights', *History and Memory*, 28:2 (2016), pp. 152–181.

Burns, W. J., *Economic Aid and American Policy toward Egypt, 1955–1981* (Albany: SUNY Press, 1985).

Calandri, E., Caviglia, D., and Varsori, A., *Détente in Cold War Europe: Politics and Diplomacy in the Mediterranean and the Middle East* (London: Bloomsbury, 2015).

Caplan, N., 'A Tale of Two Cities: The Rhodes and Lausanne Conferences, 1949', *Journal of Palestinian Studies*, 21:3 (1992), pp. 5–34.

Caron, V., *Uneasy Asylum: France and the Jewish Refugee Crisis, 1933–1942* (Palo Alto: Stanford University Press, 1999).

Carroll, M., *Pearson's Peacekeepers: Canada and the United Nations Emergency Force, 1956–1967* (Vancouver: University of British Columbia Press, 2009).

Carruthers, W., *Flooded Pasts: UNESCO, Nubia, and the Recolonization of Archaeology* (Ithaca: Cornell University Press, 2022).

Carswell, A. J., 'Unblocking the UN Security Council: The Uniting for Peace Resolution', *Journal of Conflict & Security Law*, 18:3 (2013), pp. 453–480.

Carter, D. B. and Goemans, H. E., 'The Making of the Territorial Order: New Borders and the Emergence of Interstate Conflict', *International Organization*, 65:2 (2011), pp. 275–309.

Carvin, S. and Williams, M. J., *Law, Science, Liberalism and the American Way of Warfare: The Quest for Humanity in Conflict* (Cambridge: Cambridge University Press, 2015).

Chandhoke, N., *Contested Secessions: Rights, Self-Determination, Democracy, and Kashmir* (Oxford: Oxford University Press, 2012).

Chatzicharalampous, M. and Stolte, C., 'Technologies of Emergency: Cyprus at the Intersection of Decolonisation and the Cold War', *Contemporary European History*, (2022), pp. 1–17.

Chauvel, R., 'Australia's Strategic Environment: The Problem of Papua', *Agenda: A Journal of Policy Analysis and Reform*, 11:1 (2004), pp. 39–52.

Constructing Papuan Nationalism: History, Ethnicity, and Adaptation (Washington, DC: East-West Center, 2005).

'Papuan Political Imaginings of the 1960s: International Conflict and Local Nationalisms' (2008), available at http://resources.huygens.knaw.nl/indonesischebetrekkingen1945-1969/DekolonisatieVanIndonesieEnHetZelfbeschikkingsrechtVanDePapoea/papers_pdf/chauvel, accessed on 7 December 2018.

Chem-Langhëë, B., *The Paradoxes of Self-Determination in the Cameroons under United Kingdom Administration: The Search for Identity, Well-Being, and Continuity* (Lanham: University Press of America, 2004).

Chesterman, S., 'East Timor in Transition: Self-Determination, State-Building and the United Nations', *International Peacekeeping*, 9:1 (2002), pp. 45–76.

You, the People: The United Nations, Transitional Administration, and State-Building (Oxford: Oxford University Press, 2005).

Secretary or General: The UN Secretary-General in World Politics (Cambridge: Cambridge University Press, 2007).

Chinkin, C. and Baetens, F. (eds.), *Sovereignty, Statehood and State Responsibility: Essays in Honour of James Crawford* (Cambridge: Cambridge University Press, 2015).

Chourchoulis, D., *The Southern Flank of NATO, 1951–1959: Military Strategy or Political Stabilization* (Lanham: Lexington Books, 2014).

Clavin, P., 'The Austrian Hunger Crisis and the Genesis of International Organization after the First World War', *International Affairs*, 90:2 (2014), pp. 265–278.

'The Ben Pimlott Memorial Lecture 2019 – Britain and the Making of Global Order after 1919', *Twentieth Century British History*, 31:3 (2020), pp. 340–359.

Clerc, L., et al. (eds.), *Histories of Public Diplomacy and Nation Branding in the Nordic and Baltic Countries* (Leiden: Brill, 2015).

Cohen, A., *The Politics and Economics of Decolonization in Africa: The Failed Experiment of the Central African Federation* (London: Bloomsbury, 2017).

Cohen, M., 'The United Nations Secretariat – Some Constitutional and Administrative Developments', *American Journal of International Law*, 49:3 (1955), pp. 295–319.

'The Demise of UNEF', *International Journal*, 23:1 (1968), pp. 18–51.

Collins, C. J. L., 'The Cold War Comes to Africa: Cordier and the 1960 Congo Crisis', *Journal of International Affairs*, 47:1 (1993), pp. 243–269.

Collins, M., 'Decolonisation and the "Federal Moment"', *Diplomacy & Statecraft*, 24:1 (2013), pp. 21–40.

Constandinos, A., *America, Britain and the Cyprus Crisis of 1974: Calculated Conspiracy or Foreign Policy Failure?* (Bloomington: AuthorHouse, 2009).

Cooper, A. F., Heine, J., and Thakur, R. (eds.), *The Oxford Handbook of Modern Diplomacy* (Oxford: Oxford University Press, 2013).

Cooper, F. and Packard, R. (eds.), *International Development and the Social Sciences: Essays on the History and Politics of Knowledge* (Berkeley: University of California Press, 1997).

Cooper, F. and Packard, R. *Africa since 1940: The Past of the Present* (Cambridge: Cambridge University Press, 2002).

'Development, Modernization, and the Social Sciences in the Era of Decolonization: The Examples of British and French Africa', *Revue d'histoire des sciences humaines*, 10:1 (2004), pp. 9–38.

'Writing the History of Development', *Journal of Modern European History*, 8:1 (2010), pp. 5–23.

Citizenship between Empire and Nation: Remaking France and French Africa, 1945–1960 (Princeton: Princeton University Press, 2014).

Cordier, A. W. and Foote, W., *Public Papers of the Secretaries-General of the United Nations. Volume I: Trygve Lie, 1946–1953* (New York: Columbia University Press, 1969).

Cordier, A. and Harrelson, M. (eds.), *Public Papers of the Secretaries-General of the United Nations: Volume VI, U Thant, 1961–1964* (New York: Cornell University Press, 1976).

Craig, C., *Glimmer of a New Leviathan: Total War in the Realism of Niebuhr, Morgenthau, and Waltz* (New York: Columbia University Press, 2003).

Craven, M., Pahuja, S., and Simpson, G. (eds.), *International Law and the Cold War* (Cambridge: Cambridge University Press, 2019).

de Cunha, D., *The Invention of Rivers: Alexander's Eye and Ganga's Descent* (Philadelphia: University of Pennsylvania Press, 2018).

Cunliffe, P., *Cosmopolitan Dystopia: International Intervention and the Failure of the West* (Manchester: Manchester University Press, 2020).

Dalberto, S. A., 'Hidden Debates over the Status of the Casamance during the Decolonization Process in Senegal: Regionalism, Territorialism, and Federalism at a Crossroads, 1946–62', *Journal of African History*, 61:1 (2020), pp. 67–88.

Darwin, J., 'Diplomacy and Decolonization', *The Journal of Imperial and Commonwealth History*, 28:3 (2000), pp. 5–24.

Davey, E., *Idealism beyond Borders: The French Revolutionary Left and the Rise of Humanitarianism, 1954–1988* (Cambridge: Cambridge University Press, 2015).

Declercq, R., '"From Cape to Katanga": South African Expansionism, White Settlers and the Congo (1910–1963)', *South African Historical Journal*, 72:4 (2020), pp. 604–626.

Defert, G., *L 'Indonésie et la Nouvelle-Guinée Occidentale: Maintien des frontières coloniales ou respect des identités commaunitaires* (Paris: L'Harmattan, 1996).

Delaney, D. E., *Corps Commanders: Five British and Canadian General at War, 1939–1945* (Vancouver: UBC Press, 2011).

Demetriou, C., 'Divide and Rule Cyprus? Decolonisation as Process', *Commonwealth & Comparative Politics*, 57:4 (2019), pp. 403–420.

Desgrandchamps, M., 'Entre ambitions universalistes et préjugés raciaux: La mission du Comité international de la Croix-Rouge en Afrique méridionale et centrale au début des années 1960', *Histoire@Politique*, 40 (2020), pp. 1–16

Di-Capua, Y., *No Exit: Arab Existentialism, Jean-Paul Sartre, and Decolonization* (Chicago: University of Chicago Press, 2018).

van Dijk, B., *Preparing for War: The Making of the Geneva Conventions* (Oxford: Oxford University Press, 2021).

Dikomitis, L., *Cyprus and Its Places of Desire: Cultures of Displacement among Greek and Turkish-Cypriot Refugees* (London: I. B. Tauris, 2012).

Dimitrakis, P., 'British Intelligence and the Cyprus Insurgency, 1955–1959', *International Journal of Intelligence and Counterintelligence*, 21:2 (2008), pp. 375–394.

Failed Alliances of the Cold War: Britain's Strategy and Ambitions in Asia and the Middle East (London: Bloomsbury, 2011).

Dinkel, J., *The Non-Aligned Movement: Genesis, Organization and Politics (1927–1992)* (Leiden: Brill, 2019).

Donaldson, M., 'The League of Nations, Ethiopia, and the Making of States', *Humanity*, 11:1 (2020), pp. 6–31.

Dorn, A. W. and Pauk, R, 'Unsung Mediator: U Thant and the Cuban Missile Crisis', *Diplomatic History*, 33:2 (2009), pp. 261–292.

Dorn, C. and Ghodsee, K., 'The Cold War Politicisation of Literacy: Communism, UNESCO, and the World Bank', *Diplomatic History*, 36:2 (2012), pp. 373–398.

Doyle, M. W., 'Liberalism and World Politics', *The American Political Science Review*, 80:4 (1986), pp. 1151–1169.

Drohan, B., *Brutality in an Age of Human Rights: Activism and Counterinsurgency at the End of the British Empire* (Ithaca: Cornell University Press, 2017).

Drooglever, P., *An Act of Free Choice: Decolonisation and the Right to Self-Determination in West Papua* (London: Oneworld Publications, 2009).

Dubnov, A. and Robson, L. (eds.), *Partitions: A Transnational History of Twentieth-Century Territorial Separatism* (Palo Alto: Stanford University Press, 2019).

Duffield, M. and Hewitt, V. (eds.), *Empire, Development and Colonialism: The Past in the Present* (New York: Boydell and Brewer, 2009).

Dunn, K., *Imagining the Congo: The International Relations of Identity* (New York: Springer, 2003).

Dunne, T. and Flockhart, T. (eds.), *Liberal World Orders* (Oxford: Oxford University Press/British Academy, 2013).

Durand, P.-M., 'Leçons congolaises: L'ONUC (1960–1964) ou "la plus grande des operations": Un contre-modèle?', *Relations Internationales*, 3:127 (2006), pp. 53–70.

Easter, D., 'Active Soviet Military Support for Indonesia during the 1962 West Papua Crisis', *Cold War History*, 15:2 (2015), pp. 201–220.

Easterly, W., *The White Man's Burden: Why the West's Efforts to Aid the Rest Have Done So Much Ill and So Little Good* (London: Penguin Books, 2006).

Edelstein, D., Geroulanos, S., and Wheatley, N. (eds.), *Power and Time: Temporalities in Conflict and the Making of History* (Chicago: University of Chicago Press, 2020).

Eggers, N., Pearson, J. L., and Almada e Santos, A. (eds.), *The United Nations and Decolonization* (Abingdon: Routledge, 2020).

El Shakry, O., *The Great Social Laboratory: Subjects of Knowledge in Colonial and Postcolonial Egypt* (Palo Alto: University of Stanford Press, 2007).

El-Ayouty, Y., *The United Nations and Decolonization: The Role of Afro-Asia* (New York: Springer, 2012).

Elson, R. E., 'Marginality, Morality, and the Nationalist Impulse: Papua, the Netherlands and Indonesia: A Review Article', *Bijdragen en Mededelingen betreffende de Geschiedenis der derlanden*, 122:1 (2006), pp. 65–71.

The Idea of Indonesia: A History (Cambridge: Cambridge University Press, 2008).

Enloe, C., *Bananas, Beaches and Bases: Making Feminist Sense of International Politics: Second Edition* (Oakland: University of California Press, 2014).

Escobar, A., *Encountering Development: The Making and Unmaking of the Third World* (Princeton: Princeton University Press, 1995).

Eslava, L., Fakhri, M., and Nesiah, V. (eds.), *Bandung, Global History, and International Law: Critical Pasts and Pending Futures* (Cambridge: Cambridge University Press, 2017).

Eves, R., 'Unsettling Settler Colonialism: Debates over Climate and Colonization in New Guinea, 1875–1914', *Ethnic and Racial Studies*, 28:2 (2005), pp. 304–330.

Ewing, C., 'The Colombo Powers: Crafting Diplomacy in the Third World and Launching Afro-Asia at Bandung', *Cold War History*, 19:1 (2019), pp. 1–19.

'"With a Minimum of Bitterness": Decolonization, the Right to Self-Determination, and the Arab-Asian Group', *Journal of Global History*, 17:2 (2022), pp. 254–271.

Faustmann, H., 'Independence Postponed: Cyprus 1959–1960', *The Cyprus Review*, 14:2 (2002), pp. 99–119.

Feeney, W. R., 'Sino-Soviet Competition in the United Nations', *Asian Survey*, 17:9 (1977), pp. 809–829.

Fejzula, M., 'The Cosmopolitan Historiography of Twentieth-Century Federalism', *The Historical Journal*, 64:2 (2021), pp. 477–500.

Feldman, I., 'Ad Hoc Humanity: UN Peacekeeping and the Limits of International Community in Gaza', *American Anthropologist*, 112:3 (2010), pp. 416–429.

Ferguson, J., *The Anti-Politics Machine: "Development", Depoliticisation, and Bureaucratic Power in Lesotho* (Minneapolis: University of Minnesota Press, 1998).

Ferns, N., *Australia in the Age of International Development, 1945–1975: Colonial and Foreign Aid Policy in Papua New Guinea and Southeast Asia* (London: Springer, 2020).

Fibiger, M., 'A Diplomatic Counter-revolution: Indonesian diplomacy and the Invasion of East Timor', *Modern Asian Studies*, 55:2 (2021), pp. 587–628.

Finnie, D. H., *Shifting Lines in the Sand: Kuwait's Elusive Frontier with Iraq* (Cambridge, MA: Harvard University Press, 1992).

Firestone, B. J., 'Failed Mediation: U Thant, the Johnson Administration, and the Vietnam War', *Diplomatic History*, 37:5 (2013), pp. 1060–1089.

Fisher, R. J., 'Cyprus: The Failure of Mediation and the Escalation of an Identity-Based Conflict to an Adversarial Impasse', *Journal of Peace Research*, 38:3 (2001), pp. 307–326.

Fletcher, M. E., 'The Suez Canal and World Shipping, 1869–1914', *The Journal of Economic History*, 18:4 (1958), pp. 556–573.

Foray, J. L., 'The Republic at the Table, with Decolonisation on the Agenda: The United Nations Security Council and the Question of Indonesian Representation, 1946–1947', *Itinerario*, 45:1 (2021), pp. 124–151.

Forbes, C., *The Korean War* (Sydney: Macmillan Publishers Australia, 2010).

Fouskas, V. K. and Tackie, A. O., *Cyprus: The Post-Imperial Constitution* (London: Pluto Press, 2009).

French, D., 'Nasty Not Nice: British Counter-Insurgency Doctrine and Practice, 1945–1967', *Small Wars and Insurgencies*, 23:4–5 (2012), pp. 744–761.

Fighting EOKA: The British Counter-Insurgency Campaign on Cyprus, 1955–1959 (Oxford: Oxford University Press, 2015).

'Toads and Informers: How the British Treated Their Collaborators during the Cyprus Emergency, 1955–1959', *The International History Review*, 39:1 (2017), pp. 71–88.

Fröhlich, M. and Williams, A. (eds.), *The UN Secretary-General and the Security Council: A Dynamic Relationship* (Oxford: Oxford University Press, 2018).

Fukuyama, F., *The End of History and the Last Man* (New York: Free Press, 1992).

Fullerton, G. A., *UNESCO in the Congo* (Paris: UNESCO, 1964).

Garavini, G., *After Empires: European Integration, Decolonization, and the Challenge from the Global South 1957–1986* (Oxford: Oxford University Press, 2012).

Gardner, K. J., *The Frontier Complex: Geopolitics and the Making of the India-China Border, 1846–1962* (Cambridge: Cambridge University Press, 2021).

Gatrell, P., *The Making of the Modern Refugee* (Oxford: Oxford University Press, 2013).

Gendebien, P., *L'Intervention des Nations Unies au Congo. 1960–1964* (Berlin: Walter de Gruyter, 1967), pp. 64–65.

Gerard, E., *Death in the Congo: Murdering Patrice Lumumba* (Cambridge, MA: Harvard University Press, 2015).

Gerber, L. G., 'The Baruch Plan and the Origins of the Cold War', *Diplomatic History*, 6:1 (1982), pp. 69–95

Gerits, F. and Grilli, M. (eds.), *Visions of African Unity: New Perspectives on the History of Pan-Africanism and African Unification Projects* (London: Palgrave Macmillan, 2020).

Getachew, A., 'Securing Postcolonial Independence: Kwame Kkrumah and the Federal Idea in the Age of Decolonisation', *Ab Imperio*, 3 (2018), pp. 89–113.

Worldmaking after Empire: The Rise and Fall of Self-Determination (Princeton: Princeton University Press, 2019).

Ghettas, M. L., *Algeria and the Cold War: International Relations and the Struggle for Autonomy* (London: Bloomsbury, 2017).

Ghosh, A., 'The Global Reservation: Notes toward an Ethnography of International Peacekeeping', *Cultural Anthropology*, 9:3 (1994), pp. 412–422.

Gibbs, D., *The Political Economy of Third World Intervention: Mines, Money, and U.S. Policy in the Congo Crisis* (Chicago: University of Chicago Press, 1991).

'The United Nations, International Peacekeeping and the Question of "Impartiality": Revisiting the Congo Operation of 1960', *Journal of Modern African Studies*, 38:3 (2000), pp. 359–382.

Gibler, D. M., *The Territorial Peace: Borders, State Development, and International Conflict* (Cambridge: Cambridge University Press, 2012).

Gienow-Hecht, J., 'Nation Branding: A Useful Category for International History', *Diplomacy & Statecraft*, 30:4 (2019), pp. 755–779.

Gijs, A., 'Fighting the Red Peril in the Congo, Paradoxes and Perspectives on an Equivocal Challenge to Belgium and the West (1947–1960)', *Cold War History*, 16:3 (2016), pp. 273–290.

Given, M., 'Maps, Fields, and Boundary Cairns: Demarcation and Resistance in Colonial Cyprus', *International Journal of Historical Archaeology*, 6:1 (2002), pp. 1–22.

Glazebrook, G. D., 'The Middle Powers in the United Nations System', *International Organization*, 1:2 (1947), pp. 307–318.

Goebel, M., *Anti-Imperial Metropolis: Interwar Paris and the Seeds of Third World Nationalism* (Cambridge: Cambridge University Press, 2015).

Goedde, P., *The Politics of Peace: A Global Cold War History* (Oxford: Oxford University Press, 2019).

Goktepe, C., *British Foreign Policy toward Turkey, 1959–1965* (Abingdon: Routledge, 2013).

Gordon Lauren, P., 'First Principles of Racial Equality: History and the Politics and Diplomacy of Human Rights Provisions in the United Nations Charter', *Human Rights Quarterly*, 5:1 (1983), pp. 1–26.

Gordenker, L., *The United Nations and the Peaceful Unification of Korea: The Politics of Field Operations, 1947–1950* (New York: Springer, 2012).

Gorman, D., 'Britain, India, and the United Nations: Colonialism and the Development of International Governance, 1945–1960', *Journal of Global History*, 9:3 (2014), pp. 471–490.

Goulding, M., 'The Evolution of United Nations Peacekeeping', *International Affairs*, 69:3 (1993), pp. 451–464.

Granatstein, J. L. and Suedfeld, P., 'Tommy Burns as a Military Leader: A Case Study Using Integrative Complexity', *Canadian Military History*, 3:2 (1994), pp. 63–67.

Grove, E., 'UN Armed Forces and the Military Staff Committee: A Look Back', *International Security*, 17:4 (1993), pp. 172–182.

Groves, Z., 'Transnational Networks and Regional Solidarity: The Case of the Central African Federation, 1953–1963', *African Studies*, 72 (2013), pp. 155–175.

Gupta, S., 'Frontiers in Flux: Indo-Tibetan Border: 1946–1948', *India Quarterly*, 77:1 (2021), pp. 42–58.

Guyot-Réchard, B., 'Tangled Lands: Burma and India's Unfinished Separation, 1937–1948', *The Journal of Asian Studies*, 80:2 (2021), pp. 293–315.

Haas, P. M., 'Introduction: Epistemic Communities and International Policy Coordination', *International Organization*, 46:1 (1992), pp. 1–35.

Haddad, E. A., 'Digging to India: Modernity, Imperialism, and the Suez Canal', *Victorian Studies*, 47.3 (2005), pp. 363–396.

Hadjiathanasiou, M., 'Colonial Rule, Cultural Relations and the British Council in Cyprus, 1935–55', *The Journal of Imperial and Commonwealth History*, 46:6 (2018), pp. 1096–1124.

Propaganda and the Cyprus Revolt: Rebellion, Counter-Insurgency and the Media, 1955–59 (London: Bloomsbury, 2020).

Hamblin, J. D., *The Wretched Atom: America's Global Gamble with Peaceful Nuclear Technology* (Oxford: Oxford University Press, 2021).

Hamilton, T. J., 'The UN and Trygve Lie', *Foreign Affairs*, 29:1 (1950), pp. 67–77.

Harbottle, M., *The Impartial Soldier* (Oxford: Oxford University Press, 1970).

Haron, M. J., 'The British Decision to Give the Palestine Question to the United Nations', *Middle Eastern Studies*, 17:2 (1981), pp. 241–248.

Hatto, R., 'From Peacekeeping to Peacebuilding: The Evolution of the Role of the United Nations in Peace Operations', *International Review of the Red Cross*, 95:891–892 (2013), pp. 495–515.

Hatzivassiliou, E., 'Cyprus at the Crossroads, 1959–1963', *European History Quarterly*, 35:4 (2005), pp. 523–540.

Greece and the Cold War: Front Line State, 1952–1967 (Abington: Routledge, 2006).

'Cold War Pressures, Regional Strategies, and Relative Decline: British Military and Strategic Planning for Cyprus, 1950–1960', *The Journal of Military History*, 73:4 (2009), pp. 1143–1166.

Hazzard, S., *Defeat of an Ideal: A Study of the Self-Destruction of the United Nations* (London: Little, Brown Book, 1973).

Heise, J. and Ketzmerick, M., 'Points of Division: The Role of Agency, Security and Shrinking Spaces in the UN Trusteeship State Building of Togoland and Cameroon', paper delivered at ISA, 1–3 August 2019 in Accra, Ghana.

Heiss, M. A., 'Exposing "Red Colonialism": U.S. Propaganda at the United Nations, 1953–1963', *Journal of Cold War Studies*, 17:3 (2015), pp. 82–115.

Fulfilling the Sacred Trust: The UN Campaign for International Accountability for Dependent Territories in the Era of Decolonization (Ithaca: Cornell University Press, 2020).

Heller, J., 'Failure of a Mission: Bernadotte and Palestine, 1948', *Journal of Contemporary History*, 14:3 (1979), pp. 515–534.

Heller, P. B., *The United Nations under Dag Hammarskjold, 1953–1961* (Lanham: Scarecrow Press, 2001).

Henderson, E. A., 'Hidden in Plain Sight: Racism in International Relations Theory', *Cambridge Review of International Affairs*, 26:1 (2016), pp. 71–92.

Henderson, W., *West New Guinea: The Dispute and Its Settlement* (New Jersey: Seton Hall University Press, 1973).

Hendrickx, C., 'Tshombe's Secessionist State of Katanga: Agency against the Odds', *Third World Quarterly*, 42:8 (2021), pp. 1809–1828.

Henke, M. E., *Constructing Allied Cooperation: Diplomacy, Payments and Power in Multilateral Military Coalitions* (Ithaca: Cornell University Press, 2019).

Henry, C. P., *Ralph Bunche: Model Negro or American Other?* (New York: NYU Press, 1999).

Henry, M., 'Parades, Parties and Pests: Contradictions of Everyday Life in Peacekeeping Economies', *Journal of Intervention and Statebuilding*, 9:3 (2015), pp. 372–390.

Hetherington, P. and Sluga, G., 'Liberal and Illiberal Internationalisms', *Journal of World History*, 31:1 (2020), pp. 1–9.

Hilderbrand, R. C., *Dumbarton Oaks: The Origins of the United Nations and the Search for Postwar Security* (Chapel Hill: UNC Press Books, 2001).

Hill, R. A. and Keller, E. J. (eds.), *Trustee for the Human Community: Ralph J. Bunche, the United Nations and the Decolonization of Africa* (Athens: Ohio University Press, 2010).

Hirsch, F., *Soviet Judgment at Nuremberg: A New History of the International Military Tribunal after World War II* (Oxford: Oxford University Press, 2020).

Hobson, J. M., *The Eurocentric Conception of World Politics: Western International Theory, 1760–2010* (Cambridge: Cambridge University Press, 2012).

Hodge, J. M., *Triumph of the Expert: Agrarian Doctrines of Development and the Legacies of British Colonialism* (Athens: Ohio University Press, 2007).

'British Colonial Expertise, Post-Colonial Careering and the Early History of International Development', *Journal of Modern European History*, 8:1 (2010), pp. 24–46.

Hogan, M., 'The 1948 Massacre at Deir Yassin Revisited', *The Historian*, 63:2 (2001), pp. 309–333.

Holland, R. F., *European Decolonization 1918–1981: An Introductory Survey* (London: Palgrave, 1985).

Hopkins, B. D., *Ruling the Savage Periphery: Frontier Governance and the Making of the Modern State* (Cambridge, MA: Harvard University Press, 2020).

Horne, J., 'Demobilizing the Mind: France and the Legacy of the Great War, 1919–1939', *French History and Civilization*, 2006 Seminar Papers (Published 2009), Volume 2, pp. 1–19, available at https://h-france.net/rude/vol2/horne2/.

Huber, V., 'Connecting Colonial Seas: The "International Colonisation" of Port Said and the Suez Canal during and after the First World War', *European Review of History*, 19:1 (2012), pp. 141–161.

Channelling Mobilities: Migration and Globalisation in the Suez Canal Region and Beyond, 1869–1914 (Cambridge: Cambridge University Press, 2013).

Humbert, L., *Reinventing French Aid: The Politics of Humanitarian Relief in French-Occupied Germany, 1945–1952* (Cambridge: Cambridge University Press, 2021).

Hunt, N. R., *A Colonial Lexicon: Of Birth Ritual, Medicalisation, and Mobility in the Congo* (Durham: Duke University Press, 1999).

Hunter, E., *Political Thought and the Public Sphere in Tanzania: Freedom, Democracy and Citizenship in the Era of Decolonization* (Cambridge: Cambridge University Press, 2015).

Hunter, F. R., 'Tourism and Empire: The Thomas Cook & Son Enterprise on the Nile, 1868–1914' *Middle Eastern Studies*, 40:5 (2004), pp. 28–54.

Hurd, I., *After Anarchy: Legitimacy and Power in the United Nations Security Council* (Princeton: Princeton University Press, 2008).

Hurrell, A., *On Global Order: Power, Values, and the Constitution of International Society* (Oxford: Oxford University Press, 2007).

Hyam, R., 'The Geopolitical Origins of the Central African Federation: Britain, Rhodesia and South Africa, 1948–1953', *Historical Journal*, 30 (1987), pp. 145–172.

Britain's Declining Empire: The Road to Decolonisation, 1918–1968 (Cambridge: Cambridge University Press, 2007).

Hwang, B., 'Revolutionary Armed Struggle and the Origins of the Korean War', *Asian Perspective*, 12:2 (1988), pp. 123–138.

Ikenberry, G. J., 'Liberal Internationalism 3.0: America and the Dilemmas of Liberal World Order', *Perspectives on Politics*, 7:1 (2009), pp. 71–87.

Liberal Leviathan: The Origins, Crisis, and Transformation of the American World Order (Princeton: Princeton University Press, 2012).

A World Safe for Democracy: Liberal Internationalism and the Crises of Global Order (New Haven: Yale University Press, 2020).

Ikonomou, H. A., 'The Administrative Anatomy of Failure: The League of Nations Disarmament Section, 1919–1925', *Contemporary European History*, 30 (2021), pp. 321–334.

Ikonomou, H. A., Gram-Skjoldager, K., and Kahlert, T. (eds.), *Organizing the 20th-Century World: International Organizations and the Emergence of International Public Administration, 1920–1960s* (London: Bloomsbury, 2020)

Ilan, A., *Bernadotte in Palestine: A Study in Contemporary Humanitarian Knight-Errantry* (New York: Palgrave Macmillan, 1989).

Ilan Troen, S., 'The Protocol of Sèvres: British/French/Israeli Collusion against Egypt, 1956', *Israel Studies*, 1:2 (1996), pp. 122–139.

Immerman, R. H., *John Foster Dulles and the Diplomacy of the Cold War* (Princeton: Princeton University Press, 1992).

Imy, K., *Faithful Fighters: Identity and Power in the British-Indian Army* (Palo Alto: Stanford University Press, 2019).

Inyang, E. E., 'Biafran Postage Stamps (1967–1970) and the Rhetoric of Sovereign Promise', *Nations and Nationalism*, 27:4 (2021), pp. 1213–1230.

Irfan, A. E., 'Petitioning for Palestine: Refugee Appeals to International Authorities', *Contemporary Levant*, 5:2 (2020), pp. 79–96.

Iriye, A., 'The Internationalization of History', *The American Historical Review*, 94:1 (1989), pp. 1–10.

Global Community: The Role of International Organizations in the Making of the Contemporary World (Berkeley: University of California Press, 2002).

Islam, N., 'Colonial Legacy, Administrative Reform and Politics: Pakistan 1947–1987', *Public Administration and Development*, 9 (1989), pp. 271–285.

Ivison, D., et al. (eds.), *Political Theory and the Rights of Indigenous Peoples* (Cambridge: Cambridge University Press, 2000).

Jaarsma, S. R., 'An Ethnographer's Tale: Ethnographic Research in Netherlands (West) New Guinea (1950–1962)', *Oceania*, 62:2 (1992), pp. 128–146.

'"Your Work Is of No Use to Us...": Administrative Interests in Ethnographic Research West Papua, 1950–1962)', *The Journal of Pacific History*, 29:2 (1994), pp. 153–171.

Jackson, R. O., 'The Failure of Categories: Haitians in the United Nations Organization in the Congo, 1960–1964', *Journal of Haitian Studies*, 20:1 (2014), pp. 34–64.

Jackson, S. and O'Malley, A. (eds.), *The Institution of International Order: From the League of Nations to the United Nations* (Abingdon: Routledge, 2018).

Jagtiani, S. L., '"Foreign Armies Are Functioning on Asian Soil": India, Indonesian Decolonisation and the Onset of the Cold War (1945–1949)', *Cold War History*, (2022), pp. 1–22.

James, A., 'The Soviet Troika Proposals', *The World Today*, 17:9 (1961), pp. 368–376.

The Politics of Peacekeeping (London: Cox & Wyman, 1969).

Peacekeeping in International Politics (London: Palgrave Macmillan, 1990).

Britain and the Congo Crisis, 1960–1963 (New York: Springer, 1996).

'Britain, the Cold War, and the Congo Crisis, 1960–63', *The Journal of Imperial and Commonwealth History*, 28:3 (2000), pp. 152–168.

'Canada and the Cyprus Crisis of 1963–1964: Two Mysteries and a Mistake', *The Commonwealth Journal of International Affairs*, 91:365 (2002), pp. 415–430.

Keeping the Peace in the Cyprus Crisis of 1963–64 (London: Palgrave Macmillan, 2002).

James, L., *George Padmore and Decolonization from Below: Pan-Africanism, the Cold War, and the End of Empire* (London: Palgrave Macmillan, 2014).

James, L. and Leake, E. (eds.), *Decolonization and the Cold War: Negotiating Independence* (London: Bloomsbury Academic, 2015).

James, M., '"Who Can Sing the Song of MSF?": The Politics of "Proximity" and Performing Humanitarianism in Eastern DRC', *Journal of Humanitarian Affairs*, 2:2 (2020), pp. 31–29.

'Humanitarian Fables: Morals, Meanings and Consequences for Humanitarian Practice', *Third World Quarterly*, 43:2 (2022), pp. 475–493.

Jankowski, J. P., *Nasser's Egypt, Arab Nationalism, and the United Arab Republic* (Boulder: Lynne Rienner, 2002),

Jensen, S. L. B., *The Making of International Human Rights: The 1960s, Decolonization, and the Reconstruction of Global Values* (Cambridge: Cambridge University Press, 2016).

Jerónimo, M. B. and Monteiro, J. P. (eds.), *Internationalism, Imperialism and the Formation of the Contemporary World: The Pasts of the Present* (New York: Springer, 2017).

Jerónimo, M. B. and Pinto, A. C. (eds.), *The Ends of European Colonial Empires: Cases and Comparisons* (London: Palgrave Macmillan, 2015).

Jian, C. et al. (eds.), *The Routledge Handbook of the Global Sixties: Between Protest and Nation-Building* (London: Routledge, 2018).

Johnson, E., '"The Umpire on Whom the Sun Never Sets": Dag Hammarskjöld's Political Role and the British at Suez', *Diplomacy and Statecraft*, 8:1 (1997), pp. 249–278.

'Britain and the Cyprus Problem at the United Nations, 1954–58', *The Journal of Imperial and Commonwealth History*, 28:3 (2000), pp. 113–130.

'Keeping Cyprus off the Agenda: British and American Relations at the United Nations, 1954–1958', *Diplomacy and Statecraft*, 11:3 (2000), pp. 227–255.

Jones, B. G., 'Race in the Ontology of International Order', *Political Studies*, 56:4 (2008), pp. 907–927.

Joy, R., 'Facing Decolonisation: British Agricultural Officers in Postcolonial East Africa', paper delivered at BIHG, 31 August 2018 in Exeter, Britain.

Kalb, M. G., *The Congo Cables: The Cold War in Africa – From Eisenhower to Kennedy* (Basingstoke: Macmillan, 1982).

Kalmanovitz, P., *The Laws of War in International Thought* (Cambridge: Cambridge University Press, 2017).

Katsakioris, C., 'The Lumumba University in Moscow: Higher Education for a Soviet–Third World Alliance, 1960–91', *The Journal of Global History*, 14:2 (2019), pp. 281–300.

Kattan, V., *From Coexistence to Conquest: International Law and the Origins of the Arab-Israeli Conflict, 1891–1949* (London: Pluto Press, 2009).

'The Persistence of Partition: Boundary-Making, Imperialism, and International Law', *Political Geography*, 94 (2022), pp. 1–16.

Kaufmann, C., 'When All Else Fails: Ethnic Population Transfers and Partitions in the Twentieth Century', *International Security*, 23:2 (1998), pp. 120–156.

Kearn Jr, D. W., 'The Baruch Plan and the Quest for Atomic Disarmament', *Diplomacy & Statecraft*, 21:1 (2010), pp. 41–67.

Kelén, E., *Hammarskjöld* (New York: Putnam, 1966).

Keller, R., 'The Latin American Missile Crisis', *Diplomatic History*, 39:2 (2015), pp. 195–222.

Kelly, J. D. and Kaplan, M., *Represented Communities: Fiji and World Decolonization* (Chicago: University of Chicago Press, 2001).
Kelly, S., *America's Tyrant: The CIA and Mobutu of Zaire* (New York: American University Press, 1993).
Kelsen, H., *The Law of the United Nations: A Critical Analysis of Its Fundamental Problems* (London: London Institute of World Affairs, 1950).
'Recent Trends in the Law of the United Nations', *Social Research*, 18:2 (1951), pp. 135–151.
Kent, J., 'The Neo-Colonialism of Decolonisation: Katangan Secession and the Bringing of the Cold War to the Congo', *The Journal of Imperial and Commonwealth History*, 45:1 (2017), pp. 93–130.
Ker-Lindsay, J., *Britain and the Cyprus Crisis, 1963–1964* (Berkeley: Bibliopolis, 2009).
The Cyprus Problem: What Everyone Needs to Know (Oxford: Oxford University Press, 2011).
Kille, K. J., *The UN Secretary-General and Moral Authority: Ethics and Religion in International Leadership* (Washington: Georgetown University Press, 2007).
King, P., 'Morning Star Rising? Indonesia Raya and the New Papuan Nationalism', *Indonesia*, 73 (2002), pp. 89–127.
Kıralp, Ş., 'Cyprus between Enosis, Partition and Independence: Domestic Politics, Diplomacy and External Interventions (1967–74)', *Journal of Balkan and Near Eastern Studies*, 19:6 (2017), pp. 591–609.
'Defending Cyprus in the Early Postcolonial Era: Makarios, NATO, USSR and the NAM (1964–1967)', *Journal of Balkan and Near Eastern Studies*, 21:4 (2018), pp. 367–386.
Klieman, A. S., 'The Resolution of Conflicts through Territorial Partition: The Palestine Experience', *Comparative Studies in Society and History*, 22:2 (1980), pp. 281–300.
Klose, F. (ed.), *The Emergence of Humanitarian Intervention: Ideas and Practice from the Nineteenth Century to the Present* (Cambridge: Cambridge University Press, 2015).
Kluge, E., 'West Papua and the International History of Decolonization, 1961–69', *The International History Review*, 42:6 (2020), pp. 1155–1172.
Kochavi, A. J., *Post-Holocaust Politics: Britain, the United States, and Jewish Refugees, 1945–1948* (Chapel Hill: UNC Press, 2001).
Konieczna, A. and Skinner, R., *A Global History of Anti-Apartheid: 'Forward to Freedom' in South Africa* (London: Palgrave Macmillan, 2019).
Koops, J. A., Tardy, T., Macqueen, N., and Williams, P. D. (eds.), *The Oxford Handbook of United Nations Peacekeeping Operations* (Oxford: Oxford University Press, 2015).
Kothari, U., 'From Colonialism to Development: Reflections of Former Colonial Officers', *Commonwealth & Comparative Politics*, 44:1 (2006), pp. 118–136.
Kott, S., 'International Organizations – A Field of Research for Global History', *Zeithistorische Forschungen/Studies in Contemporary History*, 8 (2011), pp. 446–450.

Krepton, M., *Winning and Losing the Nuclear Peace: The Rise, Demise, and Revival of Arms Control* (Stanford: Stanford University Press, 2021).

van der Kroef, J. M., 'Nationalism and Politics in West New Guinea', *Pacific Affairs*, 34:1 (1961), pp. 38–53.

Kuitenbrouwer, V., 'Beyond the "Trauma of Decolonisation": Dutch Cultural Diplomacy during the West New Guinea Question (1950–62)', *Journal of Imperial and Commonwealth History*, 44:2 (2016), pp. 306–327.

Kumarasingham, H., *Constitution-Making in Asia: Decolonisation and State-Building in the Aftermath of the British Empire* (Abingdon: Routledge, 2016).

Kuneralp, Z., *Sadece Diplomat* (İstanbul: ISIS, 1999).

Kunreuther, L., 'Earwitnesses and Transparent Conduits of Voice: On the Labor of Field Interpreters for UN Missions', *Humanity: An International Journal of Human Rights, Humanitarianism, and Development*, 11:3 (2020), pp. 298–316.

Kunz, D. B., *Butter and Guns: America's Cold War Economic Diplomacy* (New York: Free Press, 1997).

Kunz, J. L., 'Legality of the Security Council Resolutions of June 25 and 27, 1950', *The American Journal of International Law*, 45:1 (1951), pp. 137–142.

Kyle, K., *Suez: Britain's End of Empire in the Middle East* (New York: I. B. Tauris, 2011).

Lamarchand, R., 'The Limits of Self-Determination: The Case of the Katangan Secession', *The American Political Science Review*, 56:2 (1962), pp. 404–416.

Larmer, M., 'Nation-Making at the Border: Zambian Diplomacy in the Democratic Republic of Congo', *Comparative Studies in Society and History*, 61:1 (2019), pp. 145–175.

Larres, K., *Churchill's Cold War: The Politics of Personal Diplomacy* (New Haven: Yale University Press, 2002).

Lascurettes, K. M., *Orders of Exclusion: Great Powers and the Strategic Sources of Foundational Rules in International Relations* (Oxford: Oxford University Press, 2020).

Leake, E., *The Defiant Border: The Afghan-Pakistan Borderlands in the Era of Decolonization, 1936–1965* (Cambridge: Cambridge University Press, 2017).

'States, Nations, and Self-Determination: Afghanistan and Decolonization at the United Nations', *Journal of Global History*, 17:2 (2022), pp. 272–291.

Leake, E. and Haines, D., 'Lines of (In)Convenience: Sovereignty and Border-Making in Postcolonial South Asia, 1947–1965', *The Journal of Asian Studies*, 76:4 (2017), pp. 963–985.

Lecocq, B., *Disputed Desert: Decolonisation, Competing Nationalisms and Tuareg Rebellions in Northern Mali* (Leiden: Brill, 2010)

Lee, C. J., *Making a World after Empire: The Bandung Moment and Its Political Afterlives* (Athens: Ohio Press, 2010).

Lee, J. J., *The Partition of Korea after World War II: A Global History* (New York: Springer, 2006).

Leonardi, C., 'Patchwork States: The Localization of State Territoriality on the South Sudan–Uganda Border, 1914–2014', *Past & Present*, 248:1 (2020), pp. 209–258.

Lester, A., 'Personifying Colonial Governance: George Arthur and the Transition from Humanitarian to Development Discourse', *Annals of the Association of American Geographers*, 102:6 (2012), pp. 1468–1488.

Lester, A., Boehme, K., and Mitchell, P. (eds.), *Ruling the World: Freedom, Civilisation and Liberalism in the Nineteenth-Century British Empire* (Cambridge: Cambridge University Press, 2020).

Lester, A. and Dussart, F., *Colonization and the Origins of Humanitarian Governance: Protecting Aborigines across the Nineteenth-Century British Empire* (Cambridge: Cambridge University Press, 2014).

Leuenberger, C. and Schnell, I., *The Politics of Maps: Cartographic Constructions of Israel/Palestine* (Oxford: Oxford University Press, 2020).

Liang, Y., 'Abstention and Absence of a Permanent Member in Relation to the Voting Procedure in the Security Council', *The American Journal of International Law*, 44:4 (1950), pp. 694–708.

Lieberman, J. I., *The Scorpion and the Tarantula: The Struggle to Control Atomic Weapons, 1945–1949* (Boston: Houghton Mifflin Company, 1970).

Lijphart, A., 'The Indonesian Image of West Irian', *Asian Survey*, 1:5 (1961), pp. 9–16.

Lim, P. J., *The Evolution of British Counter-Insurgency during the Cyprus Revolt, 1955–1959* (London: Palgrave Macmillan, 2018).

Lipsey, R. *Hammarskjöld: A Life* (Ann Arbor: University of Michigan Press, 2013).

Lisle, D., *Holidays in the Danger Zone: Entanglements of War and Tourism* (Minneapolis: University of Minnesota Press, 2016).

Loffman, R. A., *Church, State and Colonialism in Southeastern Congo, 1890–1962* (Berlin: Springer, 2019).

'"My training is deeply Christian and I am against violence"': Jason Sendwe, the Balubakat, and the Katangese Secession, 1957–1964', *The Journal of African History*, 61:2 (2020), pp. 263–281.

Lofgren, W., 'In Defence of "Tommy" Burns', *Canadian Military History*, 7:4 (2006), pp. 92–94.

Loizos, P., *The Heart Grown Bitter: A Chronicle of Cypriot War Refugees* (Cambridge: Cambridge University Press, 1981).

Lopesi, L., *False Divides* (Wellington: Bridget Williams Books, 2018).

Lorenzini, S., *Global Development: A Cold War History* (Princeton: Princeton University Press, 2019).

Luard, E., *A History of the United Nations. Vol. 2: The Age of Decolonization, 1955–1965* (Basingstoke: Macmillan, 1989).

MacArthur, J., *Cartography and the Political Imagination: Mapping Community in Colonial Kenya* (Athens: Ohio University Press, 2016).

'Decolonizing Sovereignty: States of Exception along the Kenya–Somali Frontier', *The American Historical Review*, 124:1 (2019), pp. 108–143.

Macqueen, N., 'Ireland and the United Nations Peacekeeping Force in Cyprus', *Review of International Studies*, 9:2 (1983), pp. 95–108.

The United Nations Since 1945: Peacekeeping and the Cold War (London: Longman, 1999).

Peacekeeping and the International System (Abingdon: Routledge, 2006).

United Nations Peacekeeping in Africa Since 1960 (Abingdon: Routledge, 2014).

'Cold War Peacekeeping versus Humanitarian Intervention: Beyond the Hammarskjöldian Model', in F. Klose (ed.), *The Emergence of Humanitarian Intervention: Ideas and Practice from the Nineteenth Century to the Present* (Cambridge: Cambridge University Press, 2015), pp. 234–235.

Makinda, S. M., 'Sovereignty and International Security: Challenges for the United Nations', *Global Governance*, 2:2 (1996), pp. 149–168.

'The United Nations and State Sovereignty: Mechanism for Managing International Security', *Australian Journal of Political Science*, 33:1 (1998), pp. 101–115.

Mamdani, M., *Neither Settler Nor Native: The Making and Unmaking of Permanent Minorities* (Cambridge, MA: Harvard University Press, 2020).

Manela, E., *The Wilsonian Moment: Self-Determination and the International Origins of Anticolonial Nationalism* (Oxford: Oxford University Press, 2007).

'International Society as a Historical Subject', *Diplomatic History*, 44:2 (2020), pp. 184–209.

Mann, G., *From Empires to NGOs in the West African Sahel: The Road to Nongovernmentality* (Cambridge: Cambridge University Press, 2014).

Markides, D. W., 'Britain's "New Look" Policy for Cyprus and the Makarios-Harding Talks, January 1955-March 1956', *The Journal of Imperial and Commonwealth History*, 23:3 (1995), pp. 479–481.

Cyprus 1957–1963 from Colonial Conflict to Constitutional Crisis: The Key Role of the Municipal Issue (Minneapolis: University of Minnesota, 2001).

Marmon, B., 'Operation Refugee: The Congo Crisis and the End of Humanitarian Imperialism in Southern Rhodesia, 1960', *Cold War History*, 22:2 (2021), pp. 131–152.

Martin, J., *The Meddlers: Sovereignty, Empire, and the Birth of Global Economic Governance* (Cambridge, MA: Harvard University Press, 2022).

Masters, D. and Way, K., *One World or None: A Report to the Public on the Full Meaning of the Atomic Bomb* (New York: McGraw-Hill, 1946).

Matera, M., *Black London: The Imperial Metropolis and Decolonization in the Twentieth Century* (Oakland: University of California Press, 2015).

Mathys, G., 'Questioning Territories and Identities in the Precolonial (Nineteenth-Century) Lake Kivu Region', *Africa*, 91:3 (2021), pp. 493–515.

Maul, D. *Human Rights, Development and Decolonisation: The International Labour Organisation, 1950–1970* (Basingstoke: Palgrave Macmillan, 2012).

May, E. R. and Laiou, A. E. (eds.), *The Dumbarton Oaks Conversations and the United Nations, 1944–1994* (Cambridge, MA: Harvard University Press, 1998).

May, R. J., 'On the Asia-Oceania Interface: The West Papua Issue in a Regional Context', *Outre-Terre*, 58–59:1 (2020), pp. 143–179.

Mazower, M., 'An International Civilization? Empire, Internationalism and the Crisis of the Mid-Twentieth Century', *International Affairs*, 82:3 (2006), pp. 553–566.

No Enchanted Palace: The End of Empire and the Ideological Origins of the United Nations (Princeton: Princeton University Press, 2008).

Governing the World: The History of an Idea, 1815 to the Present (London: Allen Lane, 2012).

McCann, G., 'From Diaspora to Third Worldism and the United Nations: India and the Politics of Decolonizing Africa', *Past & Present*, Supplement 8 (2013), pp. 258–280.

McCarthy, H., 'Petticoat Diplomacy: The Admission of Women to the British Foreign Service, c. 1919–1946', *Twentieth Century British History*, 20:3 (2009), pp. 285–321.

'Women, Marriage and Work in the British Diplomatic Service', *Women's History Review*, 23:6 (2014), pp. 853–873.

McGarr, P. M., *The Cold War in South Asia: Britain, the United States and the Indian Subcontinent, 1945–1965* (Cambridge: Cambridge University Press, 2013).

'The Long Shadow of Colonial Cartography: Britain and the Sino-Indian War of 1962', *Journal of Strategic Studies*, 42:5 (2019), pp. 626–653.

McGregor, K. and Hearman, V., 'Challenging the Lifeline of Imperialism: Reassessing Afro-Asian Solidarity and Related Activism in the Decade 1955–1965', in L. Eslava, M. Fakhri, and V. Nesiah (eds.), *Bandung, Global History, and International Law: Critical Pasts and Pending Futures* (Cambridge: Cambridge University Press, 2017), pp. 161–176.

McMullen, C., *Mediation of the West Papua Dispute, 1962: A Case Study* (Washington, DC: Institute for the Study of Diplomacy, 1981).

Melber, H., 'Mission Impossible: Hammarskjöld and the UN Mandate for the Congo (1960–1961)', *African Security*, 10:3–4 (2017), pp. 254–271.

Mercer, G., 'Albert Einstein, Power, the State, and Peace: The Physicist as Philosopher-King in a World State', *International Social Science Review*, 69:3/4 (1994), pp. 19–26.

Michalopoulos, S. and Papaioannou, E., 'The Long-Run Effects of the Scramble for Africa', *The American Economic Review*, 106:7 (2016), pp. 1802–1848.

Milford, I., 'Federation, Partnership, and the Chronologies of Space in 1950s East and Central Africa', *The Historical Journal*, 63:5 (2020), pp. 1325–1348.

Millett, A. R., *The Korean War, Volume 3* (Lincoln: University of Nebraska Press, 2001).

The War for Korea, 1945–1950: A House Is Burning (Lawrence: University Press of Kansas, 2005).

Mitchell, T., *Rule of Experts: Egypt, Techno-Politics, Modernity* (Berkeley: University of California Press, 2012).

Mohan, J., 'Ghana, the Congo, and the United Nations', *Journal of Modern African Studies*, 7:3 (1969), pp. 369–406.

Monaville, P., 'The Political Life of the Dead Lumumba: Cold War Histories and the Congolese Student Left', *Africa*, 89: S1 (2019), pp. S15–S39.

Students of the World: Global 1968 and Decolonization in the Congo (Durham: Duke University Press, 2022).

Moran, M., *Rauf Denktash at the United Nations: Speeches on Cyprus* (Huntingdon: Eothen Press, 1997).

Morefield, J., *Covenants without Swords: Idealist Liberalism and the Spirit of Empire* (Princeton: Princeton University Press, 2005).

Morris, B., *1948: A History of the First Arab–Israeli War* (London: Yale University Press, 2008).

Moses, A. D., Duranti, M., and Burke, R. (eds.), *Decolonization, Self-Determination, and the Rise of Global Human Rights Politics* (Cambridge: Cambridge University Press, 2020).

Moss, T., *Guarding the Periphery: The Australian Army in Papua New Guinea, 1951–75* (Cambridge: Cambridge University Press, 2017).

Motadel, D., 'The Global Authoritarian Moment and the Revolt against Empire', *The American Historical Review*, 124:3 (2019), pp. 843–877.

Mote, O. and Rutherford, D., 'From Irian Java to Papua: The Limits of Primordialism in Indonesia's Troubled East', *Indonesia*, 72 (2001), pp. 115–140.

Moyn, S., *Humane: How the United States Abandoned Peace and Reinvented War* (New York: Farrar, Straus and Giroux, 2021).

Muehlenbeck, P. (ed.), *Race, Ethnicity and the Cold War: A Global Perspective* (Nashville: Vanderbilt University Press, 2012).

Muehlenbeck, P. E. and Telepneva, N., *Warsaw Pact Intervention in the Third World: Aid and Influence in the Cold War* (London: I. B. Tauris, 2018).

Muhammed, A., 'The Historical Origins of Secessionist Movement in West Papua', *Journal of Asia Pacific Studies*, 3:1 (2013), pp. 1–13.

Munro, J., *The Anticolonial Front: The African American Freedom Struggle and Global Decolonisation, 1945–1960* (Cambridge: Cambridge University Press, 2017).

van Munster, R. and Sylvest, C., *Nuclear Realism: Global Political Thought during the Thermonuclear Revolution* (London: Routledge, 2016).

Murray, G., 'Glimpses of Suez 1956', *International Journal*, 29:1 (1974), pp. 46–66.

Muschik, E., 'The Art of Chameleon Politics: From Colonial Servant to International Development Expert', *Humanity*, 9:2 (2018), pp. 219–244.

'Managing the World: The United Nations, Decolonisation and the Strange Triumph of State Sovereignty in the 1950s and 1960s', *Journal of Global History*, 12:1 (2018), pp. 121–144.

'"A Pretty Kettle of Fish": United Nations Assistance in the Mass Dismissal of Labor in the Iranian Oil Industry, 1959–1960', *Labor History*, 60:1 (2019), pp. 8–23.

Building States: The United Nations, Development, and Decolonization, 1945–1965 (New York: Columbia University Press, 2022).

'Special Issue Introduction: Towards a Global History of International Organizations and Decolonization', *Journal of Global History*, 17:2 (2022), pp. 173–190.

Musto, R. A., '"Atoms for Police": The United States and the Dream of a Nuclear-Armed United Nations, 1945–1962', *NPIHP Working Paper #15*, October 2020.

Mwangi, W., 'The Lion, the Native and the Coffee Plant: Political Imagery and the Ambiguous Art of Currency Design in Colonial Kenya', *Geopolitics*, 7:1 (2002), pp. 31–62.

Namakkal, J., *Unsettling Utopia: The Making and Unmaking of French India* (New York: Columbia University Press, 2021).

Namikas, L., *Battleground Africa: Cold War in the Congo, 1960–1965* (Palo Alto: Stanford University Press, 2013).

Naseemullah, A., *Patchwork States: The Historical Roots of Subnational Conflict and Competition in South Asia* (Cambridge: Cambridge University Press, 2020).

Nayudu, S. K., '"In the Very Eye of the Storm": India, the UN, and the Lebanon Crisis of 1958', *Cold War History*, 18:2 (2018), pp. 221–237.

'"India Looks at the World": Nehru, the Indian Foreign Service & World Diplomacy', *Diplomatica*, 2:1 (2020), pp. 100–117.

Neibuhr, R., 'Nonalignment as Yugoslavia's Answer to Bloc Politics', *Journal of Cold War Studies*, 13:1 (2011), pp. 146–179.

Newman, E. and Visoka, G., 'The Geopolitics of State Recognition in a Transitional International Order', *Geopolitics*, (2021), pp. 1–29.

Niang, A., *The Postcolonial African State in Transition: Stateness and Modes of Sovereignty* (Lanham: Rowman & Littlefield International, 2018).

Nicault, C., 'La Shoah et la création de l'État d'Israël : Où en est l'historiographie?', *Les Cahiers de la Shoah*, 6 (2002/1), pp. 161–204.

Nolan, V., *Military Leadership and Counterinsurgency: The British Army and Small War Strategy since World War II* (London: Bloomsbury, 2011).

Nordholt, H. S., 'The Jago in the Shadow: Crime and "Order" in the Colonial State in Java', *RIMA*, 25:1 (1991), pp. 74–91.

'Indonesia in the 1950s: Nation, Modernity, and the Post-Colonial State', *Bijdragen tot de Taal-, Land- en Volkenkunde*, 167:4 (2011), pp. 386–404.

Novosseloff, A., *The UN Military Staff Committee: Recreating a Missing Capacity* (Abingdon: Routledge, 2018.

Nzongola-Ntalaja, G., *The Congo: From Leopold to Kabila: A People's History* (London: Bloomsbury, 2002).

Patrice Lumumba (Athens: Ohio University Press, 2014).

O'Malley, A., 'Ghana, India, and the Transnational Dynamics of the Congo Crisis at the United Nations, 1960–1961', *The International History Review*, 37:5 (2015), pp. 970–990.

'"What an Awful Body the UN Have Become!!": Anglo American–UN Relations during the Congo Crisis, February–December 1961', *Journal of Transatlantic Studies*, 14:1 (2016), pp. 26–46.

The Diplomacy of Decolonisation: America, Britain and the United Nations during the Congo Crisis 1960–1964 (Manchester: Manchester University Press, 2018).

O'Neill, M., 'Soviet Involvement in the Korean War: A New View from the Soviet-Era Archives', *OAH Magazine of History*, 14:3 (2000), pp. 20–24.

Oren, M. B., 'Faith and Fair-Mindedness: Lester B. Pearson and the Suez Crisis', *Diplomacy and Statecraft*, 3:1 (1992), pp. 48–73.

Pak, C. Y., *Korea and the United Nations* (Leiden: Martinus Nijhoff, 2000).

Pallister-Wilkins, P., *Humanitarian Borders: Unequal Mobility and Saving Lives* (London: Verso Books, 2022).

Palumbo, M., *The Palestinian Catastrophe: The 1948 Expulsion of a People from Their Homeland* (London: Quartet Books, 1987).

Passemiers, L., *Decolonisation and Regional Geopolitics: South Africa and the "Congo Crisis", 1960–1965* (Abingdon: Routledge, 2020).

Pastor-Castro, R. and Thomas, M. (eds.), *Embassies in Crisis: Studies of Diplomatic Missions in Testing Situations* (Abingdon: Routledge, 2020).

Pearce, J., *Political Identity and Conflict in Central Angola, 1975–2002* (Cambridge: Cambridge University Press, 2015).

Pearson, J., 'Defending Empire at the United Nations: The Politics of International Colonial Oversight in the Era of Decolonisation', *Journal of Imperial and Commonwealth History*, 45:3 (2017), pp. 525–549.

The Colonial Politics of Global Health: France and the United Nations in Postwar Africa (Cambridge, MA: Harvard University Press, 2018).

Pedersen, S., 'Getting Out of Iraq – in 1932: The League of Nations and the Road to Normative Statehood', *American Historical Review*, 115:4 (2010), pp. 975–1000.

The Guardians: The League of Nations and the Crisis of Empire (Oxford: Oxford University Press, 2015).

Persson, S., 'Folke Bernadotte and the White Buses', *The Journal of Holocaust Education*, 9:2 (2000), pp. 237–268.

Phillips, A., 'Beyond Bandung: The 1955 Asian-African Conference and Its legacies for International Order', *Australian Journal of International Affairs*, 70:4 (2016), pp. 329–341.

Pillai, S., 'Fragmenting the Nation: Divisible Sovereignty and Travancore's Quest for Federal Independence', *Law and History Review*, 34:3 (2016), pp. 743–782.

Platje, W., 'Dutch Sigint and the Conflict with Indonesia 1950–62', *Intelligence & National Security*, 16:1 (2001), pp. 285–312.

Pollis, A., 'The Social Construction of Ethnicity and Nationality: The Case of Cyprus', *Nationalism and Ethnic Politics*, 2:1 (1996), pp. 67–90.

Potter, P. B., 'The Palestine Problem before the United Nations', *The American Journal of International Law*, 42:4 (1948), pp. 859–861.

Pouwer, J., 'The Colonisation, Decolonisation and Recolonisation of West Papua', *The Journal of Pacific History*, 34:2 (1999), pp. 157–179.

Prashad, V., *The Darker Nations: A People's History of the Third World* (New York: The New Press, 2008).

Prevots, N., *Dance for Export: Cultural Diplomacy and the Cold War* (Middletown: Wesleyan University Press, 2012).

Pringle, Y., 'Humanitarianism, Race and Denial: The International Committee of the Red Cross and Kenya's Mau Mau Rebellion, 1952–60', *History Workshop Journal*, 84 (2017), pp. 89–107.

Prior, C., 'Writing Another Continent's History: The British and Pre-colonial Africa, 1880–1939', available at www.gla.ac.uk/media/Media_64283_smxx .pdf Accessed on 06/04/2020, accessed on 3 June 2018.

Radmann, W., 'The Nationalization of Zaire's Copper: From Union Minière to Gecamines', *Africa Today*, 25:4 (1978), pp. 25–47.

Ramakrishna Reddy, T., *India's Policy in the United Nations* (Madison: Fairleigh Dickinson University Press, 1968).

Ravndal, E. J., '"The First Major Test": The UN Secretary-General and the Palestine Problem, 1947–9' *The International History Review*, 38:1 (2016), pp. 196–213.

'"A Force for Peace": Expanding the Role of the UN Secretary-General under Trygve Lie, 1946–1953', *Global Governance*, 23:3 (2017), pp. 443–459.

Ray, V., 'A Theory of Racialized Organizations', *American Sociological Review*, 84:1 (2019), pp. 26–53.

Razack, S., *Dark Threats & White Knights: The Somalia Affair, Peacekeeping, and the New Imperialism* (Toronto: University of Toronto Press, 2004).

Rehman, J., Shahid, A., and Foster, S. (eds.), *The Asian Yearbook of Human Rights and Humanitarian Law: Volume 5* (Leiden: Brill, 2021).

Reid, D. M., *Whose Pharaohs?: Archaeology, Museums, and Egyptian National Identity from Napoleon to World War I* (Oakland: University of California Press, 2002).

Reily, S. A. and Brucher, K. (eds.), *Brass Bands of the World: Militarism, Colonial Legacies, and Local Music Making* (Abingdon: Routledge, 2016).

Reinisch, J., 'Introduction: Agents of Internationalism', *Contemporary European History*, 25:2 (2016), pp. 195–205.

van Reybrouck, D., *Congo: The Epic History of a People* (London: Harper Collins, 2015).

Rich, W. C. (ed.), *African American Perspectives on Political Science* (Philadelphia: Temple University Press, 2007).

Richmond, O. and Ker-Lindsay, J. (eds.), *The Work of the UN in Cyprus: Promoting Peace and Development* (London: Palgrave Macmillan, 2001).

Rivlin, B. (ed.), *Ralph Bunche: The Man and His Times* (New York: Holmes & Meier, 1990).

Roberts, G., 'MOLINACO, the Comorian Diaspora, and Decolonisation in East Africa's Indian Ocean', *Journal of African History*, 62:3 (2021), pp. 411–429.

Robinson, G. B., *The Killing Season: A History of the Indonesian Massacres, 1965–1966* (Princeton: Princeton University Press, 2019).

Roehrlich, E., 'Negotiating Verification: International Diplomacy and the Evolution of Nuclear Safeguards, 1945–1972', *Diplomacy & Statecraft*, 29:1 (2018), pp. 29–50.

Inspectors for Peace: A History of the International Atomic Energy Agency (Baltimore: Johns Hopkins University Press, 2022).

Roffman, G. L., *Korean War Order of Battle: United States, United Nations, and Communist Ground, Naval, and Air Forces, 1950–1953* (Westport: Greenwood Publishing Group, 2002).

Roger Louis, W. M. and Robinson, R., 'The Imperialism of Decolonisation', *The Journal of Imperial and Commonwealth History*, 22:3 (1994), pp. 462–511.

Rosenboim, O., *The Emergence of Globalism: Visions of World Order in Britain and the United States, 1939–1950* (Princeton: Princeton University Press, 2017).

Rothschild, E., 'The Archives of Universal History', *Journal of World History*, 19:3 (2008), pp. 375–401.

Rubinstein, R. A., *Peacekeeping under Fire: Culture and Intervention* (Boulder: Paradigm Publishers, 2008).

Rutherford, D., *Laughing at Leviathan: Sovereignty and Audience in West Papua* (Chicago: University of Chicago Press, 2012).

Ryan, D., and Pungong, V. (eds.), *The United States and Decolonization: Power and Freedom* (Abingdon: Springer, 2000).

Sabaratnam, M., *Decolonising Intervention: International Statebuilding in Mozambique* (London: Rowman and Littlefield, 2018).

Said, E., *Orientalism* (New York: Random House, 1979).

Sakkas, J. and. Zhukova N, 'The Soviet Union, Turkey and the Cyprus Problem, 1967–1974', *Les cahiers Irice*, 1:10 (2013), pp. 123–135.

Saksena, P., 'Building the Nation: Sovereignty and International Law in the Decolonisation of South Asia', *Journal of the History of International Law*, 23:1 (2020), pp. 52–79.

Salem, N., *Cyprus: A Regional Conflict and Its Resolution* (London: Palgrave Macmillan, 1992).

Saltford, J., 'United Nations Involvement with the Act of Self-Determination in West Irian (Indonesian West New Guinea) 1968 to 1969', *Indonesia*, 69 (2000), pp. 71–92.

The United Nations and the Indonesian Takeover of West Papua, 1962–1969: The Anatomy of Betrayal (London: Psychology Press, 2003).

'The United Nations, West Papua and the Act of Free Choice: De-colonisation in Action?' (2008), available at http://resources.huygens.knaw.nl/indonesis

chebetrekkingen1945–1969/DekolonisatieVanIndonesieEnHetZelfbeschikkingsrechtVanDePapoea/papers_pdf/saltford, accessed on 2 April 2019.
Satia, P., *Time's Monster: History, Conscience and Britain's Empire* (London: Penguin Books, 2022 edition).
Saunier, P., 'Learning by Doing: Notes about the Making of the *Palgrave Dictionary of Transnational History*', *Journal of Modern European History*, 6:2 (2008), pp. 159–180.
Savage, P. and Martin, R., 'The OPM in West Papua New Guinea: The Continuing Struggle against Indonesian Colonialism', *Journal of Contemporary Asia*, 7:3 (1977), pp. 338–346.
Sayward, A. L., *The United Nations in International History* (London: Bloomsbury, 2017).
Schaffer, H. B., *Ellsworth Bunker: Global Troubleshooter, Vietnam Hawk* (Chapel Hill: UNC Books, 2004).
Schaufelbuehl, J. M. et al., 'Non-Alignment, the Third Force, or Fence-Sitting: Independent Pathways in the Cold War', *The International History Review*, 37:5 (2015), pp. 901–911.
Schmitz, D. F., *The United States and Right-Wing Dictatorships, 1965–1989* (Cambridge: Cambridge University Press, 2006).
Schneider, N., 'Between Promise and Skepticism: The Global South and Our Role as Engaged Intellectuals', *The Global South*, 11:2 (2017), pp. 18–38.
Scott, J. C., *Seeing Like a State: How Certain Schemes to Improve the Human Condition Have Failed* (New Haven: Yale University Press, 1998).
Seilig, L., *Lumumba: Africa's Lost Leader* (London: Haus Publishing, 2015).
Senaratne, K., *Internal Self-Determination in International Law: History, Theory, and Practice* (Cambridge: Cambridge University Press, 2021).
Shabaneh, G., *UNRWA and Palestinian National Identity: The Role of the United Nations in State-Building* (New York: City University of New York, 2005).
Shahabuddin, M., *Minorities and the Making of Postcolonial States in International Law* (Cambridge: Cambridge University Press, 2021).
Share, M., 'From Ideological Foe to Uncertain Friend: Soviet Relations with Taiwan, 1943–82', *Cold War History*, 3:2 (2002), pp. 1–34.
Shilliam, R., 'What about Marcus Garvey? Race and the Transformation of Sovereignty Debate', *Review of International Studies*, 32:3 (2006), pp. 379–400.
Shin, B., 'The Decision Process of the Trusteeship in Korea, 1945–1946: Focusing on the Change of U.S. Ideas', *Pacific Focus*, 19:1 (2004), pp. 169–211.
Siegelberg, M. L., *Statelessness: A Modern History* (Cambridge, MA: Harvard University Press, 2020).
Sievers, L. and Daws, S., The Procedure of the UN Security Council, 4th Edition website, available at www.scprocedure.org/comics-section-4-changes.
Simons, G., *The United Nations: A Chronology of Conflict* (New York: Springer, 2016).

Simpson, B., *Economists with Guns: Authoritarian Development and U.S.-Indonesian Relations, 1960–1968* (Redwood City: Stanford University Press, 2008).

'The United States and the Curious History of Self-Determination', *Diplomatic History*, 36:4 (2012), pp. 675–694.

Simpson, G., *Great Powers and Outlaw States: Unequal Sovereigns in the International Legal Order* (Cambridge: Cambridge University Press, 2004).

Sinclair, G. F., *To Reform the World: International Organisations and the Making of Modern States* (Oxford: Oxford University Press, 2017).

'Forging Modern States with Imperfect Tools: United Nations Technical Assistance for Public Administration in Decolonized States', *Humanity*, 11:1 (2020), pp. 54–83.

Skulimowska, M., 'Poland's Colonial Aspirations and the Question of a Mandate over Liberia, 1933–1939', *The Historical Journal*, (2021), pp. 1–20.

Slobodian, Q., *Globalists: The End of Empire and the Birth of Neoliberalism* (Cambridge, MA: Harvard University Press, 2018).

Sluga, G., *Internationalism in the Age of Nationalism* (Philadelphia: University of Pennsylvania Press, 2013).

Sluga, G. and Amrith, S., 'New Histories of the United Nations', *Journal of World History*, 19:3 (2008), pp. 251–274.

Sluga, G. and Clavin, P. (eds.), *Internationalisms: A Twentieth Century History* (Cambridge: Cambridge University Press, 2016).

Sluga, G. and James, C. (eds.), *Women, Diplomacy and International Politics since 1500* (Abingdon: Routledge, 2016).

Smirl, L., *Spaces of Aid: How Cars, Compounds and Hotels Shape Humanitarianism* (London: Zed Books, 2015).

Smith, L. V., *Sovereignty at the Paris Peace Conference of 1919* (Oxford: Oxford University Press, 2018).

Smith, T., *Why Wilson Matters: The Origin of American Liberal Internationalism and Its Crisis Today* (Princeton: Princeton University Press, 2017).

Sobocinska, A., *Saving the World?: Western Volunteers and the Rise of the Humanitarian-Development Complex* (Cambridge: Cambridge University Press, 2021).

Soffer, J., 'All for One or All for All: The UN Military Staff Committee and the Contradictions within American Internationalism', *Diplomatic History*, 21:1 (1997), pp. 45–69.

Somaiya, R., *Operation Morthor: The Death of Dag Hammarskjöld and the Last Great Mystery of the Cold War* (London: Penguin Books, 2020).

Spanu, M., 'The Hierarchical Society: The Politics of Self-Determination and the Constitution of New States after 1919', *European Journal of International Relations*, 26:2 (2020), pp. 372–396.

Spooner, K., *Canada, the Congo Crisis, and UN Peacekeeping, 1960–64* (Vancouver: UBC Press, 2010).

Stahn, C. and Melber, H. (eds.), *Peace Diplomacy, Global Justice and International Agency: Rethinking Human Security and Ethics in the Spirit of Dag Hammarskjöld* (Cambridge: Cambridge University Press, 2014).

Stanger, C. D., 'A Haunting Legacy: The Assassination of Count Bernadotte', *Middle East Journal*, 42:2 (1988), pp. 260–272.

Starting, R. and Davis, A. E., 'Bordering the Postcolonial State: The Relevance of Sikkim in India's Support for Indonesia's Occupation of East Timor', *Commonwealth & Comparative Politics*, 60:2 (2022), pp. 169–189.

Staples, A. L., *The Birth of Development: How the World Bank, Food and Agriculture Organization, and World Health Organization Changed the World, 1945–1965* (Ohio: Kent State University Press, 2006).

Stearns, M., *Entangled Allies: U.S. Policy toward Greece, Turkey, and Cyprus* (New York: Council on Foreign Relations, 1992).

Stergio, A., 'The Exceptional Case of the British Military Bases on Cyprus', *Middle Eastern Studies*, 51:2 (2015), pp. 285–300.

Stergiou, A., 'Soviet Policy towards Cyprus', *The Cyprus Review*, 19:2 (2007), pp. 83–106.

'Les Russes à Chypre dans l'après-guerre froide', *Outre-Terre*, 1:27 (2011), pp. 121–128.

Stern, S. M., *Averting 'the Final Failure': John F. Kennedy and the Secret Cuban Missile Crisis Meetings* (Palo Alto: Stanford University Press, 2003).

Stiles, K. W., 'The Power of Procedure and the Procedures of the Powerful: Anti-Terror Law in the United Nations', *Journal of Peace Research*, 43:1 (2006), pp. 37–54.

Stoler, A. L., *Along the Archival Grain* (Princeton: Princeton University Press, 2009).

Storr, C., *International Status in the Shadow of Empire: Nauru and the Histories of International Law* (Cambridge: Cambridge University Press, 2020).

Sultan, N. S., 'Between the Many and the One: Anticolonial Federalism and Popular Sovereignty', *Political Theory*, 50:2 (2021), pp. 247–274.

Swan, Q., *Pasifika Black: Oceania, Anti-colonialism, and the African World* (New York: NYU Press, 2022).

Terretta, M., '"We Had Been Fooled into Thinking that the UN Watches over the Entire World": Human Rights, UN Trust Territories, and Africa's Decolonization', *Human Rights Quarterly*, 34:2 (2012), pp. 329–360.

Petitioning for Our Rights, Fighting for Our Nation: The History of the Democratic Union of Cameroonian Women, 1949–1960 (Oxford: African Books Collective, 2013).

Nation of Outlaws, State of Violence: Nationalism, Grassfields Tradition and State Building in Cameroon (Athens: Ohio University Press, 2014).

Tessaris, C., 'Open Diplomacy and Minority Rights: The League of Nations and Lithuania's International Image in the Early 1920s', in L. Clerc et al. (eds.), *Histories of Public Diplomacy and Nation Branding in the Nordic and Baltic Countries* (Leiden: Brill, 2015), pp. 40–41.

Thomas, C. G. and Falola, T., *Secession and Separatist Conflicts in Postcolonial Africa* (Calgary: University of Calgary Press, 2020).

Thomas, M. and Curless, G (eds.), *Decolonisation and Conflict: Colonial Comparisons and Legacies* (London: Bloomsbury, 2017).

Thomas, M., Moore, B., and Butler, L. J., *Crises of Empire: Decolonization and Europe's Imperial States* (London: Bloomsbury, 2015).

Tilley, H., *Africa as a Living Laboratory: Empire, Development, and the Problem of Scientific Knowledge, 1870–1950* (Chicago: University of Chicago Press, 2011).

Tödt, D., '"Les Noirs Perfectionnés," Cultural Embourgeoisement in Belgian Congo during the 1940s and 1950s', Working Paper of the *Sonderforschungsbereich,* 640:4 (2012), pp. 1–23, available at http://edoc.hu-berlin.de/series/sfb-640-papers/2012-4/PDF/4.pdf.

The Lumumba Generation: African Bourgeoisie and Colonial Distinction in the Belgian Congo (Berlin: De Gruyter, 2021).

van Trigt, P., 'Scripts for a New Stage: United Nations' Observances and New Perspectives on Diplomatic History', *Diplomatica,* 1:2 (2019), pp. 145–156.

Trinidad, J., *Self-Determination in Disputed Colonial Territories* (Cambridge: Cambridge University Press, 2018).

Tudor, M., '"The Re-establishment of Satisfactory Conditions in the Congo": Examining the UN's Response to the Belgian Military Intervention in July 1960', *The King's Student Law Review and Strife Journal,* Joint Edition: Issue I (2018), pp. 1–13.

'Gatekeepers to Decolonisation: Recentring the UN Peacekeepers on the Frontline of West Papua's Re-colonisation, 1962–1963', *Journal of Contemporary History,* 57:2 (2022), pp. 293–316.

'Reputation on the (Green) Line: Revisiting the "Plaza Moment" in United Nations Peacekeeping Practice, 1964–1966', *Journal of Global History,* 16:2 (2021), pp. 227–245.

Turner, O., '"Finishing the Job": The UN Special Committee on Decolonization and the Politics of Self-Governance', *Third World Quarterly,* 34:7 (2013), pp. 1193–1208.

Tzortzis, I., *Greek Democracy and the Junta: Regime Crisis and the Failed Transition of 1973* (London: Bloomsbury, 2020).

U Thant, 'A Burmese View of World Tensions', *The ANNALS of the American Academy of Political and Social Science,* 318:1 (1958), pp. 34–42.

View from the UN (London: David and Charles, 1978).

Unger, C., *International Development: A Postwar History* (London: Bloomsbury Academic, 2018).

Urquhart, B., *Hammarskjold* (New York: Knopf, 1972).

Ralph Bunche: An American Life (New York: W. W. Norton, 1993).

Uslu, N., *The Cyprus Question as an Issue of Turkish Foreign Policy and Turkish–American Relations, 1959–2003* (New York: Nova Publishers, 2003).

Vanthemsche, G., *Belgium and the Congo, 1885–1980* (Cambridge: Cambridge University Press, 2012).

Vaughan, C., 'The Politics of Regionalism and Federation in East Africa, 1958–1964', *The Historical Journal*, 62 (2019), pp. 519–540.

Verrier, J. R., 'Is West Papua another Timor?', Parliament of Australia, *Current Issues Brief* [2000–2001], 27 July 2000.

van der Veur, P. W., 'Political Awakening in West New Guinea', *Pacific Affairs*, 36:1 (1963), pp. 54–73.

'The United Nations in West Irian: A Critique', *International Organization*, 18:1 (1964), pp. 53–73.

Search for New Guinea's Boundaries: From Torres Strait to the Pacific (Canberra: ANU Press, 1966).

Viartasiwi, N., 'The Politics of History in West Papua – Indonesia Conflict', *Asian Journal of Political Science*, 26:1 (2018), pp. 141–159.

Viola, L. A., *The Closure of the International System: How Institutions Create Political Equalities and Hierarchies* (Cambridge: Cambridge University Press, 2020).

Visser, L. (ed.), *Governing New Guinea: An Oral History of Papuan Administrators, 1950–1990* (Leiden: KITLV Press, 2012).

Vitalis, R., *White World Order, Black Power Politics* (Ithaca: Cornell University Press, 2015).

Wagner, K., *Amritsar 1919: An Empire of Fear and the Making of a Massacre* (New Haven: Yale University Press, 2019).

Waldman, S., *Anglo-American Diplomacy and the Palestinian Refugee Problem, 1948–1951* (London: Palgrave Macmillan, 2016).

Walker, L., 'Decolonization in the 1960s: On Legitimate and Illegitimate Nationalist Claims-Making', *Past & Present*, 242:1 (2019), pp. 227–264.

Wallis, J., 'It's the Little Things: The Role of International Interveners in the Social (Re)Construction of the International Peace Architecture', *Global Society*, 35:4 (2021), pp. 456–478.

Wang, G. (ed.), *Nation Building: Five Southeast Asian Histories* (Singapore: ISEAS–Yusof Ishak Institute, 2005).

Wang, Z., 'A Troubled Alliance: Sino-British Conflicts over Tibet', *The International History Review*, 44:1 (2022), pp. 1–25.

Weber, H., and Winanti, P., 'The 'Bandung spirit' and Solidarist Internationalism', *Australian Journal of International Affairs*, 70:4 (2016), pp. 391–406.

Webster, D., '"Already Sovereign as a People": A Foundational Moment in West Papuan Nationalism', *Pacific Affairs*, 74:4 (2002), pp. 507–528.

'Development Advisors in a Time of Cold War and Decolonization: The United Nations Technical Assistance Administration, 1950–1959', *Journal of Global History*, 6:2 (2011), pp. 249–272.

'Self-Determination Abandoned: The Road to the New York: Agreement on West Papua (Papua), 1960–1962', *Indonesia*, 95 (2013), pp. 9–24.

'West Papuan Independence Diplomacy, 1960–62', E-dossier, available at http://historybeyondborders.ca/?p=450.

Weinstein, B., 'Developing Inequality', *American Historical Review*, 113:1 (2008), pp. 1–18.

Weiss, H., *Political Protest in the Congo: The Parti Solidaire Africain during the Independence Struggle* (Princeton: University of Princeton Press, 1967).

Weiss, T. G., 'What Happened to the Idea of World Government', *International Studies Quarterly*, 53:2 (2009), pp. 253–271.

'The United Nations: Before, During and After 1945', *International Affairs*, 91:6 (2015), pp. 1221–1235.

Weiss, T. G., Carayannis, T., and Jolly, R., 'The "Third" United Nations', *Global Governance*, 15:1 (2009), pp. 123–142.

Weissman, S. R., *American Foreign Policy in the Congo, 1960–1964* (Ithaca: Cornell University Press, 1974).

Wempe, S. A., 'From Unfit Imperialists to Fellow Civilizers: German Colonial Officials as Imperial Experts in the League of Nations, 1919–1933', *German History*, 34:1 (2016), pp. 21–48.

'A League to Preserve Empires: Understanding the Mandates System and Avenues for Further Scholarly Inquiry', *The American Historical Review*, 124:5 (2019), pp. 1723–1731.

Wertheim, S., 'Instrumental Internationalism: The American Origins of the United Nations, 1940–1943', *Journal of Contemporary History*, 54:2 (2019), pp. 265–283.

Tomorrow, the World: The Birth of U.S. Global Supremacy (Cambridge, MA: Harvard University Press, 2020).

West, R. L., 'The United Nations and the Congo Financial Crisis: Lessons of the First Year', *International Organization*, 15:4 (1961), pp. 603–617.

Westad, O. A., *The Global Cold War: Third World Interventions and the Making of Our Times* (Cambridge: Cambridge University Press, 2012).

The Cold War: A World History (London: Penguin, 2017).

Wilde, R., *International Territorial Administration: How Trusteeship and the Civilising Mission Never Went Away* (Oxford: Oxford University Press, 2008).

Wilder, G., *Freedom Time: Negritude, Decolonization, and the Future of the World* (Durham: Duke University Press, 2015).

Williams, S., *Who Killed Hammarskjöld?: The UN, the Cold War, and White Supremacy in Africa* (Oxford: Oxford University Press, 2014).

Spies in the Congo: The Race for the Ore that Built the Atomic Bomb (London: Hurst, 2016).

White Malice: The CIA and the Neocolonisation of Africa (London: Hurst, 2021).

Wilson Centre, 'The Congo Crisis, 1960–1961: A Critical Oral History Conference', 28 November 2011.

Wimmer, A. and Schiller, N. G., 'Methodological Nationalism and the Study of Migration', *European Journal of Sociology*, 43:2 (2002), pp. 217–240.

Winter, J. and Prost, A., *René Cassin and Human Rights: From the Great War to the Universal Declaration* (Cambridge: Cambridge University Press, 2003).

Withana, R., *Power, Politics, Law: International Law and State Behaviour during International Crises* (Leiden: Brill, 2008).

de Witte, L., *The Assassination of Lumumba* (London: Verso, 2001).

'The Suppression of the Congo Rebellions and the Rise of Mobutu, 1963–5', *The International History Review*, 39:1 (2017), pp. 107–125.

Wright, K. A. M., Hurley, M., and Ruiz, J. I. G., *NATO, Gender and the Military: Women Organising from Within* (Abingdon: Routledge, 2019).

Wright, Q., 'The Goa Incident', *The American Journal of International Law*, 56:3 (1962), pp. 617–632.

Xydis, S. G., *Cyprus: Conflict and Conciliation, 1954–1958* (Columbus: Ohio University Press, 1967).

'The UN General Assembly as an Instrument of Greek Policy: Cyprus, 1954–58', *The Journal of Conflict Resolution*, 12:2 (1968), pp. 141–158.

Yates, B. A., 'Educating Congolese Abroad: An Historical Note on African Elites', *The International Journal of African Historical Studies*, 14:1 (1981), pp. 34–64.

Yehudai, O., *Leaving Zion: Jewish Emigration from Palestine and Israel after World War II* (Cambridge: Cambridge University Press, 2020).

Yiangou, A., *Cyprus in World War II: Politics and Conflict in the Eastern Mediterranean* (London: Bloomsbury, 2012).

Yoder, A., *The Evolution of the United Nations System* (Oxford: Taylor and Francis, 1997).

Young, C., *Politics in Congo: Decolonization and Independence* (Princeton: Princeton University Press, 2015).

Zaidi, W. H., *Technological Internationalism and World Order: Aviation, Atomic Energy, and the Search for International Peace, 1920–1950* (Cambridge: Cambridge University Press, 2021).

INDEX

Please note that page numbers in bold refer the reader to images.

A note for readers: one-word names are common among the Javanese population (e.g. Indonesian President, Sukarno).